# IMPROVING
# LEARNING

# IMPROVING LEARNING

## A how-to guide for school improvement

Michael N King • Jane Kovacs

Published by Quality Learning Australasia
PO Box 624
North Melbourne
Victoria 3051 Australia
www.qla.com.au

National Library of Australia Cataloguing-in-Publication entry

Creator:     King, Michael N., author.

Title:Improving learning : a how-to guide for school improvement /
    Michael N King and Jane Kovacs.

ISBN:  9780994364500 (paperback)  9780994364517 (ebook : Kindle)

Notes:  Includes bibliographical references and index.

Subjects:    School improvement programs.
    Instructional systems.

Other Creators/Contributors:
    Kovacs, Jane, author.
    Quality Learning Australasia.

Dewey Number:  371.207

Cover design by David Schembri Studios (http://www.davidschembristudios.com)
Design and layout by Scribes of Thoth (https://scribesofthoth.wordpress.com)

# Contents

# Chapter 2: Learning to Improve 15

# Chapter 3: Working on the System  47

# Chapter 4: Creating and Applying Theory

# Chapter 6: Improving Relationships 307

# Chapter 7: Making Improvement Happen

# Foreword

In the long history of school improvement, few improvement attempts have actually resulted in long-lasting improvement, much less reform or systems transformation. Michael King and Dr. Jane Kovacs of Quality Learning Australasia have made such a breakthrough. School improvement initiatives rarely last longer than a few years or the tenure of whatever politician is in office. Quality Learning Australasia has been improving schools since 2002.

In 1986, I created the concept of Total Quality Learning, which was soon shortened to Quality Learning. I first applied the concepts of Quality Learning to my own classes and then to whole school improvement. Today, Quality Learning is alive and well throughout the world. Australia is one place where Quality Learning thrives, guided by Quality Learning Australasia. I was pleased when I learned that Michael would create Quality Learning Australasia and I have been a supporter of Michael King and Jane Kovacs ever since. They have created their own applications of the concepts and continue to be a dominant force for school improvement in Australia.

I met Michael King in 1998, when he was managing the new education division of the Australian Quality Council. I had been giving keynote presentations in Australia since 1993, but had never seen sustainable application. At the behest of Dr. Myron Tribus, Michael King invited me to speak at a conference in Melbourne and then sponsored my first four-day seminar in Australia, which took place in January 1999. Since then, working collaboratively with Quality Leaning Australasia, we have given over 60 four-day seminars throughout Australia, with over 6,000 educators attending, and we are still going strong. This has had a significant impact, no doubt, but there is so much more to be done.

In this book, the authors outline Quality Learning and why it works. They provide quantitative data of the results and qualitative stories outlining the emotional commitment of people to improve. Quality Learning is more than just a set of principles or processes, it is a way of life; a way of thinking; a way of being. Once an individual adopts the philosophy, they can't go back to living in a world of boss management and working only for money. Quality Learning brings a new joy to work that has been taken away from educators. It causes a return to the initial values that caused people to become educators. Students of teachers applying Quality Learning concepts sometimes remark that it feels like they have been let out of prison.

Dr. W. Edwards Deming often remarked that people have a right to joy in their work. Students have a right to joy in their learning. Without joy in learning, there is no learning. The negative attachment will be such that students will not be enticed to learn more or apply learning in new and creative ways. We are currently in the age of creativity, where virtually all knowledge is available to every human being on the planet. What then separates us? What enables some students to succeed, while others fail to thrive? Could it be the learning experience itself? Could it be the ability to work with others and cooperate to the highest possible levels? Quality Learning provides such a framework. It unleashes human potential and creates a joy in learning that is infectious to teachers, administrators, and parents.

This book is significant and timely in that education systems are in crisis in Australia and the United States. Other countries are also experiencing the pressure to improve, brought on by global economic changes. Information technology is transforming societies. Business changes evolving through the globalisation of markets have caused a shift in what students should know when they leave high school or university. These pressures and many others require a learning system able to innovate and adapt at a rate never before required. In this book, Michael King and Jane Kovacs present a framework and methodology for navigating these stormy seas. There is no panacea, no magic wand. All improvement takes dedication and hard work. However, as Dr. W. Edwards Deming said, "It is not enough to put in your best effort. You have to know what to do and then put in your best effort." This book describes what to do. We just need to read it and put in our best effort.

I recommend that you read this book, attend a seminar and begin your Quality Learning journey. If you are already well into your journey, this book may just give you new insights or the reinvigoration you need to keep going.

David P. Langford
CEO
Langford International Inc.
June 2015

# Preface

We are passionate about improving the quality of learning in organisations, but particularly in schools. It was for this reason that we started working with schools in 1997 and then formed Quality Learning Australasia in 2002. We wanted to extend our work with educators, schools and school systems. We also wanted to continue our learning about the application of quality improvement ideas to classrooms and systems of school education.

The desire to write this book emerged quickly. Teachers, school and system leaders were asking where they could read about the quality learning approach. To our knowledge, there is no comprehensive reference about quality improvement philosophy and practices applied to learning and school improvement. We wanted to write this book to fill that gap.

In 2002, we were not ready to write; we had more to learn, data to collect, examples to collate, and experiences to reflect upon. Over the ensuing decade, we planned, drafted, shelved, revised, debated and re-drafted the manuscript.

Along the way, we have been remarkably fortunate in the support and encouragement people have bestowed upon us.

For over a decade, until his final retirement in 2005, Myron Tribus regularly gave his time to personally mentor Michael. Myron has profound understanding across many disciplines, and is particularly well known for his writings on the practical application of W. Edwards Deming's quality improvement philosophy. Myron taught us key lessons about the philosophy, but also about helping others to come to understand and apply it. Without Myron's inspiration, generosity and guidance, this book would never have been born.

Early on, Myron commented, "You meet lots of wonderful people all over the world working to improve quality." How true!

Myron introduced us to David Langford in 1998. David has become a friend to us both and a continuing source of inspiration and support. David's experiences applying the quality learning philosophy in his own classrooms and as a consultant are truly remarkable. He is an extraordinary teacher. David's insights permeate this book.

We feel privileged to have learned with so many wonderful clients, friends and colleagues. Students, classroom teachers, school leaders, parents, family members, system leaders, business leaders, other consultants, and senior executives have all demonstrated generosity and a willingness to share and learn together. Many of these people have become friends. Without their insights and examples, this book would be deficient.

Rob Palmer, Tim Grace, Diane Grantham, Tim Holness, Cliff Downey, and Lynne Macdonald each took time to provide us with detailed and invaluable feedback on the draft manuscript. The pages you read are significantly more comprehensive, fluid and coherent for their contributions.

For his remarkable skills, patience and persistence, we thank our editor, Duncan Beard. Duncan cheerfully endured our late decisions to restructure and rewrite a couple of chapters. He has provided invaluable advice, support and effort in bringing the book to you, including the design and layout. It is hard to imagine a better editor.

Finally, to our spouses, Teresa and Nandor, we offer our heartfelt thanks to each of you for the love you have demonstrated as we have pursued our passion. Without your faith, commitment and encouragement, Quality Learning Australasia would not exist and this book would never have been written.

It has taken us over a decade to bring this book to you. We sincerely hope it provides you with practical ideas and insights to improve the quality of learning, wherever you are. We have done our best. We hope it helps you.

Michael King and Jane Kovacs
June 2015

# Chapter 1:
# Introduction

Knowledge necessary for improvement comes from outside.

W. Edwards Deming, 1993, *The New Economics: For industry, government and education*, MIT, Cambridge, p. 2.

# Chapter contents

# Why another book on school improvement?

Many books have been written on school reform and the need for change in education. This book is different.

## A view from outside

This book is different because it is written by outsiders to the education system.

While we are practitioners with over 30 years' combined experience supporting education systems, our improvement experience draws on previous roles in industry and government. The different questions and perspectives brought by those not immersed in the current system can often provide new and valuable insights. There is great opportunity to learn from the improvement efforts of other systems.

> There is great opportunity to learn from the improvement efforts of other systems.

## Improvement is always possible

This book is different because it is not premised upon the need to fix things.

We are not asserting that schools, classrooms, teachers or school leaders are broken. We are of the view, however, that the system of schooling is in need of improvement. Furthermore, we are of the view that any system, process, or relationship can be improved. A school that is performing poorly can certainly improve; so can an excellent school. A newly graduated teacher can improve practice; so can an expert teacher. Everyone can be engaged in making things better; this book shows how.

> Any system, process or relationship can be improved.

## A how-to approach for everyone

This book is different because it describes an approach to improvement supported by practical how-to methods.

We do not describe yet another model of what great schools and classrooms should look like. The approach described here, unlike many others, does not assume the reader intuitively knows how-to bring about improvement. This book builds capacity for continual improvement.

The ideas and methods apply to everyone wanting to improve learning.

The ideas and methods apply to everyone wanting to improve learning — from five-year-olds to senior administrators — with outstanding results. The improvement framework drives collaborative transformation throughout the system at department, district, school, classroom, team, and individual levels: involving students, teachers, administrators, and families.

## Using proven theory and methods

The theory and practices that are presented have a long pedigree.

This book is different because it is based upon an approach proven to be effective in industry, government, and education. The theory and practices that are presented have a long pedigree. They have been applied for many decades and are now supported by developments in cognitive research.

## Improving — not just changing

This book describes how to improve the quality of learning.

This is not another book on school reform. It is different because it describes how to improve the quality of learning. The proven thinking and practical methods that are outlined within have the potential to transform school education and deliver systemic, sustainable and continual improvement, not just more change.

# Why now?

Despite increasing financial investment and over a decade of effort, the system is yet to show evidence of improvement.

A dedicated, focussed effort to improve the quality of learning is urgent and overdue. Throughout the western world, policy makers and politicians continue to search for ways to improve our systems of school education. Despite increasing financial investment and over a decade of effort, the system is yet to show evidence of improvement.

## Time to improve performance

In Australia, there is increasing debate about student-learning data and the flatlining of performance over the last ten years. Indigenous students and those from a low socio-economic background continue to perform at a significantly lower level than their peers. Standardised international testing is showing that Australian performance compared to other countries is worsening. Students in several countries now outperform our students by as much as a year in reading literacy, and as much as two years in mathematics. In the USA and UK, the data are no better.

# Time to update purposes and processes

Action is needed to transform the existing system, which is based on an outdated historical model. While the current system of school education across western nations has been shaped by individual districts, states and countries, its key characteristics remain similar. The thinking and assumptions that underpin the design of the current systems are widely shared, and have persisted since they were first established to prepare youth for the Industrial Age.

The Industrial Age school model was established to provide a basic standard of education and prepare youth for their likely future. For most, this would involve the execution of repetitive, mechanised tasks on a production line. Today, the majority of our schools continue to do what they were originally designed to do. They have improved, but not in a way that meets the needs of our changing world. The purpose of schools has changed.

> The purpose of schools has changed.

Schools are now charged with the task of developing very different skills and preparing individuals for a very different future. Employability is increasingly dependent upon the ability of an individual to think critically and creatively, solve problems, work effectively with others, and embrace new ideas and ongoing learning.

It is now widely recognised that education contributes to effective citizenship and social wellbeing. With education comes confidence and self-esteem, tolerance and acceptance, the ability to participate politically and socially, to contribute to collective goals, and to make good life choices.

Education is also critical to productivity and competitiveness at a national level in an increasingly global marketplace. To sustain competitive advantage and maintain the quality of life of its citizens, nations must be capable of continually improving and innovating. Manual jobs previously associated with the Industrial Age are being replaced by technology, or are outsourced to the cheapest supplier, no matter where they are in the world. To ensure ongoing success, organisations will increasingly outsource routine work, and instead devote time to creating greater value for clients through creativity, responsiveness, and relationships. A nation's gross domestic product increases with the level of education achieved by its citizens.

The significant challenges currently faced by our planet and those that inhabit it are many and increasing: rapid population growth, climate change, financial instability, food and water shortages, poverty, infectious disease, fishery and forest depletion, drug trafficking, peacekeeping, terrorism, and migration — all attract daily media attention. Overcoming these issues will require collaboration, creative thinking and problem solving on a scale and to a time frame never experienced before. The world's systems of education must build the capacity of individuals to make this possible.

Research and technologies developed over the last decade are changing our ideas about how our brains work and how learning takes place. New information on the role of emotion, what influences learning, motivation, and neuroplasticity have provided fresh insights; as well as opportunities to reflect on what we do in our classrooms and challenge us to identify what we could do differently, to greater effect.

> We cannot expect to keep doing more of the same and achieve the transformation the system requires to meet the changing needs of the 21st century.

An urgent transformation of the education system is critical to the wellbeing of individuals and for the broader functioning of our society. We cannot expect to keep doing more of the same and achieve the transformation the system requires to meet the changing needs of the 21st century.

## Time to end the blame game

The voices of dissatisfaction are getting louder: employers, parents, students, teachers, administrators, school leaders, and community groups are all calling for improvement. Yet we continue to waste time blaming each other for the failures and inadequacies of the system, imploring people to work harder, and applying outdated ad hoc approaches to improvement.

Stakeholder perception data reveal low levels of parent satisfaction. Other data demonstrate increasing stress levels and workloads for teachers and school leaders. A significant proportion of students become increasingly bored, de-motivated, and disengaged as they move through the system.

> The system is at a tipping point. Now is the time to work together to transform it.

The system is at a tipping point. Now is the time to work together to transform it. This book shows how we can begin to do some things differently in order to achieve a better return on our efforts and investment, and to bring about the improved outcomes we urgently need.

# Who is the book for?

This book is relevant to any individual, group or organisation committed to improving the quality of learning in school education.

It has been written specifically for the time-poor, hard-working, passionate and committed professionals who are in constant search of effective and practical means to improve student learning.

It will also provide valuable insight and information for students and their families. It also has relevance for those outside the system who are keen to learn from the experiences of education to improve their improvement efforts.

This book is relevant to any individual, group or organisation committed to improving the quality of learning in school education.

# Who are we?

Quality Learning Australasia (QLA) was established in 2002 to share knowledge and skills in applying the quality philosophy to improve school-based learning.

We continue our efforts to this day: learning, developing resources, providing professional learning and coaching. This book is an effort to capture and share what we have learned through our work with many valued clients, colleagues and friends.

This book is an effort to capture and share what we have learned through our work with many valued clients, colleagues and friends.

## Michael N. King

### BE (Hons), MBA, Grad Dip Science (Statistics), Grad Dip Education

Michael was instrumental in establishing and responsible for leading the Australian Quality Council 1996 Quality in Schools initiative, which translated industry improvement philosophies and practices to school education. Initially a joint initiative of the Victorian Department of Education and the Australian Quality Council, it was later adopted by the South Australian Department of Education and Children's Services. The program introduced quality improvement ideas and methods to over 350 schools and preschools between 1998 and 2002. The legacy of these initiatives is still evident today in many of the systemic changes made in Victoria and South Australia, and in those schools that continue to apply quality improvement as a management philosophy.

Michael established QLA in 2002 to continue to support schools in their improvement efforts, serving over 300 schools in Victoria, South Australia, New South Wales, and the Australian Capital Territory. QLA designs and delivers professional development interventions for education system leaders, school leaders, and teachers, leading to demonstrable sustainable improvements in school performance and the quality of school life. QLA also provides consultancy services to schools, districts, and systems of school education.

Michael is passionate about improving the quality of learning in our school education systems. Over nearly two decades working with school systems, he has observed that schools derive significant benefits from the adoption of a quality improvement philosophy and application of associated tools and methods. Before focussing on the school sector, he consulted in quality improvement to a variety of clients, ranging from small businesses to large corporations and government agencies.

# Jane Kovacs

## B App Sci, ME, MB, DBA

Jane spent the early years of her working life in hospitals and local government, taking on various roles in health, education, human resources, strategic planning, project management, and quality improvement. It was during this time that she was introduced to quality improvement theory and practice and directly experienced its many benefits, especially in improving the quality of work life.

Jane first started working with schools in 1999 as a project director for Business Excellence Australia (previously the Australian Quality Council). Her work involved the design and delivery of school improvement initiatives across four states and territories. She has enjoyed working with the leaders, administrators and educators of primary, secondary and special schools, and with regions, dioceses and departments applying quality improvement theory and practices.

Jane's doctoral dissertation demonstrated that schools that had applied the quality improvement approach — as a result of their participating in the Quality in Schools initiative — showed a statistically significant greater improvement than other schools.

Jane joined QLA in 2003 to focus on the school improvement work she loves. She is devoted to supporting those who share her passion to improve our school education system so that all children experience joy and success in learning.

# What is in the book?

## Content

The book comprises seven chapters, a glossary, annotated bibliography, appendices and index.

**Chapter 1: Introduction** positions the book and its authors. It provides an overview of the structure and layout. It also provides information about how to approach and make use of the book.

**Chapter 2: Learning to Improve** provides an introduction to the quality improvement approach as it applies to improving organisational performance. We introduce the underpinning theory, its history, and some key thought leaders, as well as the various tools and methods that bring the theory to life.

**Chapter 3: Working on the System** introduces systems thinking and discusses how it applies to school education. We explore tools and methods to help create shared direction with key stakeholders. We show how students, teachers and educational leaders are improving outcomes by improving systems, processes and relationships in effective, efficient and sustainable ways.

**Chapter 4: Creating and Applying Theory** discusses the dangers of blindly adopting the programs of others. We explain the importance of creating your own theory when planning for improvement. We describe how to build ownership by involving key stakeholders, using data, and identifying and addressing root causes in order to develop effective solutions.

**Chapter 5: Using Data to Improve** introduces the concept of statistical thinking. Everyone can use data to improve: easy-to-use tools help us to collect, display and understand the variation in our systems and processes to better inform decision-making and improvement. We discuss how traditional methods lead to tampering and making things worse.

**Chapter 6: Improving Relationships** explores the psychology of improvement. We contrast intrinsic and extrinsic motivation and discuss the role of leadership. We introduce powerful strategies that equip students to take responsibility for their learning and behaviour, and give them a voice in continuously improving the system of learning.

**Chapter 7: Making Improvement Happen** highlights the key insights we have gained through our experience working with schools, school systems and other organisations over the past two decades. We discuss the lessons learned from implementation. We introduce an implementation model that has been tried and proven across schools and other organisations. We conclude by suggesting what you, the reader, can do to help bring about improvement in our systems of schooling.

The **Glossary of Operational Definitions** provides a lexicon of language used throughout the book: the language of improvement.

**Appendices** provide additional material relating to the concepts, practices and tools presented in the book: Appendix 1 provides capacity matrices for material covered in chapters three to seven; Appendix 2 details quality learning school self assessment, structured around the 12 principles of quality learning; Appendix 3 answers the question: "I do not work in the school education system. What can I do?"; and Appendix 4 provides a starting point for planning a school improvement journey based upon the approach described in the book.

The **Annotated Bibliography** offers a summary of key references used in the text. Our bibliography is different to most in that it includes a brief description of each reference, to help you better understand what the reference might offer.

## Structure

Each of the following chapters comprises the following sections:

**Introduction:** The aim of the chapter; an overview of what the chapter will cover and its links to the overarching philosophy of continual improvement. A flowchart presents a visual summary of the flow of the chapter, detailing its aims and the questions to be explored along the way.

**Body:** The core content of the book is presented in detail. The body also includes explanatory stories, key quotes, textual asides featuring additional details, operational definitions, quality learning tools, suggested sources of further information, as well as links to video clips and handy templates.

**Chapter Summary:** A synopsis of the discussion, key messages and conclusions made.

**Reflection Questions:** Specific reflective questions are included to help you reflect upon the theory and make sense of it in your own unique context.

**Further Reading**: A short list of recommended references for those interested in learning or exploring key concepts and methods in more depth.

# Symbols and icons

We have included a variety of icons, fonts, colours and styles to distinguish different types of content and help you navigate your way through the book.

| Icon | Purpose |
|------|---------|
| Pull quotes | **To highlight key content**<br>Reading the pull quotes will provide an overview of the content of the book and help you locate discussions of interest. |
| Operational definition | **To create shared meaning**<br>Operational definitions appear within the text to clarify meaning where a new word, term or phrase is introduced. The Glossary of Operational Definitions provides a summary of those used in the book. |
| Resources | **To provide sources of further information**<br>Books, journal articles, and web sites are referenced. |
| Templates | **To provide links to templates**<br>Templates are made available for your use wherever possible. |
| Video Clips | **To illustrate how the theory and methods have been applied**<br>Short video clips illustrate how the methods have been applied to the school and/or classroom. These clips are freely available for viewing on the internet. |

| Icon | Purpose |
|------|---------|
| STORIES | **To share experiences**<br>We share personal examples that demonstrate how the theory, tools and methods have been applied, as well as the experiences of others, including students, teachers, principals, parents, and administrators. |
| AN ASIDE | **To provide additional information**<br>These are comments not central to the discussion in the text that may be of interest to the reader. |
| Quality learning tool | **To build capacity in the use of the quality learning tools**<br>Examples of quality learning tools are provided and explained. |

# How can I get the most from this book?

We have formatted this book in a way that makes the ideas accessible and easy to read. This includes:

- Quotes from respected individuals are included to highlight and add depth, interest and alternative perspectives to our discussion.

- Illustrations, diagrams, pictures and photos are used to enhance understanding of the information presented in the book.

- Pull quotes, chapter summaries and detailed tables of contents make it easy to skim the book for areas of interest, locate summaries of arguments, and obtain an overview of the key themes.

The introduction to each chapter and the chapter summaries can help you decide what you want to read, and in what order.

We have packed the book with practical take-away-and-start-today ideas, methods, tools and strategies, while at the same time being mindful of the need to emphasise the theory and purpose that underpins them.

The reflection questions at the end of each chapter are designed to stimulate thinking and help you to start applying what you are learning. You may like to discuss these questions with colleagues and others.

Most of all, we hope this book inspires you and builds your confidence to make a start. Don't put it off, wait for someone else to make the first move, or try to get everyone else on board. You are responsible for a system — a system that can be improved. You can apply the thinking and practices shown in this book, and you can strengthen your capacity to create and deploy your own theories for improvement.

The first step is easy: just turn the page.

# Chapter 2:
# Learning to Improve

Transformation is required: not mere change. Transformation requires Profound Knowledge.

W. Edwards Deming, 2012, *The Essential Deming: Leadership Principles from the Father of Quality*, edited by Joyce Orsini, McGraw-Hill, New York, p. 2.

# Chapter contents

# Introduction

Quality improvement is a philosophy that is profoundly different to the prevailing systems of management in use in most organisations, including those associated with school education.

This chapter introduces the quality improvement philosophy and, in doing so, provides a historical context for the chapters that follow. The origins of the quality improvement approach are introduced, as are key thought leaders, and the application of the philosophy to schools — particularly in the USA and Australia — is outlined.

> This chapter introduces the quality improvement philosophy.

The quality approach gathered momentum in the western world during the late 1980s and early 1990s with the advent of national quality awards processes in the USA, Europe, and Australia. These national processes were developed to stimulate improvement in quality, productivity, and competitiveness, with a focus on systems of management.

W. Edwards Deming was an American statistician whose contribution to quality improvement was the most significant of any individual during the twentieth century. In this chapter, we introduce Deming's work and that of key individuals known for their interpretation and application of Deming's ideas to industry, government, and education.

We describe the evolution of the application of quality improvement to school education over the past three decades, and introduce simple tools that can be used to support quality improvement efforts.

This flowchart provides a summary of the flow of the chapter.

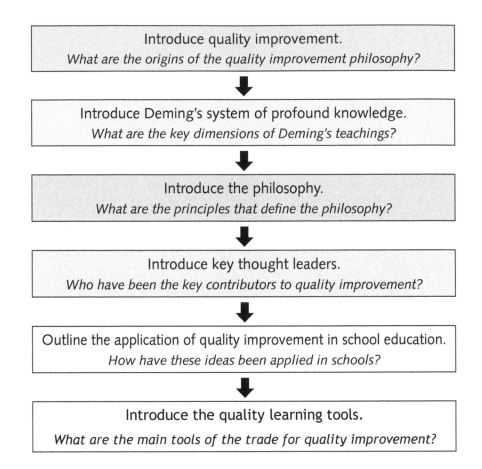

# Quality improvement as a management philosophy

People have been seeking to improve the quality of the things they do for as long as people have been striving for goals: since humanity began. Our discussion here, however, focusses on the origins of quality improvement as a management philosophy, which emerged in the 1980s in response to declining competitiveness and productivity across western nations. To create an environment of continual quality improvement, it was argued, management needed to pay attention to four areas:

1. Systems thinking, interactions and interconnectedness;

2. The importance of theory in developing knowledge and capability;

3. The impact of variation in systems and process; and

4. Psychology and the significance of intrinsic motivation.

Taken together, these areas comprise the theory of management known as quality improvement. This book is devoted to explaining this theory and its application to school education, with a chapter devoted to each of the four areas.

## Early contributions

There have been many contributors to the creation of a quality improvement management philosophy, each of whom contributed to the foundations for a new theory of management: a theory founded in deep understandings of how systems, theory, variation, and psychology work together to directly affect quality.

> There have been many contributors to the creation of a quality improvement management philosophy.

Some of these early contributors were:

• Frederick Winslow Taylor, who developed a systematic approach to economic efficiency and productivity in the 1880s and 1890s;

• John Dewey, whose 1910 work *How We Think* outlined the cognitive processes of theory and reflection and highlighted their importance;

- Walter A. Shewhart, whose struggle with preventing quality problems at the Bell Telephone laboratories resulted in his discovery of common and special cause variation, as detailed in his 1931 work, *Economic Control of Quality of Manufactured Product*; and

- Elton Mayo, an Australian, whose Hawthorne Studies in Western Electric's factory outside Chicago in the 1920s and early 1930s formed the genesis of industrial psychology and the human relations movement.

Early efforts to improve quality were largely driven by individuals and individual organisations.

These early efforts to improve quality were largely driven by individuals and individual organisations. Focus on quality improvement during the first part of the twentieth century was, in this way, fragmented and isolated, and had little impact on wider systems of management. However, these early efforts set the scene for the later work of Deming and others, which would have far more widespread influence.

# Quality and productivity as national priorities

It was not until the 1980s that quality came to widespread prominence in the western world. In the USA, the United Kingdom and Australia, there was a political recognition that poor quality was a serious impediment to productivity, competitiveness, economic growth, and national prosperity.

By the late 1980s, quality improvement was firmly on the global agenda as a management priority.

By the late 1980s, quality improvement was firmly on the agenda as a management priority. There was corporate and government funding to support it.

In Australia, the Total Quality Management Institute was formed, initially with the support of a small number of large Australian corporations, including BHP, Telecom Australia, CIG, and ICI. With support from the Australian Council of Trade Unions and the Commonwealth Government, the Total Quality Management Institute set about creating the criteria and process for a National Quality Award. The inaugural Australian Quality Awards were launched in 1988.

In the USA, Congress passed the *Malcolm Baldrige National Quality Improvement Act* of 1987, which called for the creation of criteria and a process for a National Quality Award.

The European Quality Awards were launched in 1992.

The creation of national quality awards criteria and processes accelerated understanding of the nature of quality and the conditions necessary to facilitate quality improvement. Panels of practitioners from diverse industries came together to agree and document frameworks for best practice.

The development of these criteria significantly advanced understanding of the systemic nature of the factors necessary to achieve continual quality improvement, and the obligations of management to do so. The criteria examined organisational practices in areas including: leadership, planning, the use of data and evidence, customer focus, process management, the management of people, as well as the results and performance of the organisation.

The criteria provided a lens through which an organisation's activities and results could be examined. They were designed to be generic, so that they could be applied to any enterprise. The only way this could be achieved was to focus upon common leadership and management systems that apply to all organisations.

The national quality awards criteria enabled organisations to self-assess the quality of their systems of management and to identify strengths and areas for further development.

In essence, the criteria provided a framework for organisational learning and improvement.

> The national quality awards criteria enabled organisations to self-assess the quality of their systems of management.

# Early problems with understanding and application

During the last two decades of the twentieth century, there was an explosion in the development and deployment of quality methods and approaches, driven by corporate and government attention, along with its associated funding.

Many of these methods were developed by consultants with limited experience of the history or theories of quality. Spurred on by generous funding, many joined the quality bandwagon; the common approach of discarding the old and replacing it with the new soon became evident. While connections to previous incarnations could usually be seen, each new incarnation claimed dramatic improvements on what had gone before.

In a short time, quality morphed through various approaches, programs and titles.

In a short time, quality morphed through a range of various approaches, programs and titles. The theory was diluted to a set of practices with tenuous links to any coherent or comprehensive theory.

The quality philosophy transitioned through variants including: self-managed teams, quality assurance, quality management, benchmarking, best practice, business process management, and more. Each of these approaches has merit, and many have brought tangible benefits to those who have applied them. Most have provided a contribution to the research and practice of quality improvement. In many cases, however, the proponents of these approaches claim they are *the* way to productivity and competitiveness. Where they have been attempted, however, mixed results have usually occurred, with too many showing little or no benefit.

Most of these quality variants reflect only a subset of a comprehensive theory of management.

In practice, most of these quality variants reflect only a subset of a comprehensive theory of management. In failing to address the holistic theory, they fail to deliver the potential benefits.

The many names given to various quality approaches over time also constitutes an impediment to the development of a coherent approach to a quality improvement management philosophy. Given the sheer number of programs and approaches that exist, not to mention the potential for variation in their implementation across organisations, it is not surprising that there is widespread confusion regarding quality improvement. It is predictable that people become more jaded and cynical as they hear of each "new and improved" incantation.

As the great American chemist and physicist, Irving Langmuir, is reported to have said, "There is nothing more difficult to implement than a new, good idea." Because it is good, people think they should be doing it; because it is new, they don't understand it.

At the end of the last century, quality was definitely seen as a new good idea.

## THE MANY FACES OF QUALITY IMPROVEMENT

Over the past three decades, the quality improvement philosophy has transitioned through many variants, including:

- Quality circles;
- Self-managed teams;
- Quality assurance;
- Quality management;
- Total quality management;
- Benchmarking;
- Process benchmarking;
- Breakthrough improvement;
- Best practice;
- World's best practice;
- Business process re-engineering;
- Business excellence;
- Performance excellence;
- Six sigma;
- Lean;
- Lean six sigma;
- Process management; and
- Business process management.

Each approach has drawn heavily from understandings of the quality improvement philosophy at the time of their development. The lessons learnt from these approaches have also contributed to the development of quality improvement philosophy. But the fact that quality improvement continues to morph through many variants, with so many different names and faces, makes it hard to generate a common understanding.

# Deming's system of profound knowledge

There is no substitute for knowledge.

W. Edwards Deming, 2012, *The Essential Deming: Leadership Principles from the Father of Quality*, edited by Joyce Orsini, McGraw-Hill, New York, p. 70.

W. Edwards Deming is the most significant contributor to the understanding of the theory and practices that improve quality.

While there have been many contributions to the field, Deming provided the most comprehensive, all pervasive and transformational insights into quality as a system of management.

Deming who is well known for his contribution to the economic recovery of Japan after the Second World War, died in 1993, at the age of 93. He wrote two key references, *Out of the Crisis* and *The New Economics*, and inspired hundreds, if not thousands, of individuals to apply his teaching within their spheres of influence. Toward the end of his life, approximately 20,000 people attended Deming's seminars each year. In addition to conducting public seminars, Deming worked hard to support and coach individuals to learn and apply his ideas. He was a prolific correspondent who was generous in providing feedback and guidance to those who sought it.

With Deming's passing came the loss of a focal point for quality improvement. While he was alive, there was a highly concentrated understanding of the philosophy that centred upon Deming himself. Following his death, understanding of the philosophy was inevitably diluted.

Deming's theory represents a profound and multi-disciplinary body of knowledge that provides a sound basis for a system of management.

Deming has provided a coherent and universal theory for a system of management far superior to that in common usage today.

This is not to suggest that others have not made significant contributions. Many have provided detailed expositions on various aspects of what Deming was proposing, and many have provided insights into approaches and practices that apply his ideas in a practical way.

Deming's comprehensive theory has repeatedly been shown to result in continual improvement, and research continues to support and reinforce his ideas.

---

*Sidebar quotes:*

W. Edwards Deming is the most significant contributor to the understanding of the theory and practices that improve quality.

Deming has provided a coherent and universal theory for a system of management far superior to that in common usage today.

Deming's comprehensive theory has repeatedly been shown to result in continual improvement, and research continues to support and reinforce his ideas.

During the time that we have been working on quality improvement, we have had the great fortune to have met, worked with, and learned from many Australian and world leaders in the field. We have witnessed and participated in many of the quality approaches de jour listed earlier. We have seen new theories emerge and new practices applied. We have participated in improvement efforts that have resulted in significant advances, and have noted those that have contributed to less successful ventures. Whenever our thinking or action has strayed from Deming's theory, disappointing outcomes have followed. At times, new and innovative programs promised dramatic gains and were successful in their seduction. Frequently in such cases, the significance of some aspect of Deming's theory was not fully comprehended or was ignored. As we reflect on our efforts and learn more of Deming's ideas, we find that our experiences could have been predicted by his theory.

Deming first published his system of profound knowledge in *The New Economics: For industry, government and education* in 1993. Figure 2.1 illustrates the four areas of Deming's system of profound knowledge: appreciation for a system, theory of knowledge, knowledge about variation, and psychology. These reflect the key concepts underpinning quality improvement philosophy and form the foundation for the following four chapters of this book.

Deming's system of profound knowledge: Appreciation for a system, Theory of knowledge, Knowledge about variation, and Psychology.

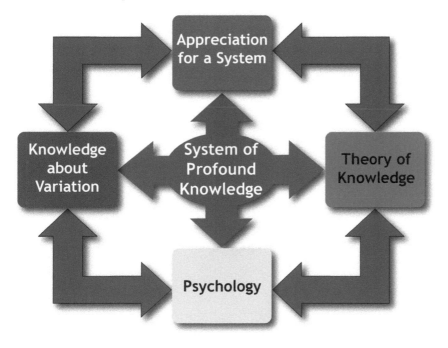

**Figure 2.1 Deming's system of profound knowledge**
Source: Adapted from W. Edwards Deming, 1993, *The New Economics: For industry, government, and education*, MIT, Cambridge.

### DEMING AND THE JAPANESE ADOPTION OF QUALITY

In Japan, at the end of the Second World War, General Douglas MacArthur was appointed Supreme Commander for the Allied Powers and was instructed to restore the country to economic stability.

Homer M. Sarasohn was appointed head of the Industry Branch of the Civil Communications Section of MacArthur's administration and oversaw the rebuilding of the Japanese telecommunications industry. By 1949, Sarasohn observed serious weaknesses in the leadership of companies: poor quality production, poor labour relations, and lack of management accountability. He determined to improve the quality of management by requiring leaders to attend management school.

W. Edwards Deming was a well-known American statistician. He had visited Japan on a number of occasions after the Second World War and outlined a vision of Japan as a world leader in quality. Deming was eventually invited to teach units of the management course.

Deming's teaching at that time included: quality is a management issue; focus on the customer; minimise the number of suppliers and work with them as a partner; trust, cooperation, and respect; statistical process control; and the Shewhart cycle (Plan-Do-Check-Act).

Over the following decades, the quality of Japanese products improved dramatically. The foundation had been laid for Japan's economic resurgence.

The full text of "The Fundamentals of Industrial Management" by Sarasohn and Protzman can be found at http://www.valuemetrics.com.au/resources003.html.

# Quality improvement principles

Stephen Covey wrote extensively on the positive role that principles can play in guiding individuals' behaviours.

> Principles are deep, fundamental truths that have universal application.

Stephen R. Covey, 1990, The 7 Habits of Highly Effective People, Simon and Schuster, New York, p. 35.

We believe that fundamental principles apply universally to organisational behaviour.

> Principles always have natural consequences attached to them. There are positive consequences when we live in harmony with the principles. There are negative consequences when we ignore them.

Stephen R. Covey, 1990, The 7 Habits of Highly Effective People, Simon and Schuster, New York, p. 123.

Deming's system of profound knowledge leads directly to a set of principles that apply to any enterprise. Each principle can be explored and analysed, providing deeper understanding of the various dimensions of the theory. The set of principles can then be reintegrated or synthesised to provide the individual with his or her own enhanced perspective.

The improvement principles provide a lens for viewing the activities and results of any organisation. Departments, districts, schools and classrooms can self-assess the degree to which their systems of management are aligned with the principles; strengths and opportunities for development can be identified. In this way, the principles provide a practical lens for learning and improvement.

Over the years, we have refined the wording of the principles to help strengthen an understanding of their original intent. What follows is our current best expression of Deming's philosophy as a set of principles. (In the spirit of continual learning and improvement, we are sure these will be refined further over time.)

## Principles of quality learning

In working with schools, we have strived to make the quality improvement philosophy accessible and relevant to the school context. One practical method learned from the Australian Quality Council is to express the theory as a set of simple principles. Obviously, this step from

*Deming's system of profound knowledge leads directly to a set of principles that apply to any enterprise.*

*The improvement principles provide a lens for viewing the activities and results of any organisation.*

Deming's original writing means the authors are overlaying their own interpretation. However, this approach is worthwhile, as it makes these ideas clear to a new audience.

The chapters that follow expand upon these principles.

The following 12 principles represent our current best expression of Deming's theory. Their simplicity frequently masks the profound nature of their implications. The chapters that follow expand upon these principles, their implications and relevance to school education.

| Systems | |
|---|---|
| **Systems:** | People work in a system. Systems determine how an organisation and its people behave and perform. |
| **Purpose:** | Shared purpose and a clear vision of excellence align effort. |
| **Processes:** | Improving systems and processes improves performance, relationships and behaviour. |
| **Clients:** | Clients define quality and form perceptions. |
| **Stakeholders:** | Sustainability requires management of relationships with stakeholders. |
| **Learning** | |
| **Planning:** | Improvement is rarely achieved without the planned application of appropriate strategy and methods. |
| **Knowledge:** | Learning and improvement are derived from theory, prediction, observation and reflection. |
| **Variation** | |
| **Data:** | Facts and data are needed to measure progress and improve decision making. |
| **Variation:** | Systems and processes are subject to variation that affects predictability and performance. |
| **People** | |
| **Motivation:** | Removing barriers to intrinsic motivation improves performance. |
| **Relationships:** | Strong human relationships are built through caring, communication, trust and respect. |
| **Leadership:** | It is everybody's job to improve the systems and processes for which they are responsible by working with their people and role modelling these principles. |

Appendix 2 presents a set of matrices designed to enable you to undertake a school self-assessment against these principles.

# Key leaders in Deming's philosophy

We have learned a great deal from those who have sought to understand and apply Deming's philosophy, and we have had the privilege to meet, converse and work with some of the key leaders in the field.

In writing this book, we have made a deliberate choice to return to the original texts of key thought leaders, and to draw from these writings. This is not to say that later advances in understanding have been limited, rather our aim has been to honour and stay close to Deming's original work.

In addition to the writings and video recordings of Deming, we have paid particular attention to a handful of individuals who worked closely with him. As frequent reference is made to these people throughout this book, a brief introduction to each is provided below.

> In writing this book, we have made a deliberate choice to return to the original texts of key thought leaders, and to draw from these writings.

## Myron Tribus

Myron Tribus is an engineer, thermodynamicist, teacher, writer, and innovator. During his working life, he has:

- Received three prestigious awards for his work on aircraft de-icing systems;
- Written a groundbreaking text relating to thermodynamics and information theory;
- Served as Dean of Engineering at Dartmouth College;
- Served as Assistant Secretary of Commerce for Science and Technology for the USA;
- Served as Senior Vice President for Research and Engineering at Xerox;
- Hosted a television science program, *Threshold*, on PBS television; and
- Been Director of the Centre for Advanced Engineering Study at MIT.

He sometimes quipped that he had trouble holding down a job.

Tribus met Deming during the mid-1980s at the time that Deming was writing his seminal work, *Out of the Crisis*, which was to be published by MIT, where Tribus was working at the time. The two men developed strong respect for one another and became good friends.

Tribus rapidly became well known for his lectures and writings on the practical application of Deming's ideas.

It was during Tribus's visit to Australia, at the invitation of Telstra Corporation in 1994, that I (Michael) first met him. In the years that followed, Tribus was generous in his support, encouragement and mentoring through many conversations, conferences, meals, and email exchanges. He would respond promptly to information and inquiries, usually with questions: very good questions that were designed to make me think and discover my own answers, or uncover gaps in knowledge or understanding.

I am most grateful for Myron's generous mentoring over the past 20 years.

---

### 💬 TRIBUS MEETS DEMING

Myron Tribus was hosting a series of video-taped interviews for students at the Centre for Advanced Engineering Studies at MIT. Each interview would focus on a different aspect of engineering or industry. To complete the series, the producer suggested that "this famous man by the name of Dr. W. Edwards Deming" might be suitable for interview.

Deming provided some interview questions, but Tribus ignored them and began with his own questions. "You have a lot of experience in industry, and you can tell me about things I don't know," he began. "For example, you can tell me how you deal with unions." Deming leaned in and retorted: "Oh! You think unions are the problem do you?" Tribus attempted to recommence the interview several times, but each time the response was similar. Both men became heated and the interview was postponed for a week. As Tribus told me many years later, "It didn't matter what I said, he made me look like an ass."

Tribus made a point of studying Deming's work closely before the rescheduled video-taping. The rescheduled interview went well and the two men went on to become good friends.

In the years that followed, Tribus became well known for his pragmatic advice and writings on the practical application of Deming's theories to industry and education. His influence has been significant. Tribus consulted to many corporations, including BHP Steel in the late 1980s, as the company was developing its corporate quality approach. This influence was later reflected in BHP's participation in the development of the Australian Quality Awards criteria. Tribus also provided advice to the US National Institute of Standards and Technology as the Baldrige criteria were being developed.

Tribus' papers on quality in education provide a clear and concise set of references that support Deming's contribution to the education sector.

---

 A comprehensive set of Tribus's papers on quality in industry and education can be found at http://www.qla.com.au/Papers/5.

# David Langford

David Langford is a remarkable educator and proponent of Deming's philosophy as it applies to education.

Langford came across Deming's work during an industry visit in Arizona while he was enrolled in a graduate course in business. Intrigued by what he saw and heard, he studied Deming's writings and sought help from corporations that were introducing his approach. From 1986, Langford was corresponding with Deming. His classroom became a laboratory for learning and applying quality improvement tools and ideas.

We first met David Langford, at the recommendation of Myron Tribus, in 1998, during the first phase of the Quality in Schools initiative in Victoria. Tribus and Langford gave well received keynote presentations at a Victorian education conference, and Langford was invited to deliver a four-day seminar in Melbourne.

Langford's seminar is based on Deming's four-day seminar. Over the course of four days, participants are introduced to Deming's system of profound knowledge, with particular attention to its application to school education. As Langford introduces the philosophy and tools, participants are encouraged to reflect upon their own experiences as educators. A tangible change in the seminar climate sets in as individuals experience a profoundly different perspective on the systems of education.

Over the years since that first seminar, we have become good friends and colleagues with David. Together, we have presented more than 60 four-day conferences across Australia.

# Russell Ackoff

Russell Ackoff was a pioneer in operations research, systems thinking, and the science of management. Ackoff and Deming found considerable common ground in their respective approaches to organisational improvement: Deming's views developed from origins in statistics, while Ackoff's came from an operations research and systems thinking background.

Ackoff became particularly well known for his research and writings on systems thinking and its relationship to human behaviour.

He died in 2009 at the age of 90.

## Peter Scholtes

Peter Scholtes has a background in adult education and organisation development. He worked closely with Deming over the last 15 years of Deming's life.

Scholtes is best known for his views on engaging employees in a more humane and effective manner than that derived from the prevailing system of management. He co-authored *The Team Handbook* and wrote the highly acclaimed work *The Leader's Handbook* in 1998. He is best known for his writings on the destructive nature of performance appraisal in organisations and what to do about it.

Michael had the pleasure of chatting with Peter and participating in several seminars conducted by him on his visits to Australia during the 1990s.

Peter died in 2009 at the age of 71.

# Quality improvement in school education

## Application in the USA

Early applications of Deming's ideas to school education were traced, by Myron Tribus, to Alaska and Arizona in the early 1980s. In Arizona, teaching and application of the tools of quality improvement were largely an add-on to the curriculum of the time.

> Early applications of Deming's ideas to school education were traced, by Myron Tribus, to Alaska and Arizona in the early 1980s.

## Mt Edgecumbe High School

Mt Edgecumbe High School, in Sitka, Alaska, deserves special mention. This was the first school to adopt Deming's ideas as a management philosophy — initially in some classrooms, and eventually across the administration. The quality approach was led by David Langford and began in his classrooms.

When Myron Tribus visited Mt Edgecumbe in 1990 he saw, for the first time, the potential of quality as a way of life in the classroom. Mt Edgecumbe provided a profound example of what is possible. He wrote:

> Mount Edgecumbe High School had presented an example:
>
> - Students in charge of their own learning
>
> - Students improving the learning processes of the school
>
> - Faculty and students working together to improve processes
>
> - Faculty, students and administration treating the school as a system
>
> - Shifting the focus from teaching to learning.
>
> Myron Tribus, "The Contribution of W. Edwards Deming to the Improvement of Education", p. 2. Available at http://www.qla.com.au/Papers/5.

## The spread of Deming's ideas

The 1990s saw the spread of Deming's ideas applied to education across the USA, and into the United Kingdom, France, and Australia. Quality, it seemed, was the new good idea de jour. During this time, many books were written on the application of Deming's ideas to education including:

- John Jay Bonstingl, 1992, *Schools of Quality: An introduction to total quality management in education*, Sage, Thousand Oaks.

- William Glasser, 1990, *The Quality School: Managing students without coercion*, HarperCollins, New York.

- Lee Jenkins, 1997, *Improving Student Learning: Applying Deming's quality principles in classrooms*, ASQC Quality Press, Milwaukee.

- David Langford and Barbara Cleary, 1995, *Orchestrating Learning with Quality*, American Society for Quality, Milwaukee.

- Franklin P. Schargel, 1994, *Transforming Education Through Total Quality Management: A practitioner's guide*, Eye on Education, Princeton.

While this list is not exhaustive, it serves as recognition, perhaps, that there was a diverse yet focussed effort to understand the application of Deming's ideas to school education. Deming's teachings were interpreted and applied across a variety of education settings.

In 1999, the scope of the Baldrige National Quality Program in the USA was expanded to include healthcare and education. This highlighted the importance of quality in education (in the USA at least), and the program promoted aspects of Deming's philosophy.

## Leander Independent School District

The Leander Independent School District in Leander, Texas, provides the only known example of wide-scale application of Deming's ideas over an extended period. The district learned from Deming, David Langford and Myron Tribus, and set about applying what they learned.

For over two decades, the district has consistently applied Deming's principles and teachings to improve the quality of learning and quality of life across the district. In this time, the district has been transformed from a small rural district to a rapidly growing and continually improving district of over 32,000 students across 37 campuses.

If you have never experienced it, it can be hard to comprehend what continual improvement looks and feels like in practice. Employees across the district find joy in their work, collaborate extensively, and share a strong and aligned sense of purpose. All key indicators across the district demonstrate continual improvement, including the following:

- Drop-out rates have fallen to below one per cent. The drop-out rate for economically disadvantaged students and minority groups is below two per cent;

- The percentage of students passing the state mathematics exam has risen from 60–70 per cent in 1994 to approximately 90 per cent (see Figure 2.2);

- The proportion of campuses rated by the state of Texas as "recognised" or "exemplary" using the Academic Excellence Indicator System has risen steadily to over 80 per cent; and

- The percentage of students completing or continuing in high school has risen steadily to nearly 94 per cent, with economically disadvantaged students at 89 per cent.

Leander serves as a magnificent example that Deming's ideas do apply to education, and that they provide dramatically different results to those seen elsewhere, results that are continually improving.

The Leander Independent School District in Leander, Texas, provides the only known example of wide-scale application of Deming's ideas over an extended period.

All key indicators across the district demonstrate continual improvement.

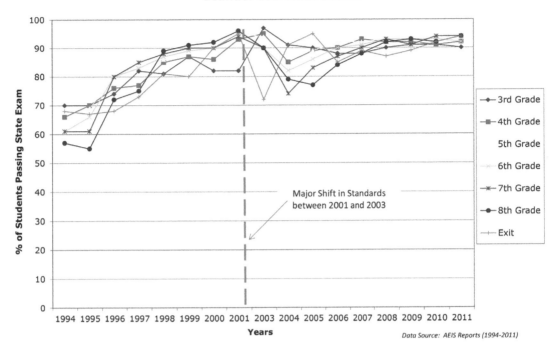

**Figure 2.2 Leander Independent School District student mathematics test scores, showing continual improvement from 1994 to 2011**

Source: Leander Independent School District, Texas.

# Application in Australia

During the 1990s, the Australian Quality Council (AQC) was engaged to lead programs to introduce Deming's ideas to schools in Victoria and South Australia. These programs ran for over five years and introduced quality improvement ideas and methods to over 300 schools and preschools.

The AQC was a small, national, not-for-profit, membership-based organisation that was formally recognised by the Australian Government as the peak body for quality. The AQC was supported by industry, the Australian Council of Trade Unions, and the Australian Commonwealth Government, with each stakeholder having representation on the AQC board.

The Quality in Schools initiative in Victoria commenced in 1997. In the years that followed, the initiative introduced over 150 schools to the quality improvement philosophy.

A similar program, Quality and Improvement in Schools and Preschools, was initiated in South Australia in 2001. Over the course of three years, this initiative engaged nearly 190 schools and preschools in quality improvement philosophy.

The legacy of these initiatives is still evident today, in many of the systemic changes since made in Victoria and South Australia and in those schools that continue to apply quality improvement as a management philosophy. Examples from a selection of these schools are scattered through this book.

The authors established Quality Learning Australasia in 2002. Our intention — and passion — is to share and build upon what we have learned about applying quality improvement philosophy to school-based learning. While our primary focus is school improvement, we enjoy working with other organisations in industry and government to continue cross-sectoral learning. It is, after all, one system.

We continue our efforts to this day: learning, developing resources, and providing professional learning and coaching. This book is an effort to capture and share what we have learned working with many valued clients, colleagues and friends.

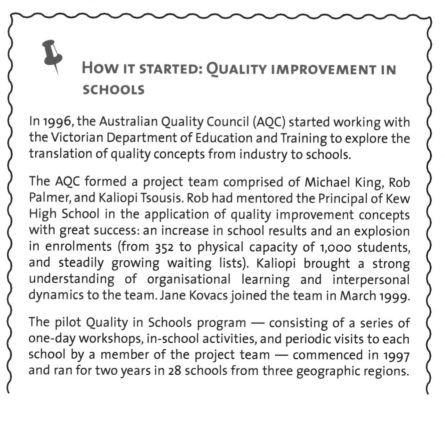

## HOW IT STARTED: QUALITY IMPROVEMENT IN SCHOOLS

In 1996, the Australian Quality Council (AQC) started working with the Victorian Department of Education and Training to explore the translation of quality concepts from industry to schools.

The AQC formed a project team comprised of Michael King, Rob Palmer, and Kaliopi Tsousis. Rob had mentored the Principal of Kew High School in the application of quality improvement concepts with great success: an increase in school results and an explosion in enrolments (from 352 to physical capacity of 1,000 students, and steadily growing waiting lists). Kaliopi brought a strong understanding of organisational learning and interpersonal dynamics to the team. Jane Kovacs joined the team in March 1999.

The pilot Quality in Schools program — consisting of a series of one-day workshops, in-school activities, and periodic visits to each school by a member of the project team — commenced in 1997 and ran for two years in 28 schools from three geographic regions.

During the second year of the pilot, it became evident that other schools were becoming interested in the project. School leaders were hearing about the benefits from their colleagues and they wanted to be part of it.

Following the pilot, the Department asked the AQC to prepare a proposal for a new group of schools to participate in the program, commencing in 1999. The AQC undertook a complete re-design for Quality in Schools Group Two, based on insights provided by Myron Tribus and David Langford and lessons derived from the pilot. It was a more integrated program that included Langford's quality learning seminar as an integral part of the overall design.

Each year, over the next five years, a new group of approximately 30 schools commenced the Quality in Schools initiative in Victoria.

In 2002, the AQC merged with Standards Australia and became known as Business Excellence Australia. Business Excellence Australia ceased to offer the Quality in Schools program to schools in 2004.

As the Quality in Schools pilot was gathering pace in Victoria, officers of the South Australian Department of Education, Training and Employment became interested in the program. A steering committee was established in Adelaide, again comprising officers from the Department and AQC. The first phase commenced in February 2001, led by Michael King with support from Trisha Howes, and was known as the Quality and Improvement in Schools and Pre-schools initiative

Phase One of this initiative ran over two years and comprised five networks, with participants from 87 schools and preschools. Phase Two commenced the following year, with 101 schools and preschools being represented. Phase Two was the final phase of the initiative in South Australia due to a change in government at the February 2002 State election and subsequent reforms.

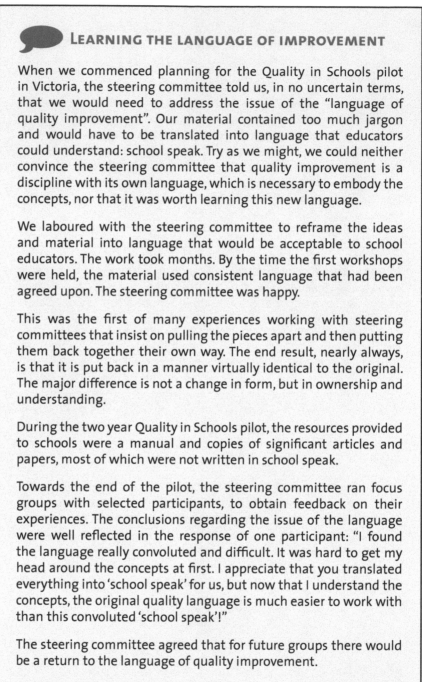

## LEARNING THE LANGUAGE OF IMPROVEMENT

When we commenced planning for the Quality in Schools pilot in Victoria, the steering committee told us, in no uncertain terms, that we would need to address the issue of the "language of quality improvement". Our material contained too much jargon and would have to be translated into language that educators could understand: school speak. Try as we might, we could neither convince the steering committee that quality improvement is a discipline with its own language, which is necessary to embody the concepts, nor that it was worth learning this new language.

We laboured with the steering committee to reframe the ideas and material into language that would be acceptable to school educators. The work took months. By the time the first workshops were held, the material used consistent language that had been agreed upon. The steering committee was happy.

This was the first of many experiences working with steering committees that insist on pulling the pieces apart and then putting them back together their own way. The end result, nearly always, is that it is put back in a manner virtually identical to the original. The major difference is not a change in form, but in ownership and understanding.

During the two year Quality in Schools pilot, the resources provided to schools were a manual and copies of significant articles and papers, most of which were not written in school speak.

Towards the end of the pilot, the steering committee ran focus groups with selected participants, to obtain feedback on their experiences. The conclusions regarding the issue of the language were well reflected in the response of one participant: "I found the language really convoluted and difficult. It was hard to get my head around the concepts at first. I appreciate that you translated everything into 'school speak' for us, but now that I understand the concepts, the original quality language is much easier to work with than this convoluted 'school speak'!"

The steering committee agreed that for future groups there would be a return to the language of quality improvement.

Only one change stuck: we still refer to "customers" in the school sector as "clients".

## A FLASH OF THE BLINDINGLY OBVIOUS

We didn't really know what we would do in the second year of the Quality in Schools pilot.

We were very clear that the first year would focus on school leadership and management systems: we would introduce quality improvement philosophy as the set of principles underpinning the Australian Business Excellence Framework; we would work with participants to have them interpret these principles from a school context; we would introduce concepts and improvement methods associated with systems; schools would complete a self-assessment using the Business Excellence Framework; the Plan-Do-Study-Act cycle would be the vehicle for school improvement teams to lead school improvement; and, finally, we would teach participants how to document processes and incorporate them into a system of school documentation.

During the second year, our intention was to mirror this approach, this time for the classroom system: interpret the principles into teaching and learning; develop understanding of the classroom as a system; undertake self-assessment against a new classroom framework developed by the steering committee; use the Plan-Do-Study-Act cycle; and so on.

During one of Myron Tribus's visits to Australia, towards the end of the first year of the pilot, we sought his advice. As always, his response was swift and to the point: "You need David Langford." The steering committee managed to convince the Victorian Department of Education that both Myron Tribus and David Langford should be invited to be keynote speakers at a Department conference in October 1998.

Both keynotes were very well received. David was invited to deliver his first four-day quality learning seminar in Australia the following January, as part of the Quality in Schools pilot.

It was during this first seminar that we had a flash of the blindingly obvious.

While the focus of David's seminar is squarely on schools, it applies to all levels of the school system — from government department, to school leader, teacher, student, and support staff — as one system. Treating school leadership differently to the classroom, as we were doing in the pilot, was not helpful. School systems frequently treat school administration, teachers and students differently, and we were engaging in the same dysfunctional practice. It is all one system, and must be managed as such. We immediately set about redesigning the Quality in Schools initiative.

# Introducing the quality learning tools

No discussion of quality would be complete without reference to the quality learning tools.

 Tool: a physical or procedural instrument.

A tape measure, saw, and nail gun are each an example of a tool: a physical instrument that may be used in the construction of a house.

When shopping, many people create a shopping list. This is an example of a different type of tool: a procedural instrument.

Sometimes, tools can be a mixture of the physical and the procedural. Emails allow people to transmit documents and messages across the globe. This tool is comprised of both a physical instrument (a computer or smart phone) and procedures relating to its use. You cannot effectively send an email, for example, without knowing the email address of the person with whom you wish to correspond, as well as the procedures by which you log-in, compose and send an email.

Tools can be as simple as a shopping list or a nail gun, or as complex as email.

Quality improvement tools are mostly procedural instruments that are simple to use.

 Quality improvement tool: a physical or procedural instrument used to improve quality.

The origin of the quality improvement tools can be traced back to Japanese industry in the 1960s. The first set of these tools went under various names, including "the seven tools of total quality control" and "the seven basic tools of quality". The list of tools changes slightly across various references, but usually includes: the Ishikawa diagram (also known as the fishbone diagram or cause and effect diagram), check sheet, Pareto chart, histogram, correlation chart (also known as the scatter diagram), control chart, and flow chart.

The seven management tools were refined, also in Japan, in the 1970s. They too go under various names, including "the seven quality

*The origin of the quality improvement tools can be traced back to Japanese industry in the 1960s.*

management tools" and "the seven management tools for quality control". (The significance of the number seven is attributed to the seven weapons of Benkei, a subject of Japanese folklore from the twelfth century). The range of tools in this group also varies by reference, but typically includes: the affinity diagram, interrelationship digraph, tree diagram, matrix diagram, process decision program chart, prioritisation matrix, and the arrow diagram (also known as the activity network diagram).

In the years since, more tools have been developed and applied to the improvement of quality, including: force field analysis, Gantt chart, nominal group technique, and multi voting.

A range of statistical data analysis and presentation tools have also been developed and applied to the improvement of quality, including: dot plots, stem and leaf plots, box and whisker plots, bar charts, column charts, area graphs, and run charts.

Toward the end of last century, more complex tools were developed. Quality function deployment, for example, is a sophisticated tool for new product design. Failure mode and effect analysis provides a structured approach to considering the risks associated with quality failures and how these risks can be minimised.

There are now literally scores, if not hundreds, of quality improvement tools.

In an educational context, quality improvement primarily relates to improving the quality of learning. All of the quality improvement tools can be relevant, in varying degrees, to an educational context. If the focus is on improving the quality of learning, there are additional tools available.

> In an educational context, quality improvement primarily relates to improving the quality of learning.

The process of learning within schools is predominantly a social process. Students are arranged into classes and frequently work collaboratively on learning activities. To support this, a range of cooperative learning tools has emerged. These tools provide simple procedures that promote structured student interaction and learning. These include tools as simple as brainstorming, to Elliot Aronson's jigsaw, and Spencer Kagan's collection of cooperative learning structures.

Additional approaches have been developed that focus on refining thinking. The best known of these are the six thinking hats, and plus, minus, interesting, both developed by Edward de Bono. Other tools in this category include Joseph Novak's concept maps and Tony Buzan's mind maps. These are sometimes known collectively as the thinking tools.

Because most of the tools are very simple, they exist in many varied forms, often with different names. While this can lead to confusion, it is a natural consequence of individuals learning and adapting the tools to their own contexts for their own uses. It is their simplicity that leads to adaptation, reframing, and the evolution of variants.

Quality improvement tools, cooperative learning tools, and thinking tools all have a role to play in improving the quality of learning. As such, they are sometimes lumped together under the title of quality learning tools.

> Quality learning tool: a physical or procedural instrument used to improve the quality of learning. Quality learning tools include quality improvement tools, cooperative learning tools and the so-called thinking tools.

There is no definitive list of quality learning tools. There is no single, agreed authority on them, nor is there likely to be. Teachers and learners are creative and will continue to draw upon the wide variety of these tools, adapt them to their needs, and create new ones to address emerging needs.

Throughout this book, reference is made to approximately 30 of these tools. The aim is not to provide a definitive guide to the tools, but to illustrate their simplicity, power and relevance to improving the quality of learning. We also aim to show how the tools promote quality improvement as a management philosophy.

It is important to remember that tools are simply tools; they are not ends in themselves. They provide efficient and effective methods that contribute to achieving desired outcomes.

David Langford has created a well-respected and comprehensive reference for the quality learning tools called *Tool Time*, which comes in four versions: education, business, health care, and lean.

---

*Sidebar notes:*

Quality improvement tools, cooperative learning tools, and thinking tools all have a role to play in improving the quality of learning.

Tools are simply tools; they are not ends in themselves.

# Chapter summary

This chapter has introduced quality improvement as a management philosophy, with origins prior to the twentieth century.

*   W. Edwards Deming was the most significant single contributor to the development of a management philosophy based on the aim of continual quality improvement. Deming expressed the philosophy as a system of profound knowledge, comprised of appreciation for a system; the theory of knowledge; knowledge about variation; and psychology.

*   Other key contributors include Myron Tribus, David Langford, Russell Ackoff, and Peter Scholtes.

*   Quality improvement theory has been expressed as 12 principles that describe the key concepts underpinning the four areas of Deming's system of profound knowledge.

*   Deming's ideas have been applied to school education since the early 1980s.

*   Quality learning tools can be applied to improve the quality of learning.

# Reflection questions

**?** What has been your understanding of quality improvement as a management philosophy? What factors have contributed to this understanding?

**?** How would you describe your organisation's or school's approach to quality improvement? How does the quality improvement philosophy reaffirm or reinform this approach?

**?** How might the set of principles of quality learning be relevant to you and to your organisation/school/classroom/context?

**?** Myron Tribus observed that Mount Edgecumbe High School provided an example by which quality had the potential to become a way of life in the classroom and observed five criteria by which this was becoming possible:

- Students in charge of their own learning;
- Students improving the learning processes of the school;
- Faculty and students working together to improve processes;
- Faculty, students and administration treating the school as a system; and
- Shifting the focus from teaching to learning.

To what degree are these criteria evident in your school? To what degree might they be desirable? Why? How can you make them come alive?

# Further reading

We recommend the following references for those who wish to read more on the quality improvement philosophy and tools.

W. Edwards Deming, 1986, *Out of the Crisis*, MIT, Massachusetts — Deming's seminal work, which describes his 14 points and the key concepts necessary for quality improvement.

W. Edwards Deming, 1993, *The New Economics for Industry, Government and Education*, MIT, Massachusetts — Deming's final publication, which captures the essence of his work in continual improvement over four decades.

David Langford, 2015, *Tool Time for Education*, version 15, Langford International, Montana — David's book is the most easy to read and use quality learning tool recipe book we have found.

Tony Miller and Gordon Hall, 2013, *Letting Go: Breathing new life into organisations*, Argyll Publishing, Glendaruel — This beautifully written book describes how the old ideas of management and control are stifling organisations and the individuals working in them and stresses the importance of systems thinking and intrinsic motivation.

Peter Scholtes, 1998, *The Leaders Handbook*, McGraw Hill, New York — A comprehensive and easy to read reference that translates Deming's theory of continual improvement into everyday language.

Myron Tribus, various papers on quality in industry and education can be found at the QLA web site: http://www.qla.com.au/Papers/5.

# Chapter 3:
# Working on the System

By understanding a system, one may be able to predict the consequences of a proposed change.

W. Edwards Deming, 1994, *The New Economics: For industry, government and education*, MIT, Massachusetts, p. 56.

# Chapter contents

# Introduction

This is the first of four chapters to introduce and explain Deming's philosophy. It introduces the first area of his system of profound knowledge — appreciation for a system — and the five improvement principles that reflect its underpinning key concepts:

**Systems:**      People work in a system. Systems determine how an organisation and its people behave and perform.

**Purpose:**      Shared purpose and a clear vision of excellence align effort.

**Processes:**    Improving systems and processes improves performance, relationships and behaviour.

**Clients:**      Clients define quality and form perceptions.

**Stakeholders:** Sustainability requires management of relationships with stakeholders.

In this chapter, we show how an understanding of systems is fundamental for organisational improvement. The particular type of system that best represents an organisation is a social system. Schools and classrooms, for example, are social systems.

We show how the two key characteristics of a social system — choice and interaction — are responsible for much of the complexity in organisations. These characteristics explain why organisations need clear purpose, vision and values to align effort and make daily interactions more productive and satisfying.

This chapter also explains how systems and processes play a critical role in delivering high quality outputs and outcomes, and examines the implications that arise from this insight. Such as the fact that the performance of organisations is governed much more by the system itself than by the actions of individuals within the system. By focussing on improving systems and processes, we can stop the damaging practice of blaming individuals for disappointing results.

A focus on such practices as system documentation, can create explicit agreed systems, processes, policies, and supporting documents. This helps to communicate, train and induct staff, eliminate waste, and continually improve how things are done.

This chapter's focus on these five principles also turns our attention to the importance of understanding and responding to the needs

---

In this chapter, we show how an understanding of systems is fundamental for organisational improvement.

and expectations of stakeholders, including clients. There are many stakeholders in most systems, with competing expectations and requirements, which need to be understood and carefully managed. The emotional engagement of all stakeholders affects organisational performance.

Finally, we explore some of the wide range of quality learning tools that can be used to apply quality improvement theory in a simple and highly practical manner, particularly system and process maps.

The following flowchart provides a summary of the chapter. Its contents are reflected as key questions we seek to answer as we explore systems.

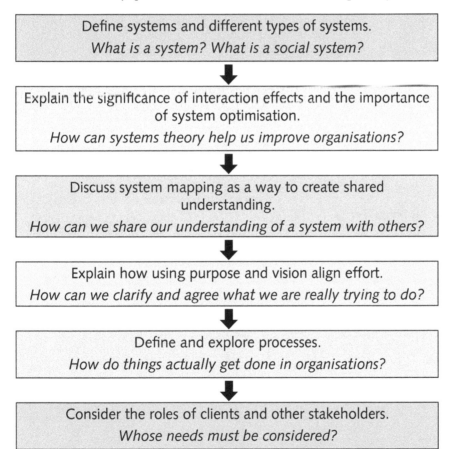

Define systems and different types of systems.
*What is a system? What is a social system?*

⬇

Explain the significance of interaction effects and the importance of system optimisation.
*How can systems theory help us improve organisations?*

⬇

Discuss system mapping as a way to create shared understanding.
*How can we share our understanding of a system with others?*

⬇

Explain how using purpose and vision align effort.
*How can we clarify and agree what we are really trying to do?*

⬇

Define and explore processes.
*How do things actually get done in organisations?*

⬇

Consider the roles of clients and other stakeholders.
*Whose needs must be considered?*

# Systems

This section of the chapter expands on the first of the twelve principles of quality learning:

> People work in a system. Systems determine how an organisation and its people behave and perform.

## What is a system?

Deming defined a system this way:

> A system is a network of interdependent components that work together to try to accomplish the aim of the system.
>
> W. Edwards Deming, 1994, *The New Economics: For industry, government and education*, MIT, Massachusetts, p. 50.

Russell Ackoff defined a system in a little more depth, as follows:

> A system is a set of two or more elements that satisfies the following three conditions:
>
> 1. The behaviour of each element has an effect on the behaviour of the whole.
>
> 2. The behaviour of the elements and the effects on the whole are interdependent.
>
> 3. However subgroups of elements are formed, each has an effect on the behaviour of the whole and none has an independent effect on it.
>
> Russell L. Ackoff, 1981, *Ackoff's Best: His Classic Writings on Management*, John Wiley & Sons, New York, pp. 15–16.

## Different types of systems

The key concept here is the relationships of parts to the whole.

When thinking about this concept, perhaps an easy system to relate to is the human body. A human body is a system; it satisfies the criteria set out in Deming's and Ackoff's definitions:

1.  The various organs in the human body have a direct effect on performance of the whole.

2. The parts of the human body are interdependent. The functioning of the heart and its effect on the body, for example, is subject to the workings of the lungs, brain, and other parts of the body.

3. It is not possible to group parts of the human body in such a way that they become independent of the whole.

## Systems within systems

Systems nest and are contained within other systems.

A school class is a system that exists within the school, which is also a system. The class is nested within the school system. The school is the containing system for the class. Similarly, a school can be nested within a district system; the district system can be the containing system for a school. In other words, systems are frequently nested within bigger systems, as is illustrated by Figure 3.1.

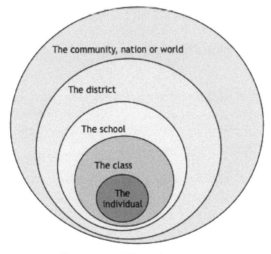

**Figure 3.1 Nested systems**

Nested systems are strongly influenced by their containing systems. The containing systems provide the environment in which the system operates.

A classroom system, for example, exists within an environment comprising the requirements, expectations and constraints imposed by the school, the district, the local community, the state, and nation. A class is expected to abide by school rules, and is required to conform to district policies and adhere to district procedures. Individual teachers are expected to abide by government legislation and regulations.

> Systems nest inside, and are contained within, other systems.

> Nested systems are strongly influenced by their containing systems.

These containing systems collectively define the environment in which the class operates. This environment imposes requirements, expectations and constraints upon the system.

It is often the requirements, expectations and constraints of the containing systems that make system reform so difficult.

This is certainly the case with school education. While individual schools may be striving to increase student responsibility for learning, for example, their efforts can be hampered by a community that expects schooling to be based on more directive, "drill and practice" methods. Similarly, a district's desire to enhance professional dialogue and sharing among teachers may be undermined by state legislation that provides bonuses only to the "best" teachers.

## Organisations as social systems

There are many different types of systems: mechanical, social, ecological, and biological.

An organisation is a social system.

Social systems choose a purpose. They can also choose the methods by which they seek to achieve their purpose. Importantly, the parts that make up a social system can also have purposes of their own and choose their methods for achieving those purposes.

An organisation has a purpose, which is frequently stated as a mission or aim. An organisation also plans the methods or strategies by which it will seek to achieve its purpose. Within an organisation, individuals and groups of individuals — such as divisions, branches and sections — can also choose their purposes and the methods by which they seek to achieve them. Social systems are usually parts of larger social systems.

It is important to apply the correct system modelling to each type of system. Some organisations are managed as if they were mechanical systems. It is usually dysfunctional to treat individuals and work groups as if they are commoditised mechanical components or interchangeable parts. An organisation does not continue to run smoothly when we simply swap parts over like tyres on a bicycle. What's more, social systems behave very differently to mechanical systems; social systems are more chaotic and dynamic while being far less predictable. Similarly, if we apply what is known as animated systems modelling to organisations, we see the widely held but dysfunctional perspective that management is the brain that controls the remainder of the organisation. This is certainly not the case.

An organisation is a social system.

Social systems choose a purpose. They can also choose the methods by which they seek to achieve their purpose.

Within an organisation, individuals and groups can also choose their purposes and the methods.

It is important to apply the correct system modelling to each type of system.

## Interactions within social systems

Because of the interactions that occur between the various elements that make up social systems, organisations are complex entities.

Let us assume for a moment that organisations are comprised only of people. We make this assumption to simplify an examination of the impacts upon the system of interactions coming from elements within the system.

If a social system were comprised of only one element — for example, a one person business — then there is only one element impacting within the system: the one person in the business.

If there are two elements in a system — a business consisting of a partnership between two people, for example — then there are three effects on this system: the effect of each individual plus the effect of their interaction.

If there are three elements, there are seven effects: the effect of each individual, the effect of the interaction between each pair of individuals, and the effect of the interaction among all three individuals.

This is illustrated in Figure 3.2.

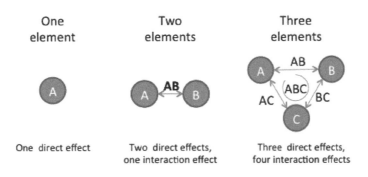

| One<br>element | Two<br>elements | Three<br>elements |
|---|---|---|
| One direct effect | Two direct effects,<br>one interaction effect | Three direct effects,<br>four interaction effects |

**Figure 3.2 Direct and interaction effects in systems**

These interactions can be positive and add to the performance of the system as a whole. They can also be negative and detract from the performance of the system. Interactions can lead to harmony, or they can lead to discord.

Interaction may reinforce efforts, or it may nullify efforts.

W. Edwards Deming, 2012, *The Essential Deming: Leadership Principles from the Father of Quality*, edited by Joyce Orsini, McGraw-Hill, New York, p. 78.

Because of the interactions that occur between the various elements that make up social systems, organisations are complex entities.

Interactions can lead to harmony, or they can lead to discord.

As the number of elements within the system grows, the number of possible interactions increases exponentially. This is shown in Table 3.1.

| No. elements | 1 | 2 | 3 | 4 | 5 | 6 | 7 | 8 | 9 | 10 |
|---|---|---|---|---|---|---|---|---|---|---|
| Direct Effects | 1 | 2 | 3 | 4 | 5 | 6 | 7 | 8 | 9 | 10 |
| Possible interaction effects | 0 | 1 | 4 | 11 | 26 | 57 | 120 | 247 | 502 | 1013 |
| Total effects | 1 | 3 | 7 | 15 | 31 | 63 | 127 | 255 | 511 | 1023 |

**Table 3.1 Direct and interaction effects in systems**

The relationship between the number of elements and the total effects can be expressed mathematically. If $n$ is the number of elements:

Total effects     = direct effects + interaction effects
$$= n + (2^n - (n-1))$$
$$= 2^n - 1$$

By the time that there are 20 elements in a system, there are over one million possible interactions. If there are 30 elements in a system, there will be over one billion possible interactions. Each of these interactions can add to or subtract from the performance of the system as a whole.

## Interaction effects dominate

Consider a workgroup of 20 individuals, such as an office or a classroom. In this social system, there will be 20 direct effects; there will be 20 people each having a direct effect on the behaviour and performance of the system. Predominantly this will be a function of choices each individual makes regarding their individual purposes at any point in time and the methods by which they choose to pursue those purposes.

Performance will also be affected by alignment of individual purposes and methods with those of the organisation. Most people have experienced the disruption caused by an individual whose behaviour is not supportive of the aims of the group. This is an example of a direct effect.

In a workgroup of 20 individuals, there will also be over one million possible interaction effects on the behaviour and performance of the system. These interactions include how the behaviour of groups of individuals (whether it be a pair of individuals, three people, or any sub-grouping) can influence the system. Sub-groups are a common feature of most groups of people (social systems). These sub-groups can exert strong influence over the behaviour and performance of the system as a whole. This influence can be disruptive — such as the influence of a small group of disinterested students, for example — but it can also be constructive — such as a group that questions assumptions, provides assistance to others, or suggests better methods.

Which effects are stronger: direct effects or interaction effects? It is certainly true that there are many more potential interaction effects than there are direct effects. In practice, the vast majority of interaction effects will have negligible impact. Some individuals and groups simply do not interact with one another to a significant degree. Yet, as we shall see in Chapter Six, a key motivator for human beings is a sense of belonging within a group. Belonging is achieved through collaboration, support, and feedback and individuals within a group are, for the most part, driven to engage and interact with one another. These interactions among individuals are hugely significant and have a profound impact on the behaviour and performance of the system. Once the group size exceeds a small number — six or seven — the impact of interaction effects is much more significant than the impact of direct effects.

> The impact of interaction effects is much more significant than the impact of direct effects.

So far we have confined our discussion to interaction occurring among people within a system. However, social systems also include non-human elements, such as resources and technology. These elements also produce interaction effects, including the interaction of individuals and groups with resources and technology systems. While these interactions should not be ignored, the dominant interaction effects within most organisations, including schools, come from interactions among people.

A further layer of complexity is added when one considers the interaction effects between elements of the system — individuals and groups of individuals — with the elements of the containing systems. People not only interact within the system, they also interact, both individually and collectively, with the people and other elements of containing systems.

The behaviour and performance of a classroom, workgroup or organisation is much more heavily influenced by the interaction among people than by the direct impact of each individual. This is an important observation, to which we will return periodically. It is in stark contrast to the commonly held assumption that one or two students (or teachers, or principals, or schools) as the primary cause of problems.

> The behaviour and performance of a classroom, workgroup or organisation is much more heavily influenced by the interaction among people than by the direct impact of each individual.

This concept is central to improving any social system.

## Systems, schools and classrooms

Schools, like all organisations, are social systems.

Schools comprise many parts that must work together if the school is to meet the needs of its community and achieve its purpose. The front office staff interact with parents, with the school executive, and with teaching staff. Teachers work together to plan and implement a curriculum that provides meaningful progression for learners. Students collaborate with one another during learning activities and on the playground.

Within the school, many interactions take place among people on a daily basis. The various parts of the school are interdependent. No amount of restructuring can reduce this interdependence.

How people work together and the methods they use when doing so are governed by systemic structures within the school. These systemic structures influence the behaviour and performance of individuals within the school as well as the behaviour and performance of the school itself.

Schools are contained within other social systems, including their communities. Factors such as population, demography, industries, remoteness, and climate all affect the operation and outcomes of the school.

Schools are also contained within various regulatory, curricula, teacher training, funding, reporting, and accountability systems. These structures vary with the region, state, or nation within which the school exists. Schools are nested and contained within the larger community, regional, state, and national systems.

These systemic factors outside the school have a direct influence on the behaviour and performance of the school and the individuals within it.

Classrooms too are social systems, full of interdependencies. These interdependencies exist among students and with the teacher. The behaviour of any element, including individual students, has a direct effect on the other elements and the performance of the whole class. Interdependence is inescapable.

The methods or processes used within the classroom are intended to support the purpose of the classroom and the school. A classroom is contained within the system that is the school, which is in turn contained within regional, state, and national systems. These containing systems directly impact upon the classroom system.

Any serious discussion about school and classroom improvement must explicitly acknowledge the impact of interaction effects within the school or classroom and the influence of containing systems. Unfortunately, this is not always the case. Many improvement efforts are focussed upon the actions of individuals, particularly those of principals and teachers, while doing little to address interaction effects.

# System behaviour and performance

There are many factors that determine the behaviour and performance of social systems, including the following.

- To improve the behaviour and performance of a system we need to not only consider how the system operates, but also to understand why it operates as it does given the context within which it exists; both analysis and synthesis are required;

- Identifying the root causes of poor performance is critical in order to make improvements that stick. However, cause and effect relationships in systems can be hard to identify;

- Optimising the system as a whole is important. Optimisation explains why we sometimes have to make sacrifices in our part of the organisation for the good of the whole; and

- Most of the problems in organisations are the results of management action (or inaction) rather than the fault of those doing the actual work.

Let us examine each of these claims more closely.

## Analysis and synthesis

Analysis involves breaking things down into smaller parts with the aim of better understanding the parts that comprise the whole. Analysis leads to understanding the parts themselves and the relationships among the parts to the whole.

The essential properties of a system as a whole are derived from the interaction among the parts of the system and with its environment. The whole has properties that none of the parts possess. Removal and study of parts of the system may reveal aspects of how the system operates, but cannot reveal why it exists or why it operates as it does. Analysis does not aid understanding of a system as a whole.

> Any serious discussion about school and classroom improvement must explicitly acknowledge the impact of interaction effects within the school or classroom and the influence of containing systems.

> Analysis leads to understanding the parts themselves and the relationships among the parts to the whole.

Synthesis requires consideration of the system as a whole, examining the environment within which it operates and its roles or functions within that environment in order to understand its behaviour. For example, we cannot explain the behaviour and performance of a school without first considering the factors outside the school that define its roles and functions within its community and society at large.

While analysis involves looking at the parts, synthesis involves looking at the whole. Analysis addresses "how"; synthesis addresses "why".

Attempts to improve school education have placed undue emphasis on analysis at the expense of synthesis. Significant effort has been expended trying to dissect and understand the operation of parts of the system, including: factors that comprise good teaching, the reasons for unsatisfactory test results, the causes of absenteeism, and why students are disengaged. There could be great gains from simultaneously exploring synthesis questions, such as: why do students choose to come to school or not, why do we need to assess student progress, why do particular students choose not to learn, why do we batch students through school by date of birth? These questions lead us to explore and understand the containing systems and their influence on our system.

## Cause and effect

If you stand in the rain, you get wet. This is an example of simple linear cause and effect: one thing leads directly to another. Piercing the skin leads to bleeding. Dropping glass on concrete causes it to shatter. Pressing the brake pedal causes a car to slow down.

In complex systems, cause and effect relationships are rarely linear or simple. Causes are usually the result of interactions among elements of the system and with containing systems. This leads to the observation of effects that are mostly symptoms arising from problems elsewhere in the system. These problems are hard to find and may have been triggered some time ago.

One of Peter Senge's laws of systems is:

> Cause and effect are not closely related in time and space.
>
> Peter Senge, 1990, *The Fifth Discipline: The art and practice of the learning organization*, Crown, New York, p. 63.

When we examine patterns within a system and its containing systems, it becomes possible to find the connections between effects and their causes.

Getting to the real or root underlying causes is critical if we are to ensure that our efforts to make improvement are successful. It is fruitless to work on symptoms.

---

*Synthesis requires consideration of the system as a whole.*

*Attempts to improve school education have placed undue emphasis on analysis at the expense of synthesis.*

*In complex systems, cause and effect relationships are rarely linear or simple.*

*Getting to the real or root underlying causes is critical if we are to ensure that our efforts to make improvement are successful.*

> ### 💬 CAUSE AND EFFECT AND PRIDE IN OUR SCHOOL
>
> A rural school decided that they had a big problem with students who lacked pride in their school. How do you begin to tackle a problem like that?
>
> The school applied the Plan–Do–Study–Act improvement process to their problem. A critical step in this process involves a cause and effect analysis of the system under study.
>
> The leadership team asked staff to brainstorm the possible causes they thought were contributing to a lack of student pride in the school. When they prioritised the causes identified, they determined that the root or most significant cause was associated with school bag and litter mess in the main school corridor.
>
> They worked with students to agree how best to address this issue. Hooks were installed for bags and litter bins placed in the corridor.
>
> Identifying root causes and engaging students in the improvement process led to identification of a solution that was welcomed by the students and resulted in less litter mess and a more tidy corridor.

## System optimisation

📖 Optimisation is the process of orchestrating the efforts of all components towards achievement of the stated aim.

W. Edwards Deming, 1994, *The New Economics: For industry, government and education*, MIT, Massachusetts, p. 53.

A good choir provides an excellent example of an optimised system. While a choir may include many talented soloists, it is the way that the voices blend together in harmony and balance that leads to a joyful performance: optimisation of the whole. To have individual choristers optimise their solo performance is to sub-optimise the sound of the choir as a whole.

That illustrates another feature of systems:

If the whole is optimized, the components will not be.

W. Edwards Deming, 1994, *The New Economics: For industry, government and education*, MIT, Massachusetts, p. 74.

If a child's learning and development is to be optimised at school, the teaching of individual subject areas will not be. In order to optimise the learning of mathematics, for example, a mathematics faculty would seek

*If a child's learning and development is to be optimised at school, the teaching of individual subject areas will not be.*

to have the lion's share of available teaching time and other resources. This would be at the expense of English, arts and science. To optimise science would sub-optimise learning in other areas.

The reference point that enables system optimisation is the agreed aim or purpose of the system.

# Improving systems

The first step that can be taken to improve system performance is to cease blaming individuals for disappointing results.

## Stop the blame game

During the first half of the last century, Joseph Juran undertook studies at Western Electric to examine production defects and nonconformities. He analysed the causes of both over a defined period of time. Each of the causes were categorised as "management-controllable" or "worker-controllable". Worker-controllable defects and nonconformities resulted directly from the actions of the worker. Had the worker been doing his job properly these defects and nonconformities would have been prevented. Anything outside the control of the worker was categorised as management-controllable. This included factors such as inadequate training, poor machine maintenance, sub-standard materials, and equipment deficiencies. In other words, anything that is outside the control of the worker is caused by other factors within the system (or the containing systems), which is the domain of management, not the worker.

Juran's research led to the often quoted 85/15 rule:

> Wherever there is a problem, 85% of the time it will be the system and not the fault of an individual.

In order to bring about improvement, this finding requires us to turn our attention to the system, rather than focus upon individuals.

As discussed earlier, the behaviour and performance of a system is the product of the interactions among its elements or parts, rather than the quality of the parts themselves. Until now, we have focussed largely on individual people as elements of the system, but we also recognise that the system includes other elements, such as technology, equipment and materials. Interaction effects include the interactions among these elements as well as the interaction of these elements with people and interactions among people.

---

*Sidebar notes:*

The reference point that enables system optimisation is the agreed aim or purpose of the system.

Anything that is outside the control of the worker is caused by other factors within the system (or the containing systems), which is the domain of management.

In order to bring about improvement, we must turn our attention to the system, rather than focus upon individuals.

The behaviour and performance of a system are also a function of the characteristics of the containing system. It follows that a significant proportion of the performance of a system is driven more by structural factors that are characteristics of the containing system and interaction among the elements, than by the individual elements of the system itself. In social systems, behaviour and performance are dominated by the impact of structural factors rather than the actions of individuals working within the system.

Deming referred to these ideas in the following way.

> In my experience, most troubles and most possibilities for improvement add up to proportions something like this:
>
> 94% belong to the system (responsibility of management)
>
> 6% are attributable to special causes
>
> No amount of care or skill in workmanship can overcome fundamental faults of the system.
>
> W. Edwards Deming, 1994, *The New Economics: For industry, government and education*, MIT, Massachusetts, p. 35.

We expand on Deming's special causes later, but for now the message is clear: most of the time it is the system itself and the containing system within which it operates, not merely the components of the system or the people within it, that produces the observed performance.

Peter Senge observed that:

> When placed in the same system, people, however different, tend to produce similar results.
>
> Peter Senge, 1990, *The Fifth Discipline: The art and practice of the learning organization*, Crown, New York, p. 42.

In most schools, the distribution of student performance from one year to the next remains fairly constant. Students in any chosen year level tend to perform similarly to the students that went before them. Teachers' mark books from year to year look remarkably similar, only the names are different. This is an excellent example of the system producing the results, not the people.

It is the system that produces the performance. In order to improve performance, we must understand the nature of the systems in which we operate and focus our efforts on working on the system to improve it.

*In social systems, behaviour and performance are dominated by the impact of structural factors rather than the actions of individuals working within the system.*

*In order to improve performance, we must understand the nature of the systems in which we operate and focus our efforts on working on the system to improve it.*

Einstein described insanity as doing the same thing over and over again and expecting a different result. This is the equivalent to working only in the system and expecting outcomes to improve.

Exhortations, rewards, blame and punishments do nothing to improve the system. They upset people, interfere with relationships and make things worse.

A colleague of ours, Lynne Macdonald, observed:

> In schools, parents blame teachers for their children not learning; teachers blame parents; students blame teachers; teachers blame students; principals blame teachers. Where does it get us? Nowhere. So we have to eliminate this blame game.

Lynne Macdonald, retired principal, Plenty Parklands Primary School, Victoria, QLA Case Study 3 DVD.

Most organisations' problems derive from the system, not the people. Our best efforts cannot compensate for a dysfunctional system. This leads to the sad but true corollary: pitch a good player against a dysfunctional system and the system wins nearly every time.

## Work in and on the system

Educators work very hard in their system. This is what they have been trained to do. This is what they have been told is their job.

Working in the system is only the first of three types of work in which everyone must be engaged if improvement is to be ongoing.

These three types of work are:

1. Daily routines;

2. Improving systems and processes; and

3. Innovation projects.

 Daily routines: the everyday, getting-the-job-done type of work, working in the system.

For a teacher, daily routines include the everyday work of planning, teaching, assessment, and so on. For a school leader this includes responding to emails, meeting with stakeholders, preparing returns and reports, and the like. Daily routines get the job done. Daily routines are what most people understand they are paid to do.

---

**Margin notes:**

Exhortations, rewards, blame and punishments do nothing to improve the system.

Our best efforts cannot compensate for a dysfunctional system.

Working in the system is only the first of three types of work.

Daily routines get the job done.

📖 Improving systems and processes: working on the existing system to improve it.

Improvement does not just happen. It requires conscious effort.

Everyone has responsibility for specific systems and processes, and it is their responsibility to improve those system and processes — continually.

For a classroom teacher, this means continually improving the systems and processes that directly affect the learning of their students. In other words, teachers are required to continually improve their methods and practices. Improving systems and processes increases organisational efficiency and effectiveness.

For a school leader, this means continually improving the systems and processes that support or hinder student learning, such as student welfare, staff development, curriculum planning, pedagogy, and the like. (As we shall see, this improvement activity cannot effectively be undertaken alone, it requires a collaborative effort.)

If the person with responsibility for a process or system does not lead improvement of that system or process, who will?

📖 Innovation projects: projects that seek to meet organisations' emerging needs through the creation of new systems and processes. Innovation projects work on the system to create new products, services, and ways of working.

In commercial enterprises, innovation projects include the development of completely new products and services, and the adoption of new technologies. In a school context, innovation projects can relate to new technologies, new programs, and system reforms. Innovation projects prepare organisations for the future.

Innovation projects are widely regarded to be the domain of senior management. This is not strictly the case.

Everyone in an organisation needs to be engaged, to varying degrees, in each of these three types of work. The more senior the role, the more time needs to be spent working on the system, improving systems and processes, and engaging in innovation projects. Less senior staff members spend more time on daily routines: working in the system.

Figure 3.3 illustrates the proportion of time we suggest should be devoted to each type of work within a school education system.

> Improving systems and processes increases organisational efficiency and effectiveness.

> Innovation projects prepare the organisation for the future.

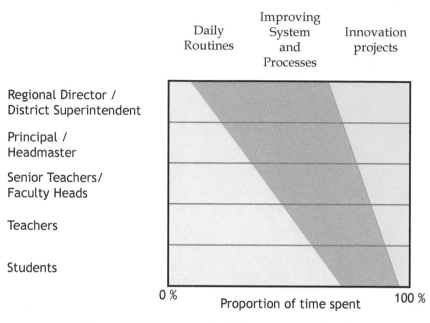

**Figure 3.3 Time spent in different types of work**
Source: Adapted from Myron Tribus, 1992, "The Germ Theory of Management".
Available at http://www.qla.com.au/papers/the-germ-theory-of-management/2112871002

As Figure 3.3 indicates, everybody should be involved in all three types of work, but in different proportions:

• Students spend most of their time (60–70 per cent) doing the routine, core business of learning. These are their daily routines of working in the system. Students also work on the system. They contribute some of their day to improving the systems and processes within which they operate and for which they are personally responsible. In other words, they spend some of their day (about 20 per cent) working with their teachers to improve classroom systems and processes, as well as improving their personal systems and processes associated with their learning. Students can also be called upon to contribute to the innovation projects of the school (perhaps 5–10 per cent of their time), participating in a technology trial for example.

• Teachers spend the majority of their time (50–60 per cent) on the daily routines of teaching, working in the system. Teachers also work on the system. They spend a significant proportion of the day (about 25 per cent) improving their key systems and processes, and those of the school. Some of their time is devoted to supporting innovation projects (approximately 10–15 per cent).

- Senior teachers, faculty heads, deputies and assistant principals spend a lot of their time (40–50 per cent) working on the system, improving the systems and processes of the school. They also have daily routines to complete, working in the system, as well as contributing to the innovation projects of the school, working on the system.

- The school principal, headmaster or headmistress places a strong emphasis on the future directions of the school. They explore emerging community needs, societal trends, emerging regulatory requirements, political developments, technological developments and educational trends to set future directions for the school. They champion innovation (devoting roughly 20–30 per cent of their time to innovation related activities) and play a strong role in supporting school improvement activities (about half of their time). The majority of their work involves working on the system. They also have daily routines to perform, working in the system (taking up 20–30 per cent of their time).

- Senior executives such as regional directors or district superintendents are primarily devoted to innovation projects (about 25–30 per cent of their time is devoted to such activities) and improving systems and processes (50–60 per cent of their time is allocated here). Daily routines and working in the system is inescapable, even at these levels of seniority (although they spend only 10–15 per cent of their time on such activities).

You may disagree with the percentages we have proposed above: for many people these numbers are radical. As it happens, the specific numbers are designed to be provocative and are far less important than the concepts. We are advocating that significantly more time needs to be spent on improvement and innovation than is currently the case in most organisations. Without this conscious effort, improvement will not be continual.

Everyone needs to engage, to appropriate degrees, in all three types of work if continual improvement is to be achieved. Completing daily routines alone does not result in improvement.

Innovation projects have significant implications for change across organisations. These changes are usually widespread and disruptive to existing systems and processes. These changes can and frequently do result in improvement, but results are not guaranteed. Improvement from innovation projects comes in fits and starts.

*Everyone needs to engage, to appropriate degrees, in all three types of work if continual improvement is to be achieved.*

Only by engaging everyone in improving systems and processes will ongoing improvement occur across the organisation. For this to happen, working on the system must be explicitly acknowledged as a key aspect of everyone's job, and it must be explicitly reflected in the plans and planning processes of the organisation.

*Working on the system must be explicitly acknowledged as a key aspect of everyone's job.*

It is not usual for everyone in schools and school systems to be actively involved in improvement. District and school improvement plans typically highlight the priorities of senior management. Task forces and improvement teams are established to address strategic priorities, but these projects have little relevance for the majority of staff. Improvement is seen as belonging to others, so those not directly involved in high-level improvement teams focus their attention on daily routines.

Our emphasis throughout this book is on improving systems and processes, with limited reference to innovation projects. This is not to say that innovation projects are unimportant, rather, they are an existing feature of our current management approach that already receive sufficient attention. Improving systems and processes is not promoted widely, so we place emphasis upon it.

## A FEW WORDS ABOUT IMPROVING LEARNING

When educators hear the words "improving" and "learning" used together, they nearly always think the same thing: that improving learning means moving students from an existing level of performance to a higher level. Improving learning is interpreted as increasing the capacity of their students, otherwise known as growth.

While we do want to see improvements in the capacity of learners over time, this is core business that is delivered through daily routines; it is not a part of working on the system. Working on the system involves teachers working with their students to improve systems and processes. More specifically, it involves working on improving the systems and process of learning (not teaching) for which the teacher is responsible. In a traditional classroom, only the teacher has the authority to change classroom systems and processes. If they do not devote effort to improving systems and processes, no one else can.

Our concept of improving learning is about increasing the capacity of teachers and their processes. By improving systems of learning, teachers are able to support and guide their students to learn to a deeper level at a more rapid rate. Each year, the learning will be even deeper and more rapid. This is continually improving learning.

# Change the job of the manager

People work <u>in</u> a system. The job of a manager is to work <u>on</u> the system, to improve it, continuously, with their help.

Myron Tribus, 1993, "Quality Management in Education", *Journal for Quality and Participation*, Jan–Feb, p. 5. Available at http://www.qla.com.au/Papers/5.

We have discussed the importance of recognising the need to work in and on systems, and how continual improvement needs to be an explicit part of everyone's job. This means that we need to engage those working in the system in improvement of the system.

Individuals within an organisation enact the daily routines of the organisation. These routines encompass the methods and practices used to get the job done. The individuals that enact these routines are the ones closest to the front line. In manufacturing this is sometimes called the factory floor, in mining it is the coal face, in education it is sometimes called the chalk face.

It is front line individuals that have most hands-on experience with the system. They are most intimate with the system and know most about its operation. They know the actions and interactions within the system. They see, first-hand, the impact of deficiencies and errors elsewhere in the system. A manager's knowledge of interactions is of vital importance to planning for improvement. Of course, a manager also has the authority to allocate resources to improvement efforts.

People working in the system have a detailed understanding of the actions they take on a daily basis. This understanding is of immense value when planning for improvement.

Managers and leaders also bring valuable understanding to improving systems. With their wider span of influence, they frequently have a broader understanding of the interactions in an organisation. As discussed earlier, the performance of a system is governed more by the interactions among its parts and containing systems than by the actions of its individual parts. A manager's knowledge of interactions is of vital importance to planning for improvement. Of course, a manager also has the authority to allocate resources to improvement efforts. Managers working collaboratively with their people can harness the immense depth of understanding that is necessary to improve systems in a demonstrable and sustainable manner.

There is another crucial reason to include those who work in the system in working on improvement of that system. If front line staff participate in the creation of improvement plans, they are more likely to be supportive of the implementation of these plans than if the plans are simply imposed upon them.

> We need to engage those working in the system in improvement of the system.

> It is front line individuals that have most hands-on experience with the system. They are intimate with the system and know most about its operation.

> If front line staff participate in the creation of improvement plans, they are more likely to be supportive of the implementation of these plans.

What does this look like in practice? Firstly, individuals lead improvement of the systems for which they are personally responsible, as the owners of those systems. Secondly, individuals contribute to improvement teams working on the systems and processes with which they are involved.

> Students learn in a system. The job of a teacher is to work on the system, to improve it, continuously, with their help.
>
> Myron Tribus, 1993, "Quality Management in Education", *Journal for Quality and Participation*, Jan–Feb, p. 6. Available at http://www.qla.com.au/Papers/5.

Classroom teachers are personally responsible for the daily routines within their classrooms. In the first instance, they work collaboratively with their students to improve these systems. This aspect of their improvement work is an ongoing and a regular part of their life in the classroom. Tools such as the parking lot, force field analysis and cause and effect diagram (explained below) are in regular use to this effect. Secondly, classroom teachers participate in teams to improve other systems in which they take part. For example, they may participate in an improvement team working on the student welfare system, the curriculum development system, or the assessment and reporting system.

Of particular importance here is the role of the student. Students are actively engaged in the improvement of systems in which they take part. They work collaboratively with their teacher to improve classroom systems in a way that goes beyond common understandings of student voice: seeking, listening to, and valuing the views and opinions of students. While student feedback is identified by John Hattie as one of the greatest influences on learning (see John Hattie, 2009, *Visible Learning: A synthesis of over 800 meta-analyses relating to achievement*, Routledge, New York), what we are proposing here goes beyond just listening to and responding to student feedback. Rather, we are proposing that students be actively and routinely engaged in designing and making improvements to classroom and school operations. In this way, students become regular and active contributors to system improvement.

Myron Tribus's principle that the manager's job is to continuously work on and improve the system with the help of the people who work in the system, has implications beyond the classroom.

Principals are called upon to work with their staff and students to bring about improvement to the school as a system. Regional directors and district superintendents are called upon to work with their principals, teachers, and students to bring about improvement across the school system. This is a vastly different standpoint to the commonly held view that leaders should direct and control organisations and their improvement efforts.

---

**Margin notes:**

Individuals lead improvement of the systems for which they are personally responsible, and contribute to improvement teams working on the systems and processes with which they are involved.

We are proposing that students become actively and routinely engaged in designing and making improvements to classroom and school operations.

# Reflection questions

**?** What is your experience of individuals and groups within your organisation choosing their own purpose and methods? How has your organisation aligned the efforts of those working within the organisation?

**?** What is the nature of the interaction effects in your organisation? Are they predominantly positive or negative? What is their impact upon the system's behaviour and performance?

**?** Think of some things that have recently gone wrong or problems that exist in your organisation. Which of these are due to individuals? Which are due to the system? How do you know? How do the proportions compare to Juran's 85/15 rule or Deming's 94 per cent to 6 per cent proposition?

**?** At your school, to what degree do mark books and test results reflect similar performance from year to year? What does this mean?

**?** What proportions of your work time do you spend on daily routines; improving systems and processes; and innovation projects? How does this impact upon the continual improvement of your organisation? How could you change your approach to the time you spend on these different types of work?

**?** To what degree are staff and students at your school actively involved in improving school and classroom systems and processes? What are they currently working on to improve?

# Quality learning tools to understand and explore systems

The following tools help you to align effort and explore the range of causes that may result in a given effect. Use of these tools can reduce the temptation to reactively "jump to solution" by imposing a discipline on the consideration of a wide range of possible causes. The tools promote a shift in thinking from simple linear cause and effect to consideration of the interactions among effects. They assist with identifying the many causes within the system under consideration, as well as the causes coming from the external environment or containing systems. Root underlying causes must be identified and addressed if lasting improvement is to be achieved.

#  System map

If leaders are to work with their people to improve systems, they need a method to agree and document these systems. One of the most effective approaches is a system map.

 A system map: a pictorial representation of the elements that comprise a system.

Based on Deming's flow diagram (see Figure 3.4), the system map provides a set of key questions about a system. Engaging key stakeholders in dialogue and creating a shared understanding of the answers to these questions helps everyone to better understand the nature of the system, and the key interactions within the system and with containing systems.

> The system map provides a set of key questions about a system.

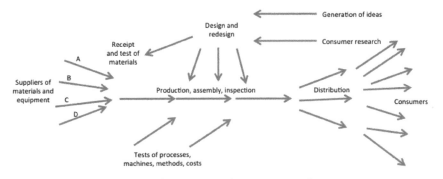

**Figure 3.4 Flow diagram: production viewed as a system**

Source: W. Edwards Deming, 1993, *The New Economics: For industry, government and education*, MIT, Cambridge, p. 58.

A system map documents answers to the following questions.

1.  What is the **purpose** (aim or mission) of the system?

2.  What is the **vision** (image of the desired future state) for the system?

3.  What are the **values** (qualities to which the organisation aspires in behaviour and relationships) of the system?

4.  Who are the **people** comprising the system?

5.  Who are the **clients** (recipients and direct beneficiaries) of the system?

6.  Who are the **suppliers** (individuals and enterprises that provide the inputs) to the system?

7.  Who are the other **stakeholders** (individuals and enterprises with a vested interest in the activities and outcomes) of the system?

8.  What are the **inputs** (external resources) to the system?

9.  What are the **outputs** (tangible products and services) and outcomes (benefits to clients and stakeholders) of the system?

10. What are the **key processes** (sequences of actions) that enable the organisation to achieve its purpose and serve the clients of the system?

11. What are the **results measures** (indicators of success, based on performance and perceptions) for the system?

12. What are the **process measures** (indicators of process performance) for the processes within the system?

13. How is **feedback** (information about the system) used to improve processes and performance?

The system map is not a static document. Answers to these questions change and are refined over time. As more is learned about the system and as improvements are made to the system, the system map is updated to reflect these changes. A system map captures the current shared understanding about the key elements that comprise a system.

> A system map captures the current shared understanding about the key elements that comprise a system.

Figure 3.5 provides a template for creating a system map. Configured as a flow diagram, it captures the questions to be answered to complete a system map. The dotted line represents a boundary that separates the internal elements of the system from the elements external to it — when documenting a school system, it can be helpful to think of this boundary as the school fence. Following the template are some examples of system maps of different school-based systems.

Download a system map template at www.qla.com.au

Video Clip 3.1: Year 2 classroom system map
http://www.qla.com.au/Videos/3

Source: Roxburgh Homestead Primary School, Victoria.

Video Clip 3.2: Systems thinking across the school
http://www.qla.com.au/Videos/3

Source: Plenty Parklands Primary School, Victoria.

What is the **PURPOSE** *(aim or mission)* of the organisation?

What is the **VISION** *(image of the desired future state)* for the organisation?

What are the **VALUES** *(qualities to which the organisation aspires in behaviour and relationships)* of the organisation?

Who are the **PEOPLE** *(individuals and groups)* working in relationship with one another, with clients, suppliers and other key stakeholders?

Value Adding Processes and Relationships

What are the **PROCESSES** *(sequences of actions)* that enable the organisation to meet its purpose and serve its clients?

What **FEEDBACK** *(information about the system)* is used to improve products, processes and performance?

What are the **OUTCOMES** *(benefits to clients and stakeholders)* from the activities of the organisation?

Who are the **CLIENTS** *(recipients and beneficiaries of the products and services)* of the organisation?

What are the **OUTPUTS** *(tangible deliverables)* from the activities of the organisation?

What are the **RESULTS MEASURES** *(measures of success)* for the organisation?

What are the **PROCESS MEASURES** *(indicators of process performance)* for the organisation?

Who are the **SUPPLIERS** *(individuals and organisations who provide inputs)* to the

What are the **INPUTS** *(external resources)* required by the organisation?

Who are the **OTHER STAKEHOLDERS** *(individuals and organisations with a vested interest in the success)* of the organisation?

**System Map**

© Copyright 2015 QLA_Version 14.0

QLA
learning + improvement
w w w . q l a . c o m . a u

New Zealand: PO Box 1850, Wellington, 6140 Phone +64 273 021 747

Australia: PO Box 624, North Melbourne, Victoria 3051 Phone +61 3 9370 9944 Fax +61 3 9370 9955

Figure 3.5 This template provides the questions to be answered to complete a system map

## System Map

**QLA** — learning • improvement

www.qla.com.au

*Who are the SUPPLIERS (individuals and organisations who provide inputs) to the organisation?*
- Global network of colleagues
- Seminar venues
- Mail house
- Office suppliers, printers and stationers
- Suppliers of telecommunication products and services
- Legal and accounting advisors
- Government departments
- Industry bodies
- Professional associations

*What are the INPUTS (external resources) required by the organisation?*
- Knowledge of schools and the education system
- Knowledge of industry improvement approaches and strategies
- Printed materials
- Equipment and supplies
- Venues and catering
- ICT hardware and software, web hosting, phone, fax, email, internet
- Legal, accounting and taxation advice

*Who are the OTHER STAKEHOLDERS (those not already listed with a vested interest in the success) of the organisation?*
- Partners (our families, Langford International Inc.)
- Regulators
- Mentors
- QL consultants (with whom QLA has a relationship)
- QL practitioners
- Competitors
- Teacher Institutes (BOSTES, VIT, TQI)

*What is the PURPOSE (aim or mission) of the organisation?*
Helping schools and school systems to improve learning by learning how to improve.

*What is the VISION (image of the desired future state) for the organisation?*
We are the first choice in improving learning and learning how to improve.
Clients are our advocates because we add significant value. We have data that quantifies the difference we make.
We know our chosen markets and their needs.
We have a sustainable network of colleagues who share in our vision for Quality Learning and support our work.
We are recognised by influencers as making a substantial system-wide contribution to improving learning.
We employ sound practices, based on the philosophy we espouse.
We love our work, working with each other and our clients. We enjoy a sense of achievement.
We enjoy productive relationships with all stakeholders.
Whatever we choose to do, we do it superbly well.

*What are the VALUES (qualities to which we aspire in behaviour and relationships) of the organisation?*
Success: Getting better together. Making a positive difference.
Integrity: Consistency in what we think, say and do. Being trustworthy.
Learning: Constantly looking for ways to increase our capacity for effective action.
Fun: Enjoying what we do. Celebrating success.

*What are the CRITICAL SUCCESS FACTORS (things the organisation must get right for survival and success)?*
Clients and Markets - Develop a growing number of loyal clients in our chosen markets (including deliberate strategies for client relationship management, marketing, promotion and planned development of the business)
Product and Service Development and Delivery - Develop products and services and deliver them superbly well (develop offerings that maximise client success, represent value for money and are attractive to clients. Deliver them superbly well.)
Stakeholder Relationships - Maintain and extend key stakeholder relationships (ensure all key stakeholder groups' needs and expectations are understood and that we deliver value for all of them)
Sustainability and Success - Ensure long-term viability (sustain a good cash-flow, manage risk and return a modest surplus)
Infrastructure - Establish Quality support processes and infrastructure (to diligently apply the philosophy to our own operations, minimising waste to ensure we are efficient and effective)
Leadership, Learning and Improvement - Actively plan to learn and improve (challenge our paradigms, use data to inform planning and action, extend our leadership and work to improve everything we do)
QLA People - Find joy in our work and take care of ourselves (live the philosophy, have fun, celebrate success, maintain work-life balance and look after our individual productive capacities)

*Who are OUR PEOPLE (individuals and groups) working in the organisation?*
Jane Kovacs, Michael King and others as aligned with growth strategy.

*What are the PROCESSES (sequences of actions) that enable the organisation to achieve its purpose and serve its clients?*

**Client Relationship Management (C)**
- Client needs analysis & diagnostic
- Client interaction/communication
- Client value/satisfaction evaluation

**Administration (A)**
- System documentation
- Filing and office management
- Inventory management
- Mailing
- Printing
- Travel

**ICT (T)**
- Client database development & management
- Technology support
- Web site administration

**Governance (G)**
- Management meetings
- Regulatory compliance

**Product and Service Development (D)**
- Product & service design & development
- School example collection & publication
- Web site development
- Resource development, production, review
- School Stakeholder Perception Surveys

**Risk Management (R)**
- Accounting, tax & legal advice
- Insurance
- Professional development
- School example & image permissions
- Work cover and OH&S
- ASIC
- First aid training

**Delivery (E)**
- Proposal preparation/agreement
- Consulting to clients
- Seminar management
- Resource sales

**Finance (F)**
- Accounts payable
- Accounts receivable
- Asset management
- Banking
- Debtors
- Invoicing
- Purchasing
- Salaries & expenses
- Superannuation
- ATO Requirements
- Manage cash flow
- Reporting

**Stakeholder Relations (S)**
- Stakeholder relationship management
- Stakeholder needs analysis
- Supplier selection and management

**Marketing (M)**
- Annual Catalogue production & issue
- Blog posts
- eNewsletter

**Planning (P)**
- Budget preparation (including pricing)
- Calendar of events
- Event planning
- Stakeholder strategy development
- Strategic & operational planning
- Risk management planning

*What are the RESULT MEASURES (indicators of success) for the organisation?*
- Client satisfaction with products and services
- Client outcomes
- Client interactions / proposals / acceptance rates
- FQL participation rates
- QLS / QLMC attendance
- Consulting workload
- Staff satisfaction
- Resource sales
- Web site hits and visits
- Cash flow, P&L, Balance Sheet

*Who are the CLIENTS (recipients and beneficiaries of the products and services) of the organisation?*

Individuals who are serious about improving learning:
- School leaders, administrators and teachers
- School regions/districts /state departments
- Australian teacher training institutions
- Selected organisations in other sectors
- Selected markets offshore

*What are the OUTPUTS (tangible deliverables) and OUTCOMES (benefits to clients and stakeholders) from the activities of the organisation?*

QLA Products:
- Quality Learning programs
- Consulting, facilitation and training services
  - Quality Learning
  - Other
- 4-day Quality Learning Seminar
- Other LtI offerings
- Quality Learning resources and materials
- QLA Web site

Third Party Products:
- Publications
- Videos and CDs
- Posters

For Our School System Clients:
- Improving student learning outcomes
- Improving student responsibility, engagement and love of learning
- Improving teacher morale
- Improving leadership and management of schools
- School communities working together to improve

For Our Other Clients:
- Teacher education institutions adopting the principles and practices of Quality Learning and Improvement
- Wider understanding and application of quality improvement principles and practices across government and industry

For Our Suppliers:
- Long-term, mutually beneficial relationship with QLA

For Our Other Stakeholders:
- Value from stakeholder involvement with QLA

New Zealand: PO Box 1850, Wellington, 6140 Phone +64 273 021 747
Australia: PO Box 624, North Melbourne, Victoria 3051 Phone 03 9370 9944 Fax 03 9370 9955
www.qla.com.au

**Figure 3.6 The system map for Quality Learning Australasia**

**Figure 3.7 A system map can be creatively represented in many ways**
Source: Mungindi Central School, NSW.

**Figure 3.8 A Year 2 classroom system map**
Source: Roxburgh Homestead Primary School, Victoria.

# ✖ Fishbone diagram

Developed in the 1940s by Kaoru Ishikawa, an eminent Japanese authority on quality, the fishbone diagram is also known as the Ishikawa diagram and the cause and effect diagram.

The diagram is created by a team of individuals with an intimate knowledge of the system under consideration.

The first step is to agree on the effect for which causes are sought. The effect is written in a prominent place at the head of the fish as a reminder to team members during the identification of the causes.

The team uses brainstorming to list the possible causes of the given effect. These are categorised and noted on the appropriate bones of the fishbone diagram. Some frequently used categories include: materials, methods/processes, resources, people, environment, and information.

Once the possible causes are identified, the relative contribution of each can be evaluated. This evaluation can be objective, through data collection, or subjective, though prioritisation based on team opinions and experience.

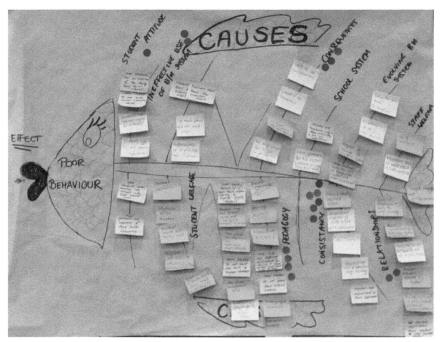

**Figure 3.9 A fishbone diagram used to identify and document the causes of poor student behaviour**

Source: Foundations in Quality Learning Seminar, Armidale, NSW.

# ⚒ Five whys

The five whys tool was developed within the Toyota Motor Corporation as a means to identify the underlying causes of problems. When root causes are identified and addressed, the problem can be fixed and stay fixed.

The process is very simple: the issue under investigation is identified and noted, and "why?" is asked five times (the number of repetitions is not immutable, but in most cases five repetitions have been found to be sufficient to uncover root causes of problems).

5 – Why's

**Why Do I Study Maths At School?**
- *To get through life. It is a building block of life and enables you to prosper in whatever job you choose.*

**Why do we need maths to get through life?**
- *Maths is an 'everyday requirement'. Most jobs require us to use mathematical skills and we need to use maths someway or another every day.*

**Why is maths used every day?**
- *We need to measure, to construct buildings, to calculate or pay bills, to buy food and clothing and other family needs.*

**Why do we need to calculate, measure, construct and buy?**
- *If you can't calculate your bills you may not earn what you should, or pay too much and if you can't provide food, clothing and shelter you will be hungry and naked.*

**Why do need to have food and not be naked?**
- *Because you will starve and freeze to death!*

**Figure 3.10 Five whys: Year 8 mathematics classroom**
Source: Macleod College, Victoria.

### THE FIVE WHYS: MANAGING BEHAVIOUR IN THE CLASSROOM

Some years ago a teacher from a secondary school in Victoria told us the following story.

A class was being constantly disrupted by the inappropriate behaviour of a student. Instead of responding in the usual manner by removing the child from the classroom, the teacher took the student to one side and applied the five whys tool to investigate the cause of the behaviour.

The student revealed that he found it difficult to make friends with others in the classroom, and that the behaviour was a means of getting attention and connecting with others.

The teacher worked to help the student learn strategies to develop relationships with others. This was a far more productive and long-lasting solution than would have been achieved by reacting to the symptom and removing the student from the classroom.

The following video clips show students using five whys in the classroom.

Video Clip 3.3: Why do I come to school? Year 4
http://www.qla.com.au/Videos/3

Source: Plenty Parklands Primary School, Victoria.

Video Clip 3.4: Why do I come to school? Year 2
http://www.qla.com.au/Videos/3

Source: Mungindi Central School, NSW.

# ⚒ Force field analysis

The force field analysis tool helps to identify the forces that drive and restrain a system as it strives to achieve a goal. It is most commonly constructed using brainstorming with a team of individuals, including those who work within the system and those with a broader understanding of how the system fits within its context and containing systems.

Once the forces that drive and restrain a system are identified, the relative contribution of each can be established, either through further data collection or by the team. Applying effort to minimise or eliminate the most significant restraining forces provides the greatest leverage to improving the system.

---

### 💬 FORCE FIELD ANALYSIS: LEARNING MATHEMATICS

Students in a Year 9 mathematics class were asked to work in pairs and identify forces that help them to learn mathematics (driving forces) and forces that hinder their learning of mathematics (restraining forces).

Their responses were compiled into lists of driving forces and restraining forces and they prioritised each list using nominal group technique (see Chapter Four). The tallies were plotted to reveal the greatest contributors and barriers to their learning. This is shown in Figure 3.11. The class then worked together to explore how to address the most significant restraining forces and agree upon improvements to their system of learning.

---

| DRIVING FORCES | | RESTRAINING FORCES | |
|---|---|---|---|
| 157 | Understanding the work | Homework | 214 |
| 143 | Get good marks | Teacher moves on too fast | 214 |
| 136 | Being pushed to do my best | Other students' behaviour | 196 |
| 131 | Teacher | Not having time for homework | 181 |
| 121 | Working with a partner | Being side-tracked | 175 |
| 99 | My career path / future job | Maths after lunch on Friday | 169 |
| 97 | Calculator | People who don't want to learn | 157 |
| 96 | Encouragement | The pressure to perform at your best | 145 |
| 92 | Family | Not always enjoyable | 142 |
| 86 | Explanation of ideas | Time | 135 |
| 78 | Formulas | It's too hard! | 128 |
| 77 | Challenge | Continuously getting distracted | 124 |
| 72 | Examples | Talking while explanations are being given | 114 |
| 71 | Studying | Makes you do some homework | 111 |
| 68 | Seeing friends | Tiredness | 110 |
| 44 | Text book | Hard work | 100 |
| 42 | You need it in everyday life | Boredom | 96 |
| 34 | You have to do it | People trying to teach you their way | 91 |
| 33 | Soduku | Slower people in class | 86 |
| | | Teacher being away / changing teachers | 84 |
| | | Failing yourself | 74 |
| | | Being in top class | 68 |

Figure 3.11 Force-field analysis: learning mathematics

# ✕ Interrelationship digraph

Having identified and prioritised the most significant causes or restraining forces, where should improvement efforts be focussed? It is tempting to seek solutions to causes or forces with the highest rating, but if these ratings have been undertaken subjectively there are risks. Typically, people rate most highly the causes or restraining forces that they feel are the most significant, but these may not represent underlying causes.

An interrelationship digraph is a powerful tool to examine the interaction among related causes in order to identify one or more underlying causes.

- Six to eight of the most significant causes or restraining forces are identified and are drawn in a circle, like the numbers on a clock face.

- The cause and effect relationship between each pair of causes is considered in turn and the question is asked: "Is there a relationship between these two causes?"

- If the answer is yes, a line is drawn between the two items and a second question is asked: "Which causes the other, the most?"

- An arrowhead is drawn from the cause pointing into the item that is an effect.

- After each pair has been considered, the number of arrowheads in and out of each item is counted and noted on the chart. The items with the most outward arrows are the stronger causes: the root causes. Those with more inward pointing arrows are the effects of other causes.

To achieve the most sustainable improvement to the system, strategies can then be developed to address these root causes.

---

### 💬 INTERRELATIONSHIP DIGRAPH: IS STUDENT EFFORT REALLY THE PROBLEM?

Teachers at a school were convinced that the most significant cause of disappointing performance was a lack of student effort.

Use of the interrelationship digraph tool revealed that student effort was more of an effect than a cause. As such, working to improve student effort would be ineffective.

Their analysis of the interrelationship digraph convinced them that low "teacher expectations", "lack of purpose and goals" in the learning programs, and "relationships" with students were the real causes. With this new perspective, the teachers worked together to develop strategies to address these causes.

---

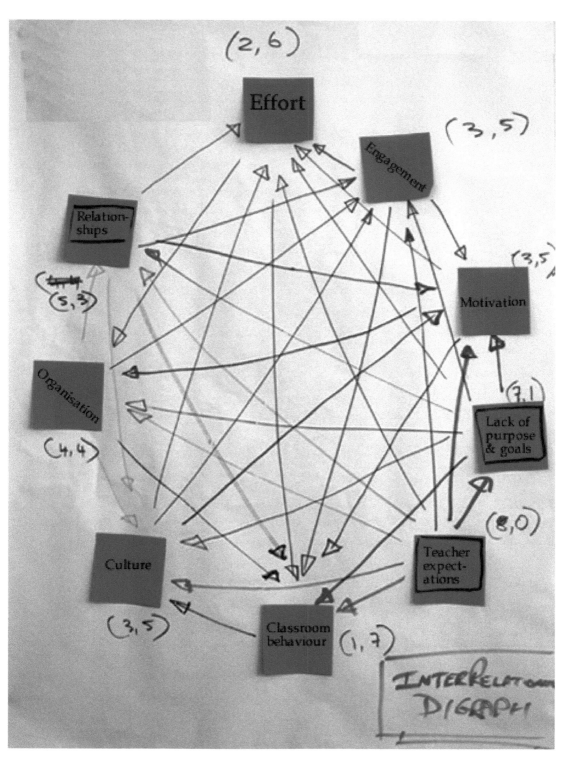

**Figure 3.12 Interrelationship digraph**
Source: Suburban high school in Victoria.

# ⚒ System's progress

System's progress, developed by David Langford, provides a simple framework for considering and documenting "where were we", "where are we now" and "where do we want to go". It provides a means by which changes in a system over time can be reflected upon, agreed, documented, and next steps determined.

| Where were we? | Where are we now? | Where do we want to go? |
|---|---|---|
| Individual teachers doing "their own thing" | A collegiate style | Continue to strengthen the school community |
| Limited sharing of classroom practice | Collaboration among staff | Structured planning and sharing time |
| Limited understanding of the work of other groups in the school | Opportunities to share | Extend the "quality start" program |
| No use of common tools | Common language and common tools | Extend the consistent use of tools by staff and students |
| Low ICT [information and communications technology] awareness and usage | Staff and students using QL [quality learning] tools. Plan-Do Study Act used routinely | Integrate ICT |
| No clear vision or shared direction | Moving to integration of ICT | Enhance students' capacity to manage their own learning: goal setting, planning, monitoring progress |
| Systems and processes not in place | Clear vision and purpose | |
| | Students aware of class routines and tools | |
| Inconsistent application of school values | School values are embedded | Further refine collection and use of data |
| Three year plan was department directed | Long term planning is school directed | Data shows continual improvement in all key areas |
| Limited student involvement in planning and decision making | Staff and students have greater input to school direction. Shared leadership | |
| Students not responsible for their learning | Students taking greater responsibility for their learning | |
| Lack of data to inform planning | Using data to reflect and improve. Clear signs of trends of improvement in school-wide data | |
| Staff meetings focussed on "nuts and bolts" | Feedback from staff and students is sought and valued | |

**Figure 3.13 System's progress used during planning**

Source: A primary school in SA.

# Purpose

This part of the chapter expands on the second principle of quality learning:

> Shared purpose and a clear vision of excellence align effort.

## The importance of purpose

It is widely accepted that people are hard-wired to care about purposes, and that we suffer in the absence of purpose. People have desires, from the base to the transcendent, and seek the means to satisfy these desires.

> It is the nature of purposeful systems — and people are purposeful systems — to desire, and one can desire nothing without desiring the ability to satisfy it.

> Russell L. Ackoff, 1999, *Ackoff's Best: His classic writings on management*, Wiley and Sons, New York, p. 140

Much of the joy in life comes from identifying one's purposes, and the triumph of overcoming the challenges to achieve them.

Research repeatedly demonstrates that people are purposeful and goal-driven. Much of the joy in life comes from identifying one's goals, and the triumph of overcoming the challenges to achieve them. Most fulfilling, it seems, are purposes aimed at the service of others. Viktor Frankl summarises this beautifully:

> Being human always points, and is directed, to something, or someone, other than oneself — be it a meaning to fulfil or another human being to encounter.

> Viktor E. Frankl, 1959, *Man's Search for Meaning*, Beacon Press, Boston, p. 133.

In the industrial era, enterprises were seen as purposeful, but the workers within enterprises were considered to be machine-like and without purpose.

We have already discussed how social systems, like individuals, are purposeful entities. In the industrial era, however, enterprises were seen as purposeful, but the workers within enterprises were considered to be machine-like and without purpose. Compliance was required, and jobs were reduced to low-level, intrinsically meaningless tasks that could be completed with a minimum of education and skill. As Kenneth Thomas writes:

> Workers came to think of this sort of work as a necessary evil (or devil's bargain) – forty to sixty hours of meaningless labour in exchange for economic survival ... something to withdraw from emotionally, to numb out from and get through.

> Kenneth W. Thomas, 2002, *Intrinsic Motivation at Work*, Berrett-Koehler, San Francisco, p. 22.

During this era, leaders were the "keepers of the purposes". They alone knew the overall aim, the purpose of work tasks, how they fitted together and contributed to the whole. Handling uncertainties and complexities were the domain of management. Workers were required only to follow instructions, rules and mandates. (Where does this still sound familiar today?)

Contrary to this approach, for people to function most effectively, they need to feel free to make choices regarding their purposes and methods. Which task should I do next? To which of these competing demands should I give priority? How shall I tackle this? Who should I consult on this issue? How shall I manage this situation? These are the questions faced by individuals that require them to make meaningful choices. This sort of questioning is a key characteristic of social systems, one that makes social systems so complex.

For an organisation to function most effectively, people need guidance on how to make choices, not rules and regulations. This guidance comes from purpose.

> Without a clear notion of purpose, workers cannot make intelligent choices about work activities, and they are also deprived of a sense of the meaningfulness of their work.
>
> Kenneth W. Thomas, 2000, *Intrinsic Motivation at Work: What really drives employee engagement*, Berrett-Koehler, San Francisco, p. 15.

In many organisations, purpose is documented as a mission statement.

A statement of purpose, or mission statement, should be brief, general, and point to the future. The mission states a noble purpose and should explain why, if the organisation did not exist, someone would feel compelled to create it.

*For an organisation to function most effectively, people need guidance on how to make choices, not rules and regulations. This guidance comes from purpose.*

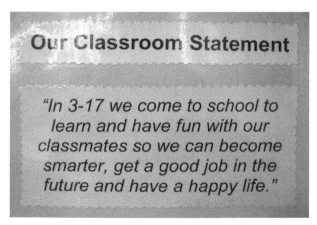

**Our Classroom Statement**

*"In 3-17 we come to school to learn and have fun with our classmates so we can become smarter, get a good job in the future and have a happy life."*

**Figure 3.14 Purpose statement from Year 3 class**
Source: Plenty Parklands Primary School, Victoria.

Purpose provides clarity at the activity level and at the system level.

Purpose provides clarity at the activity level and at the system level. Once purpose is clear, individuals can base their decisions on an understanding of the purpose to which they are contributing. They can align their contributions and evaluate them against the purposes to which they contribute.

> It is important that an aim never be defined in terms of activity or methods. It must always relate directly to how life is better for everyone.
>
> W. Edwards Deming, 1993, *The New Economics: For industry, government and education*, MIT, Cambridge, p. 52.

The benefit of shared purpose extends well beyond making choices at the activity level. When individual purposes and organisational purposes are in alignment, there is a multiplier effect that comes from aligned effort. The overriding purpose — the system purpose — can unify and galvanise all parts of the organisation towards the common aim. Purpose provides criteria by which to optimise the system towards achievement of the common aim. Alignment occurs most naturally when the purpose is exciting and inspiring.

The overriding purpose — the system purpose — can unify and galvanise all parts of the organisation towards the common aim.

Shared purpose is a pre-requisite for system optimisation. Unless there is a clear purpose that all elements of the system understand and share in common, it is not possible for each element to align effort towards achievement of that purpose. If individuals or groups are not aware of, do not understand, or do not commit to a unifying purpose, then they cannot align their efforts towards that goal and the system will be sub-optimised.

If individuals or groups are not aware of, do not understand, or do not commit to a unifying purpose, then they cannot align their efforts towards that goal and the system will be sub-optimised.

If we wish people to take responsibility for a task, or students for their learning, they cannot do so in the absence of understanding the purpose of these actions.

# The importance of vision

Key to achieving a quality outcome for any endeavour is an initial understanding of what quality will look like — a vision of excellence. When a worthwhile task is about to commence, start with a question: What would it look like to do this with a high degree of quality? In other words: What is our vision of excellence for this?

While purpose or mission describes the aim, vision describes what it will look like when it is done superbly well.

While purpose or mission describes the aim, vision describes what it will look like when it is done superbly well.

At its simplest level, a shared vision is the answer to the question,
"What do we want to create?"

Peter Senge, 1990, *The Fifth Discipline: The art and practice of the learning organization*,
Crown, New York, p. 206.

Many organisations have vision statements. A vision statement describes
what it will be like if the aim is achieved. It need not be brief, but it
needs to be inspiring and compelling, not boring.

---

**At Yarra Primary School:**

- Our curriculum is innovative, creative and challenging.

- Together we create a holistic education that prepares
  students for success.

- Our teachers are inspiring, enthusiastic and motivating people
  who work together to deliver quality education.

- We have a respectful, caring and safe learning environment.

- We value and maximise our resources and facilities to
  continuously improve learning.

- Our community is committed and involved.

---

**Figure 3.15 School vision statement**
Source: Yarra Primary School, Victoria.

The vision needs to exist not just on paper, but also in the collective
minds of key stakeholders. The vision needs to be shared among the
stakeholders of the organisation if it is to galvanise their efforts. This
requires more than a manager standing before the crowd declaring,
"I have a vision, let me share it with you."

> The vision needs
> to be shared
> among the
> stakeholders of
> the organisation
> if it is to
> galvanise their
> efforts.

 Shared vision: a picture in the collective minds of key stakeholders
for a given point of time in the future.

Myron Tribus points out that vision statements should contain "testable
propositions" which provide "some way of demonstrating the integrity of
what is undertaken". In other words, it should be possible to evaluate the
extent to which the organisation is taking the vision seriously.

It's not what the vision is, it's what the vision does.

Peter Senge, 1990, *The Fifth Discipline: The art and practice of the learning organization*,
Crown, New York, p. 154.

Some people have strong views on the nature and structure of mission,
purpose, and vision statements. From our perspective, what really

matters is that all stakeholders have a mutual understanding of why an organisation exists and what it is trying to create. Only when this mutual understanding exists can effort be aligned and the system optimised.

Figure 3.16 illustrates the nature of alignment in organisations.

**Figure 3.16 Aligning efforts through shared purpose and vision**

# Quality criteria

The need for a shared vision applies just as much at the task level as it does at the system level. At the systems level, a vision is agreed; at the task level, quality criteria are agreed.

Identifying specific quality criteria establishes a vision of excellence by specifying the key features that distinguish excellence from mediocrity. For example, engaging junior primary students in developing quality criteria for handwriting provides a powerful reference point for them to self-evaluate the quality of their own handwriting. They can also use the quality criteria to set improvement goals for themselves. Developing quality criteria is a process of engaging people in specifying the distinguishing features of excellence that will guide them in their endeavours, not imposing criteria upon them.

### 📌 SETTING THE BAR HIGHER

When students are involved in setting quality criteria to guide their learning, teachers are frequently surprised at the very high standard they set. Students are usually quite capable of working with the teacher to identify the quality criteria for their assignments, projects, handwriting, and other activities. (Of course, the teacher can ensure that students don't miss any of the essential criteria.)

Our experience has shown that when students use quality criteria to self-assess their learning, they are generally more rigorous and less generous in their self-evaluation than their teachers.

Many schools use rubrics to assist in the evaluation of quality. Quality criteria are similar but subtly — and significantly — different to rubrics.

Rubrics usually provide a scale against which quality can be evaluated, from poor to excellent. Each rubric provides this quality scale for a range of characteristics associated with a piece of work. Rubrics are frequently used as assessment tools, to rate students' work. Students may or may not have prior access to the rubrics.

Quality criteria define a target level for quality. They establish a target at which all but the most challenged learners can aim.

Rubrics usually define the various levels of quality, for example from "fail", through "pass" to "high distinction". If students have access to the rubric, they can evaluate their current level of quality, and they can determine their aspirations. If a student wants to know what is required to achieve a "high distinction", it is clear what is required. However, if a student seeks to do the bare minimum to get through, this is also clear. In this way, rubrics can encourage mediocrity.

Quality criteria can help to raise the benchmark for all students. With quality criteria all students are expected to meet or exceed the agreed criteria. Efforts that don't meet the quality criteria are reworked until they do.

As David Langford frequently said to his students, "In my class there is only 'good work' and 'get to work' — which are you? How can I help you meet the standard?"

> Quality criteria define a target level for quality.

> Rubrics can encourage mediocrity.

---

**💬 PREPARING TO LEARN**

Many schools that we have worked with have developed processes to ensure that the first days of the school year are devoted to developing shared agreements with students to set up their learning environment. Many develop a system map with their students.

An example of this is Warrnambool East Primary School in Victoria. At the beginning of each year, every classroom spends time creating its own Learning to Learn Plan. Students devote two weeks of team-building activity and discussion to developing their plan. The plan reflects a shared commitment to a vision for the class, their agreed values, behaviours and purpose.

The Learning to Learn Plan provides an ongoing reference for students to align their efforts and behaviour. It is revisited for two days at the start of each term to re-establish commitment.

The principal, teachers and students of schools using this approach report a dramatic change in the culture of the school, compared to when they used to start the year by launching straight into curriculum. Student behaviour, engagement, learning and relationships are greatly improved.

# Values and behaviours

Values define how people within the organisation aspire to behave.

In addition to being explicit about their purpose and vision, many organisations are also explicit about their values and expected behaviours.

Values define how people within the organisation aspire to behave as they work with others towards the agreed purpose and vision.

It is the aspiration of most organisations to have staff and stakeholders who are emotionally engaged and behaving well.

Most organisations aspire to have staff and stakeholders who are emotionally engaged and behaving well. Being explicit about the behaviours that are considered desirable provides a solid foundation for interactions and conversations that encourage the desired behaviours.

Our experience with many schools has shown that taking a practical approach and engaging stakeholders in dialogue regarding expected behaviours is very productive. These conversations usually elicit a strong and positive response, with many desirable behaviours being identified independently by staff, students, parents, and community. People of all ages draw from their experiences and beliefs to identify those behaviours that make individuals well-rounded, decent human beings.

The behaviours identified by staff, students, parents and community can be brought together and categorised into themes from which values are identified. Through engaging in this process, the school community builds ownership of the identified values and behaviours. Ideally, these behaviours are the same for all stakeholder groups: students, staff, board, parents, and visitors.

We have also found it most helpful to express the behaviours as directly observable I-statements. Commencing the behavioural statement with "I" takes responsibility for behaviour to a personal level. The behaviour I wish to see in others starts with me; I do not expect anything of others I am not prepared to role model myself.

Expressing behaviour in directly observable terms — I *am* on time, rather than I *will* be on time, for example — clearly defines it. This makes behaviour explicit, easy to understand, observe, and measure.

Figure 3.17 illustrates a set of values and the behaviours associated with them as identified by Aranda Primary School in the ACT.

## Aranda Primary School, ACT Values and Behaviours

### Communication
*Reaching a shared understanding*
> I use good manners
> I listen to others and value their opinions
> I raise concerns and offer suggestions in a polite and productive manner
> I ask questions if I don't understand
> I share my ideas confidently and respectfully
> I praise others for a job well done

### Success
*Achieving through cooperation, persistence, resilience and learning*
> I am an active learner
> I am persistent
> I am resilient
> I do my best
> I follow through and finish what I start
> I celebrate success

### Respect
*Polite and thoughtful in dealing with others*
> I am polite
> I respect myself
> I respect other people, their ideas and property
> I work well with others
> I give everyone a "fair go"
> I accept difference and celebrate diversity
> I treat others the way I want to be treated

### Caring
*Friendly and helpful to others*
> I behave safely
> I help others when I see they need support
> I am kind and considerate
> I am friendly, welcoming and a good friend to others

### Integrity
*Consistency in word and deed*
> I do what I say I will do
> I am honest and trustworthy
> I take responsibility for my actions

**Figure 3.17 Example of I-statement behaviours to demonstrate agreed values**

Source: Aranda Primary School, ACT.

Once identified and agreed, the behaviours can be used as the basis for self- and peer-assessment, as illustrated in Figure 3.18. Students and staff periodically self-assess the degree to which they have demonstrated these behaviours. They can then set goals for improvement. They may ask others to assess their behaviour. While this can be a little confronting, reflecting upon how others' view us can be very insightful.

The conversations that follow self- and peer-assessment of behaviours can be very powerful in shaping interactions within an organisation and aligning behaviours across it. Being clear about behavioural aspirations and basing these on deep understandings of what it takes to be a decent human being will change the nature of conversations and interactions within an organisation. These changed conversations, over time, have a significant positive effect on behaviour within the organisation and the resultant culture.

Mutually agreed values and behaviours can eliminate the need for complex school rules. They have also been found to reduce the need for disciplinary action.

> Behaviours can be used as the basis for self- and peer-assessment.

> Being clear on behavioural aspirations will change the nature of conversations and interactions within an organisation.

> Mutually agreed values and behaviours can eliminate the need for complex school rules.

| | Rarely (10%) | Sometimes (25%) | Moderately (50%) | Mostly (75%) | Nearly | Always |
|---|---|---|---|---|---|---|
| **Name** ........................................................ **Date**............................. <br><br> **Assessed by:** .................................................................... <br><br> **To what extent are our agreed behaviours in action?** | | | | | | |
| **Innovation:** We believe that developing and applying new processes and practices leads to: <br> ▪ creative and original ideas <br> ▪ new opportunities <br> ▪ a culture of change <br> ▪ life-long learning | | | | | | |
| I am open to new ideas | | | | | | |
| I look to do ways to do things more effectively | | | | | | |
| I challenge my own learning | | | | | | |
| I apply new models | | | | | | |
| **Quality:** We believe that the use of quality concepts that measure improvement leads to: <br> ▪ a culture of constant improvement <br> ▪ quality processes and practices <br> ▪ meeting expectations <br> ▪ raising standards | | | | | | |
| I have high expectations | | | | | | |
| I value the use of quality processes and practices | | | | | | |
| I look for ways to improve my work practices | | | | | | |
| **Collaboration:** We believe that the inclusion of all stakeholders in decision-making processes leads to: <br> ▪ a culture of listening, learning and sharing <br> ▪ stronger networks <br> ▪ effective communication <br> ▪ maximisation of outcomes | | | | | | |
| I am honest and open with my colleagues | | | | | | |
| I respect the positive input of others | | | | | | |
| I acknowledge other's prior learning and knowledge | | | | | | |
| I share my learning | | | | | | |
| I encourage the expression of a range of opinions | | | | | | |
| I listen to learn rather than listen to respond | | | | | | |
| I facilitate and encourage innovation and new opportunities | | | | | | |
| I use processes to promote collaboration and cooperation | | | | | | |
| I listen and learn with and from others | | | | | | |
| **Contextualisation:** We believe that schools and their communities identifying and addressing particular needs and circumstances leads to: <br> ▪ informed decision-making <br> ▪ improved teaching and learning <br> ▪ maximisation of student outcomes | | | | | | |
| I assess each situation so that quality improvement can occur | | | | | | |
| I seek out strategies to maximise student outcomes | | | | | | |
| I apply ideas | | | | | | |

**Figure 3.18 Values self-assessment**

Source: Country Areas Program Team, NSW.

**AGREEING ON A SCHOOL PURPOSE, VISION AND VALUES? ASK THE KIDS!**

We encourage schools to involve all of their students — of all ages — in having input to school purpose, vision and values (and to include staff, families and as many community members as can be mustered). Older students can assist the younger ones to write down their valuable ideas and contributions.

When collating the input from stakeholders and when drafting the purpose, vision and values, let the students take charge. Students usually approach this task with rigour and without preconceived ideas or assumptions. They stay true to stakeholder input and use direct, easy to understand language.

To derive the very best direction, purpose, vision and values, get the adults out of the way and let the students take the lead.

# Aligning purpose, vision and values

The above discussion regarding purpose, vision and values for an organisation is just as relevant to the individual parts that make up an organisation — such as classrooms in a school — as it is to the organisation as a whole.

Sub-systems — such as faculties, classrooms, and committees — are also social systems that also need clear purpose, shared vision, and agreed values and behaviours.

Alignment of these sub-systems to the encompassing system is crucial if this system is to be optimised. While the purposes of sub-systems are not identical to the purpose of the whole system, alignment of these systems will make clear how the sub-system contributes to the whole. Similarly, the vision of subsystems will be different from but aligned to that of the whole. The values and behaviours of the sub-system are, on the other hand, usually identical to that of the whole.

Sub-systems — such as faculties, classrooms, and committees — are social systems that also need clear purpose, shared vision, and agreed values and behaviours.

# Reflection questions

**?** What is the purpose of your organisation, school or classroom? How has this been agreed and documented?

**?** What has been your experience with organisation, school or class vision? To what degree does shared vision align effort? How?

**?** Think of an important activity or project that you are currently working on. What are the quality criteria for this? What characteristics distinguish excellence from mediocrity? Have these criteria been specified before now? How might this help you?

**?** What has been your experience of organisational values and behaviours? What might be done to make values real and alive within your organisation?

# Quality learning tools to create shared purpose and vision

Each of the tools described below provides a method for individuals and/ or groups to clarify their purposes.

## Paper passing purpose tool (P³T)

The paper passing purpose tool (P³T) was developed by David Langford. This tool enables a group of people to share their ideas about the purpose of an activity, team or organisation.

Seated around a table (or multiple tables if the group is large), each individual has a sheet of paper on which they write a statement that reflects their understanding of the purpose.

These sheets of paper are then systematically shared with other members in the team by being progressively passed to the person on the right. Upon receiving each sheet from the person on their left, each individual reads the statement of purpose, and underlines key words and phrases that he or she agrees with.

Once everyone has read all of the sheets and underlined the words and phrases that resonate with them, they will have received their own sheets back.

A tally of the most underlined words and phrases is then made. (If there is more than one table group, the tallies can be combined).

A purpose statement can be drafted based on the collected words and phrases. It is important not to try to explicitly use all the words and phrases, but rather to capture the shared intentions.

A consensogram (see Chapter Six) can be used to gauge consensus around the final statement.

Video Clip 3.5: Purpose of Hargraves Public School
http://www.qla.com.au/Videos/3
Source: Hargraves Public School, NSW.

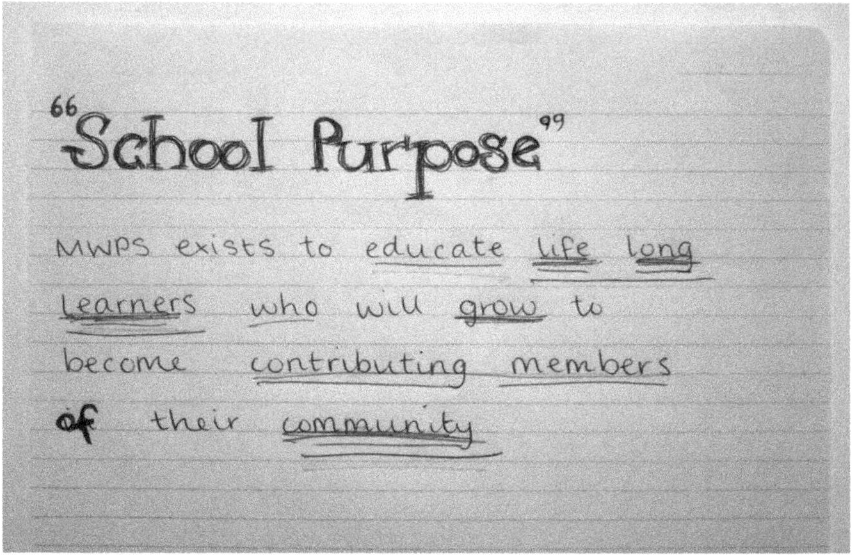

**Figure 3.19 A P³T sheet, showing words and phrases underlined by team members**

Source: Mount Waverley Primary School, Victoria

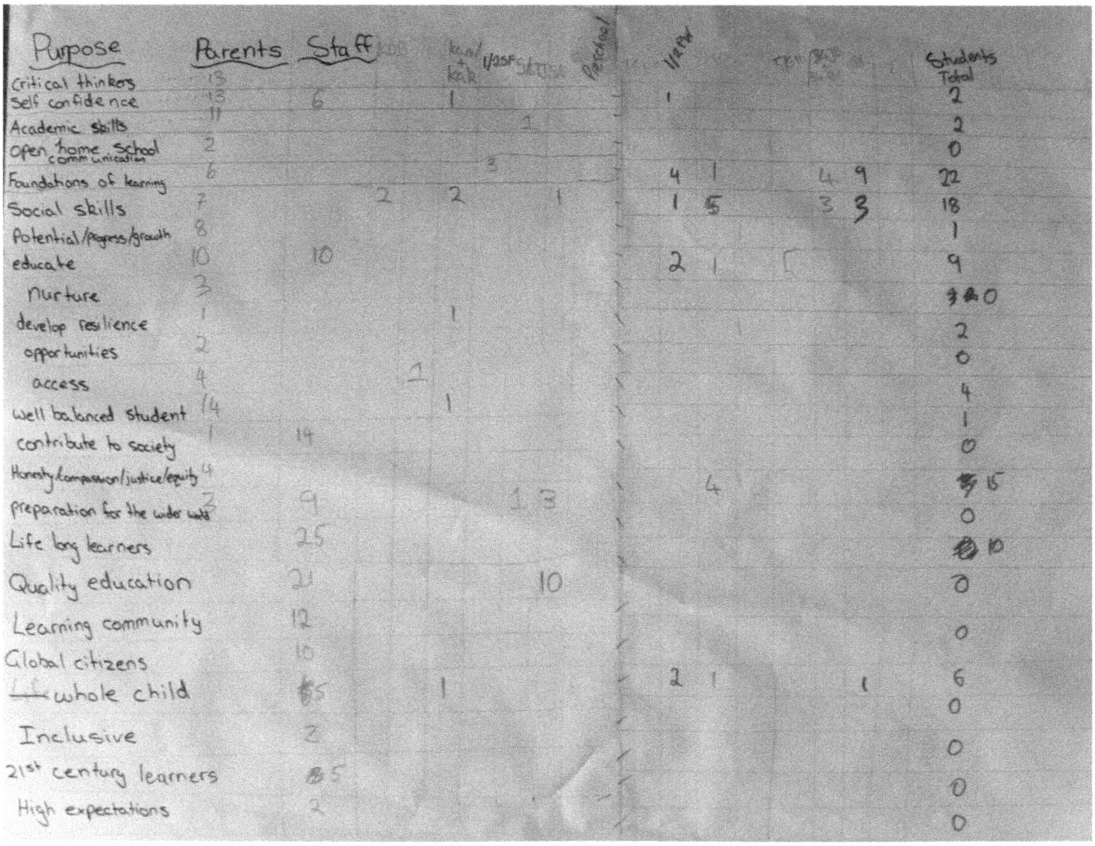

**Figure 3.20 A tally sheet of findings from a P³T**

Source: Aranda Primary School, ACT.

### 🗨 P³T: ARANDA PRIMARY SCHOOL'S SHARED PURPOSE STATEMENT

Staff, students and members of the Aranda Primary School in the ACT used the P³T tool to derive a shared purpose statement for the school.

Students created a tally sheet of the words and phrases from each class as well as staff and community members (see Figure 3.20). The students then drafted a purpose statement for the school based on the tallies they had collated.

All stakeholder groups were invited to provide comments about what they thought was good about the purpose statement drafted by the students, and what could be improved (see plus delta in Chapter Six). Students discussed the purpose statement in class, staff members at a staff meeting, and parents received a note home asking for comment. Once feedback was collated, the purpose statement was amended and finalised:

> Aranda Primary School provides students with a quality education. Students learn both academic and social skills to become well rounded individuals who are prepared for life outside school. Students become critical thinkers, self-confident and able to contribute to society. They learn how to learn, interact with others and have fun.

**Figure 3.21 Students prepare a purpose statement**
Source: Aranda Primary School, ACT.

# ✖ Purpose, outcomes, process, evaluation (POPE)

The POPE tool is excellent for bringing focus to meetings, programs, projects, and teams. It helps to keep the meeting on task and increases the likelihood that the needs of the attendees will be met.

- Begin by agreeing the purpose (P) of the meeting or team (the $P^3T$ can be useful for this).

- Use structured brainstorming (see Chapter Six) to involve everyone in creating a list of desired outcomes (O). (If the list is too long, you can use the hot dot tool (see Chapter Six) to prioritise outcomes).

- The process (P) is the agenda or set of steps the team will work through to achieve the desired outcomes. (Check with team members that they agree that the proposed process steps appear sufficient to achieve the desired outcomes. Modify the process if necessary.)

- The evaluation (E) phase establishes how participants will determine the degree to which the meeting was a success. Achievement of the desired outcomes is a usually key focus for the evaluation.

---

### 💬 POPE: CLARIFYING THE AIMS FOR YOUNG SMALL SCHOOLS' NETWORK

The Young Small Schools' Network in NSW set aside three days through the year for facilitated team meetings. At the first meeting, the POPE tool was used to clarify the aims of the team. The POPE was then reviewed at each subsequent meeting to ensure the aims were still relevant and that the team remained focussed upon the desired outcomes.

---

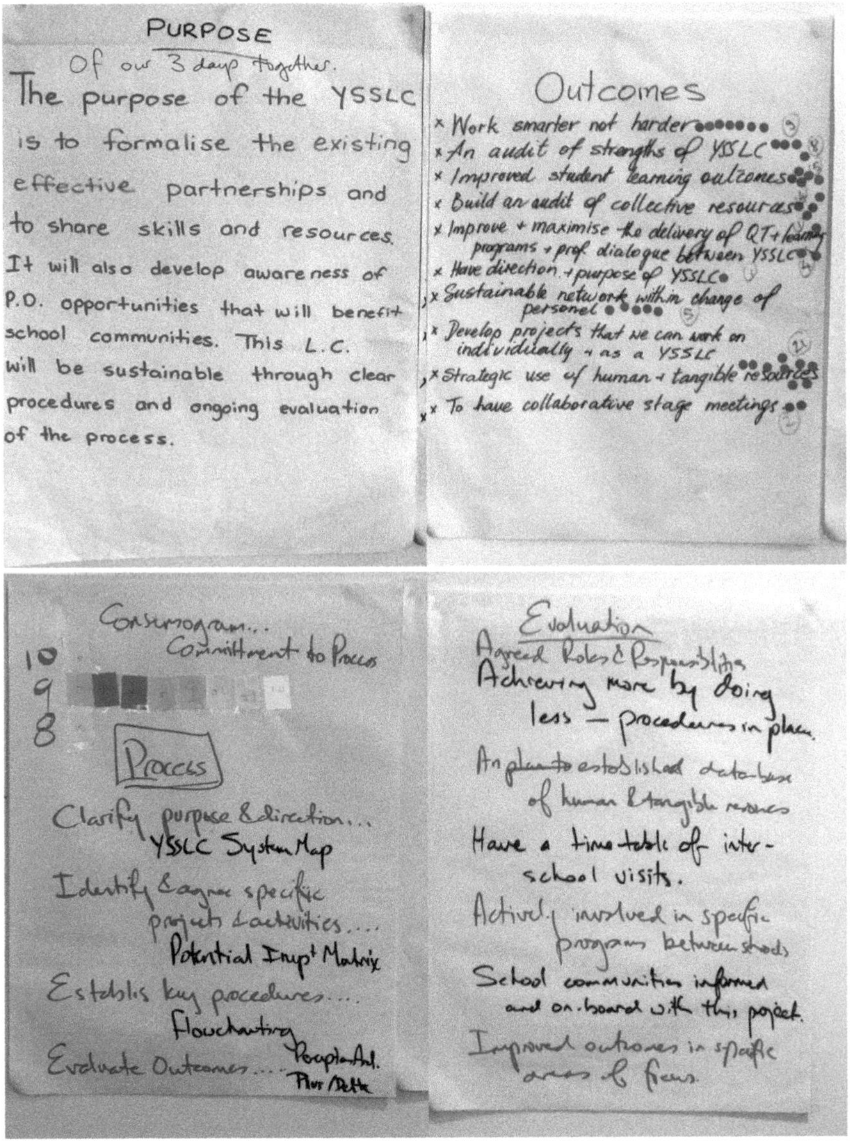

**Figure 3.22 POPE tool**

Source: Young Small Schools' Network, NSW.

# ⚒ Imagineering

Originally coined by Alcoa, the term imagineering comes from combining the words imagination and engineering. It is closely related to Russell Ackoff's "idealised redesign". We also call it "a vision of excellence".

Quite simply, imagineering involves imagining the perfect or ideal situation, free of current constraints, and then engineering the vision to reality.

---

### 💬 IMAGINEERING: THE VISION FOR ARANDA PRIMARY SCHOOL

The staff, students and community at Aranda Primary School in the Australian Capital Territory engaged in an imagineering exercise. They used the process to create the following vision statement for the school.

**The Vision for Aranda Primary School**

Our school:
- is welcoming, friendly, fun, happy and safe.
- offers a dynamic and engaging curriculum that is future focussed and meets the needs of each student and those of our community.
- is well resourced with excellent staff, facilities, equipment and technology.
- is aesthetically pleasing and environmentally sustainable.

Our community:
- is inclusive. The contributions of staff, students and families are valued as they work together for the benefit of all.
- fosters a strong ethos of collaboration and teamwork among all members of the school community.

Our students:
- are engaged and inspired. They accept responsibility for their learning and experience the joy of learning.
- develop a solid foundation in core curriculum areas, in particular literacy and numeracy.
- experience and develop their passions.
- are challenged to reach their potential and are successful as a result.

---

### IMAGINEERING: QUALITY CRITERIA AT MUNGINDI CENTRAL SCHOOL

Year 2 students at Mungindi Central School, NSW, used imagineering to develop quality criteria for a range of their learning activities.

They called the quality criteria their "five star criteria". They created five star criteria for developing a draft piece of writing, which refer to previously developed criteria for handwriting. ("Sookin'" is a term the students use to describe frustrated and acting out behaviours.)

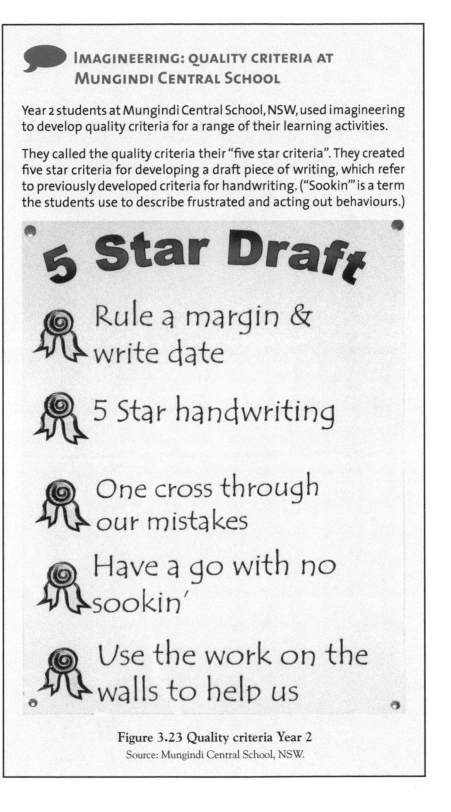

**Figure 3.23 Quality criteria Year 2**
Source: Mungindi Central School, NSW.

### IMAGINEERING: EXPOSITION WRITING AT THEODORE PRIMARY SCHOOL

Year 6 students at Theodore Primary School in the Australian Capital Territory, worked with their teacher to develop quality criteria for exposition writing, shown in Figure 3.24.

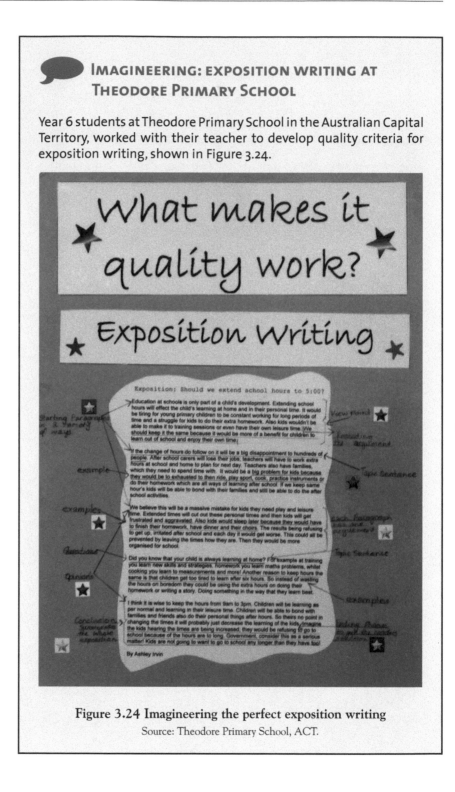

**Figure 3.24 Imagineering the perfect exposition writing**
Source: Theodore Primary School, ACT.

# Processes

The following pages expand on the third principle of quality learning:

Improving systems and processes improves performance, relationships and behaviour.

## What is a process?

The work of every organisation is accomplished through processes.

 Process: a sequence of actions that are enacted to achieve a purpose.

A process consists of actions that are completed in sequence. The actions of a process are activities or tasks, things that are done by people, computers and machines. Nothing is achieved without taking action.

A sequence of actions, tasks or activities defines a process. Getting up in the morning and going to school is a process. It includes actions such as waking up, having breakfast, taking a shower, getting dressed, packing a school bag, and walking to school. These actions are completed in sequence.

A process is, then, a way of doing something: a method.

Processes are means by which the work of an organisation is accomplished.

Processes are purposeful. A sequence of actions is enacted in order to meet some purpose. The process of sending an email is enacted with the purpose of sharing information with the recipient. The process of cooking a meal is enacted with the purpose of preparing food to nourish people.

Sometimes processes have a multi-faceted purpose. The process of cooking a meal, for example, may serve the purpose of providing nourishment as well as the purpose of providing enjoyment for those who eat it.

Processes may by consciously designed, defined and documented, or they may be informal and made as needed. Either way, the sequence of actions comprises the process. The greater the number of contributors to a process and the more frequently the process is enacted, the greater the benefit from clearly defining and documenting it.

Processes are the means by which the work of an organisation is accomplished.

Processes are
usually repeated,
in sequence,
time after time.

Processes are usually repeated, in sequence, time after time, but they can also be one-off. Most processes in everyday life tend to be repeated on a regular basis. Schools routinely report to parents in a formal manner twice per year, for example. The reporting process comes around two times each year and follows the same process steps each time. Home learning (homework) process cycles around most days after school. A few processes may occur only once. A special centenary celebration of a school's birthday will come around only once. Even so, the preparation, implementation and evaluation of the celebration still comprise a process: it has a sequence of actions that are enacted for a purpose.

If we wish to
improve an
outcome we
must turn out
attention to
improving the
processes that
produced the
outcome.

It is processes that realise objectives and create outcomes. If we wish to improve an outcome we must turn our attention to improving the processes that produced the outcome.

Processes are nested within and are elements of systems. Being elements of a system, processes have functions or roles that contribute to the aim of the system. Processes contribute to the purpose of the system but cannot achieve that purpose on their own. Like systems, processes are purposeful. In this way, processes are sub-systems within the larger system. Where systems can be large and complex, processes are usually less so.

Peter Scholtes was fond of clarifying the difference between systems and processes by using the analogy of ships and boats. Ships are to systems as boats are to processes. You can put a boat in a ship, but you cannot put a ship in a boat. From a practical perspective, this sums it up quite nicely.

Earlier in this chapter we discussed the notion that systems determine performance much more than individuals. On a smaller scale, the same applies to processes. The consequence of this is that, once again, we must cease looking for scapegoats for poor performance and unhappy outcomes.

> It is important to work on the process that produced the fault, not on him that delivered it.
>
> W. Edwards Deming, 1994, *The New Economics: For industry, government and education*, MIT, Massachusetts, p. 39.

Instead of asking
"whose fault is
this?", we can
ask "how did
our systems and
processes allow
this to happen?"

An understanding of this leads to a change of questioning when things don't go as desired. Instead of asking "whose fault is this?", we can ask "how did our systems and processes allow this to happen?"

Fix the process, not the blame.

# Process inputs, outputs and outcomes

In industry, processes are frequently viewed as part of a chain known as SIPOC, an acronym constructed from:

- **Suppliers**: individuals and enterprises that provide the inputs;

- **Inputs**: external resources required by the process;

- **Process**: sequences of actions enacted;

- **Outputs**: tangible products and services created by the process; and

- **Customers**: recipients of the products and services.

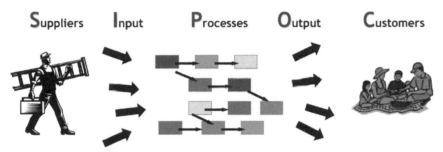

**Figure 3.25 SIPOC**

Source: Adapted from Peter R. Scholtes, 1998, *The Leaders Handbook: A guide to inspiring your people and managing the daily workflow*, McGraw Hill, New York, p. 59.

This view of processes highlights the flow from suppliers to customers. It acknowledges that processes consume tangible resources (inputs) from individuals and organisations (suppliers) and transform the inputs into tangible products and services (outputs) for people (customers).

Customers receive and benefit from the product and service. Thus, the purpose of a process is always centred on the customer.

The outputs of a process are tangible products or services. For example, one of the products of a school, under this definition, is a student's report card. This is a tangible booklet or report that is delivered to the student and parents by the school. A tangible product of the school planning process, for example, is the school's plan. Processes produce products or services and these products and services are delivered to customers.

Some educators can be reluctant to engage with the notion that schools have customers or clients. It would appear that the language of commerce and industry can be a barrier when introducing the notion of processes serving customers. Once the conversation shifts to acknowledging that a school exists to serve students and families, resistance to the concept usually diminishes.

> Processes consume tangible resources (inputs) from individuals and organisations (suppliers) and transform the inputs into tangible products and services (outputs) for people (customers).

The student
is NOT the
product.

## 📌 STUDENTS ARE NOT A PRODUCT

When first considering the SIPOC model in the context of schools, confusion can arise regarding the product.

Myron Tribus provided clarity:

> The student is NOT the Product.
> The Education of the Student is the Product.
>
> Myron Tribus, 1993, "The Transformation of American Education to a System for Continuously Improved Learning", p. 10. Available at http://www.qla.com.au/Papers/5.

This is a very helpful distinction for two reasons. Firstly, to regard students as the product is to suggest they can be worked upon in the way that raw materials are manipulated in a factory. This is a rather inhumane and dysfunctional perspective. Secondly, focussing on education as the product promotes valuable discussion regarding a vision of excellence for this product.

In addition to producing tangible outputs, processes can also produce outcomes, which are less tangible.

The outputs of a school enrolment process, for example, could include a welcome letter to children and parents. The output of a planning process is usually a plan.

Outcomes are derived from outputs, and are usually intangible. For example, the outcomes of an enrolment process include the ability to participate in the activities of the school. The desired outcomes of a planning process are not so much about the creation of a plan, as aligning the efforts of those involved in achieving the goals outlined in the plan.

The primary
output of a
school is not
children, but
the childrens'
education.

The primary output of a school is not children, but the childrens' education. The outcomes derived from this output are many and relate to the benefits this education brings to the child and the community. Some schools and districts choose to specify their desired outcomes as a graduate profile: a statement of the specific benefits that students will derive from attending school.

## The Leander ISD
# Graduate Profile

*Leander ISD students are well prepared to enrich our world and excel in a global society. Each student is challenged, encouraged, and supported to achieve the highest level of knowledge, skills, and character.*

### Academics
*Students are academically prepared for college, career, and life and equipped to achieve their highest potential. Students demonstrate:*
- Knowledge, understanding, and application of
  - i. English and language arts,
  - ii. mathematics,
  - iii. science,
  - iv. social studies, and
  - v. U.S. constitutional studies
- Familiarity with a second language

### Character Development
*Students understand the importance of positive interactions with others as a foundation for living successful lives. Students personify the 10 Ethical Principles:*
- Honesty - telling the truth
- Integrity - doing the right thing even when no one is looking
- Promise-keeping - doing what you say you are going to do
- Loyalty - supporting someone or something
- Concern for Others - caring for and helping others
- Law-abidance/Civic duty - obeying rules and laws/making the world a better place
- Respect for Others - being polite and kind to everyone and everything
- Fairness – treating everyone equally
- Pursuit of Excellence - doing everything the best you can, looking for ways to improve
- Accountability - taking responsibility for your actions, and taking pride in what you do right

### Communication
*Students communicate and collaborate effectively. Students demonstrate:*
- Proficiency in written communication
- Proficiency in oral communication, individually and in groups, including speaking, active listening, and constructive dialogue
- Proficiency in preparing and delivering presentations
- Ability to work collaboratively as a team
- Adaptability and flexibility in response to the audience and environment
- Effective use of current technology

### Effective, Productive, and Lifelong Learning
*Students possess the aptitude, attitude, and skills necessary for the continuous pursuit of knowledge throughout life. Students demonstrate:*
- Problem-solving skills
- Creative and critical thinking skills
- Proficiency in accessing, managing, and processing information
- Competency using various learning tools, techniques, and technologies
- Perseverance, resiliency, and self-discipline to successfully set goals, develop action plans, manage time, monitor progress, and evaluate results
- Ability to learn through collaboration
- Ability to reflect and use feedback to continuously improve
- Discerning research skills

### Personal Growth and Expression
*Students apply their unique talents for personal growth and fulfillment. Students demonstrate:*
- Passion for and ownership of learning
- Self-awareness of skills, interests, aptitudes, and learning styles
- Personal development and expression through artistic, physical, and intellectual disciplines
- Proactive physical wellness
- Understanding of fiscal responsibility
- Awareness of life opportunities in college and career guidance

### Social Awareness, Contribution, and Stewardship
*Students are active contributors in the community and prepared to participate in our global society. Students demonstrate:*
- Contribution and service to community
- Stewardship of resources
- Understanding the benefits of a democratic government, free enterprise and entrepreneurship
- Leadership skills
- Understanding the value of cultural diversity

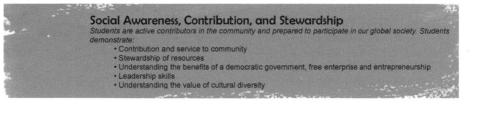

**Figure 3.26 Graduate profile**

Source: Leander Independent School District, Texas.

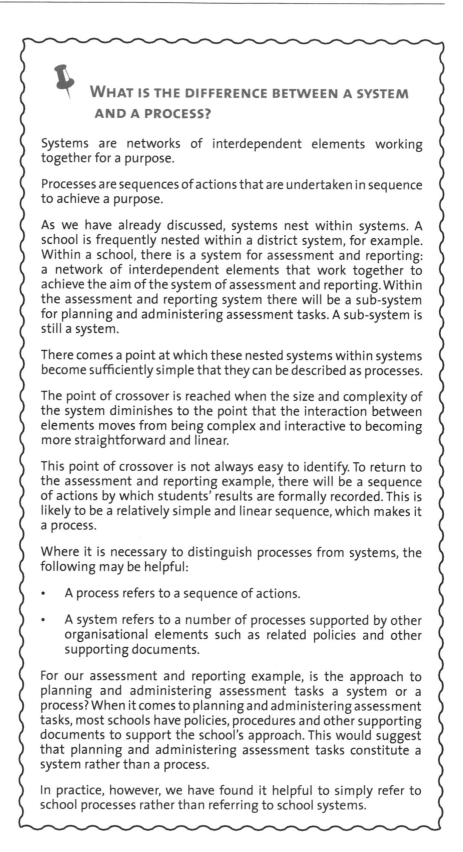

## WHAT IS THE DIFFERENCE BETWEEN A SYSTEM AND A PROCESS?

Systems are networks of interdependent elements working together for a purpose.

Processes are sequences of actions that are undertaken in sequence to achieve a purpose.

As we have already discussed, systems nest within systems. A school is frequently nested within a district system, for example. Within a school, there is a system for assessment and reporting: a network of interdependent elements that work together to achieve the aim of the system of assessment and reporting. Within the assessment and reporting system there will be a sub-system for planning and administering assessment tasks. A sub-system is still a system.

There comes a point at which these nested systems within systems become sufficiently simple that they can be described as processes.

The point of crossover is reached when the size and complexity of the system diminishes to the point that the interaction between elements moves from being complex and interactive to becoming more straightforward and linear.

This point of crossover is not always easy to identify. To return to the assessment and reporting example, there will be a sequence of actions by which students' results are formally recorded. This is likely to be a relatively simple and linear sequence, which makes it a process.

Where it is necessary to distinguish processes from systems, the following may be helpful:

- A process refers to a sequence of actions.

- A system refers to a number of processes supported by other organisational elements such as related policies and other supporting documents.

For our assessment and reporting example, is the approach to planning and administering assessment tasks a system or a process? When it comes to planning and administering assessment tasks, most schools have policies, procedures and other supporting documents to support the school's approach. This would suggest that planning and administering assessment tasks constitute a system rather than a process.

In practice, however, we have found it helpful to simply refer to school processes rather than referring to school systems.

# Processes, relationships and behaviour

With the exception of highly automated processes, people enact most of the actions that comprise a process. This requires time and effort.

Many processes require different people to enact tasks in sequence. Consider, for example, the process by which schools conduct parent-teacher interviews or student-led conferences. In most schools, this process requires enormous effort on the part of the classroom teachers, members of the school executive, front office support staff, and sometimes students.

The perceived efficiency and effectiveness of processes within an organisation have a direct effect on the quality of relationships within the organisation.

A healthy process is efficient and effective:

1.  The process has a high likelihood of achieving its purpose;

2.  The process consumes minimum resources; and

3.  There is mutual agreement that the purpose is of significant value.

Processes that do not meet these criteria rob people of pride in their efforts. Having to enact processes that are deemed to be of limited value or are viewed as inefficient is toxic to relationships. Poor processes raise unnecessary tensions and frustrations among individuals and groups, and they can steer conversations and interactions into negative territory.

The first step in ensuring that a process is efficient and effective is to reflect — with stakeholders in the process — upon the purpose or objectives of the process.

Where there is divided opinion regarding the value of the process purpose, it will be necessary to create a shared understanding of the importance of the outcomes. Most frequently, a divided opinion on the worth of a process purpose derives from differences in the perceived value of the outcomes. Appealing to the higher purpose, the system purpose, can provide context for reflecting on the relative contribution of different processes to the aim of the system as a whole. This is not to suggest that people should be told a process is important, rather, stakeholders can be encouraged to share their perspectives with one another and, by doing so, a collective and shared understanding can be derived.

> People enact most of the actions that comprise a process.

> Poor processes raise unnecessary tensions and frustrations among individuals and groups.

In recent years considerable efforts have been expended to improve the planning process in schools across Australia. School planning for improvement has been a national priority. Initially, many schools saw school planning as a compliance requirement: something to be done because the government demanded it. This perspective has been gradually shifting and school planning is increasingly seen as a process that contributes significantly to establishing priorities and focussing improvement efforts. It has taken several years for school communities to reach mutual agreement that the objectives of the planning process are of sufficient value for the school to make a commitment to doing it well, and for their own benefit.

Only when there is mutual agreement that the objectives of a process are of significant value will any efforts towards improving the efficiency and effectiveness of the process be truly supported by key stakeholders.

Once this mutual agreement is reached, the second step in ensuring that a process is efficient and effective is to reflect with stakeholders on the ability of the process to meet the process objective. In what way and to what degree does each action contribute to achievement of the objective of the process? In what ways might the process be modified to increase the achievement of the process objective? Simultaneously, ways to minimise the resources consumed by the process can be identified. In schools these resources are mostly time and effort. The primary target at this point will be to reduce waste.

Processes build cooperation among stakeholders when:

- They are seen to be working towards valued objectives;
- They achieve these objectives consistently, with minimum effort and resources; and
- They are productive and easy to work with.

# Processes and waste

Waste in a process results from using more resources (including time, money, and effort) than necessary in order to achieve the aim of the process.

There are many forms of waste, which can be categorised under three main headings: rework, non-value adding activities, and unnecessary checking. The dominant kinds of waste apparent in schools include the following.

**Sidebar quotes:**

> Only when there is mutual agreement that the objectives of a process are of significant value will any efforts towards improving the efficiency and effectiveness of the process be truly supported by key stakeholders.

> There are many forms of waste, which can be categorised under three main headings: rework, non-value adding activities, and unnecessary checking.

Rework:

- Rework: doing things more than once, correcting errors, answering the same question more than once, re-teaching, remedial programs, repeated repairs.

- Poor record keeping and inventory management: being unable to find records, documents, forms, files, equipment and resources.

- Poor planning: duplication of effort, unrealistic timelines and demands, overspending, underspending, teaching something a student is not ready to learn or has already learned.

- Staff turn-over: loss of experience, up-skilling costs.

Non-value adding activities:

- Over-processing: excessive bureaucracy, steps that add no value, busy-work, "shush and colour", "shut-up sheets", damage control, responding to many complaints.

- Waiting time: being unable to proceed; waiting for the computer, email, principal, department, government, parent, student or teacher.

- Over-production and excess inventory: making and having more than is required.

- Accidents: damage to people and equipment, absenteeism.

- Low asset utilisation: equipment out-of-order, idle equipment, items sitting on shelves, empty rooms, buildings empty over-night and during holidays.

Unnecessary checking:

- Inspection: checking someone else's work, looking for faults and errors, checking paperwork, "rubber stamping". (Inspection is justified only when mistakes are inevitable and intolerable: we don't object to pre-flight aircraft inspections, or testing a new pace-maker before surgery, for example.)

Each of these items results in wasted resources.

Waste relates directly to the concept of loss. When someone is required to complete and submit a form for the second time because it has been misplaced, the time and effort devoted to this rework is not available for other activities; it is lost.

Time devoted to process steps that add no value is lost. Money devoted to excess inventory is not available for other priorities; it is lost. The potential of equipment is lost when it sits idle.

The aim of all improvement efforts is to reduce waste and minimise loss.

*The aim of all improvement efforts is to reduce waste and minimise loss.*

For many years there has been a rule of thumb that 30 per cent of what is done in organisations is waste of one form or another. This has led in recent years to the concept and tools of lean-manufacturing. This has largely been an adaptation of the Toyota Production System being applied across industry and government, with the intention of reducing waste and minimising loss.

Discussions with our colleagues over the years suggest that the proportion of waste in education is significantly greater than 30 per cent. Some of our colleagues estimate that waste in schools is close to 80 per cent. We believe it may be even higher. This is particularly so when one considers:

- Time spent on tasks not related to learning;

- Time spent waiting for the teacher or other students;

- Students being taught things they already know;

- Students being taught things they are not yet prepared to learn; and

- Setting low expectations on students' learning.

By making the steps in a process explicit — mapping a process — we can begin to see waste, including rework, non-value adding activities, and unnecessary checking.

> Some of our colleagues estimate that waste in schools is close to 80 per cent. We believe it may be even higher.

> By making the steps in a process explicit — mapping a process — we can begin to see waste.

---

### 💬 WASTING TIME: LINING UP TO LEARN

A Victorian Primary School teacher decided to work with her students to improve the lining-up process, which was a source of great frustration to students and the teacher every day.

They collected data that showed they were wasting an average of 20 minutes a day lining up in the morning and after recess and lunch. (The teacher calculated that she had spent over a year of her teaching career waiting for students to line up.)

Relationships suffered as students who were early or on time were effectively punished by having to wait for those who were late. Late students jostled for position at the front of the line.

By working together to improve the process, they now have an extra 20 minutes a day to devote to more worthwhile and enjoyable learning activities.

In a school of 350 students, 20 minutes lost to every student every school day equates to nearly 1,000 person-days lost from learning per year.

# Mapping processes

In many organisations, some processes are carefully described and documented. Most schools, for example, have quite clearly defined processes for managing staff grievances, acquitting funding allocations, and enrolling students.

Other processes are less formally documented, which increases the risk that individuals will develop different understandings regarding how the process operates.

One of the most powerful ways to understand and make processes explicit is to create a process map.

> Process map: a pictorial representation of the sequence of actions that comprise a process.

Process mapping requires breaking processes down into their individual actions and documenting these in a concise visual manner. Process maps reveal the relationships between actions and among those enacting them.

Process maps enable us to see, discuss and share our understanding about how things are done, as well as who does what, why and when.

In a classroom, it is the teacher who leads the process discussion with students. Together they develop process maps for the classroom, building ownership and understanding. When processes are made explicit, students understand what happens, what they need to do, why, when and how. They do not have to ask the teacher these questions continually.

As our colleague, Rachelle, says:

> If you, as the teacher, are holding all of the classroom processes in your head, when are you finding time for teaching and learning?

Rachelle Hedger, Year 2 Teacher, Roxburgh Homestead Primary School, Victoria.

Perhaps the most important aspect of process mapping is that it captures the memory of what gets done, eliminating the need to reinvent the process each time. People who work in schools can usually tell many horror stories of processes that are reinvented from year to year.

*Process maps enable us to see, discuss and share our understanding about how things are done.*

*Process maps can eliminate the need to reinvent processes each time they are run.*

**Figure 3.27 A process map of the morning process for a Year 1 class**

Source: Plenty Parklands Primary School, Victoria.

> ### REINVENTING PROCESSES IN SCHOOLS
>
> A new senior teacher arrives. The person they are replacing ran the school concert/athletics carnival/interschool sports day/middle school camp/homework club. Even though each activity has taken place dozens of times before, nothing has been documented, or what documents do exist are on the laptop that departed with the person who just left.
>
> What to do? Start again and design from scratch, of course.
>
> This is not a welcoming prospect for the new senior teacher. Never fear, she did something similar at her old school. "After all, isn't that why they employed me?" she thinks, as she resigns herself to the mammoth job ahead. But this state of affairs is about to deliver a double dose of waste.
>
> Firstly, the incoming teacher redesigns the process. She creates a new process, quite possibly from scratch, which involves a lot of rework.
>
> Secondly, the new teacher imposes the new process on other staff members. Invariably, their response is something along the lines of, "This isn't how we did it last year", or, quite frequently, "This won't work for us, we can't possibly ...", or, eventually, "Okay, here comes another one!"
>
> The consequences of interaction of this sort can be far worse, with the new teacher coming into conflict with other staff members because of their different (unstated) expectations about how the (undocumented) processes should work.

Mapping processes and capturing how things get done, by whom, and when, benefits everyone. It is not hard to do, but does require discipline.

Before beginning to map a process, it is important to determine which version of the process is to be mapped. For any process, there are several possible versions:

- **The process as you think it is**: what individuals believe the process to be. Of course, this usually varies from individual to individual;

- **The process as it really is**: what actually happens in practice (also known as the as-is process). This is frequently more complex that the process as you think it is; and

- **The process as it could be**: what people would like the process to be (also known as the to-be process). A better process than as it really is.

From our experience, the best starting point is usually the process as it really is.

Mapping the process, as-is, generates a mutual agreement about the current situation, stimulates discussion about the presence of various forms of waste in the existing process, and provides an agreed base-line for further improvement.

The four common approaches to process mapping are:

1.  SIPOC Modelling;

2.  Top-down flowcharting;

3.  Standard flowcharting; and

4.  Deployment flowcharting.

In a school setting, standard flowcharting and deployment flowcharting tend to be the most useful. These tools are discussed later in this chapter.

> In a school setting, standard flowcharting and deployment flowcharting tend to be the most useful.

Video Clip 3.6: Deployment flowchart for spelling
http://www.qla.com.au/Videos/3

Source: Sherbourne Primary School, Victoria.

Video Clip 3.7: Classroom processes
http://www.qla.com.au/Videos/3

Source Plenty Parklands Primary School, Victoria.

# School processes

All organisations, large and small, enact hundreds of processes. To make it easier to adopt a process-based approach, industry quite commonly categorise their processes using the three broad categories:

All organisations, large and small, enact hundreds of processes.

- Management: processes that provide direction and capability for core processes;

- Core: processes that enact the primary reason for an organisation's existence. This is typically where direct value is added for customers; and

- Support: processes that manage the supporting infrastructure of the organisation.

In the school context, we have found it productive to adapt these categories to:

- Leadership: processes that shape school direction and outcomes. These include processes related to planning, the management of external stakeholder relationships, and the processes of ongoing review and improvement;

- Learning: processes that enact the reason the school exists. These include processes related to curriculum, learner wellbeing, assessment and reporting, as well as the school's learning programs; and

- Administration: support processes that enable the school to operate. These include people (internal stakeholder) management processes, finance, facilities, technology, and risk management.

This architecture is illustrated in Figure 3.28.

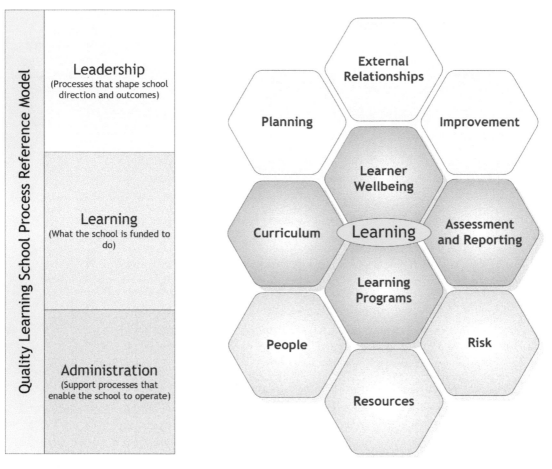

Figure 3.28 Overview of school processes

Each of these process groups can be further broken down into specific processes, as illustrated by Figures 3.29–3.31.

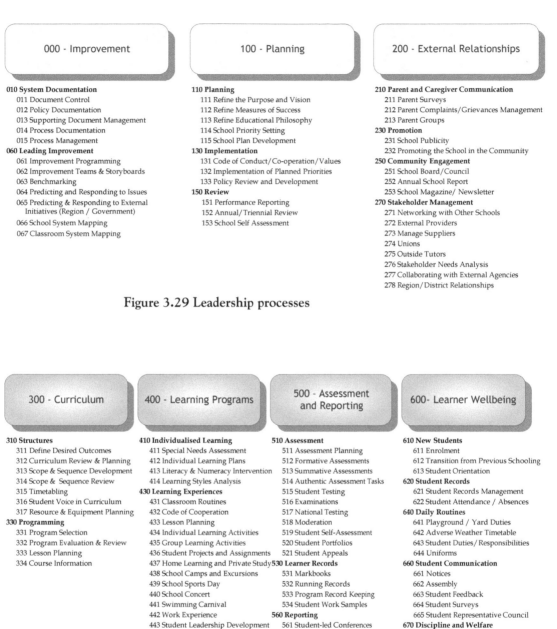

**000 - Improvement**

**010 System Documentation**
  011 Document Control
  012 Policy Documentation
  013 Supporting Document Management
  014 Process Documentation
  015 Process Management
**060 Leading Improvement**
  061 Improvement Programming
  062 Improvement Teams & Storyboards
  063 Benchmarking
  064 Predicting and Responding to Issues
  065 Predicting & Responding to External
     Initiatives (Region / Government)
  066 School System Mapping
  067 Classroom System Mapping

**100 - Planning**

**110 Planning**
  111 Refine the Purpose and Vision
  112 Refine Measures of Success
  113 Refine Educational Philosophy
  114 School Priority Setting
  115 School Plan Development
**130 Implementation**
  131 Code of Conduct/Co-operation/Values
  132 Implementation of Planned Priorities
  133 Policy Review and Development
**150 Review**
  151 Performance Reporting
  152 Annual/Triennial Review
  153 School Self Assessment

**200 - External Relationships**

**210 Parent and Caregiver Communication**
  211 Parent Surveys
  212 Parent Complaints/Grievances Management
  213 Parent Groups
**230 Promotion**
  231 School Publicity
  232 Promoting the School in the Community
**250 Community Engagement**
  251 School Board/Council
  252 Annual School Report
  253 School Magazine/ Newsletter
**270 Stakeholder Management**
  271 Networking with Other Schools
  272 External Providers
  273 Manage Suppliers
  274 Unions
  275 Outside Tutors
  276 Stakeholder Needs Analysis
  277 Collaborating with External Agencies
  278 Region/District Relationships

**Figure 3.29 Leadership processes**

**300 - Curriculum**

**310 Structures**
  311 Define Desired Outcomes
  312 Curriculum Review & Planning
  313 Scope & Sequence Development
  314 Scope & Sequence Review
  315 Timetabling
  316 Student Voice in Curriculum
  317 Resource & Equipment Planning
**330 Programming**
  331 Program Selection
  332 Program Evaluation & Review
  333 Lesson Planning
  334 Course Information

**400 - Learning Programs**

**410 Individualised Learning**
  411 Special Needs Assessment
  412 Individual Learning Plans
  413 Literacy & Numeracy Intervention
  414 Learning Styles Analysis
**430 Learning Experiences**
  431 Classroom Routines
  432 Code of Cooperation
  433 Lesson Planning
  434 Individual Learning Activities
  435 Group Learning Activities
  436 Student Projects and Assignments
  437 Home Learning and Private Study
  438 School Camps and Excursions
  439 School Sports Day
  440 School Concert
  441 Swimming Carnival
  442 Work Experience
  443 Student Leadership Development
  444 Extension Programs
**460 Program Integration**
  461 Drug Education
  462 Religious Education
  463 Physical Education
  464 Bike Education

**500 - Assessment and Reporting**

**510 Assessment**
  511 Assessment Planning
  512 Formative Assessments
  513 Summative Assessments
  514 Authentic Assessment Tasks
  515 Student Testing
  516 Examinations
  517 National Testing
  518 Moderation
  519 Student Self-Assessment
  520 Student Portfolios
  521 Student Appeals
**530 Learner Records**
  531 Markbooks
  532 Running Records
  533 Program Record Keeping
  534 Student Work Samples
**560 Reporting**
  561 Student-led Conferences
  562 Parent - Teacher Interviews
  563 Reporting to Parents

**600- Learner Wellbeing**

**610 New Students**
  611 Enrolment
  612 Transition from Previous Schooling
  613 Student Orientation
**620 Student Records**
  621 Student Records Management
  622 Student Attendance / Absences
**640 Daily Routines**
  641 Playground / Yard Duties
  642 Adverse Weather Timetable
  643 Student Duties/Responsibilities
  644 Uniforms
**660 Student Communication**
  661 Notices
  662 Assembly
  663 Student Feedback
  664 Student Surveys
  665 Student Representative Council
**670 Discipline and Welfare**
  671 Class Placement
  672 Pastoral Care & Student Counseling
  673 At-risk Student Referral
  674 Exclusions, Suspensions, Expulsions
  675 Integration
  676 Student Health
**690 Departing Students**
  691 Student Graduation / Exit
  692 Transition Beyond School

**Figure 3.30 Learning processes**

| 700 - People | 800 - Resources | 900 - Risk |
| --- | --- | --- |

**710 Staff Communication**
  Collegial Sharing
  Team Meetings
  Staff Meetings
  Meeting Scheduling
  Professional Networks
  Daily Notices / Bulletin
  Staff Surveys
  Messages for Staff
**730 Staff Welfare**
  Equal Employment Opportunity/Merit & Equity
  Staff Leave
  Staff Attendance
  Payroll
  Privacy
  Governance procedures
**750 Staffing**
  School Leadership and Team Structures
  Recruitment
  Position Descriptions and Role Statements
  Staff Induction
  School Support Professionals/ Specialists
  Relief Teacher Booking
**770 Performance Development**
  Performance Review
  Professional Learning
  Pre-Service Teacher Management
  Reportable Conduct

**Finance**
  Budgeting              Fundraising
  Financial Reporting    School Fees
  Financial Audit        Grants
  Purchasing / Purchase Order   Borrowing
  Accounts Payable       Petty Cash
  Purchasing Student Supplies   Bad Debts
  Expense Claims         Census
**Facilities**
  Asset Audit
  Equipment Register
  Borrowing Register
  Keys
  Maintenance
  Facilities Hire/Rental
  Use of Off-site Facilities
  After Hours Access / Security
  Lost Property
  Management of Library Resources
  School Bus
  School Uniforms
  Canteen
**Technology**
  Management of Hardware
  Management of Software
  File Management
  Password and access management
  Computer Maintenance and Replacement

**Student Health and Safety**
  Employment Screening and Notification
  Visitors / Trespassers
  Child Protection and Mandatory Reporting
  Student Supervision
  Internet Use
  Drugs / Medications
  Contractor / Volunteer Management
  Messages for Students
**School Community Health and Safety**
  First Aid
  Accidents and Injuries
  Emergency Treatment
  Critical Incident
  Permission Forms
  Harassment
  Hazardous Substances
  Emergency Procedure - Evacuation
  Emergency Procedure – Lock Down
  Fire Safety Assessment
  Building Certification
**Compliance**
  Insurance
  Registration
  Audits
  Departmental Reporting
  Responding to Region/Department Requests
  Teacher Qualifications, Registration, Accreditation
    and Training Record Keeping

**Figure 3.31 Administration processes**

Similar process reference models have been created for use in different organisations. In presenting this reference model for schools, our aims are to:

- Highlight the range and complexity of processes that schools are required to manage, regardless of size;

- Provide an inventory of processes to assist schools to identify where they might begin process documentation and improvement; and

- Promote process awareness, process thinking, and process management.

# Process improvement

*If we seek to improve outcomes we must work to improve the processes that create those outcomes.*

Processes deliver outcomes, so if we seek to improve outcomes we must work to improve the processes that create those outcomes.

The following sections discuss process-based essentials of continual improvement.

## Improve processes to improve performance

Time and effort is consumed though enacting processes. This time and effort is always finite. Working harder to get a better outcome is rarely a sustainable option.

The key to improving performance is to create better processes: processes that efficiently and effectively deliver the outcomes we care about. The place to start is with the most important processes, those that deliver products and services to our clients.

Having identified important processes, we can work to improve their effectiveness, primarily by removing waste. We will have more to say about how to do this in the following chapter. The key message here is to recognise that the only way to sustainably improve performance is to improve systems and processes.

> The only way to sustainably improve performance is to improve systems and processes.

## Use a structured improvement process

All elements of a system are interdependent. Processes are elements of systems and, as such, are interdependent. To make changes to any process will have consequences for other processes within the system. These consequences are frequently not predicted and are unintended. Changes to the student behaviour management process, for example, will probably impact upon the student welfare process and, quite likely, learning and teaching processes.

It is for this reason that process improvement is most successfully undertaken using a structured approach that carefully studies the current situation — both the process in question and its relationship to the bigger system — before identifying possible changes.

> Process improvement is most successfully undertaken using a structured approach.

Fixing things is not process improvement. Placing students in a remediation program because they cannot read may help those students, but it is not process improvement. Merely fixing things is not improvement. It does not provide better methods and it does not prevent recurrence. Putting out fires merely stops things getting worse, for now.

> Merely fixing things is not improvement. It does not provide better methods and it does not prevent recurrence.

We will discuss a more structured Plan–Do–Study–Act approach to process improvement later.

## Embed continuous improvement into processes

Every time a process is enacted, there is an opportunity to learn more about the process and to use this knowledge to improve the process for next time.

Continual improvement can be built into processes, either by including a review and improve step among the last steps of the process, or by reviewing the process at regular intervals.

Continual improvement can be built into processes.

The aim of the review step is to gather feedback from participants and clients of the process regarding the process operation and outcomes. This feedback can be collated and examined. From the findings, agreement can be reached regarding actions that can be taken to improve the process.

The improve step refers to updating the process documentation and ensuring that key stakeholders are aware of the improvements and trained as necessary.

## CONTINUALLY IMPROVING OUR SCHOOL PROCESSES

At the end of the reporting to parents process at Riverside Primary School in Tasmania, the staff conduct a routine process post-mortem. It is a simple affair. Representative staff from each work area, and anyone else who wants to participate, meet 15 minutes before school one morning.

Each member of staff reviews the deployment flowchart for the reporting process. Using a plus delta tool (see Chapter Six), they reflect on each step in the process and identify things that went well and things that could have been better.

They also identify items on the flowchart that are not clearly expressed so that these can also be improved for the benefit of new staff in the future.

The ideas are recorded and the flowchart is amended accordingly.

By morning recess, the flowchart has been updated. The specific deadlines for the following year have been inserted, and the new version has been saved on the electronic record system.

The flowchart of the improved process is now ready to be printed, briefly discussed at a staff meeting, and put into action when the next reporting process begins.

Video Clip 3.8: Process review
http://www.qla.com.au/Videos/3
Source: Riverside Primary School, Tasmania.

Many processes lend themselves to review and improvement at the end of each cycle. This is relatively simple to do, and is most effective when undertaken immediately after the process is complete.

Many processes lend themselves to review and improvement at the end of each cycle.

However, it is not sufficient to simply collect improvement ideas at the end of the process. These must be acted upon and the documentation updated immediately before memories fade and the improvements are lost.

Building review and improvement steps into key processes can prevent a good deal of waste by ensuring continual incremental improvements to processes.

# Processes, roles and responsibilities

Senior managers in most organisations have a chart that shows the chain of command, communication and reporting lines, and descriptions of each individuals' responsibilities.

According to Peter Scholtes, this became standard practice following a very nasty head-on train wreck that occurred on the west coast of the USA in 1841. The enquiry into the cause of the tragic accident found it was difficult to identify who was at fault, and subsequently recommended a radically new structure of organisation and accountability: the now common organisation chart. The development of this new approach to management was underpinned by the premise that the primary cause of problems was dereliction of duty.

An organisation chart shows lines of accountability. It can be used to quickly identify culprits, those to be blamed and punished when things go wrong in the organisation. Scholtes calls this "train wreck management".

Organisation charts typically describe a functional view of an organisation: reporting lines, budget divisions, and accountability break-downs. They do not reflect process flow or identify the major processes of an organisation. Yet we have already established that processes are the means by which the work of an organisation is accomplished.

Organisation charts do not reflect process flow or identify the major processes of an organisation.

Processes frequently cut across organisational boundaries. The process of enrolling a student involves the front office staff, senior administrators, and classroom teachers. Unless processes are considered from an end-to-end perspective, it can become easy for things to fall through the cracks.

For this reason, an increasing number of organisations are placing people in charge of processes. They are frequently called process owners.

The process owner is responsible for the wellbeing of the process: the efficiency and effectiveness of the process. This responsibility applies across the whole process, from start to finish, frequently across the organisation's structural boundaries. The process owner agrees to be accountable for the end-to-end process, including:

- The purpose of the process, and how this fits with the purpose of other processes, and the organisation overall;

- The clients of the process, their needs and their satisfaction with the process and its outputs and outcomes;

- Organisation policies, supporting documents and legal requirements that enable the process and impact upon its operation;

- Measures of process performance, measured quantitatively and through qualitative data; and

- Continual improvement of the process and its associated policies and supporting documents.

While a process owner takes care of the health or wellbeing of the end-to-end process, this does not mean that they enact all the actions in the process. In many cases, the process owner will not be responsible for enacting any steps. It is important, however, for everyone engaged in the process to know who is responsible for each action within the process. In most school settings, the process owner is also accountable for process performance, and is responsible to ensure the well-being and continual improvement of the process.

A useful tool in clarifying roles and responsibilities is the process accountability matrix. This matrix makes it clear who is:

- **Accountable** for the wellbeing of the process: the process owner;

- **Responsible** for taking action within the process; and

- **Consulted** during execution of the process.

In this way, the process accountability matrix summarises process ownership as well as responsibilities for enacting steps in the process, which are detailed in deployment flowcharts. These tools are described at the end of this section.

We are aware of only a handful of schools that have implemented this innovation. More schools can benefit from doing so.

The process accountability matrix is of particular benefit during periods of staff turnover. Incoming staff can be easily briefed on the processes for which they are accountable and the processes within which they have responsibilities. Deployment flowcharts and associated policies and supporting documents provide the details.

## NAMADGI SCHOOL EXECUTIVE ARC CHART (Accountable, Responsible, Consulted)

**NOTES:**
- The Accountable person changes R and C in the grid.
- Only one Accountable person per role
- It is fine to add or change categories.
- Process charts are the responsibility of the Accountable person

| Process | Co-Principal | Co-Principal | DP (Primary) | DP (Secondary) | SLC (Pre/Sp Needs) | SLC (Early Ch) | SLC (Upper Prim/HR) | SLC (Secondary) | SLC Pastoral Care | Behaviour Support Partner | Lit Num Field Officer | Business Manager | Row updated? | Hyperlink Process Chart saved in 790 |
|---|---|---|---|---|---|---|---|---|---|---|---|---|---|---|
| **Curriculum** | | | | | | | | | | | | | | |
| Define Desired Outcomes (Primary) | A | | R | | R | | | | | | | | | |
| Define Desired Outcomes (Secondary) | | A | | R | R | | | | | | | | | |
| Timetabliing (early childhood) | R | C | A | | R | R | | | | C | C | | | |
| Timetabling (primary) | R | C | A | | R | | R | | | C | C | C | | |
| Timetabling (secondary) | C | R | | A | | | | R | R | C | C | | | |
| Reporting (primary) | | | | | | A | | | | | | | | |
| Reporting (secondary) | | | | | | | | | A | | | | | |
| Modified reports (secondary) | | | | | | | | | A | | | | | |
| Scope and sequenciing (Primary) | | | A | | R | R | R | | | | | R | | |
| Scope and sequencing (Secondary) | | | A | | | | | R | | | | R | | |
| Resource and equipment planning (Primary) | R | C | A | | R | R | R | | | | | | | |
| Resource and equipment planning (Secondary) | C | R | | A | | | | R | | | | | | |
| Program selection (primary) | | | A | | | | | | | | | | | |
| Program Selection (secondary) | | | | A | | | | R | R | R | R | | | |
| Program review and evaluation | | | | | | | | | | | | | | |
| Curriculum development | | | | | | | | | | | | | | |
| Course information (Secondary) | | C | | C | | | | | A | | | | | |
| **Learning Programs** | | | | | | | | | | | | | | |
| Lesson Planning split to EC P Sec | | | | | R | R | R | R | C | C | C | | | |
| Special Needs Assessment | C | C | C | C | A | R | R | R | R | C | C | | | |
| Individual Learning Plans | R | R | C | C | A | C | C | C | C | C | C | | | |
| Literacy and Numeracy Intervention | ? | ? | R | R | R | R | R | R | C | C | A | | | |
| Special Needs Review Days | C | C | C | C | A | R | R | R | C | C | | | | |
| Incursions | A | C | C | C | R | R | R | R | C | | | R | | |
| Excursions | A | C | C | C | R | R | R | R | R | | | R | | |
| Whole School Events | A | A | | | | | | | | | | | | |
| Work Experience | | | R | A | C | C | C | C | C | C | C | | | |
| Student Leadership | R | | | | | | | R | A | | | | | |
| Namadgical | R | R | R | R | R | R | A | R | | | | R | | |
| Whole School Assemblies | | A | R | R | | | | | | | | | | |
| End of Year Events | | | | | | | | | | | | | | |
| Beginning of Year Events | | | | | | | | | | | | | | |
| **Learner Wellbeing** | | | | | | | | | | | | | | |
| Initial Enrolment | R | R | R | R | C | C | C | C | | | | A | | |
| Yr 6 Transition | | | A | | | | | | | | | | | |
| EC Transitions | | | A | R | R | R | R | R | | | | C | | |
| New Student orientation | | | R | C | | | | | | C | C | A | | |
| Student records management | R | R | R | R | R | R | R | R | R | C | | A | | |
| Census | | | C | C | R | R | R | R | R | | C | A | | |
| Student non-attendance Secondary | | | | A | | | | | | | | | | |
| Student non-attendance Primary | | | A | | | | | | | | | | | |
| Playground duties | | | A | | C | C | R | C | R | C | | | | |
| Adverse weather times | | A | | | C | C | R | C | R | C | | | | |
| Student duties (Ambassadors)  ?? 'A' person ?? | | | | | C | C | C | | C | | | R | | |
| Uniforms | R | A | R | R | R | R | R | R | | | | | | Y |
| Student recognition | | | | | R | R | R | R | A | | | | | |
| Class placement Primary | | | A | R | R | R | R | R | R | C | C | C | | |
| Class placement Secondary | | | A | R | R | R | R | R | R | C | C | C | | |

**Figure 3.32 A process accountability matrix**

Source: Namadgi School, ACT.

# Documenting organisational systems

It is possible to create shared understanding and capture the best practice of an organisation. Developing a system of documentation captures and communicates the collective knowledge of the organisation.

This includes the following components (some of which have been discussed earlier):

- **System maps** capture the mutual agreements of stakeholders as to the purpose, vision, values and other key elements that comprise the overall system and key sub-systems;

- **Process maps** describe how things are done, when, and by whom;

- **Policies** provide a statement of intent, describing what an organisation will do in a specific area of endeavour, and, frequently, why this will be done. Policies are enacted through processes; and

- **Supporting documents** are standard templates, letters, forms and other documents called upon during the execution of a process.

Bringing all these documents together in a systematic manner and making them freely available to those who need them can reduce frustration and rework. It can also provide a foundation for continual improvement and facilitate induction, training and ongoing coaching. The process reference model discussed earlier can provide a structure for this documentation.

> *Developing a system of documentation captures and communicates the collective knowledge of the organisation.*

---

### 💬 CAPTURING OUR SCHOOL MEMORY

Romsey Primary School is a rural Victorian state school situated 50 kilometres north of Melbourne. The school has approximately 29 staff and 400 students.

The Principal and Assistant Principal decided to make a start with documenting the school "System Memory" during one school holiday period. The task was commenced primarily so that everything was in the one place and could be easily found, and to capture the many improvements they were making to the school.

They started by gathering together all of the current polices and processes that were scattered around the school on various computers, bookshelves, and in filing cabinets.

They agreed a format for their policies and processes (flowcharting).

Priority areas where review and documentation would be of immediate benefit were identified. These related to the policies and procedures most needed by staff who were new to the school — what new employees needed to understand in order to settle in quickly.

They consulted with staff to determine a list of all school processes (using the affinity diagram tool — see Chapter Five), and asked them to prioritise (using the hot dot tool — see Chapter Six) what most needed improving.

Improvement teams were established for the emergent priorities, with policy and process documentation a required output of each of the teams. A member of the leadership team, trained in the Plan–Do–Study–Act improvement process, was appointed to each of the improvement teams. Key stakeholders of the policy and process made up the other members. They quickly realised that there were lots of gaps among existing policies and processes.

The system they have designed is three-tiered, with policies, processes, and supporting documents. It is numbered so that processes and policies correlate. There are two tables of contents, numerical and alphabetical.

The system is totally electronic. The initial idea of paper copies was abandoned when hardcopy versions proved too difficult to keep current and distribute to all who need them. The electronic manual has hyperlinks between policies, processes, and supporting documents.

All staff reference the manual regularly. They had a rare incident where a teacher did not follow the agreed excursion process. "All hell broke loose" when office staff found out and were faced with significant rework.

They have prepared an induction manual (an extract of the main manual) with key policies and procedures needed by new staff.

One person has been appointed as the system gatekeeper and is responsible for updating the manual.

Staff discuss ideas for improvement with the leadership team. The manual undergoes constant review as policies and processes are enacted, with review cycles built into processes. There is an annual structured staff review, during which new opportunities for improvement are identified and prioritised. "This way, whatever is not working well will be brought to our attention." There are always improvement teams at work in the school.

The Principal reports that this approach to system documentation has provided the school with a memory of what it has done, and helps determine what needs to be done. "It has significantly reduced rework and saved lots of time. We no longer reinvent processes when we do them again next year."

It has taken three to four years to build the system and embed it into day-to-day school operations.

The advice to those starting out with documenting their system is to keep it simple and start with small, easy to document policies and processes.

Video Clip 3.9: School system documentation
http://www.qla.com.au/Videos/3

Source: Romsey Primary School, Victoria.

# Reflection questions

**?** Think of a regular activity you undertake in your organisation. Which process is this activity a part of? What is the output? Who is the customer for this process? Create a process map of the process. What have you learned? What would you improve about the process?

**?** What has been your experience of the impact of processes on relationships and behaviour?

**?** Which of the various forms of waste are visible to you in organisations? Which forms of waste are most common? Which forms of waste are most obvious? What proportion of resources do you estimate are wasted in your organisation?

**?** Where are process maps used in your organisation? In what ways do they benefit or hinder the organisation? Which include review and improvement steps at the end? Which might benefit from doing so?

**?** To what degree are process responsibilities clear in your organisation? Where might you start to improve this situation? Create an accountability and responsibility chart for the key processes in your organisation. What did you learn?

**?** To what degree have organisational systems been documented in your organisation? How might this be improved?

# Quality learning tools to understand and explore processes

## ✕ Top-down flowchart

A top-down flowchart provides an overview of a process.

It can be useful in identifying and emphasising the major steps in a process, especially large and complex processes with many decision points. Each of the key process steps is broken down into its component sub-steps.

Top-down flowcharts do not of themselves identify decision points in a process, nor do they clarify who is responsible for each activity within the process.

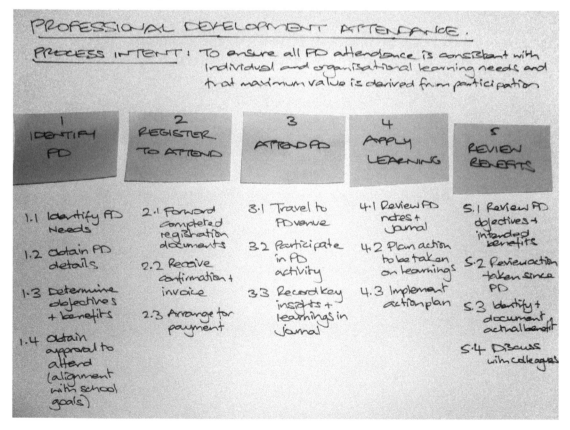

**Figure 3.33 A top-down flowchart of a school professional development process**

# SYMBOLS USED IN FLOWCHARTING

It is useful to use standard symbols when preparing standard and deployment flowcharts. This ensures that everyone preparing and using the flowcharts can easily read and interpret them.

The symbols we use have been adapted from Business Process Modelling Notation (BPM-N) Standards. These symbols are commonly used in standard and deployment flowcharts across the world.

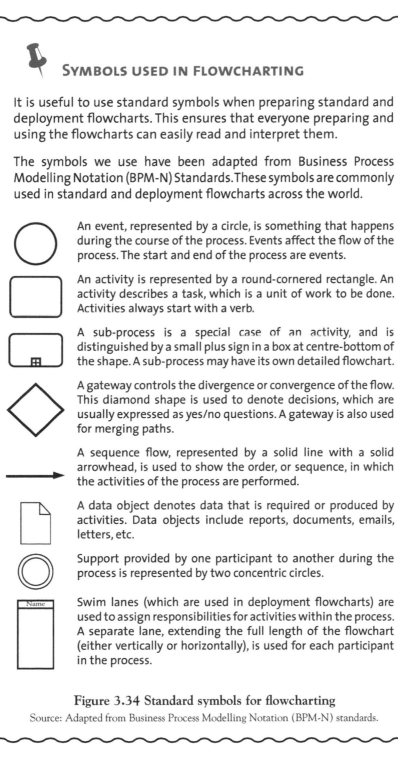

An event, represented by a circle, is something that happens during the course of the process. Events affect the flow of the process. The start and end of the process are events.

An activity is represented by a round-cornered rectangle. An activity describes a task, which is a unit of work to be done. Activities always start with a verb.

A sub-process is a special case of an activity, and is distinguished by a small plus sign in a box at centre-bottom of the shape. A sub-process may have its own detailed flowchart.

A gateway controls the divergence or convergence of the flow. This diamond shape is used to denote decisions, which are usually expressed as yes/no questions. A gateway is also used for merging paths.

A sequence flow, represented by a solid line with a solid arrowhead, is used to show the order, or sequence, in which the activities of the process are performed.

A data object denotes data that is required or produced by activities. Data objects include reports, documents, emails, letters, etc.

Support provided by one participant to another during the process is represented by two concentric circles.

Swim lanes (which are used in deployment flowcharts) are used to assign responsibilities for activities within the process. A separate lane, extending the full length of the flowchart (either vertically or horizontally), is used for each participant in the process.

**Figure 3.34 Standard symbols for flowcharting**

Source: Adapted from Business Process Modelling Notation (BPM-N) standards.

# ⚒ Standard flowchart

A standard flowchart can be used to establish the sequence of activities in a process. There is an example of a standard flowchart at the beginning of most chapters of this book.

Figure 3.35 shows a standard flowchart that was developed by Year 1/2 students at Calwell Primary School in the ACT. Figure 3.36 shows a standard flowchart from Roxburgh Homestead Primary School, which details the process to be followed should a student go missing.

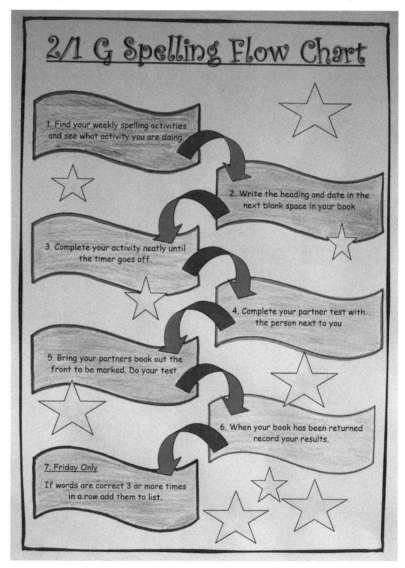

**Figure 3.35 Standard flowchart: Year 1/2 spelling process**
Source: Calwell Primary School, ACT.

# Title - Student Missing Flowchart

Purpose - to enable any staff members to deal with a student who has been reported missing.

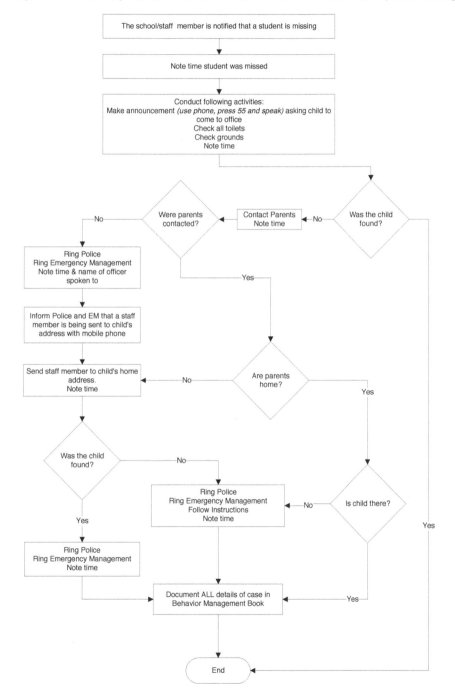

**Figure 3.36 Standard flowchart: student missing process**

Source: Roxburgh Homestead Primary School, Victoria.

# ⚒ Deployment flowchart

The deployment flowchart was developed by Myron Tribus. Unlike the standard flowchart, the deployment flowchart includes a time progression down (or across) the page, and includes a cast of characters that provide columns (or rows) in which the activities undertaken by each character can be placed. In industry, these columns are increasingly becoming known as swim lanes. Swim lanes allow any participant in the process to quickly examine the activities they enact as part of a process, and how these activities relate to others in the process.

Figure 3.37 shows a deployment flowchart developed by high school students at Seaford 6-12 School. Note that the teacher and student each have columns — swim lanes — that identify the tasks for which they are responsible.

Video Clip 3.10: Documenting school processes
http://www.qla.com.au/Videos/3

Source: Romsey Primary School, Victoria.

Video Clip 3.11: Classroom processes
http://www.qla.com.au/Videos/3

Source: Seaford 6-12 School, SA.

## Seaford 6-12 School 10-01
**Planning Work** - Process that supports your organisation
Deployment Flowchart. Date Term 1 2007

**Process Intent:** To support your organisational skills in completing a personal task

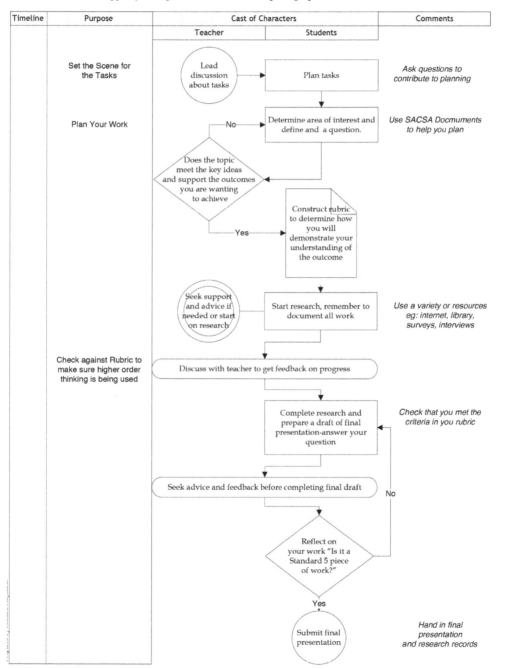

Figure 3.37 Deployment flowchart: Year 10 planning work process
Source: Seaford 6–12 School, SA.

# ⚒ **Process accountability matrix**

A process accountability matrix can be used to map the responsibilities associated with particular roles within an organisation against specific processes or group of processes.

Figure 3.38 shows a high level process accountability matrix, based upon the school process reference model. For each process a role may be:

- **Accountable** for the wellbeing of the process (the process owner);

- **Responsible** for taking action within the process; or

- **Consulted** during execution of the process.

## School Process Reference Model - Possible Responsibilities

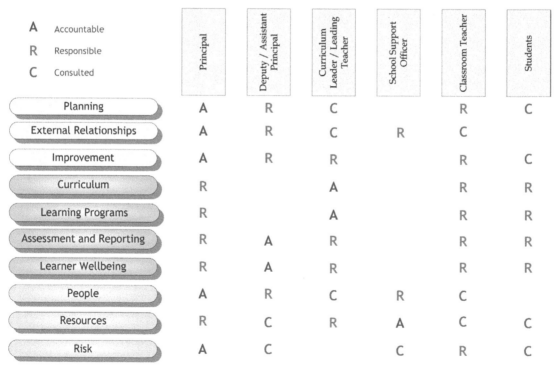

| A Accountable<br>R Responsible<br>C Consulted | Principal | Deputy / Assistant Principal | Curriculum Leader / Leading Teacher | School Support Officer | Classroom Teacher | Students |
|---|---|---|---|---|---|---|
| Planning | A | R | C | | R | C |
| External Relationships | A | R | C | R | C | |
| Improvement | A | R | R | | R | C |
| Curriculum | R | | A | | R | R |
| Learning Programs | R | | A | | R | R |
| Assessment and Reporting | R | A | R | | R | R |
| Learner Wellbeing | R | A | R | | R | R |
| People | A | R | C | R | C | |
| Resources | R | C | R | A | C | C |
| Risk | A | C | | C | R | C |

**Figure 3.38 Process accountability matrix**

Figure 3.39 shows a process accountability matrix for a school's communication processes, which often provide a common source of complaint and frustration when responsibilities are not clear.

| | Principal | Deputy | Teachers | Specialists | Office Manager | Office Staff | Students |
|---|---|---|---|---|---|---|---|
| Staff meetings | A | R | R | C | C | | |
| Team meetings | | A | | C | | | |
| Notice Board | R | R | R | R | A | | |
| Phone Messages | C | A | | C | A | R | |
| Reporting to Parents | A | R | | R | C | | C |
| Notes to Parents | R | A | R | R | | C | R |
| Parent Complaints | A | R | | C | C | | R |
| School Newsletter | R | | R | R | | R | R |
| School Magazine | A | R | | C | R | C | C |
| Annual School Report | A | R | R | | R | | |

Figure 3.39 Process accountability matrix for school communication

# Clients

We now expand on the fourth principle of quality learning:

Clients define quality and form perceptions.

## Who are clients?

Let us begin with an operational definition:

Clients: the recipients and beneficiaries of the products produced and the services provided by an organisation.

### Direct and indirect clients

This definition gives rise to a range of possible clients:

- The direct recipients of a product (the purchaser of a book, for example);

- Those who directly experience and benefit from a service (such as the patient whose tooth cavity is filled by the dentist); and

- Those who benefit from a product or service but are not the direct recipients (for example, citizens who enjoy a safe community but rarely interact with police).

A key distinction here is between direct and indirect clients.

> Direct clients are the immediate recipients of the product or service provided by the organisation. Indirect clients benefit in some other way.

Direct clients are the immediate recipients of the product or service provided by the organisation. Indirect clients benefit in some other way. (Employers, for example, are indirect clients of a school in that they benefit from the educational services provided by the school to the students, who in turn may become employees.)

Both direct and indirect clients care about the quality of products and services, but only direct clients have first-hand experience with products and services. Indirect clients usually experience the outcomes of the organisation rather than the outputs.

## The school and clients

Families are direct clients of a school in that they are direct recipients of reports of their child's learning progress. Students are direct clients as they receive (or, more precisely, co-create) their education, which they take with them into the future.

The direct clients of a school are students and families or care givers.

There are many indirect clients of schools, including siblings, the next educational institution to receive a student (whether this be a high school, college, university or vocational training institution), and potential employers.

The direct clients of a school are students and families or care givers.

### WE ARE SCHOOLS, WE DON'T HAVE CUSTOMERS

In 1997, when we first began working with Australian schools, we sought to explain the quality improvement philosophy. Because our experience had previously been with businesses and government, a steering committee made up of principals and education department officials was established to guide our work with the first groups of schools.

The committee made it quite clear that we would have to ensure that the concepts we were endeavouring to convey were expressed in "school speak": we needed to translate the quality improvement concepts and language into something that could be readily digested by school educators.

We learned a great deal from the process of explaining the concepts and words and working with these educators to find language appropriate to schools.

The steering committee objected strongly to use of the term "customer" in the school context. Customers, in their eyes, were people who purchased products and services, like customers in shops. We later discovered that this was a widely held perspective across the school sector.

We agreed to call the customers of a school "clients".

> ### 💬 IT ALL SOUNDS GREEK TO ME
>
> A high school in Melbourne was experiencing decreasing enrolments. It gathered data to try to ascertain why this was the case. The data revealed that in recent years the demographic of the client base had changed from a predominantly Greek background to mainly Chinese.
>
> Greek was the only language currently being offered as part of the curriculum. Chinese parents did not want their children to learn Greek, so they enrolled their children in other schools that offered languages they felt were more appropriate to their needs.
>
> The school changed the language it offered, which, in addition to other positive changes made at the school, saw enrolments improve dramatically. Over time, people began moving into the area in order to enrol their children at the school.

# Clients and their perceptions

*As clients experience products and services, they form perceptions about them.*

As clients experience products and services, they form perceptions about them. They reflect upon their experiences with the product or service and the extent to which these experiences disappoint, satisfy, or delight them.

In the 1980s, Noriake Kano developed a framework that describes three classes of characteristic that impact upon the perceptions formed by clients:

- **Basic**: characteristics that are so fundamental they are simply taken as given. For example, parents expect their children will be kept safe from injury at school, and that they will be sheltered from rain, hail, sleet and snow. They also have a basic expectation that their children will learn. Failure to exhibit basic characteristics usually results in complaints. Get them right and almost nothing is said.

- **Performance-related**: characteristics that clients are looking for in a product or service (sometimes known as spoken requirements). The more these characteristics are present, the greater the client satisfaction. Some parents are looking for their schools to provide specific language or music programs, to offer child-care before and after school, or to provide regular and meaningful reports on their child's progress. These are examples of performance-related characteristics. Organisations need to understand what clients regard as performance-related characteristics, and then deliver them.

- **Delight**: characteristics that the client was not expecting but when provided, even in small doses, enhance client satisfaction. Clients cannot usually articulate these characteristics, but once experienced, they can quickly become performance-related (and then basic) characteristics. Parents who have not experienced student-led conferences, in place of parent-teacher interviews, for example, are frequently delighted by the experience.

Organisations need processes to listen to the voice of the client. Without such processes, organisations are unlikely to have a comprehensive understanding of the characteristics by which their clients are judging quality. They will also remain unaware of the relative importance of each characteristic and how performance is being judged.

> Organisations need systems and processes to listen to the voice of the client.

- **Basic** requirements will rarely be uncovered by asking the clients about their needs, unless, of course, they are not currently being met. Complaints can be a good indicator of basic requirements not being met.

- **Performance-related** characteristics can be identified though qualitative research — asking clients in one-on-one interviews or focus groups. (The perception analysis tool, described later in this chapter, can be used to identify the relative importance of competing characteristics as part of the voice of the client process).

- **Delight** factors will not usually be identified by speaking with clients. By knowing the clients well and the things that matter to them in their lives, sometimes a good judgement can be made as to possible delight characteristics.

There is general consensus that basic requirements must be met first. Attention can then be paid to performance-related requirements. Only when both of these are firmly in place, when processes are delivering to these needs consistently and with a high degree of satisfaction, should effort be expended on delight factors.

Clients make choices based upon their perceptions of the quality of an organisation's offering. They do this in consideration of the characteristics that are important to them. Producers of products and services may not agree with the characteristics upon which a client has formed their perceptions of quality. Producers can disagree with the importance placed upon particular characteristics. They can believe clients have ignored key characteristics. But producers cannot make clients' purchasing decision. They cannot prevent unhappy clients telling others of their dissatisfaction. Schools cannot make choices for parents and students about which school to attend. Schools cannot prevent unhappy parents complaining to other parents and potential parents.

> Clients make choices based upon their perceptions.

Clients are the arbiters of quality, based on their own criteria.

Clients are the arbiters of quality, based on their own criteria. Clients' perceptions are their reality and contribute significantly to their decision making. In this way, clients define quality.

Schools need to listen to students and parents intently and without discounting what they have to say. While it can be tempting to dismiss a parent's concern about bullying, for example, this will not make the concern go away. If a parent is dissatisfied, you can be certain they will be telling others about it.

## UNDERSTANDING PARENTS' PERCEPTIONS

We worked with a primary school that was considering adoption of the International Baccalaureate (an educational program that leads to an internationally recognised qualification). There was a view among some stakeholders in the school that the program would raise the profile of the school in the community and attract more students. The school was already performing well by most measures.

Working with the school leadership, we ran a series of focus groups with parents to understand what they saw as the performance-related characteristics of the school. The views of the parents were recorded and then collated into a list of characteristics.

Further analysis was completed by asking a random sample of parents to rate the importance of each characteristic and their perception of the school's current performance against it.

The data indicated that parents were more concerned with aspects related to communication with the school and supporting their child's learning than they were about the choice of curriculum or school programs.

The school chose to focus upon those factors raised by the parents as opportunities for improvement rather than to adopt the International Baccalaureate.

(The results of this perception analysis can be seen in Figure 3.47)

# Internal clients

So far, we have been discussing clients of the organisation as a whole. Given that organisations contain sub-systems, it follows that sub-systems also have clients: internal clients.

Work areas create products and offer services to other work areas. Teachers submit forms to the office, for example, and the office staff are thus internal clients of the teachers. These products and services contribute to the aim of an organisation. In the same way that clients of an organisation are the arbiters of quality, so too are the work areas that are the recipients of the sub-system product or service: internal clients. In most cases, internal clients directly serve external clients or support others who do. Internal clients form perceptions regarding the extent to which their requirements are satisfied by the products and service they receive from their internal supplier.

Just as organisations need systems and processes to listen to the voice of the client, so too do work areas within organisations.

Everyone in an organisation is engaged in enacting processes that produce products and services. These products and services are intended for others within or outside the organisation. Central office staff manage the logistics for professional development workshops for school staff, for example. Participants in professional development are their clients, who will form perceptions about the quality of the training. Staff preparing the workshops must pay close attention to the needs of participants if they are to deliver a high quality workshop, in the eyes of the participants.

Everyone in an organisation needs to understand who their clients are and to ensure they listen carefully to the voice of their clients.

> Internal clients directly serve external clients or support others who do.

> Just as organisations need systems and processes to listen to the voice of the client, so too do work areas within organisations.

# Reflection questions

**?** Who do you think of as being the clients of a school? Why?

**?** What processes are used by your school to listen to the voice of the client? How are the ideas collected by these processes used?

**?** What are some of key internal supplier–client relationships within your organisation?

**?** Who are your clients?

# Stakeholders

The following pages expand on the fifth principle of quality learning:

> Sustainability requires management of relationships with stakeholders.

Having discussed clients and people within an organisation, in this section we turn our attention to other individuals and groups that have an interest in the activities and outcomes of the organisation: stakeholders. Stakeholders have competing demands and an organisation must find a way to manage and balance the complexity that comes about because of this.

Let us be clear who we are referring to when we speak about the stakeholders of a system.

 Stakeholders: individuals, groups and organisations with an interest in the activities and outcomes of a system.

In social systems there are four main categories of stakeholder:

- **Clients**: the recipients and beneficiaries of products and services;

- **Our people**: those who regularly come to work within the system — leaders, workers and volunteers;

- **Suppliers**: people and organisations external to the system who provide resources necessary for the system. These resources can be materials, equipment, information, policy, and/or regulations. Publicly funded enterprises, such as schools, also have suppliers of funding (who also supply accountability policies and obligations with this funding); and

- **Other stakeholders**: people and organisations (and other systems) external to the system that are neither clients of the system, nor suppliers to it, yet have an interest or stake in the activities and outcomes of the system. For schools, this group frequently includes other schools, unions, community groups, and local residents. Also included here are silent stakeholders: future generations and the environment (which is significantly affected by the performance of the system).

In some situations, it can be useful to define a fifth category of stakeholder:

- **Partners**: people and organisations external to the system who are both clients of and suppliers to the system. A district office, for

In social systems there are four main categories of stakeholder: clients, our people, suppliers, and other stakeholders.

example, is frequently seen as both a client of a school — in that it directly receives reports and information from the school — and is a supplier to it — as it supplies resources such as funding, policy, and professional learning programs.

**Figure 3.40 An affinity diagram listing stakeholders**
Source: Aranda Primary School, ACT.

# Managing the competing demands of stakeholders

Stakeholders have different needs and expectations of an organisation. These competing demands must be carefully managed.

It will be obvious that different stakeholders have different needs and expectations. The needs of students are very different from those of teachers, which in turn can be contrasted with the needs of parents or politicians.

Stakeholders have different needs and expectations of an organisation. These competing demands must be carefully managed. The first step is to understand the needs and expectations of each stakeholder group. A school's primary stakeholders are students, staff, and parents or families. While there are common needs and expectations among these groups, there are also differences.

In our experience, when asked for their views on the purpose and vision for their school, students, staff and families each indicate they are looking to the school to help their students be prepared for their future. Similarly, they all want this be achieved in a respectful and supportive environment. While these requirements are common, there are also differences in their stated needs and expectations. Students nearly always highlight fun and friends as key attributes they are looking for at school. Staff nearly always mention curriculum and pedagogy as key requirements. Families tend to be the most vocal about the need for good academic results, though this is not the case for all families.

> One of the great challenges for leaders is to find an appropriate balance among these competing needs.

One of the great challenges for leaders is to find an appropriate balance among these competing needs. Uniting stakeholders in agreement regarding the purpose of an organisation goes a long way towards finding this balance. By necessity, this involves exploring and sharing the various perspectives of key stakeholder groups, and then building consensus across them. Once an organisation's purpose is understood and agreed, different perspectives can be considered and weighted in this light.

Failing to respond to the needs of any stakeholder group can spell trouble for an organisation. Developing strong relationships with stakeholders enables an organisation to promote a mutual understanding of their competing demands and develop a strategy that addresses these needs.

Sarasohn and Protzman expressed this beautifully on the very first page of their training manual over half a century ago:

> The business enterprise must be founded upon a sense of responsibility to the public and to its employees. Service to its customers, the wellbeing of its employees, good citizenship in the communities in which it operates — these are cardinal principles fundamental to any business. They provide the platform upon which a profitable company is built.
>
> Homer M. Sarasohn and  Charles A. Protzman, 1949, *The Fundamentals of Industrial Management: CCS management course*, p. 1.

## PERSPECTIVES ON SCHOOL PURPOSE AND VISION

Students, teachers and families have different perspectives on the purpose and vision of their school.

Over the years, we have assisted dozens of schools as they worked with their families, staff and students to clarify their aspirations and jointly agree the purpose and vision for their school. The process usually involves working with each group separately to identify and prioritise their views on the purpose and desired vision for the school. Every school is unique, so stated purposes and visions tend to be unique to each school and suited to its specific context. But there are common themes too.

A review of data from approximately ten Australian schools (representing a mix of primary and secondary schools across four states and territories) reveals the following common themes:

- A place of pride
- Choice of subjects
- Clean
- Curriculum
- Engaged students
- Focus on the whole child
- Fun
- Friends
- Good academic results
- Great resources
- Great teachers
- Passion for learning
- Pedagogy
- Positive school spirit
- Respectful and supportive
- Safe and happy
- Students future ready
- Students learn how to learn
- Technology

The majority of schools sampled referred to each of these themes. While the wording and expression may have varied from school to school, these themes were common.

Of particular interest is the degree to which each stakeholder group raises these themes. Some themes, such as "safe and happy", "respectful and supportive", and "students future ready" are referred to by all three stakeholder groups in equal measure. Other items tend to be raised by only one group. For example, students identify "fun" and "friends" as being important elements of their schooling. Similarly, teachers tend to raise "curriculum" and "pedagogy". Other themes are raised by two of the three groups: students and families want "great teachers", though teachers tend not to mention this; staff and families want "engaged students", while students tend not to mention this.

Figure 3.41 illustrates these different perspectives. Each theme is represented by a bubble, the size of which indicates the frequency with which it is raised: the bigger the bubble, the more commonly it is mentioned. The closer the bubble is to one of the three corners (students, staff, or families), the stronger that stakeholder expression of that item. For example, the item being tight in the students' corner indicates that only students tend to mention "fun". Alternatively, "respectful and supportive" sits in the centre of the triangle, indicating it was identified by students, staff, and families in equal proportion.

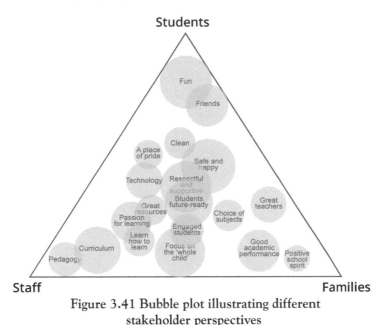

Figure 3.41 Bubble plot illustrating different stakeholder perspectives

These data illustrate two important points.

Firstly, they indicate the importance of taking the time to find out the perspectives of each stakeholder group, directly from that stakeholder group. Attempts to second-guess the perspective of another group are likely to completely miss themes held dear to that group.

Secondly, there are many points of commonality among stakeholders, which provide the basis for agreement. Each stakeholder group mentioned most themes, at least to some degree. This commonality provides a starting point for generating and documenting a shared perspective that is agreeable to all stakeholder groups. Once the unique perspectives of individual groups are identified, they can be discussed and incorporated into this new shared perspective.

# Emotional engagement

It has been well documented that organisations with emotionally engaged employees outperform those with disengaged employees. Fully engaged employees feel a sense of confidence, pride and passion for their enterprise and are keen to contribute to its success. Employee engagement has been shown to be a predictor of organisation performance.

Similarly, clients that are fully engaged demonstrate a strong emotional bond with an organisation and are loyal to it. This is in contrast to clients who are attitudinally and emotionally neutral, and those who harbor negative feelings towards an organisation.

This spectrum of engagement applies to all stakeholders.

> For an organisation to thrive, it requires the full emotional engagement of all key stakeholders.

For an organisation to thrive, it requires the full emotional engagement of all key stakeholders. Schools need teachers who are confident, proud and passionate. Schools need students who are fully engaged in their learning and the experiences offered by their school. Schools need parents who feel positive about the school and are active participants in the partnership with the school to support their children's learning and development.

If emotional engagement is so important, how can it be developed and enhanced? Chapter Six — in which we discuss the centrality of purpose, choice, mastery and belonging — examines this question in detail. For now, however, let us consider the interactions that affect engagement.

> Engagement ebbs and flows with the many interactions individuals have with the products and processes of an organisation.

Engagement ebbs and flows with the many interactions individuals have with the products and processes of an organisation, with themselves and with others. Clients who consistently enjoy positive experiences with an organisation's products and services gradually develop positive emotional engagement. Bad experiences can result in anger or outrage. We have already pointed out that bad processes are toxic to relationships and that good processes enhance relationships. (This is particularly important for those working within an organisation.) The conversations one has with oneself — self-talk — also has a direct bearing on our degree of emotional engagement. Positive self-talk enhances confidence and passion, negative self-talk suppresses them. Finally, the interactions we have with others, our colleagues, supervisors and clients, also directly affect our level of emotional engagement. If these relationships are positive and supportive, then higher levels of engagement can follow. If these relationships are negative and destructive, our motivation and engagement suffer.

In short, engagement is developed through products, processes, and relationships. Of these, it is processes and relationships that most strongly influence the levels of engagement of those working within an organisation. We have discussed processes at some length, so let us turn our attention to relationships.

Human relationships are all about the connections and interactions between people. The heart of any relationship is communication. Communication includes acknowledgement of one another, one-on-one spoken conversations, group discussion, sharing information, and confirming understanding. Of these, the most powerful influence on relationships is one-on-one spoken conversations.

If leaders wish to improve the level of engagement of their stakeholders, then they must focus upon changing the nature of the interactions within and among stakeholders. Communication is the key. Specifically, leaders can seek to change the nature of conversations within and among stakeholders, for it is these conversations that set the tone of an organisation. The most powerful way to change conversations is by asking different questions; new questions that are based on underpinning principles that drive personal and organisational excellence. We will return to this point in Chapter Six.

> It is processes and relationships that most strongly influence levels of engagement of those working within an organisation.

## STAKEHOLDERS IN A COMPANY

Many would argue that the purpose of a company is to make a profit. We do not agree.

A company does need to return a profit in order to have funds available to reinvest in its future and to compensate shareholders for investing their hard-earned cash. If a company does not return sufficient profit to reinvest in its future, it will run down and go out of business. If it does not earn sufficient profit to provide a return to investors, these investors may withdraw their financial support.

But these factors represent constraints to be managed as part of the operation of a company, not a reason for its existence.

We have discussed the importance of clients. As key stakeholders, if their needs are not met, they may take their patronage elsewhere. Serving clients is the reason an organisation exists.

If people who work within an organisation are not compensated fairly for their efforts and if they do not find joy in their work, they will not be emotionally engaged and may leave the organisation. They are also unlikely to provide joy to their clients, internal or external. Meeting the needs and expectations of this key stakeholder group is another important consideration.

Other stakeholders of the company also have needs and expectations to be managed. The Taxation Office, for example, expects (in fact, demands) that assessed taxes are paid, and that they are paid on time. Regulatory authorities require compliance with statutes and regulations. There will be community groups that have a significant impact on the operations of an organisation.

These stakeholders all present an organisation with different, sometimes conflicting considerations and constraints to its ongoing operations.

Leaders of all organisations are faced with the challenge of working within constraints, while seeking to harmonise (rather than compromise) the competing requirements of stakeholders.

# Reflection questions

**?** List the key stakeholders of your organisation. Which are suppliers, clients, people working in the organisation, and partners?

**?** What are the needs and requirements of the stakeholders of your organisation? Can you assess the current performance of your organisation in meeting these needs? You can use a perception analysis (see below) to assist in this task. What have you learned?

**?** Who are the key stakeholders in your school? Through which processes are their competing needs and requirements identified and managed?

# Quality learning tools to engage with clients and other stakeholders

The following tools are useful for gaining insight into the perceptions of stakeholders. They assist understanding the views and requirements of stakeholders.

Remember, clients and the people working in the system are also stakeholders, and these tools work well with them too.

##  Parking lot

The parking lot tool has nothing to do with motor vehicles. Rather, it is a tool that provides a place to capture ("park") feedback, concerns, questions, and issues that arise during a meeting or other process. The aim of the parking lot tool is to capture these thoughts without interrupting the flow of the process, ensuring that they are not lost, ignored, or forgotten.

The early parking lots were simply pieces of flip chart paper onto which ideas were recorded, either as a list or on sticky notes.

We use a version of the parking lot developed by David Langford (Figure 3.42), and have found it to be very effective in classrooms, staff rooms, meetings and other learning environments.

This parking lot has four quadrants in which thoughts and comments can be recorded, usually anonymously, using sticky notes:

- + What is going well?
- Δ What can we improve?
- ? What are the questions?
- ! What are the issues or ideas?

Teachers have found the parking lot to be a very effective tool to provide the basis of class meetings. During the week, students and the teacher can note comments on the parking lot as they arise. When the class meeting comes (often weekly), the comments can be discussed in turn and agreements reached. Some principals use the parking lot to gather staff and community feedback on school operations or specific issues.

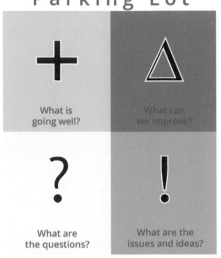

**Figure 3.42 Parking lot**

Source: David P. Langford, 2015, *Tool Time for Education*, version 15, Langford International, Montana, p. 96.

**Figure 3.43 Year 5 student with a classroom parking lot**

Source: Plenty Parklands Primary School, Victoria.

Video Clip 3.12: Classroom parking lot
http://www.qla.com.au/Videos/3

Source: Plenty Parklands Primary School, Victoria.

# ✖ Perception analysis

Perception analysis is a powerful tool used to identify stakeholder (particularly client) needs and priorities. It also provides an efficient way to assess how well a current system and processes are meeting client needs, and where improvement efforts may be required.

The perception analysis tool is a matrix comprising four columns.

* The first column, client requirement, is used to document a list of client needs. This is usually determined through face-to-face discussions or focus groups with selected representative stakeholders. (Care must be taken with this first activity to focus on identifying needs and not solutions; for example, a "school report to a parent" is a solution, while "understanding the learning progress of my child" is a need).

* In the second column, stakeholders are asked to rate the importance of each need on a scale of one to ten — with ten being very important and one being very unimportant. This can be undertaken with a larger group of stakeholders. (Note that this is a rating rather than a ranking of needs; some needs may have similar ratings.)

* The third column is used by stakeholders to rate the current performance of the system in meeting each of their listed needs. A number between one and ten is recorded against each need, reflecting how well the current system is performing in meeting that need. (Again, this is a rating, not a ranking.)

* The fourth column can be used to record any comments, insights or ideas as to the needs or ratings of importance or performance.

Once the data have been recorded, look for those client requirements that are considered important, but against which system performance is judged to be poor. This is readily identified as the difference or gap between ratings of importance and performance. The larger the gap between importance and performance, the greater the opportunity for improvement. Those requirements with a large gap are the ones that need to be considered first when working on the system or process to improve it.

| Client Requirement | Importance<br>10 = very important<br>1 = of little importance | Current Performance<br>10 = consistently high performance<br>1 = very poor performance | Comments |
|---|---|---|---|
|  |  |  |  |
|  |  |  |  |
|  |  |  |  |
|  |  |  |  |
|  |  |  |  |
|  |  |  |  |
|  |  |  |  |
|  |  |  |  |

## Perception Analysis

New Zealand: PO Box 1850, Wellington, 6140  Phone +64 273 021 747
Australia: PO Box 624, North Melbourne, Victoria 3051  Phone +61 3 9370 9944 Fax +61 3 9370 9955

### Figure 3.44 Perception analysis template

This perception analysis template is available from www.qla.com.au

| Client Requirement | Importance<br>10 = very important<br>1 = of little importance | Current Performance<br>10 = consistently high performance<br>1 = very poor performance | Comments |
|---|---|---|---|
| · need to be organised | 10 | 7 | - Need more processes to be put in place. |
| · need to be persistent | 10 | 7 | - If they can't find their answers immediately they tend to give up. |
| · I need to be held responsible for my choices. | 8 | 6 | - Most of the responsibility is driven by teachers. |
| · I need to know who I can ask for help when I need it? | 10 | 7 | - Able to identify who but do not always follow it through. |
| · I need to know where I can find information when I need it? | 10 | 5 | - Too reliant on teachers and google.<br>- Don't visit libraries, contact experts (Human Interaction). Ex Alexander... |
| · I need to know how I learn best? (Multiple Intelligences) | 7 | 9 | - Learning styles<br>- Personal/Interpersonal Dev Learn |
| · I need to know what tools are available and how to use them? | 7 | 7 | - Thinking tools, organisers, charts, software, ICT. |
| · I need to know how to communicate and problem solve? | 10 | 6 | - Don't use the language of learning |

### Figure 3.45 An example of perception analysis
Source: Participants in a Plan–Do–Study–Act workshop, Victoria.

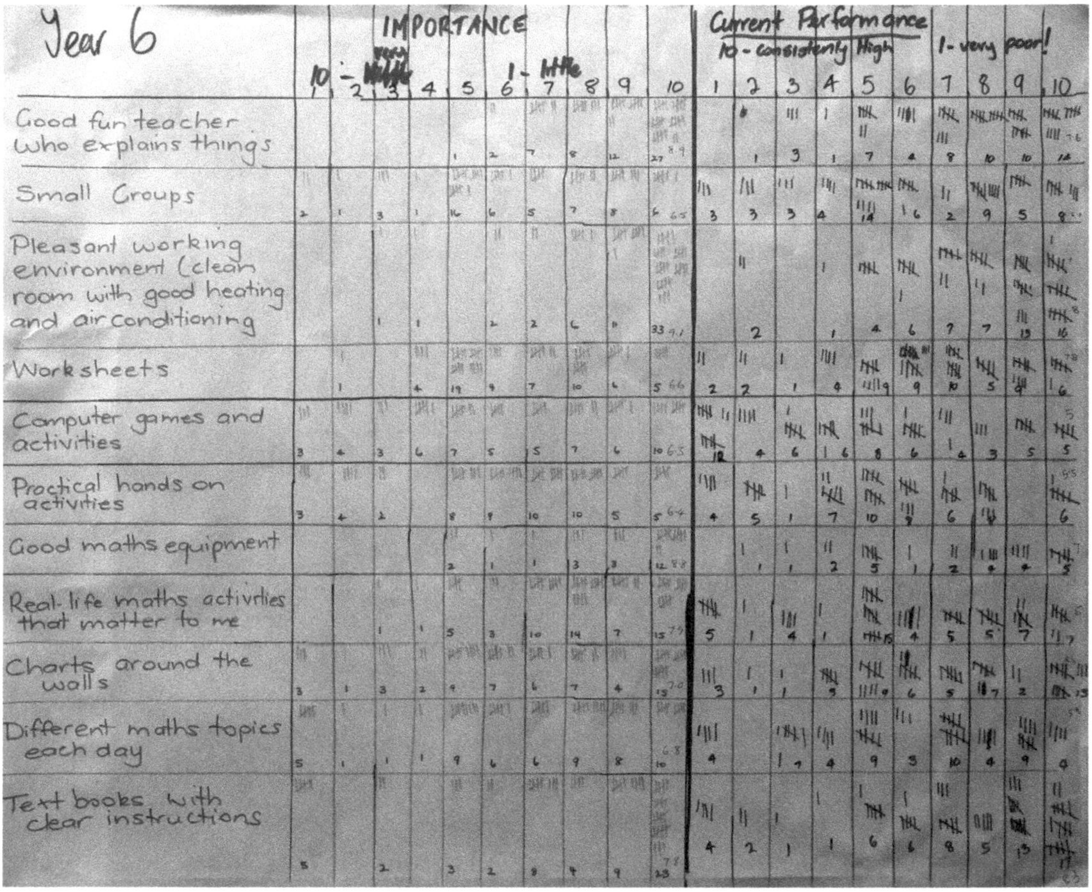

**Year 6**

| | IMPORTANCE | | | | | | | | | | Current Performance | | | | | | | | | |
| | 10 - will | | | | 1 - little | | | | | 10 - consistently High | | | | | 1 - very poor! | | | | |
| | 1 2 | 3 | 4 | 5 | 6 | 7 | 8 | 9 | 10 | 1 | 2 | 3 | 4 | 5 | 6 | 7 | 8 | 9 | 10 |
|---|---|---|---|---|---|---|---|---|---|---|---|---|---|---|---|---|---|---|---|---|

Figure 3.46 Perception analysis tally sheet
Source: A network of schools in NSW.

Figure 3.47 illustrates the result of a perception analysis undertaken with a parent community in a graphical form that shows, for each item, the difference or gap between the average importance rating and the perceived performance rating.

A negative number, such as appears at the top of the graph, indicates that the requirement is considered to be important and is not being met to a high degree by the school's current performance.

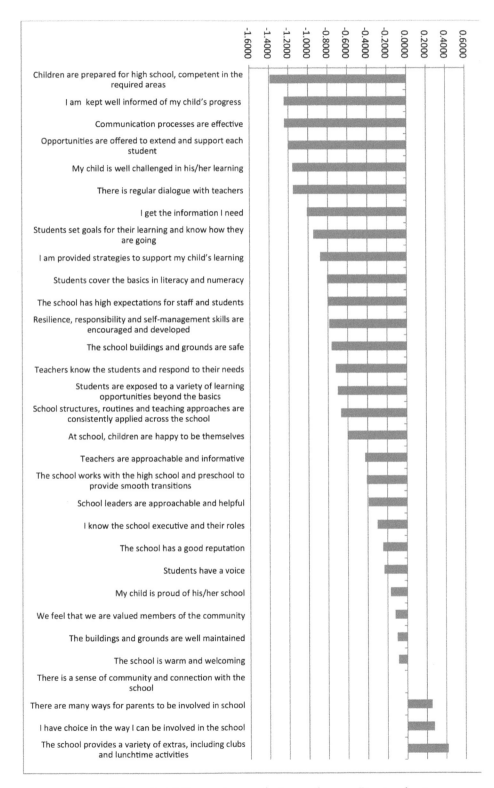

**Figure 3.47 Perception analysis results as a Pareto chart**

Source: Primary school in the ACT.

# Chapter summary

In this chapter, we have examined the five principles relating to the first area of Deming's system of profound knowledge, appreciation for a system:

**Systems:**   People work in a system. Systems determine how an organisation and its people behave and perform.

**Purpose:**   Shared purpose and a clear vision of excellence align effort.

**Processes:**   Improving systems and processes improves performance, relationships and behaviour.

**Clients:**   Clients define quality and form perceptions.

**Stakeholders:**   Sustainability requires management of relationships with stakeholders.

In doing so, we have explained that:

- Schools and classrooms are social systems;

- Social systems exhibit specific characteristics, the most significant of which are interdependence among elements of the system and with the containing system, and the capacity of elements to choose their own purpose and methods;

- Systems drive performance more than individuals;

- Shared purpose and vision are required to galvanise effort towards a common aim and to optimise the system;

- Improving processes is the key to sustainable improvement;

- Improving processes is aimed at eliminating waste and reducing loss, thus improving efficiency and effectiveness;

- Everyone has a role to play in improving systems and processes;

- System documentation makes explicit agreed processes, policies, and supporting documents. This helps to minimise and eliminate waste; communicate, train and induct staff; and continually improve how things are done in the organisation;

- There are many stakeholders in most social systems. Clients, the people being served, are a key stakeholder of any system;

- Stakeholders have competing expectations and requirements. These need to be understood and carefully managed;

- Emotional engagement of all stakeholders affects organisational performance;  and

- There are quality learning tools that help to bring these ideas to life and which can provide practical strategies to take action. These include:  paper passing purpose tool (P³T); purpose, outcomes, process, evaluation (POPE); imagineering; top-down flowchart; standard flowchart; deployment flowchart; process accountability matrix; parking lot; and perception analysis.

# Further reading

We highly recommend the following references for those who wish to read more on this aspect of the improvement theory:

Russell L. Ackoff, 1999, *Ackoff's Best: His classic writings on management*, Wiley and Sons, New York — Ackoff was a master of systems theory, and this work provides a wonderful collection of his best writings.

Peter R. Scholtes, 1998, *The Leader's Handbook*, McGraw-Hill, New York — A comprehensive and easy to read work on leading organisations towards continual improvement.

Quality Learning Australasia, 2011, *Understanding systems: system mapping*, QLA – A how-to guide for system mapping.

Quality Learning Australasia, 2011, *Understanding processes: process mapping*, QLA – A how-to guide for process mapping.

Quality Learning Australasia, 2014, *Understanding systems: system documentation*, QLA – A how-to guide for documenting systems.

Additional references can be found in the annotated bibliography.

# Chapter 4:
# Creating and Applying Theory

The theory of knowledge helps us to understand that management in any form is prediction.

W. Edwards Deming, 1994, *The New Economics: For industry, government and education*, MIT, Massachusetts, p. 104.

# Chapter contents

# Introduction

In this chapter we introduce the second area of Deming's system of profound knowledge — theory of knowledge — and explore the two principles that underpin and reflect the key concepts related to this area of his improvement theory:

**Planning:**  Improvement is rarely achieved without the planned application of appropriate strategy and methods.

**Knowledge:**  Learning and improvement are derived from theory, prediction, observation and reflection.

Planning is a critical part of organisational improvement that underpins learning and the creation of knowledge. Our aim in this chapter is to explore the good and bad practices of planning as a critical basis for learning and continual improvement.

We show that there are opportunities to improve the processes of planning for improvement in schools by:

- removing the requirement to specify numerical goals or targets;

- expanding the plan to include key daily routines in order to make the plans more relevant to all staff;

- deferring the specification of specific action plans until the appropriate system and root cause analysis has been completed; and

- ensuring that improvement plans focus upon sustainable systems and processes, rather than becoming to-do lists.

Planning is the process by which organisations develop their theory for improvement. The implementation of plans provides the experiences needed to reaffirm or re-inform this theory. Using a structured improvement process, such as the Plan–Do–Study–Act cycle enables individuals and teams to create and test theories for improvement.

This chapter highlights some current ineffective practices, such as schools enacting planning as a compliance rather than a learning activity, and copying the practices or programs of others, rather than developing their own robust theories for improvement.

The flowchart below is a summary of the flow of the chapter and its contents.

> Our aim in this chapter is to explore the good and bad practices of planning as a critical basis for learning and continual improvement.

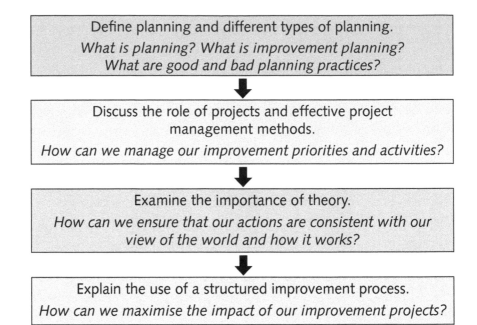

# Planning

The following pages expand on this principle of quality learning:

> Improvement is rarely achieved without the planned application of appropriate strategy and methods.

## What is planning?

The following definition of planning has been adapted from the work of Russell Ackoff.

 Planning: a process of making and evaluating a set of interrelated decisions, before taking action, in order to increase the likelihood of achieving some desired future state through the actions taken.

The key aspects of this definition are:

1. Planning is a process;

2. Sets of decisions are interrelated; and

3. The aim is a desired future state, which would be unlikely without specific actions.

 Plan: the product of a planning process that articulates the intended actions to be taken in pursuit of the desired future state. A plan documents an agreed theory for action.

Planning is a process, the output of which is a plan. Planning involves making evaluations and choices about possible courses of action, before taking action, in order to achieve the vision of an organisation.

> Planning involves making evaluations and choices about possible courses of action.

Plans and planning are about creating a desired future, so it is logical for planning to start with mutual agreement among stakeholders regarding the desired future. This brings us back to the concepts of purpose and vision, as discussed in Chapter Three. In order to plan for a desired future, we must reach mutual agreement among the stakeholders about what this desired future is.

Once this is agreed, the immediate question follows: by what method will we achieve our desired future state? A plan documents agreement about the best methods to achieve vision and purpose. It represents a theory for improvement.

> A plan documents agreement about the best methods to achieve vision and purpose. It represents a theory for improvement.

In the school education system, planning occurs on many levels, from state to region and district education systems, from whole school planning to team and individual planning. The focus of our discussion here will be whole school planning and individual planning. However, the same principles we discuss also apply to states, regions, districts, committees, and teams.

## Different types of planning

In addition to varying levels of organisational planning, planning can also be aimed at different activities in which an organisation might engage, including:

- **Operational planning**, which focusses on the management of an organisation's ongoing activities;

- **Improvement planning**, which focusses on priorities for improvement as an organisation seeks to achieve its vision;

- **Financial planning**, which focusses on the allocation of funds to an organisation's operations and improvement efforts; and

- **Professional development planning**, which focusses on strategies to build individuals' capacity to take effective action within an organisation.

This list is not exhaustive.

The focus of planning affects the range of stakeholders required to take action as a result of the plan. Strategic plans are usually the domain of senior management. Operational plans, on the other hand, may be written in such a way that everyone in an organisation can see the contribution of their activities. Typically, organisations will develop an overarching or strategic plan, complimented by a set of annual operating plans to detail the activity to be undertaken each year. This occurs so that implementation of the plan may be effectively managed.

Given that this book is about the practices of improvement, our discussion will focus on whole school improvement planning. This is not to downplay the significance of other facets of planning, but rather to target our attention to planning that supports school improvement.

# The role of individual planning

All people in an organisation need to be engaged in working on the system if the organisation is to be improving continually.

At the individual level, planning provides a mechanism to make working on the system an explicit part of everyone's role. Individual plans outline the desired future state resulting from the contribution of the individual. This will result in the creation of intended outcomes for daily routines, the desired outcomes from improving systems and processes, and from innovation projects. Individual plans can also outline professional learning priorities and the resulting strategy or actions proposed for that individual.

Ideally, development and monitoring of individual plans will be tightly coupled with an organisation's performance development process.

# What is good planning?

Good planning is a process for learning. A plan represents an organisation's theory regarding what is required to achieve desired objectives. As a plan is implemented and evaluated, this theory can be validated or reinformed according to the outcomes of the plan. This process represents an opportunity for learning.

> Planning is a process for learning.

Let us consider a set of criteria for excellent planning (reflecting our experiences with the planning processes of various organisations over many years) which will provide a basis to reflect on the improvement planning activities of schools and other organisations. The distinguishing features of an excellent planning process are:

- Planning is viewed and enacted as a learning process across the organisation;

- The planning process involves key stakeholders of the organisation and is based on their input. The plan is owned and committed to by key stakeholders. Stakeholders can see their role reflected in the plan. Their contribution to the improvement of the organisation is clear;

- Planning is a reflective, evidence-based process informed by data obtained from a range of sources;

- The planning process and plan align and contribute to the purpose and vision of the organisation or system, and reflects its philosophy, values and beliefs;

- Priorities, desired outcomes (or goals), strategies, and timelines are clearly articulated in the plan. They are realistic and achievable;

- Plans are developed through the application of a structured process that includes root cause analysis;

- A few effective measures have been identified against each of the priorities. These are measures that will provide the greatest insight into the achievement of the priorities: to monitor progress and to evaluate the impact of improvement strategies;

- The plan is accessible and meaningful to everyone in the organisation;

- The plan targets the development or improvement of products, services or processes;

- The planning process and resultant plans align as they cascade through the various levels within and across the organisation;

- The planning process facilitates and supports a structured and regular review of the implementation of the plan. The plan is dynamic and is easily updated and modified as the organisation learns. The theory contained within the plan is reinforced through experience; and

- The planning process delivers demonstrable, sustainable and continual improvement.

# Problems with planning

Let us use the criteria above to discuss the planning practices that currently take place in many schools.

## Planning as compliance not learning

Australian government schools are required to participate in a review and planning process that results in the development of a multi-year plan, annual operating plans, and preparation of an annual report.

The mandated planning processes for government schools in Australia are surprisingly similar across the various states and territories. For the most part, Australian government schools are required to participate in a review and planning process that results in the development of a multi-year plan, annual operating plans, and preparation of an annual report. A typical cycle is illustrated in Figure 4.1.

The multi-year plan is given a variety of names across jurisdictions, but essentially serves the same purpose: to outline the longer term — three- to four-year — improvement priorities and intended outcomes. These improvement priorities are frequently linked to state, territory, and national priorities.

In most jurisdictions, schools are required to establish targets — specific numerical goals — to monitor progress towards the intended outcomes for each priority.

This multi-year plan also specifies key initiatives and actions — frequently called strategies — which the school intends to undertake to achieve the desired outcomes.

The annual improvement plan identifies the key improvement strategies that will be addressed during that year. This plan usually details specific actions, time-lines, responsibilities, and, in many jurisdictions, specific numerical goals or targets.

An annual report is prepared each year to report performance and progress, usually against the multi-year plan.

In most states and territories these are all public documents published on each school's web site.

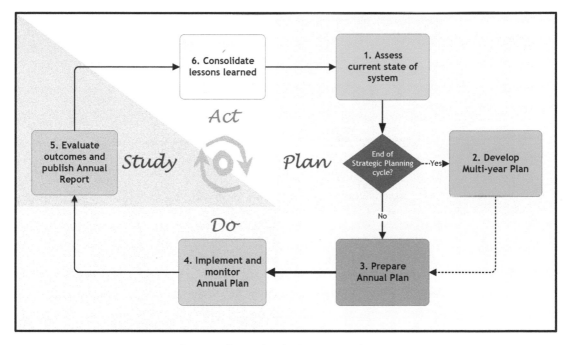

**Figure 4.1 Typical Australian school planning cycle**

School's reactions to these mandated processes is highly variable. Of primary concern is that the planning process is often seen as yet another externally imposed "thing to be done", on top of a crowded program of daily work.

As a consequence, plans are frequently viewed as a compliance requirement, rather than recognised and valued as part of an ongoing process of improvement. Plans are often documented, approved, shelved and forgotten until reporting time.

## Whose plan is it?

In many schools, the school executive prepare the plans, with little input from the staff that will be required to implement them.

Plans have much greater chance of success if those who have a stake in the plan and its outcomes have contributed in a meaningful way to the planning process. This is particularly true of those who will be called upon to implement the plan.

> The most important (but not the only) benefit of planning is not derived from use of its product, a plan, but from engaging in its production.
>
> Russell L. Ackoff, 1981, *Ackoff's Best: His classic writings on management*, John Wiley & Sons, New York, p. 111.

Plans can be broadly classified as improvement plans or operational plans.

### Improvement plans

Improvement plans specify improvement priorities and strategies for a coming period. They typically focus upon the innovation projects of an organisation and key projects to improve specific processes. As such, they detail specific improvement projects.

Therefore, improvement plans are only of direct relevance to those actively involved in the identified improvement projects. It is easy for other individuals to dismiss improvement plans as irrelevant to them, because they are not involved in these improvement projects or have only a minor role to play in them. Improvement plans do not, in general, make clear that everybody has improvement work do to. Leading improvement is often seen as the domain of senior management.

### Operational plans

Operational plans, however, cover all the planned activities of an organisation, including improvement priorities and core processes. Operational plans recognise the value that teachers and other school staff contribute to the ongoing operations of a school — working in the system — as well as their contributions to improvement — working on the system.

---

*Plans have much greater chance of success if those who have a stake in the plan and its outcomes have contributed in a meaningful way to the planning process.*

*Improvement plans are only of direct relevance to those actively involved in the identified improvement projects.*

It is through operational plans that improvement can be made an explicit part of everybody's job. Operational plans specify the key innovation projects and improvement projects for which teams will be formed (as would be specified in an improvement plan). Operational plans also highlight that each individual has important daily routines to perform and that they will be responsible to lead improvement activities of their own.

Operational plans allow every individual to see the contributions they make to an organisation through daily routines, improving systems and processes, and innovation projects.

## Actions or strategies?

Australian government schools improvement plans are generally required to be quite specific about the improvement actions to be undertaken. This is particularly the case for annual improvement plans.

This creates two potential problems. Firstly, it may lead schools to "jump to solution" during the planning process; reacting in a trigger-happy manner to fix a problem without fully understanding the issues involved, often with unintended negative consequences. Secondly, requiring detailed actions fails to recognise the distinction between a plan and a strategy, as identified by Myron Tribus some 20 years ago.

> IN A PLAN you know what you want to do and you know exactly how to do it. You start from the desired outcome and work backwards. *Each step in a plan is designed to support the steps which follow.*
>
> IN A STRATEGY, you know what you want to do but you cannot say exactly how to do it. There are things to be learned along the way. *In a strategy, each step is determined by what is learned at the previous step.*
>
> Myron Tribus, 1993, "The Transformation of American Education to a System for Continuously Improved Learning", p. 7. Available at http://www.qla.com.au/Papers/5. (Emphasis in original).

This distinction can help to explain why some staff do not support their school improvement plans: when actions are specified in a plan, solutions are imposed; when a plan is strategy-based, more rigour can be applied to developing solutions and ownership is achieved through collaborative effort.

There is frequently a great deal to be learned about the workings of the school, which leads to a better solution when taken into account. Studying the current state of a system, the driving and restraining forces

*Operational plans allow every individual to see the contributions they make to an organisation through daily routines, improving systems and processes, and innovation projects.*

*When a plan is strategy-based, more rigour can be applied to developing solutions and ownership is achieved through collaborative effort.*

acting upon it, and the root causes underlying the opportunities for improvement can ensure that a plan addresses the real issues, not just the symptoms.

If a careful examination of the system is not completed before the steps of an improvement plan are agreed, the plan is unlikely to succeed. For this reason, improvement plans need not provide detailed specification of the actions to be taken. This is particularly true of multi-year or strategic plans. These plans can still specify desired outcomes and the overall approach that will be taken towards achieving them, but detailed actions are not necessary during this phase of the improvement process.

## Plans or to-do lists?

For improvement plans to bring about sustainable improvement, they must focus on the development or improvement of an organisation's products, services, and processes. All improvement efforts will result in changes to the organisations processes, whether it be in the form of defining, refining and documenting organisational processes and their associated policies and supporting documents, or in the form of creating new processes.

Unfortunately, many school improvement plans read more like lists of things to do: tasks to be completed. Unless the implementation of the improvement plans results in improved and documented organisational processes, the impact of the actions is difficult to sustain.

## Targets and goals: a numerical nightmare

Many schools are required to set targets as part of their planning processes. Targets in this context are specific numerical goals: desired numbers to be achieved within a particular timeframe, such as increasing mean reading test scores by five per cent within 12 months.

Targets are an area where schools typically experience difficulty in the planning process. In general, when it comes to improvement, targets prove to be more of a hindrance than a help, and can be destructive rather than productive. The pre-conditions for establishing meaningful targets generally do not exist within the current school system.

We will discuss targets at some length in Chapter Five.

## Barriers to improvement planning

There are four obstacles within current planning practices that need to be overcome:

- Limiting plans to improvement priorities and ignoring the daily routines of most people;

- Expecting plans to resemble to-do lists rather than focussing upon the development of sustainable systems and processes;

- Requiring a greater level of detail regarding planned improvement actions than is necessary or appropriate; and

- The requirement for plans to include targets — specific numerical goals.

When these obstacles are addressed, the school planning process is more likely to become enthusiastically adopted and more effective in guiding improvement. Later discussion in this chapter describes how these shortcomings can be overcome and how the planning process can be improved. But first let us look at issues related to implementation of plans.

# Implementation

Planning is about deciding what to do in order to achieve a desire future; implementation is about getting on and doing it. Implementation is hard work.

> The planning process comes to nothing if plans are not acted upon with discipline and rigour.

The discipline and rigour with which plans are implemented are highly variable. Some schools are good at managing implementation, monitoring and reporting on the progress of their improvement projects. Others have a more lackadaisical approach — scattered, poorly conceived improvement efforts may progress, or not, depending on the demands of daily routines — and lack good processes to implement and track progress against their plans. Not surprisingly, in this situation, progress towards the desired future state is not rapid.

The planning process comes to nothing if plans are not acted upon with discipline and rigour. A study of top performing Australian organisations identified effective execution as an essential element of the success of these organisations (Graham Hubbard et al., 2007, *The First XI: Winning organisations in Australia*, second edition, Wiley, Sydney).

> The research identified effective execution of plans and strategies as the pivotal elements of success.
>
> Graeme Cocks, 2012, "The Pathway to Organisational Excellence: An Australian perspective", *Australian Educational Leader*, 34:1, p. 10.

This finding is not surprising. If plans are not implemented, then, of course, improvements will not be realised.

A deep commitment is required not only to being clear and transparent about what is being planned, but also to enact good process in the implementation of the plan, including:

- Carefully allocating resources to achievement of plans;

- Ensuring that rigorous measures are in place and that these are regularly reported upon to understand how the execution of the plan is progressing;

- Implementing the plan on time and within budget; and

- Learning from mistakes and improving the process so mistakes are never repeated.

Until schools and school systems develop the rigour and disciplines of effective execution, school improvement will be sub-optimised.

> Until schools and school systems develop the rigour and disciplines of effective execution, school improvement will be sub-optimised.

## Improvement projects

Joseph Juran, a highly influential American quality control specialist, defined the term "breakthrough" (which was very popular in the late 1980s and early 1990s) as "an improvement to unprecedented levels of performance". He pointed out:

> All breakthrough is achieved *project by project*, and in no other way.
>
> Joseph Juran, 1988, *Juran's Quality Control Handbook*, fourth edition, McGraw-Hill, New York, p. 22.

To achieve significant improvement of the type necessary to make progress towards an organisation's vision, improvement projects are needed. Improvement plans need to be broken down into finite, definable projects that can be managed over the life of a plan.

> Improvement plans need to be broken down into finite, definable projects that can be managed over the life of a plan.

 Project: a temporary endeavour undertaken to meet specific goals and objectives with a defined beginning and end. Projects are usually subject to specific time and resource constraints.

Projects contrast strongly with daily routines. Whereas daily routines involve the ongoing enactment of an organisation's processes, projects are temporary endeavours to improve an organisation's processes, to create new products, services or processes, or to build infrastructure.

So strong is the contrast between daily routines and projects that the Universal Improvement Company defines a project as "any piece of work aside from routine operations". In short, working in the system is accomplished by process; working on the system is accomplished project by project.

This presents a challenge for schools, which are accustomed to establishing committees rather than project teams.

Committees are a common feature of routine school structure. They usually carry responsibilities associated with management and improvement in specific areas of school endeavour, but are problematic in that they have an ongoing role, and have a tendency to lose momentum and focus.

Project teams, on the other hand, are formed for specific, defined timeframes and purposes. Guided by a specific purpose and structured processes, project teams usually realise greater success. They stay focussed and can maintain the energy necessary to see through the improvement, due to a tight, specified timeframe and an effective progress reporting process.

At any time, any organisation will be engaged in a finite number of improvement projects. These improvement projects are likely to include:

- Innovation projects that will introduce new organisational systems and have far-reaching implications for the daily routines of many people across the organisation;

- Projects to improve organisation-wide processes, again with potentially far-reaching implications for the daily routines of many;

- Projects to improve processes within parts of the organisation; and

- Projects aimed at relatively small scale improvements to local processes.

Management has a vital role to play in ensuring the success of these projects, both individually and as a system of projects. In particular, management has a responsibility to work with staff to:

- Prioritise and sequence the projects identified in the improvement plan;

- Establish project teams, including project leaders;

- Ensure there is shared understanding and agreement of each project's objectives, scope, timeframes, and interdependencies;

Working in the system is accomplished by process; working on the system is accomplished project by project.

Project teams are formed for specific, defined timeframes and purposes.

Management has a vital role to play in ensuring the success of projects.

- Encourage disciplined application of the project methodology by each project team;

- Monitor progress of the full set of projects;

- Coordinate between projects where there are interdependencies;

- Reach agreement regarding recommendations from the project team, including implementation plans; and

- Provide direct support to the teams where this is required.

A steering committee is usually formed to manage and coordinate the organisation-wide projects and attend to these responsibilities. Depending on the size of an organisation, it may also be appropriate to establish project steering committees within parts of the organisation to manage and coordinate local projects. These local steering committees will also liaise with the primary steering committee regarding interdependencies between local projects and major projects. Steering committees receive reports from project leaders and convene regularly to monitor progress and identify where additional support may be required. In small organisations, the steering committee may be the senior leadership team.

Schools in general have neither well developed project management methodologies, nor the management structures and disciplines to execute their improvement plans.

Most large corporations have well developed project methodologies and well established project steering committees to maximise the impact of their improvement projects. Our study of schools, at least in Australia, reveals that schools in general have neither well developed project management methodologies, nor the management structures and disciplines to execute their improvement plans in this manner. This is a significant capability gap. Until these structures and disciplines are more strongly established, school improvement efforts will continue to provide disappointing results. This is not a criticism of schools or those that work within them, rather it is an observation of a systemic failure, which needs to be addressed by senior administrators and policy makers.

The project team, charged with the responsibility of undertaking a particular project derived from an improvement plan, follows a specific and agreed methodology, which includes:

- Careful planning;

- Disciplined execution;

- Continual monitoring and reporting of progress; and

- Identification of lessons learned, including future improvement opportunities, from the project.

The Plan–Do–Study–Act (PDSA) cycle is an example of such a methodology. We will discuss PDSA later in this chapter. Before doing so, however, let us reflect upon what might be required to manage the set of improvement projects that may be derived from an improvement plan.

# The system map and planning

In Chapter Three, we described how organisations are social systems and showed how the elements that comprise the organisation can be documented as a system map, which provides a one-page description of the mutually agreed shared understanding of the elements that comprise a system. We also discussed how improvement is achieved by improving systems and processes, and that planning must focus on systems and processes if it is to generate sustainable improvement.

*Planning must focus on systems and processes if it is to generate sustainable improvement.*

The improvement priorities for a system can be captured on the system map as critical success factors: those things that an organisation must get right in order to survive and thrive. Critical success factors describe key priorities for the organisation that relate to both its daily work and its improvement work. In most organisations, the improvement work doesn't just happen; there must be a deliberate and planned approach. Organisations need to actively plan to ensure that they take action on those things they must get right. Critical success factors, therefore, provide the key priorities for an organisation's plan.

*The improvement priorities for a system can be captured on the system map as critical success factors, which provide the key priorities for an organisation's plan.*

Figure 4.2 shows how a cluster of Victorian schools used this approach to planning to agree how they would work together. Their first step was to create a system map to describe the key elements of the cluster system. This provided a mutual agreement of the elements comprising the system in which and on which they were working.

These critical success factors were carried forward to become key priorities in the cluster plan shown in Figure 4.3. For each critical success factor, goals were established. Strategies were then developed to take action towards the goals.

Figure 4.4 shows an example from Fadden Primary School in the ACT, which also used a system map to record mutual agreements regarding the key elements of the school system and agreed direction for the school. Critical success factors have been used as the priorities in Fadden Primary School's strategic plan shown in Figure 4.5.

# System Map

## Thomastown Innovations & Excellence Cluster

*Version 3 15 March 2005*

*Who are the* ***SUPPLIERS*** *(individuals and organisations who provide inputs) to the organisation?*

- Local Welfare Agencies
- Pre-schools
- Local Businesses
- DE&T NMR
- Whittlesea Youth Commitment Group
- DE&T Central Office
- DE&T Accountability Division
- Local Government (Whittlesea Council)
- Government
- Consultants
- Police

*What are the* ***INPUTS*** *(external resources) required by the organisation?*

- Policy and guidelines
- Financial resources
- Human resources
- Research
- Expert advice
- Counselling and support
- Infrastructure
- Police in Schools Program
- Consultancy services
- Professional development
- Advocacy
- Sponsorship
- Parenting skills
- Information
- Financial incentives/opportunities
- Advertising and promotion
- Clients
- Student early learning capacities
- Resources (stationery, ICT, books etc.)

*Who are the* ***OTHER STAKEHOLDERS*** *(those not already listed with a vested interest in the success) of the organisation?*

- Unions
- Broader Community

*What is the* ***PURPOSE*** *(aim or mission) of the organisation?*

To achieve optimal learning and social outcomes for every Middle Years Student through improved classroom teaching practice

*What is the* ***VISION*** *(image of the desired future state) for the organisation?*

**Our Teachers:**

- Have excellent classroom practices based upon up-to-date knowledge
- Share common goals and knowledge of middle years practices
- Are motivated to improve outcomes for middle years students
- Undertake regular and relevant professional development
- Are aware of and share the goals of the Cluster
- Have increased knowledge and application of the Quality Learning philosophy, practices and tools

**Our Parents:**

- Trust the school is meeting their child's needs
- Have the opportunity to participate in and support their child's education

**Our Broader Community:**

- Has a positive view of the schools in our Middle Years Cluster

**Our Students:**

- Have increasing ownership of their learning
- Have improved their learning outcomes
- Value learning
- Have improved motivation and engagement
- Find learning more enjoyable
- Perform to their individual potential
- Have improved social competence
- Enjoy a seamless transition from primary to secondary school

*What are the* ***VALUES*** *(qualities to which we aspire in behaviour and relationships) of the organisation?*

**Respect** – We value difference and diversity **Open Communication** – We value the full expression of the thoughts and opinions of others
**Love of Learning** – We value learning as an integral part of our community
**Cooperation (Teamwork)** – We value and work to balance the needs of individual, schools and the Cluster

*What are the* ***CRITICAL SUCCESS FACTORS*** *(things the organisation must get right for survival and success)?*

- Teachers display effective teaching practices that result in improved student outcomes
- We are committed to and support the efforts of the Cluster in achieving is purpose and vision
- We use data to measure progress and inform improvement
- We have developed an infrastructure that can sustain the Cluster beyond its initial three year term

*What are the* ***RESULT MEASURES*** *(indicators of success) for the organisation?*

- **Academic Achievement** (AIM Data, TORCH, PAT Tests, VCE Data)
- **Parent Satisfaction** (inc. Enrolments)
- **Student Satisfaction** (Welfare) (Attendance, Student opinion survey, Discipline, Social Competence)
- **Teacher Satisfaction** (PD Logs, Staff Morale Survey)
- **Cluster Satisfaction** (PD sessions, Resource sharing, Meeting Attendance)
- **Financial Performance** (Cluster Budget)
- **Teaching Practice**

*Who are the* ***PEOPLE*** *(individuals and groups) working* *__in__* *the organisation?*

- School Councils
- Staff from the Cluster Schools
- Cluster Planning Group

*What are the* ***PROCESSES*** *(sequences of actions) that enable the organisation to meet its purpose and serve its clients?*

- **Financial and Resource Management** – (Budgeting and Accountability processes)
- **Reporting** – (DE&T and NMR reporting Processes, Staff and Parent Reporting processes)
- **Infrastructure - Planning and Meetings** – (Cluster Planning and Cluster Management Meeting processes)
- **Professional Development** – (Planning and Delivery processes)
- **Curriculum Provision** – (Teaching and Learning processes, Curriculum Planning and Scoping and Sequencing processes, Change Management process)
- **Transition** – (Transition Planning and Transition processes)
- **Data Collection and Analysis** – (Progress Monitoring processes, Data Collection and Analysis processes)
- **Research** (Research, Networking with outside organisations and individuals, Evaluation Processes

*Who are the* ***CLIENTS*** *(recipients and beneficiaries of the products and services) of the organisation?*

- Students
- Parents

- Local Community
- Universities and other tertiary institutions
- Employers

*What are the* ***OUTPUTS*** *(tangible deliverables) and* ***OUTCOMES*** *(benefits to clients and stakeholders) from the activities of the organisation?*

- Improved Student Learning Outcomes
- Provision of Quality Professional Development
- Students as Effective Community Members
- Increased student attendance
- Improved communication and sharing across the Cluster
- Improved community involvement and perceptions
- Improved Classroom Teaching practices


Canberra: PO Box 897, Belconnen, ACT 2616 Phone 02 6251 3870 Fax 02 6251 3871
Melbourne: PO Box 624, North Melbourne, Victoria 3051 Phone 03 9370 9944 Fax 03 9370 9955

**Figure 4.2 Cluster system map**

Source: Thomastown Innovation and Excellence Cluster, Victoria.

# Thomastown Innovation & Excellence Cluster: Action Plan 2005-2007 Draft 2 15 March 2005

| CSF | Goal | Strategy | Importance | Urgency | Leader | Timing | Resourcing |
|---|---|---|---|---|---|---|---|
| Teachers display effective teaching practices that result in improved student outcomes | Research drives relevant and regular professional development | Employ an Educator who maintains a current knowledge of best pedagogical practice and facilitates learning within the Cluster | H | H | BT | | |
| | | Research and evaluate current pedagogical practices within our Cluster and beyond. Make recommendations to the Cluster Management Team regarding shared needs and priorities | H | H | E | | |
| | Professional development contributes to improved teaching practice and student outcomes | Schedule and conduct or facilitate shared professional development sessions | H | M | E | | |
| | | Provide time and develop structures for teachers to engage in professional dialogue and implement best practice | H | M | E | | |
| | | Develop processes for documenting and sharing agreed identified best practices | M | L | E | | |
| We are committed to and support the efforts of the Cluster in achieving is purpose and vision | The Cluster is well networked with outside organisations and undertakes purposeful research to inform improvement efforts | Establish network with other clusters | M | M | E | | |
| | | Attend DE&T Cluster professional development and networking sessions | H | H | E | | |
| | Adequate resources are allocated (time and personnel) for Cluster plan implementation | Allocate, monitor and review the Cluster budget in line with Action Plan strategies | H | H | BT | | |
| | | Develop a job description and appoint an Educator to implement the Cluster Plan | H | H | BT | | |
| | | Agree on a process for resource allocation | H | H | E | | |
| | | Establish relevant structures to facilitate the implementation and review of the Cluster Action Plan | H | H | E | | |
| | Communication amongst Cluster schools and within individual schools is open, regular and effective to build commitment among staff | Schedule and conduct ongoing Cluster Management Meetings. Agree base agenda and develop and action process for recording meeting agreements and actions | H | H | E | | |
| | | Develop agreed and documented processes for communication | H | M | E | | |
| | | Develop a schedule for communication between schools and key stakeholders | H | M | E | | |
| | There is ongoing monitoring and review of the Cluster Action Plan | Use ongoing Cluster Management Meetings to review and monitor progress of plan. | H | H | E | | |
| We use data to measure progress and inform improvement | Processes are in place to collect agreed Key Performance Indicators that are used to improve classroom practice and Cluster performance | Conduct research to identify data collection tools that will identify specific areas of improvement. Where necessary develop local tools | H | M | E | | |
| | | Collect an d collate baseline data | H | H | E/RB | | |
| | | Develop a timeline for the collection, collation, analysis, reporting and actioning of data to improve practice | H | H | RB | | |
| We have developed an infrastructure that can sustain the Cluster beyond its initial three year term | Processes are in place to ensure ongoing networking and communication within the Cluster | Develop Cluster Plan to be implemented beyond the three year term | M | M | VH | | |
| | | Explore the role of a facilitator to monitor the sustainability of the cluster beyond the three year term of the Educator | M | L | E | | |
| | | Develop processes to provide for ongoing shared professional development and the maximisation of other resources | M | M | E | | |
| | The Cluster continues to access funding to support its improvement efforts | Establish processes to research funding sources and monitor availability | M | M | E | | |

**Figure 4.3 Action plan**

Source: Thomastown Innovation and Excellence Cluster, Victoria.

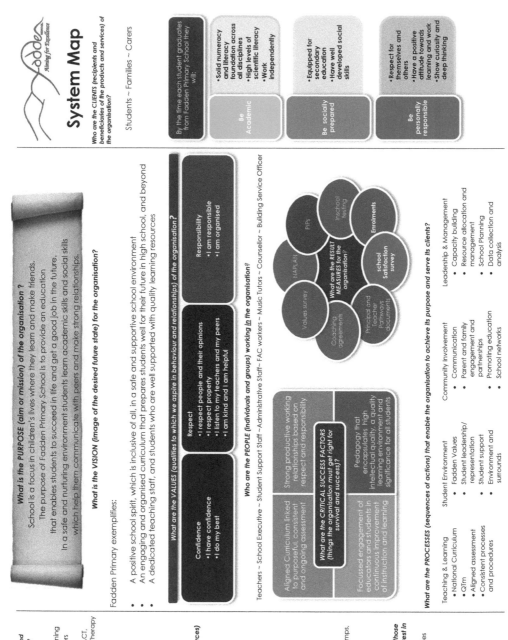

**Figure 4.4 School system map**

Source: Fadden Primary School, ACT.

# School Strategic Plan for Fadden Primary School 2012-2015

Example

| Priority | Desired Outcomes | Performance Measures | Projects |
|---|---|---|---|
| Aligned curriculum linked to purposeful, consistent and ongoing assessment. | Improving student learning outcomes. Purposeful and aligned curriculum. Staff capable and confident to use data effectively to guide learning and teaching. | Fadden school improvement survey demonstrates increased teacher confidence with data analysis and use<br><br>NAPLAN results demonstrate increased percentage of students above expected growth and a decrease of students in the lower percentiles. | Develop staff capacity to collect, analyse and discuss a range of student assessment data<br><br>Introduce and evaluate aligned mathematics pedagogy K-6<br><br>Align reading and writing teaching, assessment and student feedback approach K-6 |
| Focussed engagement of educators and students in continuous improvement of instruction and learning. | All staff are engaged in continual improvement of teaching practice through a structured program of lesson observation, feedback and reflection. | Fadden school improvement survey demonstrates improved teacher engagement with lesson observation and feedback and lesson study | Develop and align staff coaching and mentoring processes to build sustainability and accountability with clear links to student outcomes |
| Pedagogy that encapsulates high intellectual quality, a quality learning environment and significance for all students. | Improving student learning outcomes. Effective pedagogy across the school. Effective learning environments in all classrooms. | Increasing percentage of students in top two NAPLAN bands and decreasing percentage of students in bottom two bands<br><br>ACER PAT maths and reading comprehension data demonstrate improving student growth<br><br>Fadden school improvement survey demonstrates teacher engagement with lesson study<br><br>PIPS results demonstrate growth above system mean | Implementation of high quality pedagogy in all classrooms<br><br>Ensure all school curriculum are relevant, current and of high intellectual quality<br><br>Develop a culture of reflective practice |
| Strong productive working relationships based on respect and responsibility. | Productive working relationships based upon agreed Fadden School Values. | Staff, student and parent satisfaction survey results show improved communication and understanding of the school values. | Develop awareness, understanding, use and practice of the Fadden values of respect, confidence and responsibility for all stakeholders<br><br>Introduce improved practices and procedures for communication between school and families |

Example 18: Example School Strategic Plan (based upon Fadden Primary School, ACT)

**Figure 4.5 Extract from school strategic plan**
Source: Fadden Primary School, ACT.

# Reflection questions

**?** Does your organisation focus on operational planning, improvement planning, or some other form of planning? What distinguishes these types of planning from one another?

**?** To what degree does your organisation view planning as a compliance requirement or as a valuable learning process? Why?

**?** To what degree does your organisation exhibit effective execution or implementation of its plans? How could this be improved?

**?** Do planning processes in your organisation tend to focus on systems and processes, or are they more like to-do lists? How could you change the current strategies within your current plan to focus on processes and systems?

**?** How does your organisation manage improvement projects? What systems and structures are in place to support project teams? How effective are these? Why?

**?** How effective is the planning process in your school? How might it be improved?

**?** What are the critical success factors for your organisation? How are these addressed in your current plan?

# Quality learning tools to support planning

The following tools can be used to support planning processes within any system.

 **Bone diagram**

The bone diagram provides a structured way of thinking about planning for system improvement. It was developed by George Noyes at the Defence Systems Management College, Fort Belvoir, Virginia, USA, and is promoted by David Langford in his popular *Tool Time* books. Bone diagrams incorporate two other tools — imagineering and force field analysis.

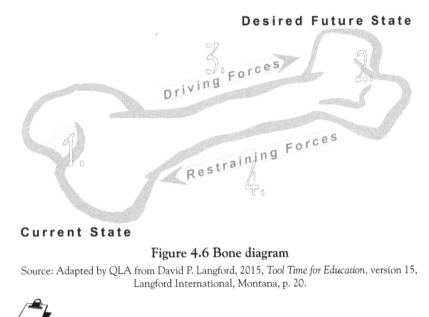

**Figure 4.6 Bone diagram**

Source: Adapted by QLA from David P. Langford, 2015, *Tool Time for Education*, version 15, Langford International, Montana, p. 20.

Download a bone diagram template from www.qla.com.au

The bone diagram requires the user to first identify the current state of the system. This is reflected upon and recorded in area one.

Imagineering is then used to define and document the desired future in area two.

Finally, a force field analysis is used to identify and document those forces that are driving system change towards the desired state and those forces that are restraining improvement, in areas three and four respectively.

Developing a bone diagram within a team is a great way to develop mutual agreement about the current and desired states of a system, as well as the forces driving and restraining progress towards the desired future state.

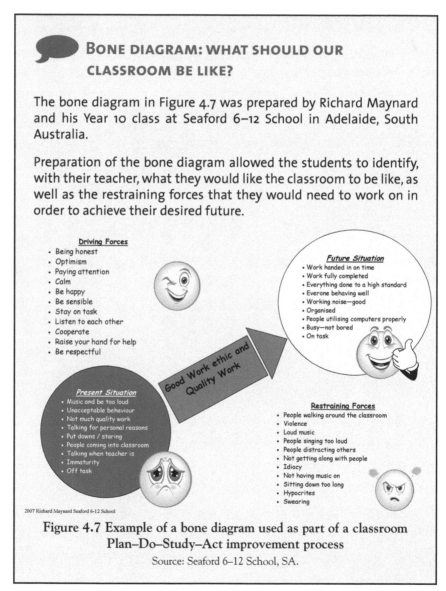

**BONE DIAGRAM: WHAT SHOULD OUR CLASSROOM BE LIKE?**

The bone diagram in Figure 4.7 was prepared by Richard Maynard and his Year 10 class at Seaford 6–12 School in Adelaide, South Australia.

Preparation of the bone diagram allowed the students to identify, with their teacher, what they would like the classroom to be like, as well as the restraining forces that they would need to work on in order to achieve their desired future.

**Driving Forces**
- Being honest
- Optimism
- Paying attention
- Calm
- Be happy
- Be sensible
- Stay on task
- Listen to each other
- Cooperate
- Raise your hand for help
- Be respectful

**Future Situation**
- Work handed in on time
- Work fully completed
- Everything done to a high standard
- Everone behaving well
- Working noise—good
- Organised
- People utilising computers properly
- Busy—not bored
- On task

Good work ethic and Quality Work

**Present Situation**
- Music and be too loud
- Unacceptable behaviour
- Not much quality work
- Talking for personal reasons
- Put downs / staring
- People coming into classroom
- Talking when teacher is
- Immaturity
- Off task

**Restraining Forces**
- People walking around the classroom
- Violence
- Loud music
- People singing too loud
- People distracting others
- Not getting along with people
- Idiocy
- Not having music on
- Sitting down too long
- Hypocrites
- Swearing

2007 Richard Maynard Seaford 6-12 School

**Figure 4.7 Example of a bone diagram used as part of a classroom Plan–Do–Study–Act improvement process**

Source: Seaford 6–12 School, SA.

# ⚒ Gantt chart

A Gantt chart is a project planning and monitoring tool, which is in common use for project management all over the world. It was first developed a century ago and is named after its developer, Henry Gantt, an American mechanical engineer and management consultant.

The Gantt chart shows, in graphical form, the phases, timing and responsibilities for the activities required to complete a project. It is ideal when all the steps in the action plan are agreed.

A Gantt chart is a matrix. The rows of the matrix list the activities to be completed, usually grouped into phases. The columns of the matrix represent time, usually in weeks or months. The cells of the matrix are shaded to form bars that indicate when each activity is to be undertaken. There can also be a column to indicate who is responsible for each activity.

Progress can be evaluated against the plan to identify activities that were completed on time, those running ahead of time, and those that are running late.

The Gantt chart is a powerful tool for use with adults, but students also find them very helpful in planning their major learning activities. Gantt charts help students learn how to plan, time manage, and track their learning.

Figure 4.8 shows how Claire, a Year 12 student from Seaford 6–12 School in Adelaide, South Australia, used a Gantt chart to help plan and implement her tourism report.

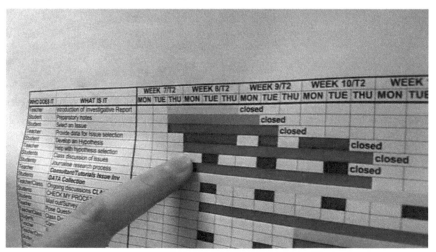

**Figure 4.8 Year 12 tourism project Gantt chart**
Source: Seaford 6–12 School, SA.

Video Clip 4.1: Planning with a Gantt chart
http://www.qla.com.au/Videos/3
Source: Seaford 6-12 School, SA.

 Download a Gantt chart template from www.qla.com.au

# 🔧 Hot dot

The hot dot tool is a simple prioritisation tool that can be used by any group, from very young children to adults.

Each person is given a number of sticky dots (usually up to a third as many dots as there are items to be prioritised) plus one hot dot, which is usually red.

Individuals stick their dots on a master list of items. The hot dot is placed next to the item that they believe is the top priority, while the other dots are placed next to other items they believe are important.

Final priorities are determined by tallying the number of dots against each item. Some groups like to assign points to the dots, for example, three points for each hot dot and one point for each other dot.

**Figure 4.9 Year 5 student hot dotting (prioritising) ideas on an affinity diagram**
Source: Hargraves Public School, NSW.

# Knowledge

The following pages expand on the principle of quality learning:

Learning and improvement are derived from theory, prediction, observation and reflection.

## What are theory and prediction?

People make innumerable predictions each day. Will I need to mow the lawns this weekend? Which of these movie choices will I find most enjoyable? How will my friends respond to this news? Is this meeting likely to be a productive use of my time? Who will win the most gold medals at the Olympic Games? These questions all call for prediction.

In a similar manner, planning calls for prediction. We decide what time to leave for work in the morning. In doing so, we are making a prediction about how long it will take to get to work, so that we can leave early enough to be there on time. When considering alternate courses of action, we need to predict the likely outcomes of each option and select the most desirable option. We cannot make a rational plan without prediction.

*We cannot make a rational plan without prediction.*

It follows that to manage is to predict. Predictions need not be complex. I have a hunch it will rain this afternoon, and, I expect I am not likely to win the lottery: both are predictions.

*To manage is to predict.
To predict is to apply theory.*

How do we make predictions? Theory. To predict is to apply theory.

Rational prediction requires theory and builds knowledge through systematic revision and extension of theory based on comparison of prediction with varied short-term and long-term results.

W. Edwards Deming, 2012, *The Essential Deming: Leadership principles from the father of quality*, edited by Joyce Orsini, McGraw-Hill, New York, p. 62.

Theory organises our ideas and enables us to make sense of the world. It is from our understanding of the world that we make predictions. Given that each individual sees the world differently, individuals can have quite different theories.

Here is our definition of theory.

Theory: a coherent system of concepts that represents a view of how the world works. Theory can be used to make predictions about the outcomes of proposed actions.

Note that this definition acknowledges the interdependent nature of the concepts that comprise our theory. Note also that the definition is action oriented, linking our conception of the world with our actions within it.

"If I stand in the rain, I will get wet and cold" is a theory. Concepts included in this theory include sky, clouds, rain, moisture, water, humidity, temperature, wind, clothing, comfort and discomfort. These concepts are interdependent: rain comes from clouds, temperature has a direct effect on comfort, and so on. This theory is also action oriented, as it predicts an outcome (getting cold and wet) from the action (standing in the rain).

### TESTING, NOT PROVING, THEORIES

Theories can be tested by observation or experiment. I can stand in the rain and observe whether I do, in fact, become wet and cold. If I do, the evidence supports my theory. If by standing in the rain, in the tropics for example, I observe that I become wet but not cold, I will need to revise my theory to take account of this new evidence.

We cannot make a prediction without theory.

> Rational prediction requires theory and builds knowledge through systematic revision and extension of theory based on comparison of prediction with observation.
>
> W. Edwards Deming, 1994, *The New Economics: For industry, government and education*, MIT, Massachusetts, p. 105.

Theories cannot be proven. No number of examples can prove a theory. Evidence can be cited that supports the theory, but this does not prove the theory. Years of experience and research may support our propositions, but they do not constitute proof of the theory.

Theories can, however, be disproven. Logical inconsistencies can be uncovered and counter-examples can be identified. One unexplained example is sufficient for a theory to require revision or even abandonment.

Testing theories against observations and through experiments provides evidence that reinforces or reinforms them. Carefully observing the outcomes of our actions enables us to refine and improve our theories. This is a learning process. Experience alone teaches nothing unless it is studied with the aid of theory.

> Theory by itself teaches nothing. Application by itself teaches nothing. Learning is the result of dynamic interplay between the two.
>
> Peter R. Scholtes, 1998, *The Leader's Handbook*, McGraw-Hill, New York, p. 32.

We all have theories about many things. Every plan, program, model, framework, and initiative represents a theory.

In a structured approach, once a theory is established, plans can be prepared to apply the theory, thus creating experience with the theory. One can then reflect upon the theory and the experience to refine and improve the theory. This is a learning cycle.

The learning cycle — illustrated in Figure 4.10 — can be found in many places and is the basis of effective planning processes, scientific method, action research, and plain common sense.

*Experience alone teaches nothing unless it is studied with the aid of theory.*

*Every plan, program, model, framework, and initiative represents a theory.*

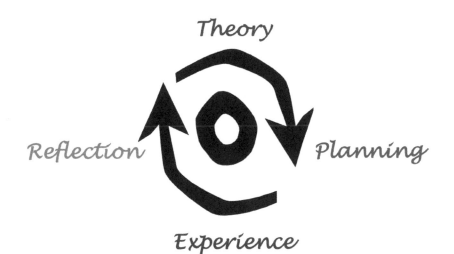

**Figure 4.10 The learning cycle**

# Creating shared understanding: Operational definitions

Theory enables us to make sense of the world as we see it.

How we see the world is a very individual thing. The diversity of our previous experiences leads us to have different views of the world, with consequently different theories. For example, Sara, a mathematics teacher, may believe that Ashley, one of her Year 9 students, is lazy. This is a theory. Jayden, an English teacher, may believe that Ashley is hard working. This is another theory. These two theories appear incompatible. How can these incompatible views be reconciled? By examination of the evidence.

Examination of just any evidence, however, will not resolve the situation, for it is not immediately apparent what evidence should be examined. To test whether Ashley is lazy or hard working we must define what we are looking for and how we will make judgement. We must come up with a definition for each term, against which we can test the evidence. Such a definition is called an operational definition.

An operational definition provides a basis for testing for conformance to a definition. Is Ashley lazy? That depends on our definition.

> An operational definition is a procedure agreed upon for translation of a concept into a measurement of some kind.
>
> W. Edwards Deming, 1994, *The New Economics: For industry, government and education,* MIT, Massachusetts, p. 108.

In this example, Sara and Jayden may agree to resolve the disparity in their theories by agreeing an operational definition for "hard-working" and collecting data to determine if Ashley's behaviour is consistent with their agreed definition. They could then use the same definition, if they wished, to measure the number of students in their classes that are hard-working. Operational definitions enable people to create shared meaning about concepts.

Operational definitions put meaning into concepts in a way that promotes shared understanding and a capacity to collect consistent data.

Operational definitions are also required in order make our theories explicit and share them with others.

Here are some examples of slippery terms, words that mean one thing to one person and something different to another and which produce an

---

An operational definition provides a basis for testing for conformance to a definition.

Operational definitions enable people to create shared meaning about concepts.

illusion of consensus that often falls apart under pressure. These slippery terms highlight the need for operational definitions: taxable income, number of students funded, cash reserves, workload, staff morale, literacy, numeracy, at risk, special needs, gifted, talented, on-task, engaged, socio-economic status, poverty, advanced skills teacher, expert teacher, leader, leadership, teaching, and learning.

# Learning, not copying

Copying the practices of others will not lead to sustainable improvement. Every school is unique, and the practices that work in one setting may not work in another.

Firstly, the context, or containing system, in which every school operates is unique. A one-teacher school in a remote indigenous community, for example, operates in a totally different context to a large, affluent, urban school. These are contrasting social systems, existing in radically different communities of unique constraints and opportunities.

> The context, or containing system, in which every school operates is unique. The practices that work in one setting may not work in another.

Let us examine an example and test it in each setting: the challenge of community engagement. In an isolated indigenous community in Australia, this challenge usually revolves around how to establish meaningful dialogue with elders and families. In many cases, the families and other members of the community do not have positive or happy memories of their own schooling, and are frequently uncomfortable in a school setting. They question the value of school education, based on their own experiences. Many parents are also distrustful of teachers who are posted to the school for limited periods and who have little or no personal investment in their community. These families can actively seek to have as little to do with the school as possible. In an affluent urban school, on the other hand, parents are more likely to be professionals who managed to survive, and probably thrive, in the education system. They place a high value on the school education of their children. These families can be openly critical of their school's practices and, sometimes, the personnel. It can be hard to moderate these parents' desire to influence school operations. Clearly, the policies and processes required for meaningful community engagement in these two situations will need to be radically different.

Secondly, there is variation in the individual and collective philosophies evident within each school. This variation can be evident in the school's purpose, vision and values. It is always reflected in an organisation's behaviour, stemming from school policies and processes. In essence, this variation derives from differing theories regarding how the world works and different views about what is important.

Each school is a unique social system that operates in a unique context. In Chapter Three we saw that every system is comprised of interdependent parts that work together to achieve the aim of the whole system. The nature of interdependence is such that it is not possible to change just one part of a system; change in one area impacts elsewhere.

If we seek to improve a system, we need to have a theory for improvement. We need to be able to explain the workings of our current system in order to predict the impact of our proposed changes. When changes are implemented, we are able to study the outcomes in a way that will reinforce or reinform our theory.

Copying others' practices, without due consideration of the system in which they are to be implemented, the appropriateness of the theory behind the practices, and the congruence of that theory to existing theories, will result in incoherence and disappointing results.

> To copy an example of success, without understanding it with the aid of theory, may lead to disaster.
>
> W. Edwards Deming, 2012, *The Essential Deming: Leadership Principles from the Father of Quality*, edited by Joyce Orsini, McGraw-Hill, New York, p. 79.

The most common example of this at the school level is implementation of "tried and true" programs.

Programs can be seen as the panacea for the ills of a school. "All we need is a behaviour management program," and, "We should pick up the XYZ program, I heard it works really well at the school up the road," are not uncommon utterances in many schools.

Across education systems, there are endless waves of imposed and prescriptive interventions. Schools in networks, coaching, and professional learning communities are some recent examples. We are not saying that these programs and approaches do not have merit, but they must be carefully considered in the context of the system in which they are to be introduced.

Mindless copying leads to what has been described as "fad surfing": catching waves of change, enjoying an exhilarating ride, leaving the wave as the waters become shallow, and then paddling out, with significant effort, to pick up the next wave. Great fun perhaps, but exhausting and ultimately going nowhere.

*Copying others' practices will result in incoherence and disappointing results.*

*Across education systems, there are endless waves of imposed and prescriptive interventions.*

This is not to say that others do not have good ideas. Rather, caution should be taken in implementing others' theories, practices, processes and reforms without due consideration to their appropriateness to one's own context.

This theme emerges consistently in school improvement literature. Michael Fullan, for example, describes it this way:

> Neither off-the-shelf programs nor research per se provides the answer. Professionals working together is what counts.
>
> Michael Fullan, 2010, *All Systems Go: The change imperative for whole system reform*, Corwin, Thousand Oaks, p. 59.

So how can we benefit from others' good ideas without copying? The answer lies in adapting rather than adopting.

Here are some questions that can help you sift through a range of proposed programs and initiatives to determine which might be most useful in your context, and which may not fit.

- For what problem is this the solution? What is the purpose of the proposed action?

- What is the theory behind the proposed program or initiative? Why does it work?

- To what degree is the proposed program or initiative consistent with the purpose, vision and values of our school and community?

- What are the systemic actions and interactions that the proposed program or initiative is targeting, and how do these proposed changes fit with our existing systems and approaches? What else will need to change if we are to derive the intended benefits?

- What are the likely downsides of implementation? Is it going to be worth it?

- What would it look like to do this superbly well?

In practice, we can do better than wait for others' research and solutions to come along. We can all create our own solutions, drawing upon the learning of others, but uniquely tailored to our specific context.

The Plan–Do–Study–Act cycle provides a theory and methods for doing so. Before discussing the Plan–Do–Study–Act cycle, however, let us first explore one form of copying that is particularly problematic for schools: programs.

---

*Sidebar:*

Caution should be taken in implementing others' theories, practices, processes and reforms without due consideration to their appropriateness to one's own context.

We can all create our own solutions, drawing upon the learning of others, but uniquely tailored to our specific context.

# Why a programmatic approach usually fails

Schools are, to a large degree, driven by programs. Literacy programs, numeracy programs, science programs, sports programs and music programs are all examples of typical school educational programs. Many schools run other programs, such as breakfast club, after-school care, anti-bullying, and mental health, to name just a few. There are hundreds of programs available across a wide range of curriculum areas.

In a school context, a program can be thought of as an organisational system. Programs are useful in that they clarify what is to be done, by whom, and when. They frequently provide specific direction on how key tasks are to be undertaken: how each lesson is to be conducted, for example. They can also provide the key learning materials and resources needed to run the program. Programs can make teachers' jobs easier, as activities and resources are already designed and detailed.

New programs are frequently seen as solutions to existing problems; spelling results are poor, so a new spelling program is needed, for example. Programs may have been seen to work in other settings, and become attractive. It is not uncommon to hear school leaders expressing excitement and optimism about the latest program the school has picked up from a neighbouring, interstate or overseas school.

Sadly, new programs often fail to live up to expectations because too often they are implemented as actions without sufficient attention being paid to theory.

Every school is different. Some differences can be dramatic, others subtle. There are differences within the school and in the containing systems within which the school operates.

In addition to the obvious and significant differences in student population, there are other more subtle and important differences. What are the collective beliefs and understandings about students' performance and learning? What are the shared understandings about the ability, readiness and desirability of student's accepting responsibility for their learning? What are the roles of recognition and reward in stimulating or subverting student learning?

In other words, what is the school's current theory about optimising student learning? Schools frequently fail to understand and articulate how a proposed new program will support and extend their current theory.

Unless a school can articulate the manner in which a new program is supportive of their theory and how and why it is expected to improve performance, they are probably making things worse.

Implementing a new program takes time and effort. Teachers need to be trained and to integrate the new program into their existing work. This frequently involves them in new and different behaviours, which requires focussed effort over time. When new programs fail to deliver quickly according to expectations, they are commonly dropped. With this development, teachers must again make changes.

Chopping and changing programs is demoralising for everyone concerned. It leads people to lose confidence in those responsible for such decisions, and increases resistance to the next proposed program.

This is not to say that programs and approaches developed by others cannot be useful. Where the rationale for a program is clearly understood and is aligned to the dominant theories in use by the organisation, a program can make a significant contribution. It is where the rationale is not examined or understood and where it is in conflict with the organisations' beliefs that programs usually fail.

The challenge is to adapt, not adopt, programs. The most successful adaptations of programs see the concepts and methods of the new program become integrated into the culture of the organisation. "This is not some fancy new program, it is part of how we do things around here."

> The challenge is to adapt, not adopt, programs.

The programmatic approach is not unique to the schools' sector. Industry and government are similarly prone to adopting others' programs. In quality improvement, for example, there has been a steady parade of programs over past decades: business excellence, performance excellence, total quality management, voice of the customer, benchmarking, business process reengineering, six sigma, lean, and more recently, business process management.

In a similar manner, enterprises are subjected to endless waves of the latest fashionable management theory. New books are released that highlight the newest and greatest management innovation. Managers are exhorted to adopt this latest practice or risk being left behind. It can be hard, even for discerning managers, to separate signal from noise. Only the leading organisations have found a way to articulate their own unique approaches, such as The Toyota Way, that evolve over time as new insights and practices are introduced and assimilated. Only these organisations have truly articulated their own theory of management.

# Creating a theory for improvement

Continual improvement is derived, in large measure, from the efforts of individuals and teams working together to improve the systems and processes for which they are responsible, with the help of those working in those systems and processes. How should this happen? Or — as Deming was fond of asking — by what method?

## A scientific approach

Firstly, we need to recognise that an improvement project is not an event; it is a process. It calls for a sequence of actions to be enacted as a project in the pursuit of improvement. So our improvement projects need to follow a defined process.

> We need to recognise that an improvement project is not an event; it is a process.

In Chapter Three we argued that the only way to sustainably improve performance is to improve processes. It follows, then, that if we want to improve our ability to bring about improvement, we need to focus our attention on the improvement process itself.

Improvement is a process. Like all processes, it can be mapped, studied and improved. Improvement calls for theory, prediction, observation, and reflection: a scientific method. Over a century ago, the influential American psychologist and educational philosopher John Dewey analysed reflective thought and identified five distinct steps in reflection:

> Improvement is a process. Like all processes, it can be mapped, studied and improved.

(i) a felt difficulty;
(ii) its location and definition;
(iii) suggestion of possible solution;
(iv) development of reasoning of the bearings of the suggestion;
(v) further observation and experiment leading to acceptance or rejection; that is, the conclusion of belief or disbelief.

John Dewey, 1910, *How We Think*, D. C. Heath and Co., Boston, p. 72.

Dewey here describes a structured process for learning through theory, prediction, observation, and reflection. This is the learning cycle that was introduced earlier and illustrated in Figure 4.10.

## Plan–Do–Study–Act (PDSA)

During the 1930s, Walter Shewhart developed a similar line of thinking to Dewey regarding the scientific method. This became known as the Shewhart or Deming cycle, and is more commonly known today as the Plan–Do–Study–Act (PDSA) cycle.

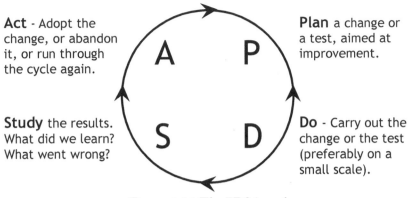

**Act** - Adopt the change, or abandon it, or run through the cycle again.

**Plan** a change or a test, aimed at improvement.

**Study** the results. What did we learn? What went wrong?

**Do** - Carry out the change or the test (preferably on a small scale).

**Figure 4.11 The PDSA cycle**

Source: W. Edwards Deming, 1993, *The New Economics: For industry, government and education*, MIT, Cambridge, p. 132.

The PDSA cycle provides a basic frame upon which an improvement process can be developed.

There are, of course, many variants of the improvement process, with many and varied names. We have heard these approaches referred to as action research, scientific method, and common sense. (Common sense, however, is not necessarily common practice.) In overview, the concepts are the same.

The Plan–Do–Study–Act cycle is a structured process for improvement based on a cycle of theory, prediction, observation, and reflection.

Our observations from experience in industry, government and education are similar to those expressed by Deming. There is a strong tendency for people to want to race through the "plan" stage and get straight into the "do" stage.

> Step 1 is the foundation of the whole cycle. A hasty start may be ineffective, costly and frustrating. People have a weakness to short-circuit this step. They cannot wait to get into motion, to be active, to look busy, to move into Step 2.
>
> W. Edwards Deming, 1994, *The New Economics: For industry, government and education*, MIT, Massachusetts, p. 135.

Schools in particular find it difficult to make time for the reflective step of "study". Many individuals and teams just want to get into the action and be seen to be making changes, rather than reflecting on whether the change has been an improvement, or just a change.

The Plan–Do–Study–Act cycle is a structured process for improvement based on a cycle of theory, prediction, observation, and reflection.

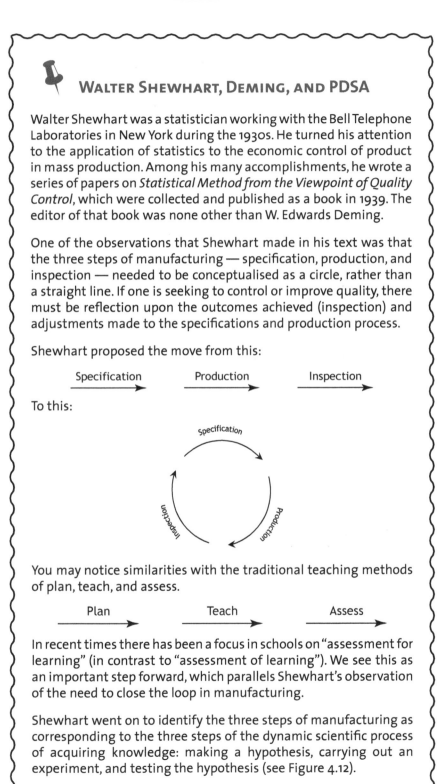

### WALTER SHEWHART, DEMING, AND PDSA

Walter Shewhart was a statistician working with the Bell Telephone Laboratories in New York during the 1930s. He turned his attention to the application of statistics to the economic control of product in mass production. Among his many accomplishments, he wrote a series of papers on *Statistical Method from the Viewpoint of Quality Control*, which were collected and published as a book in 1939. The editor of that book was none other than W. Edwards Deming.

One of the observations that Shewhart made in his text was that the three steps of manufacturing — specification, production, and inspection — needed to be conceptualised as a circle, rather than a straight line. If one is seeking to control or improve quality, there must be reflection upon the outcomes achieved (inspection) and adjustments made to the specifications and production process.

Shewhart proposed the move from this:

Specification ⟶        Production ⟶        Inspection ⟶

To this:

You may notice similarities with the traditional teaching methods of plan, teach, and assess.

Plan ⟶        Teach ⟶        Assess ⟶

In recent times there has been a focus in schools on "assessment for learning" (in contrast to "assessment of learning"). We see this as an important step forward, which parallels Shewhart's observation of the need to close the loop in manufacturing.

Shewhart went on to identify the three steps of manufacturing as corresponding to the three steps of the dynamic scientific process of acquiring knowledge: making a hypothesis, carrying out an experiment, and testing the hypothesis (see Figure 4.12).

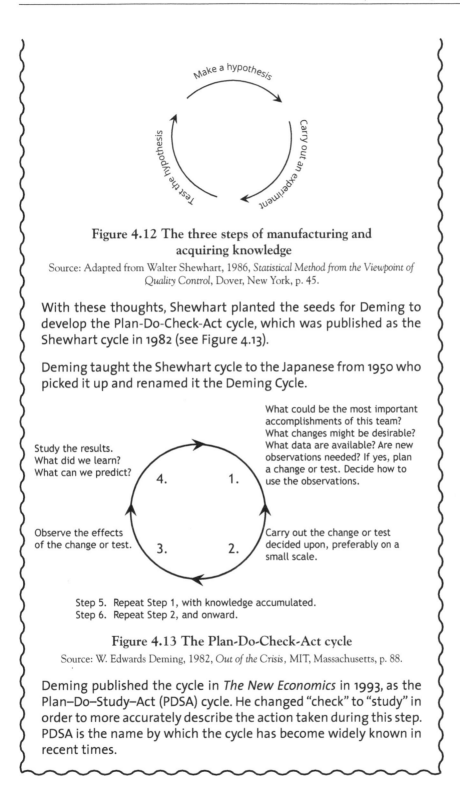

**Figure 4.12 The three steps of manufacturing and acquiring knowledge**

Source: Adapted from Walter Shewhart, 1986, *Statistical Method from the Viewpoint of Quality Control*, Dover, New York, p. 45.

With these thoughts, Shewhart planted the seeds for Deming to develop the Plan-Do-Check-Act cycle, which was published as the Shewhart cycle in 1982 (see Figure 4.13).

Deming taught the Shewhart cycle to the Japanese from 1950 who picked it up and renamed it the Deming Cycle.

Step 5.  Repeat Step 1, with knowledge accumulated.
Step 6.  Repeat Step 2, and onward.

**Figure 4.13 The Plan-Do-Check-Act cycle**

Source: W. Edwards Deming, 1982, *Out of the Crisis*, MIT, Massachusetts, p. 88.

Deming published the cycle in *The New Economics* in 1993, as the Plan–Do–Study–Act (PDSA) cycle. He changed "check" to "study" in order to more accurately describe the action taken during this step. PDSA is the name by which the cycle has become widely known in recent times.

### 💬 PDSA APPLIED TO YEAR 1 WRITING

Trevor, a Year 1 teacher at Roxburgh Homestead Primary School in Victoria, learned about the PDSA cycle and decided to use it to improve his students' writing skills. He worked with his students to identify some goals and measures of success. The goals were: use of capital letters, full stops (periods), spaces, writing in straight lines, and use of words the student knows. From these goals, the student agreed a measurement scale for each item: "yes", "no", and "sort of". He then prepared a template for the students to plan, write, review, and improve their stories.

In Figure 4.14 and Video Clip 4.2, one of Trevor's students, Jordan, tells the story of how he planned his story (Plan), wrote his story (Do), and studied the results (Study) using the agreed measures. Jordan identified that he needed to improve writing in straight lines, which he did (Act) by preparing his good copy.

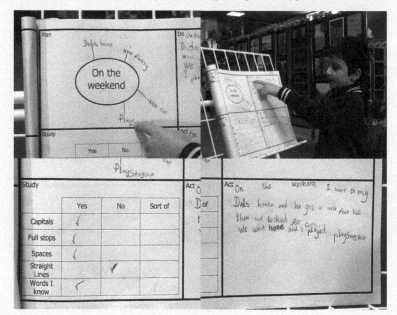

**Figure 4.14 Year 1 student uses the PDSA process to improve writing skills**

Source: Roxburgh Homestead Primary School, Victoria.

Video Clip 4.2: Plan–Do–Study–Act (PDSA) Year 1 writing
http://www.qla.com.au/Videos/3
Source: Roxburgh Homestead Primary School, Victoria.

## A more detailed and structured PDSA process

Where an improvement opportunity is of a significantly complex nature, a more detailed and in depth application of the PDSA process is necessary.

Our work in industry, government and education over the past two decades has shown the nine step PDSA process, illustrated in Figure 4.15, to be particularly effective. This nine step process described here has been compared with dozens of alternate models of PDSA and refined over the past two decades.

In developing such a process, there is a balance to be struck between the technical considerations of having a robust process that will deal with diverse contexts and issues, and the simplicity that makes the improvement process accessible and practical for busy people. Over the years, we have continually sought to simplify the model to make it more accessible. For nearly a decade, the nine steps have remained constant, but the specific actions and tools comprising each step have been progressively refined.

Where an improvement opportunity is of a significantly complex nature, a more detailed and in depth application of the PDSA process is necessary.

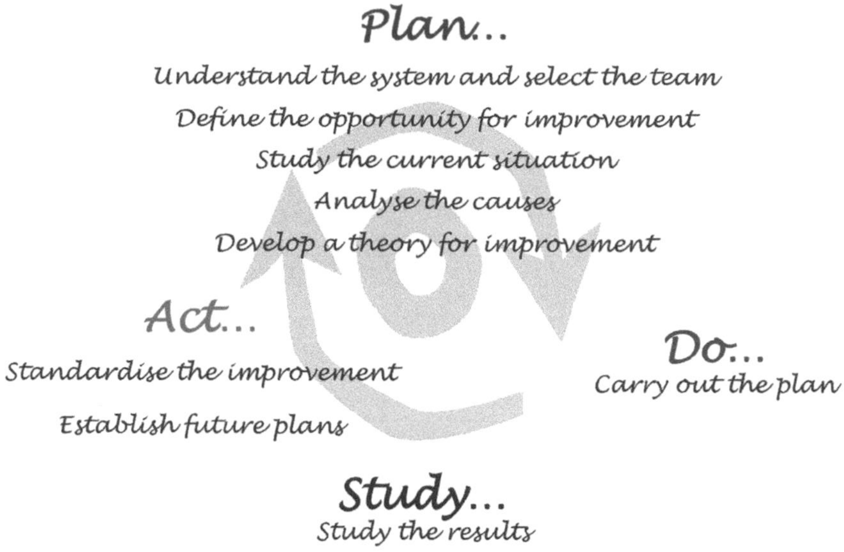

*Plan...*
*Understand the system and select the team*
*Define the opportunity for improvement*
*Study the current situation*
*Analyse the causes*
*Develop a theory for improvement*

*Act...*
*Standardise the improvement*
*Establish future plans*

*Do...*
*Carry out the plan*

*Study...*
*Study the results*

**Figure 4.15 The nine step PDSA process**

As we reflect upon what might be necessary considerations in an improvement process, let us recap the key points we have made so far.

To achieve sustainable improvement, we need to:

• Be clear about our mutually agreed purpose;

• Establish a shared vision of excellence;

• Use operational definitions to ensure clarity of understanding and measurement;

• Focus upon improving systems, processes and methods (rather than blaming individuals or just doing things);

• Identify the root causes of our dissatisfaction, not the symptoms;

• Carefully consider the systemic factors driving and restraining improvement, including interaction effects within the system and with containing systems;

• Identify strengths to build upon as well as deficiencies to be addressed;

• Identify the clients of our improvement efforts and understand their needs and expectations;

- Achieve a balance in addressing the competing, and sometimes contradictory, needs and expectations of stakeholders in our improvement efforts;

- Be clear about our own theory for improvement, and use this to predict outcomes;

- Reflect on the outcomes of our efforts, in the context of our theory for improvement, in order to refine our theory for improvement; and

- Not copy others' practices without adequate reflection about their proper implementation in a new context — adapt not adopt.

These requirements are reflected in the detailed nine step PDSA improvement process shown in Figure 4.16.

We have framed the PDSA improvement process as a series of questions to be answered by the improvement team (or individual). These questions address the considerations necessary to achieve sustainable improvement as detailed above.

The process also refers the user to specific quality learning tools that can be used to address the questions.

The PDSA cycle has been used to great effect by individuals and teams for a wide range of improvement activity, including: teams of teachers working on whole-school issues; classroom teachers working with their students to improve classroom systems and processes; and student teams addressing whole-school issues. PDSA can also be used as the basis of student projects, individually and in teams.

> The PDSA cycle can be used by individuals and teams for any improvement activity.

The point here is not that this is the perfect process for improvement — there is no such thing. It is a process for improvement that can be adapted (not adopted), applied, studied, and improved. It can be used as a starting point for others, like you, who may wish to create a process of their own.

There are enormous benefits to an organisation in having a standard improvement process: an agreed improvement process, such as the one illustrated, that everybody follows. This can be standard across the school or whole district. The benefits of doing so derive directly from having a common and widely used model, language, set of concepts, and agreed tools. Everyone uses the same approach, from students to superintendent. Not only does this get everyone aligned in their approach, but it provides a common language and a process that can itself be reviewed and improved, with the contribution of everybody in the organisation.

> There are enormous benefits to an organisation in having a standard improvement process.

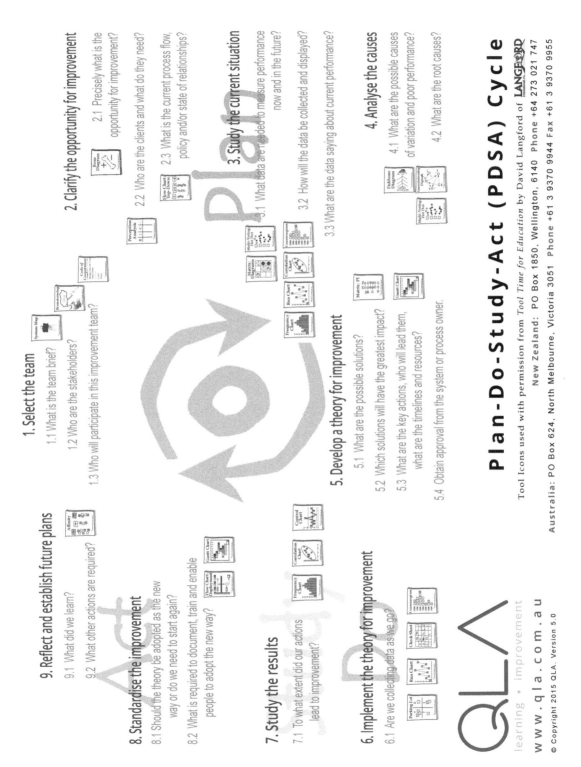

Figure 4.16 The detailed nine step PDSA cycle

# Using PDSA storyboards

In most situations, an improvement team will work through the PDSA improvement process to address particular opportunities for improvement. The team will usually comprise four to eight representatives of key stakeholder groups. In most cases, it is not practical for the team to include everybody affected by the improvement activities, as the team would be too large.

Just as a storyboard is used in film making to illustrate a narrative, a PDSA storyboard can be created to illustrate the activities and findings of the PDSA team.

> Storyboard: a graphic organiser of illustrations or images displayed in sequence with the aim of visualising a narrative.

A PDSA storyboard is a powerful and practical way for a team to document their activities and findings and to communicate the improvement process to stakeholders.

> PDSA Storyboard: a graphic organiser of tables, charts, tools and other illustrations displayed in sequence with the aim of capturing, recording, visualising and sharing the progressive activities, findings and decisions of a PDSA team.

During the team's progress through the improvement project, they will be considering the questions asked by the detailed nine step PDSA process, collecting evidence, and recording their answers. They can also record how the tools helped them arrive at their various conclusions.

Periodically, the team will need to meet with stakeholders to share the team's findings and seek input. The PDSA storyboard supports this. It also helps the team to quickly reconnect with where they are up to in the improvement process each time they reconvene.

A PDSA storyboard is a powerful and practical way for the team to document their activities and findings.

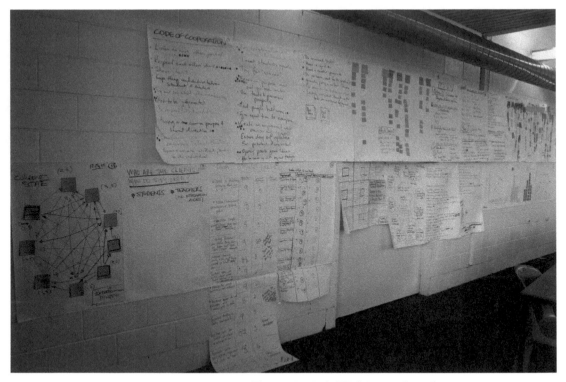

**Figure 4.17 A PDSA storyboard**
Source: Suburban high school in Victoria.

The storyboard in Figure 4.17 was created to document the activities and findings of an improvement team over the course of an improvement project, which lasted several months.

More recently, we have seen an increasing use of electronic storyboards. Digital photographs provide a wonderful way to quickly capture a storyboard.

Most importantly, a PDSA storyboard provides the team with a reference document that acts as a point of reflection and review for the team and which can be used to great effect for sharing the team's work with others. The storyboard not only explains the improvement project, but it also helps to enhance understanding of the tools and the improvement process itself.

A PDSA storyboard provides the team with a reference document that acts as a point of reflection and review for the team and which can be used to great effect for sharing the team's work with others.

### A TUB FULL OF STORYBOARDS

When I (Michael) visited a middle school in Leander Independent Schools District in Texas some years ago, the Principal asked me if I would like to see some of their improvements. Of course, I said "yes". The district had been working with David Langford for some years, so I knew I was in for a treat.

The Principal took me to her office and led me to a large cardboard tub in the corner. The tub was nearly a metre in diameter and was filled with large scrolls of paper. "What would you like to see?" she asked. "These are all our improvement storyboards for the past three years. Whenever a team works on an improvement project, they capture their efforts and learning as a story board."

Sure enough, I selected a few at random, and each one told the story of the investigations, actions, tools, data and conclusions that the team were making through the process.

"During the improvement process," she explained, "the storyboard lives on the wall down the corridor. Staff members who are not on the team are invited to read the storyboard, add their comments on sticky notes if they wish, and consult with team members if they have questions." I had noticed the beginnings of a storyboard on the corridor wall on our way to her office.

"Once the improvement project is completed," she continued, "we keep all the storyboards here in my office. This way they are available for anyone who needs them. We find ourselves sharing them with other schools in the district, as well as visitors like you. We also return to them if we are addressing similar issues, or revisiting the area for improvement."

It was clear to me that the storyboards had become an important and valuable part of the improvement culture at that school.

## Evidence of improvement

How will an improvement project team know if their improvement efforts have been successful? In too many cases, improvement efforts in schools can falter or result in change that is not improvement.

The improvement process calls for the team to identify measures — quantitative indicators — that can be used to measure performance before and after the improvement actions in order to determine the degree to which things have become better (or worse).

The improvement process calls for the team to identify measures to determine the degree to which things have become better.

Without objective evidence, the team and stakeholders will not know the degree to which their improvement efforts have been successful. As Deming is reported to have said, "In God we trust, all others must bring data."

This raises many challenges, not the least of which is that all data exhibit variation. We must address these challenges and learn how to interpret data in the presence of variation. This is the focus of the next chapter.

> Without objective evidence, the team and stakeholders will not know the degree to which their improvement efforts have been successful.

---

## PDSA IN PRACTICE

Over the years, we have seen the Plan–Do–Study–Act cycle used many times, frequently with remarkable results. Here are some examples.

### STUDENT WORK ETHIC

A high school in Victoria was concerned that they had a problem among their students. The students were neither turning in their work on time, nor completing it with a high degree of quality. The staff were of the view that the students were lazy and lacked a good work ethic. To address this, they began a PDSA improvement project. The improvement team was comprised of school leaders, teachers and students.

When the improvement team reached Step 2.3: "Who should benefit most from this improvement and what do they need?", they decided that they had better seek the views of students. The team used the perception analysis tool (detailed in Chapter Three) to obtain the views of staff and students. The students were clear in their feedback: the learning was seen as largely irrelevant and meaningless; teachers were frequently ill-prepared, disorganised and late to class; and teachers were not excited by what they were teaching. Staff reported, among other things, that staff meetings were neither purposeful nor efficient.

These data helped the school recognise that they had systemic issues to address, not defective students. The improvement team then focussed upon some of the key leadership and support systems that were identified to be the root causes.

### YEAR 5/6 MATHEMATICS

Mr Phypers began a PDSA when the classroom parking lot tool (see Chapter Three) became congested with suggestions to improve his teaching of mathematics.

Working together with his students, they made improvements to the mathematics program. Students' enjoyment of mathematics increased dramatically, as did their performance.

## STUDENTS LEADING SCHOOL IMPROVEMENT TEAMS

The student leadership team at Hallett Cove School in South Australia is comprised of student representatives from Years 5 to 11. The team collectively identified a range of issues about the school's operations that concerned them, including: litter; teacher-student relationships; student enthusiasm and attitudes to learning; activities for students before school, during lunch times, and after school; and use of information and communication technologies.

Ten multi-age student improvement teams were formed, with about six members on each team. Students prioritised the list of issues and each team selected one of the priority issues as its focus. Each team was supported by an adult school leader with experience in PDSA and the tools.

Over the course of five days, the student teams were trained in the PDSA cycle and tools, using their issue as the topic. Each team worked through the cycle step by step, collecting and analysing data, identifying root causes, developing a theory for improvement, and drafting recommendations, including a proposed implementation plan.

On the final day, each team presented their findings to the Principal, senior leaders and school board members. Student teams supported their presentation and recommendations with a formal report. The majority of the students' recommendations were accepted and students played a pivotal role in the implementation of the recommendations.

Video Clip 4.3: Student improvement teams
http://www.qla.com.au/Videos/3
Source: Hallett Cove R-12 School, SA.

# Reflection questions

**?** Which commonly used terms at your school would benefit from operational definitions? (Some examples: number of students funded, cash reserves, workload, staff morale, literacy, numeracy, at risk, special needs, gifted, talented, on-task, engaged, socio economic status, poverty, advance skills teacher, expert teacher, leader, leadership, teaching and learning).

**?** What proportion of your available working day do you spend in each PDSA area: Planning, Doing, Studying, and Acting? What about the classroom teachers and students that you know?

**?** What has been your experience of schools adopting (or adapting) others' programs?

**?** To what degree is plan–teach–assess seen as a cycle at your school? How do you know?

**?** What has been your experience of improvement projects using a structured improvement process (or not)? In the light of the points made in this chapter, what observations would you now make about this?

# Quality learning tools to create knowledge

All of the tools given as examples in this book, not just the few that follow, can be gainfully applied to the improvement process.

## Operational definition

We have previously discussed the importance of creating an operational definition in order to achieve shared understanding of the precise meaning of a concept. Without operational definitions, terms can be vague, ambiguous and misunderstood.

The paper passing purpose tool (P³T), introduced in Chapter Three, can be used to great effect in creating operational definitions. We have more to say about using operational definitions for measurement in Chapter Five, but here our focus is on creating operational definitions that can provide clarity to groups of individuals for the purposes of discussion and action.

> ### OPERATIONAL DEFINITION: BEING ON TIME IN YEAR 2
>
> Students in a Year 2 class at Theodore Primary School in the ACT had difficulty getting to school on time at the start of each day.
>
> They agreed an operational definition for "on time". This is shown in Figure 4.18.
>
> This definition provided a basis for them to collect data and prepare a graph of the number of students who were on time each day. They used this data to monitor progress over time.
>
> The class also prepared a list of the reasons why they were late (Figure 4.19), which they published in the entrance corridor for students to share with their parents. Instances of lateness diminished considerably.

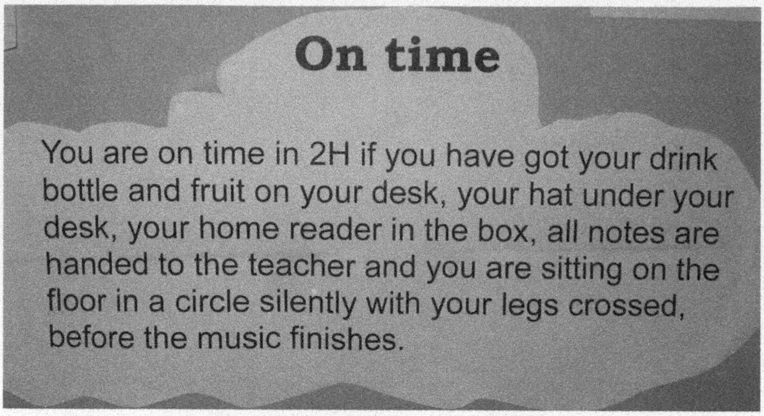

# On time

You are on time in 2H if you have got your drink bottle and fruit on your desk, your hat under your desk, your home reader in the box, all notes are handed to the teacher and you are sitting on the floor in a circle silently with your legs crossed, before the music finishes.

**Figure 4.18 Year 2 operational definition for "on time"**
Source: Theodore Primary School, ACT.

Why are we late to school?

- lots of traffic lights
- lots of cars in the way
- broken down car
- didn't get dressed on time
- didn't eat my breakfast on time
- because I didn't listen to my Mum
- because I slept in
- Mum was sick
- I watched too much TV
- Playing on my X-Box

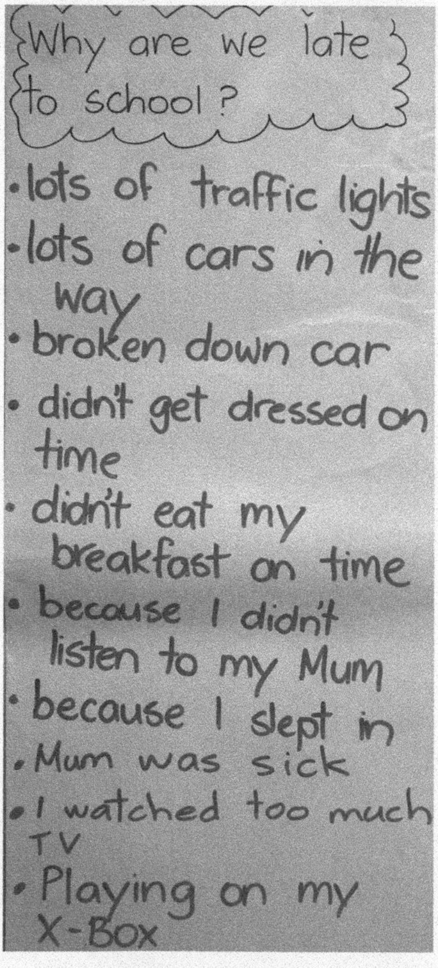

**Figure 4.19 Why we are late to school**
Source: Theodore Primary School, ACT.

### OPERATIONAL DEFINITION: BULLYING IN YEAR 2/3/4

Students in Year 2/3/4 class at Mungindi Central School in New South Wales, developed an operational definition for bullying.

Not only did the students work with their teacher to come up with a specific definition — "when people make you feel sad, scared or unsafe" — they also clarified the definition by identifying and documenting what bullying looks like.

Creating an operational definition for bullying provided the students and their teacher with several benefits. Firstly, it provided a common language that enabled them to discuss what was and what wasn't bullying behaviour. Secondly, it enabled students to identify when they may have been bullied and when they may have engaged in bullying behaviour themselves.

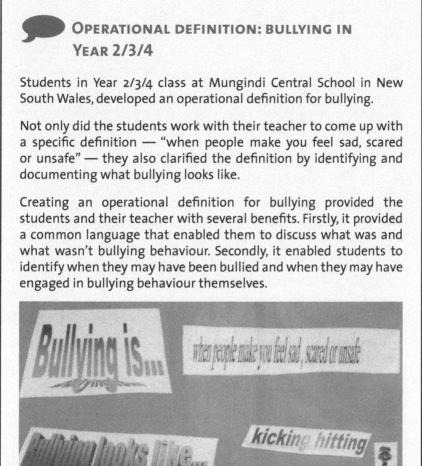

Figure 4.20 Operational definition for bullying
Source: Mungindi Central School, NSW.

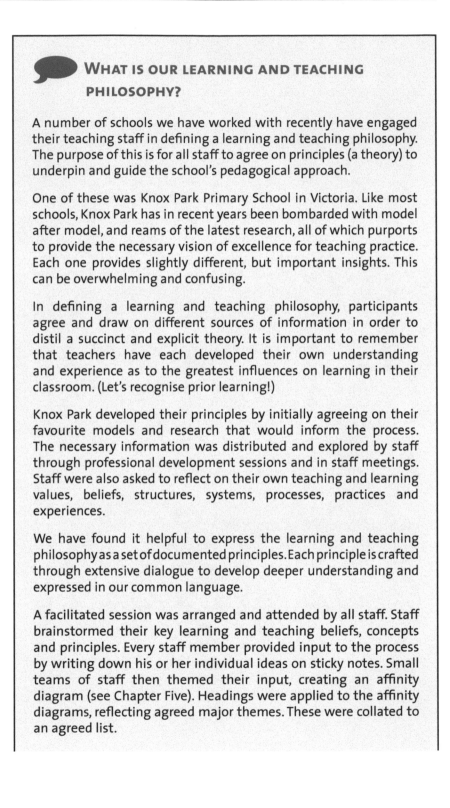

## What is our learning and teaching philosophy?

A number of schools we have worked with recently have engaged their teaching staff in defining a learning and teaching philosophy. The purpose of this is for all staff to agree on principles (a theory) to underpin and guide the school's pedagogical approach.

One of these was Knox Park Primary School in Victoria. Like most schools, Knox Park has in recent years been bombarded with model after model, and reams of the latest research, all of which purports to provide the necessary vision of excellence for teaching practice. Each one provides slightly different, but important insights. This can be overwhelming and confusing.

In defining a learning and teaching philosophy, participants agree and draw on different sources of information in order to distil a succinct and explicit theory. It is important to remember that teachers have each developed their own understanding and experience as to the greatest influences on learning in their classroom. (Let's recognise prior learning!)

Knox Park developed their principles by initially agreeing on their favourite models and research that would inform the process. The necessary information was distributed and explored by staff through professional development sessions and in staff meetings. Staff were also asked to reflect on their own teaching and learning values, beliefs, structures, systems, processes, practices and experiences.

We have found it helpful to express the learning and teaching philosophy as a set of documented principles. Each principle is crafted through extensive dialogue to develop deeper understanding and expressed in our common language.

A facilitated session was arranged and attended by all staff. Staff brainstormed their key learning and teaching beliefs, concepts and principles. Every staff member provided input to the process by writing down his or her individual ideas on sticky notes. Small teams of staff then themed their input, creating an affinity diagram (see Chapter Five). Headings were applied to the affinity diagrams, reflecting agreed major themes. These were collated to an agreed list.

A small team of staff volunteered to draft a principle to reflect each of the agreed themes, informed by the details on each of the sticky notes. The resultant draft was then shared with, wordsmithed a little by, and finally (and quickly) agreed to, by all staff.

Figure 4.21 shows the principles of learning and teaching they agreed to.

The principles are used as an ongoing reference to develop, review and continually improve consistency, policy and practice across the school.

Naturally, the principles are dynamic. Like any theory or hypothesis to be effective in an ongoing way it will need to be regularly reviewed and reaffirmed or reinformed by further research and experiences, over time.

## Knox Park PS: Philosophy of Teaching & Learning

1. Provide an engaging, stimulating and fun learning environment to enable students to become lifelong learners
2. Implement consistent whole school teaching methods through agreed systems and processes
3. Achieve individual success through differentiated learning and goal setting
4. Respect all relationships. Accept individuality and foster inclusiveness in a safe environment
5. Empower students through student-centred learning and constructive feedback and encourage students to take responsibility for their learning
6. Value our role as educators and through targeted professional development strive for continual improvement
7. Acknowledge the importance and impact of all aspects of our school environment on educational outcomes and personal growth
8. Celebrate and recognise achievement and improvement within the school community
9. Use a variety of tools and strategies for feedback to improve
10. Support students to be intrinsically motivated and autonomous learners

**Figure 4.21 Principles of teaching and learning**

Source: Knox Park Primary School, Victoria.

# 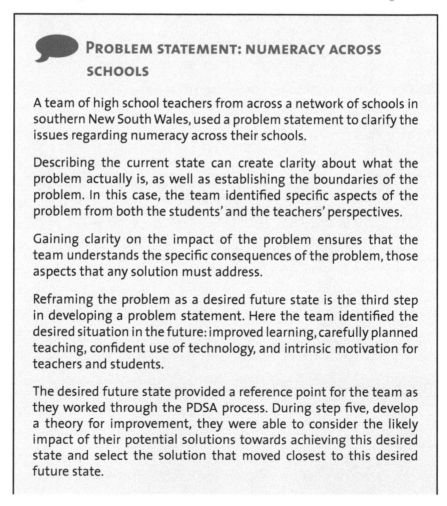 Problem statement

The problem statement is a simple tool for clarifying and reaching agreement regarding the nature of a problem. It is comprised of three parts:

1.  A description of the current situation or existing state of the problem;

2.  A description of the impact of that situation on the people and the system; and

3.  A description of the desired situation.

In describing the desired future state, it is important to take care to describe the situation, not specific solutions. Solutions come later. The aim at this point is to reach agreement about the existing problem or situation.

Frequently, when preparing a problem statement, teams may need to create an operational definition for terms that are unclear or vague.

> ### PROBLEM STATEMENT: NUMERACY ACROSS SCHOOLS
>
> A team of high school teachers from across a network of schools in southern New South Wales, used a problem statement to clarify the issues regarding numeracy across their schools.
>
> Describing the current state can create clarity about what the problem actually is, as well as establishing the boundaries of the problem. In this case, the team identified specific aspects of the problem from both the students' and the teachers' perspectives.
>
> Gaining clarity on the impact of the problem ensures that the team understands the specific consequences of the problem, those aspects that any solution must address.
>
> Reframing the problem as a desired future state is the third step in developing a problem statement. Here the team identified the desired situation in the future: improved learning, carefully planned teaching, confident use of technology, and intrinsic motivation for teachers and students.
>
> The desired future state provided a reference point for the team as they worked through the PDSA process. During step five, develop a theory for improvement, they were able to consider the likely impact of their potential solutions towards achieving this desired state and select the solution that moved closest to this desired future state.

Problem Statement

Current
* Teachers confused about program delivery in
numeracy
* Teachers overwhelmed about incorporating technology
into classrooms.
* Student engagement low
* Student's limited understanding of language of maths
* Significant number of students not taking ownership of
learning.

Impact
* Drop in student growth in numeracy 5-7
* Students are off task, not taking up skills & knowledge
* Lack of focus on key curriculum content
* Technology not being used to full capacity

Desired
* Improved growth in target group 5-7
* Explicit, focussed & planned sequence in teaching &
learning
* Confident technology users
* Intrisically motivated teacher & student learners

**Figure 4.22 Problem statement**
Source: Sunraysia Schools Network, NSW.

# ✖ Lotus diagram

A lotus diagram is a graphical organiser for breaking ideas into their component parts. The topic is placed in the centre of the lotus diagram and key components recorded in the eight boxes surrounding the central topic. Each of these key components is then broken down, in turn, to record sub-components.

Download a lotus diagram template from www.qla.com.au

## LOTUS DIAGRAM: UNPACKING WORK ETHIC

A team of teachers at a large Catholic High School in New South Wales used a Lotus Diagram to unpack and document the components that comprise the concept of work ethic.

Beginning by placing the topic — "work ethic" — in the centre of the lotus diagram, the team then brainstormed eight key aspects of the topic. These were noted in the boxes immediately surrounding the central box.

Each of these aspects, working clockwise from "motivation" to "enjoyment", was then copied to the centre of each of the outer boxes of the lotus diagram.

The team then considered each of these aspects in turn. They discussed, agreed and noted the components that contribute to that aspect. For instance, they agreed that displaying work, having input into their learning, choice, and self respect all contribute to pride.

Finally, the team used coloured dots to note which components they believed needed to be changed and those that should not be changed. This provided the team with greater clarity as to what they might focus upon in developing potential solutions.

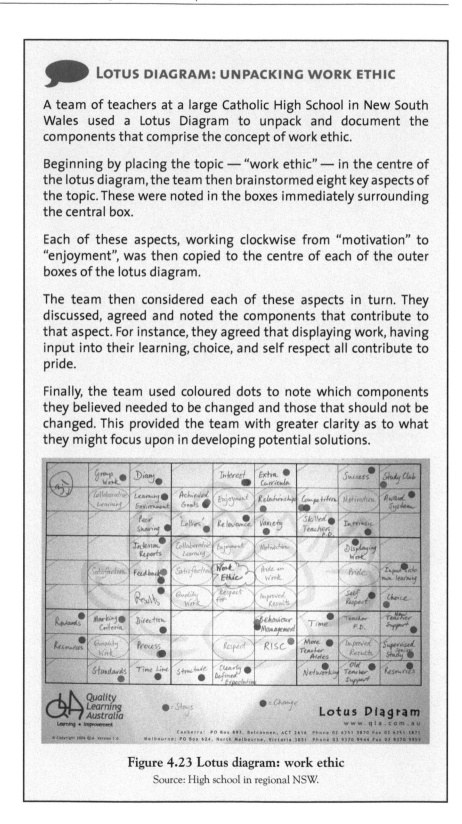

**Figure 4.23 Lotus diagram: work ethic**

Source: High school in regional NSW.

### 🗨 LOTUS DIAGRAM: CLASS PROCESSES

Students at St. Joseph's Primary School in Quirindi in New South Wales used a lotus diagram to focus on class processes. This was written in the centre of the lotus diagram.

The class then identified seven class processes, which they listed around the central topic, clockwise from "morning process" to "job process". These process names were then copied to the centre box of each outer grid.

Next, they considered each process in turn and identified the key steps in each, noting these around the process name. (When Figure 4.24 was collected, they had not completed this step for the "job process".)

Finally, they noted the order of the steps of some (not all) processes by placing a number in the top left corner of the box in which the step is written. For example, the "morning process" is comprised of five steps, beginning with "walk quietly to bags" as step one and finishing with "after roll call and note collection proceed to desk" at step five.

This lotus diagram enabled the students and teacher to agree and document their key class processes. All students were able to contribute to the agreements regarding how things work in their class and know what is expected of them in enacting these processes.

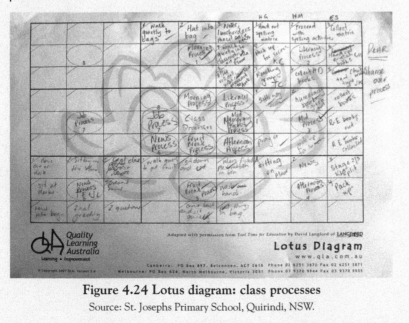

**Figure 4.24 Lotus diagram: class processes**
Source: St. Josephs Primary School, Quirindi, NSW.

# Potential improvement matrix

A potential improvement matrix captures the possible solutions to address identified issues or root causes, and supports selection of the most appropriate solutions through careful prioritisation. The potential improvement matrix encourages individuals and teams to identify and consider a range of possible solutions, not just "jump to solution" (react to fix a problem without fully understanding the issues involved or considering a range of options, often with unforeseen consequences).

For each issue, or root cause of variation and poor performance, a range of possible solutions is identified. Where it is not clear what a solution may look like in practice, practical actions can be documented. Each possible solution is rated for its likely impact in achieving the desired state, and it is rated for "do-ability": how easy it will be to implement. Each possible solution is then considered in the context of the ratings given, and a decision is taken to implement the solution, defer the solution, or abandon the solution.

Figure 4.25 shows a potential improvements matrix used by a team of teachers at a high school in South Australia to reflect upon the need for a stronger sense of shared direction across the school.

| Root Cause | Possible Solutions | Practical Actions | Potential Impact<br>10 = Very significant/positive<br>0 = No impact | Do-ability<br>10 = Very easy<br>0 = Seemingly impossible | Implement? |
|---|---|---|---|---|---|
| | Devise a mission statement<br>PURPOSE | All stakeholders write a response to the following question "What is the purpose of our school"<br>- Underline important words + phrases<br>- Group words on sticky notes<br>- Compile consensogram using data<br>- Use data to develop a purpose statement | 9 | 7 | ✓ |
| | Determine the vision of our school<br>VISION | All stakeholders write a response to the following question "What would a perfect school look like?"<br>- Use data to create an affinity diagram<br>- This diagram will assist in writing a school vision | 10 | 7 | ✓ |
| | Establish what values are important to our school<br>VALUES | Brainstorm what values are important to our school. Sort the responses into groups. Hot Dot. These become our school values (Top 5)<br>Inservice all staff on values statement | 10 | 5 | ✓ |
| | Develop a maintenance plan to ensure consistency and practicality through revision<br>LIVING | Display values in all classrooms and throughout the school<br>Use W.I.L.F.<br>Include values in all assemblies and in point giving<br>Use language in communication with stakeholders<br>Classes develop powerpoints to make values relevant to students | 10 | 4 | ✓ |

Quality Learning Australia
Learning . Improvement

**Potential Improvement Matrix**
www.qla.com.au
Canberra: PO Box 897, Belconnen, ACT 2616 Phone 02 6251 3870 Fax 02 6251 3871
Melbourne: PO Box 624, North Melbourne, Victoria 3051 Phone 03 9370 9944 Fax 03 9370 9955



**Figure 4.25 Potential improvement matrix**

Source: A high school in SA.

Download a potential improvement matrix template from www.qla.com.au

# Chapter summary

In this chapter we have examined the principles relating to the second area of Deming's system of profound knowledge, theory of knowledge:

**Planning:**   Improvement is rarely achieved without the planned application of appropriate strategy and methods.

**Knowledge:**   Learning and improvement are derived from theory, prediction, observation and reflection.

In doing so, we have explored the following ideas:

- Planning is a process of evaluating possible actions and selecting those most likely to achieve the desired future;

- Improvement planning focusses upon possible improvement actions;

- There are opportunities to improve the processes of planning for improvement in schools by:

  - Removing the requirement to specify numerical goals or targets;

  - Expanding the plan to include key daily routines in order to make it more relevant to all staff;

  - Deferring the specification of action plans until the appropriate system and root cause analysis has been completed; and

  - Ensuring that improvement plans focus upon sustainable systems and processes rather than becoming to-do lists.

- Significant improvement is achieved project by project;

- Effective execution of plans is critical to success;

- Improvement projects need to be monitored and coordinated, usually by senior leaders;

- Learning occurs through the dynamic interaction of theory and experience;

- Planning is a process that facilitates learning, leading to improvement;

- Operational definitions provide clarity of meaning among stakeholders;

- Copying others' approaches and programs is usually unsuccessful — the aim should be to adapt, not adopt;

- A structured improvement process, such as Plan–Do–Study–Act, enables teams to create a theory for improvement and then test the theory. Such processes enhance learning and improve the likelihood of success;

- Storyboards enable teams to capture progress during their project and share their findings with others; and

- There are quality learning tools that help to bring these ideas to life and which can provide practical strategies to take action. These include: bone diagram; Gantt chart; hot dot; operational definition; problem statement; lotus diagram; and potential improvement matrix.

# Further reading

David P. Langford, 2015, *Tool Time for Education*, version 15, Langford International, Montana — David Langford's *Tool Time for Education* is a valuable resource for continually improving learning environments. *Tool Time* provides instructions for approximately 60 quality learning tools, many of which are discussed throughout this book. It also illustrates how these tools can fit within the Plan–Do–Study–Act learning and improvement cycle.

Quality Learning Australasia, 2010, *The Plan-Do-Study-Act (PDSA) improvement cycle*, QLA.

Quality Learning Australasia, 2014, *Planning for school improvement*, QLA.

# Chapter 5:
# Using Data to Improve

Use of data requires knowledge about the different sources of uncertainty.

W. Edwards Deming, 1994, *The New Economics: For industry, government and education*, MIT, Massachusetts, p. 103.

# Chapter contents

# Introduction

This is the third of four chapters to introduce and explain the theory of improvement.

In this chapter we explore the third area of Deming's system of profound knowledge — knowledge about variation — and the two underpinning principles of quality learning:

**Data:** Facts and data are needed to measure progress and improve decision making

**Variation:** Systems and processes are subject to variation that affects predictability and performance.

Mathematics and statistics raise strong emotions for many people, as Peter Scholtes observed:

> Math and statistics have traditionally been taught in such a way that the only point of interest is whether students will be bored to death or scared to death.
>
> By the time people become managers, they have taken a vow of statistical abstinence.
>
> Peter R. Scholtes, 1998, *The Leader's Handbook*, McGraw-Hill, New York, p. 30.

While many readers may have misgivings about data and statistics, we encourage you to discover the discipline of statistical thinking which, like systems thinking, provides a new way of viewing the world.

Fundamental to statistical thinking is the use of data as the voice of a system — performance, process, perception, and input measures give the system a voice. In this chapter, we argue that learning to listen to the voice of the system and responding accordingly to the variation it reveals is essential if the system is to be optimised and improved.

> In this chapter, we argue that learning to listen to the voice of the system and responding accordingly to the variation it reveals is essential if the system is to be optimised and improved.

While some figures are necessarily unknown and unknowable, and data can certainly be misused (such as often occurs due to the imposition of numerical goals or targets, ratings and rankings), data can be used productively for three main purposes: to monitor performance, to adjust system operations, and to understand the system operation and behaviour.

This chapter also explains that variation exists in all systems, and can be observed within groups, between groups and over time. Common cause variation, for example, which establishes the natural limits of variation for a system, is always present and is built into the system. Special cause variation, on the other hand, is the result of unique events or situations.

We contend that management need to respond differently to special cause variation than they do to common cause: special cause variation needs to be case managed, while common cause variation can only be managed by changing the system.

In discussing how to respond appropriately to variation, this chapter shows how the common practice of tampering with a system — making changes in the absence of an understanding of the variation impacting upon the system — makes things worse.

The following flowchart is a summary outlining the flow of the chapter and its contents.

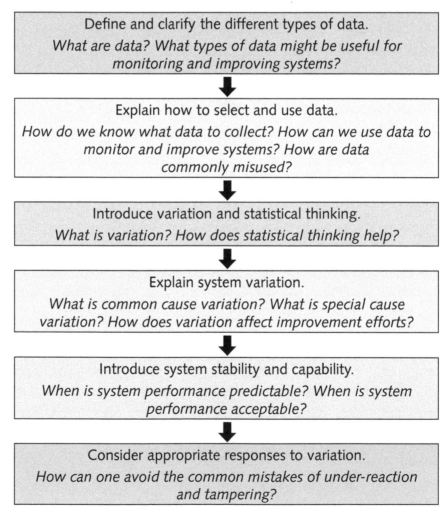

**Define and clarify the different types of data.**
*What are data? What types of data might be useful for monitoring and improving systems?*

⬇

**Explain how to select and use data.**
*How do we know what data to collect? How can we use data to monitor and improve systems? How are data commonly misused?*

⬇

**Introduce variation and statistical thinking.**
*What is variation? How does statistical thinking help?*

⬇

**Explain system variation.**
*What is common cause variation? What is special cause variation? How does variation affect improvement efforts?*

⬇

**Introduce system stability and capability.**
*When is system performance predictable? When is system performance acceptable?*

⬇

**Consider appropriate responses to variation.**
*How can one avoid the common mistakes of under-reaction and tampering?*

# What are data?

This section of the chapter expands on the following principle of quality learning:

> Facts and data are needed to measure progress and improve decision making.

Everyone sees the world differently.

Our life experiences have all been different, providing us with access to a rich diversity of world views and perspectives. As a result of both genetic variation and upbringing, all brains are wired differently. Each individual forms a different perception of their observed reality.

> What you see depends upon what you think before you look.
>
> Myron Tribus, personal communication.

Sometimes the difference in perception is small, sometimes it is significant.

In working to improve systems, we need to develop an understanding of these systems in a way that is as free of personal bias as possible, to develop an objective and shared understanding of the world. A good way to approach this is to collect facts and data.

Facts and data can be used to help see the world more objectively. Facts and data provide the means to measure progress towards achieving a system's purpose and vision, and to inform and improve planning and decision making.

*Facts and data can be used to help see the world more objectively.*

Before going further, let us clarify and define a few concepts.

Firstly, what do we mean by data and statistics?

 Data: facts, statistics or pieces of information.

 Statistic: a number that summarises observations.

Data can be subjective or objective.

 Subjective data: data related to the thoughts, opinions and perceptions of people.

 Objective data: data that are derived from observation and are free of personal feelings, interpretations and prejudices.

Objective data can provide an unbiased view of a system and, as such, are more clinical and focussed upon observations than subjective data. This is not to say that objective data are better than subjective data. Nor is it to say that individuals or organisations should only ever seek objective data. Both are required in order to seek and understand different perspectives of systems. Objective data provide insight into performance, and subjective data provide insight into the perspectives of the people working in and served by a system. Both subjective data and objective data are required to understand social systems.

*Subjective data and objective data are both required to understand social systems.*

Data can also be qualitative or quantitative.

 Qualitative data: data that relate to characteristics or qualities.

 Quantitative data: data that relate to quantities.

Qualitative data are descriptive. Quantitative data are expressed as numbers.

*Qualitative data are descriptive. Quantitative data are expressed as numbers.*

Qualitative data can aid understanding of the nature of systems and processes. A vision of excellence for an oral presentation, for example, is a list of observable qualities — quality characteristics — that are known to distinguish excellent presentations from mediocre and poor presentations. Similarly, when students give teachers their opinions on what was good about a unit of learning and what could be improved next time, they are providing valuable qualitative data. These data are also subjective.

Quantitative data relate to counts and measures, such as the number of students reaching achievement benchmarks, the number of students in a class, or the number of different countries of birth represented at a school.

We use measurement to create quantitative data.

 Measurement: a process of assigning numbers to observations.

A tape measure can be used to measure the width of a desk. The number of students present in a class at roll call can be counted. The time that it takes to walk to the bus stop can be observed and recorded. In each of these examples, numbers are assigned to observations: a measurement is taken.

*Quantitative data can be derived from qualitative data.*

Quantitative data can be derived from qualitative data. For example, the number of positive comments or the number of suggestions for improvement provided by students can be counted. These are also measurements.

# Data as the voice of the system

In order to understand the wellbeing of people, data can be collected by making observations and asking questions. These data can provide insight regarding peoples' wellbeing, and give people a voice to which the organisation can respond. The data can focus attention upon what is going well and where improvement is required.

In a similar manner, to understand the wellbeing of a system, data can be collected by making observations and asking questions. In this case, however, the questions and observations relate to the wellbeing of the system rather than that of people. The questions to be asked of the system take the form of observations to be made about system operation and performance. These observations are defined in such a way that numbers can be assigned to them. In this way, questions about system operation and performance become measures that provide data. Identifying what is to be measured, is, in effect, asking the system to tell us how it is performing. These data provide insight into the wellbeing of the system and give the system a voice. These data can also provide insights into where improvement is needed.

Data are thus the voice of the system. To care for systems and to improve them, we need to learn to ask the right questions and learn how to interpret the answers. In other words, we need to learn how to listen to the voice of the system. We do this by choosing useful measures and learning how to interpret the data.

> Data provide insights into the wellbeing of the system.

> We need to learn how to listen to the voice of the system. We do this by choosing useful measures and learning how to interpret the data.

## Types of measures

There are four sets of measures that can be used for monitoring and improving systems:

- Performance measures;

- Process measures;

- Perception measures; and

- Input measures.

### Performance measures

Data can be collected to summarise the degree to which the aims of the system have been met. These data are called performance measures.

Performance measures: measures of the outcomes of a system that indicate how well the system has performed. Performance measures answer the question: how did we go?

Performance measures relate to the aims of the system. They are used to quantify the outputs and outcomes of the system. In this way, performance measures relate to the key requirements of stakeholders as reflected in the aims of the system.

Performance measures provide historical data. Also called lag indicators, they relate to data collected after the event.

Examples of performance measures for a school include:

- Student graduation and completion rates;

- Student test results;

- Expenditure to budget; and

- Parental engagement with student learning.

It is important to collect and monitor performance measures for three reasons:

1. To understand the degree to which the aims of the system are being met;

2. To compare performance of one system with that of another similar system; and

3. To monitor changes in performance over time.

Performance measures have two major deficiencies:

1. They report what has happened in the past; and

2. They generally provide no insight into how to improve performance.

## USING ONLY THE REAR VIEW MIRROR

Myron Tribus remarked that managing by performance measures alone is like trying to drive a car by watching only the rear view mirror.

We also need measures that help us to understand the road ahead and allow us to predict when to make adjustments. We need to know the speed at which we are travelling, how much fuel we have remaining, and how far we have come so we can predict how much further we have to go. In short, we also need process measures.

## Process measures

Data can be collected within a system that can predict, ahead of performance measures, how the system is performing. These are process measures.

Process measures: measures collected within the system that are predictive of system performance and which can be used to initiate adjustments to processes. Process measures answer the question: how are we going?

Process measures can be used to monitor progress and predict final outcomes. Most importantly, process measures are used to identify when changes need to be made to a system in order to bring about improved performance. Process measures are used to predict performance and identify when changes to the operation of the system are required.

> Process measures are used to predict performance and identify when changes to the operation of the system are required.

Examples of process measures include:

- Regular student self-assessment, peer-assessment and teacher assessments;
- Home learning and assessment task completion rates; and
- Monthly financial reports.

Each of these process measures is collected and reported regularly. This enables intervention when a process appears to be at risk of delivering unsatisfactory outcomes — before it is too late. With student learning this is critical so that mediation — improvements to learning — can be made, ensuring that high levels of learning are maintained.

## Perception measures

Data can be collected from stakeholders in a system regarding their thoughts and opinions about the system. These are perception measures.

 Perception measures: measures collected from the stakeholders in the system and are used to monitor their thoughts and opinions of the system. Perception measures answer the question: what do people think of the system?

Perception measures increase understanding of peoples' experience of the system; they tell us what people think of the system. Given that people make choices based on their perceptions, whether these are accurate or not, perception measures provide valuable insights that can be useful in predicting and explaining behaviour.

Perception measures can be collected for the following stakeholder groups:

- **Clients**: the recipients and direct beneficiaries of products and services;

- **People working within the system**: leaders, staff, students, and volunteers;

- **Suppliers**: those who provide the inputs necessary for the system to function;

- **Partners**: those who work collaboratively with the people working in the system, as both clients and suppliers, to achieve the purpose and vision of the system; and

- **Other stakeholders**: those with a vested interest in the activities and outcomes of the system who do not fall into the above categories.

Examples of perception measures include:

- Opinions of product and service quality;

- Satisfaction with the system and its operation; and

- Thoughts and opinions about specific aspects of the system.

> Perception measures tell us what people think of the system.

# Quality Learning
# Staff Questionnaire Example
# Quality Learning College

Your Name: _____
*(Optional)*

Date: _____

## Notes on completing the questionnaire:

Thank you for completing this questionnaire. Please read the statements carefully, there is a mixture of positively and negatively worded statements.

Your responses will be treated confidentially. A report providing a summary of all responses will be provided to the school. Individuals' responses will not be identified.

|   | | Strongly Disagree | Disagree | Mildly Disagree | Mildly Agree | Agree | Strongly Agree |
|---|---|---|---|---|---|---|---|
| 1 | I am very happy with the progress of my students | 1 | 2 | 3 | 4 | 5 | 6 |
| 2 | I often feel excluded | 1 | 2 | 3 | 4 | 5 | 6 |
| 3 | I am proud of what I do and achieve at school | 1 | 2 | 3 | 4 | 5 | 6 |
| 4 | My students always achieve high standards | 1 | 2 | 3 | 4 | 5 | 6 |
| 5 | Staff are not valued equally | 1 | 2 | 3 | 4 | 5 | 6 |
| 6 | I am not involved in setting direction for the whole school | 1 | 2 | 3 | 4 | 5 | 6 |
| 7 | My students have what it takes to be good students | 1 | 2 | 3 | 4 | 5 | 6 |
| 8 | The school values are rarely discussed | 1 | 2 | 3 | 4 | 5 | 6 |
| 9 | All my colleagues work well together | 1 | 2 | 3 | 4 | 5 | 6 |
| 10 | I regularly set explicit and challenging learning goals for myself | 1 | 2 | 3 | 4 | 5 | 6 |
| 11 | I feel I am not supported in doing my job | 1 | 2 | 3 | 4 | 5 | 6 |
| 12 | Being part of this school is important to me | 1 | 2 | 3 | 4 | 5 | 6 |
| 13 | Students do not treat staff with respect | 1 | 2 | 3 | 4 | 5 | 6 |
| 14 | I am bored by the things we do at school | 1 | 2 | 3 | 4 | 5 | 6 |
| 15 | Students feel that their views are valued | 1 | 2 | 3 | 4 | 5 | 6 |
| 16 | I feel strong ties with others at this school | 1 | 2 | 3 | 4 | 5 | 6 |

**Figure 5.1 Example of a school stakeholder perception measure questionnaire (staff)**

## Input measures

Data can be collected relating to the quantity, quality and other characteristics of key inputs — anything put in, taken in, or operated on by the system. The collections of data that relate to inputs are known as input measures.

 Input measures: measures collected at the boundary of the system and quantify key characteristics of the inputs that affect system operation. Input measures answer the question: what are the key characteristics of the inputs to the system?

Inputs to a system affect system performance. In the manufacturing sector, the key characteristics of many system inputs, such as material thickness or lubricant viscosity, can be controlled by requiring the suppliers of these inputs to conform to certain specifications. Other key process input variables cannot be controlled in this manner and process adjustments are necessary based on measurements of these inputs. For example, farmers cannot control rainfall, but they can adjust their rates of irrigation based on rainfall measurements.

Very few teachers can control the prior learning of their students, but they do adjust their classroom processes based on this input characteristic. Similarly, very few schools can control the value that their students' families place on education, but they can adjust school processes based on data about this.

*Input measures quantify key characteristics of the inputs to a system that directly affect system operation.*

Input measures quantify key characteristics of the inputs to a system that directly affect system operation. Input measures relate directly to the performance measures of the previous system. For example, a student's prior learning is an input measure for her current system of learning and a performance measure of her previous system of learning.

Input measures — data relating to critical characteristics of key inputs to a system — are required to ensure that appropriate actions are taken within the system to accommodate changes and variation in inputs. They are also required if systems are to become robust to input variation.

The core process in a school is learning (not teaching). The learning process is subject to enormous variation in inputs. Key process input variables include students' prior learning, motivation to learn, family background, home support and peer pressure, to name a few. Any classroom of students will display enormous variation in these inputs. It is not uncommon, for example, to have a class of 13-year-olds with chronological reading ages varying from seven to 18 years. Understanding input variation is crucial to designing learning processes that cater to the many and varied needs of all students.

At a whole school level, there is variation among teachers. Teachers' knowledge of the content they are required to teach is not uniform, nor is their knowledge of students' learning processes or the programs in use at the school. Experience with school and education system compliance requirements can also be highly variable. School processes need to take account of this input variation.

In a school context, most of the system inputs relate to people. For this reason, schools sometimes speak of input measures as demographic or people measures.

Examples of input measures include:

*   Student demographics, including family first language and socio-economic indicators;

*   Students' prior learning; and

*   Teacher qualifications and experience.

## Measures for a school system

To recap, there are four sets of measures that can be used for monitoring and improving systems:

1.   Performance measures;

2.   Process measures;

3.   Perception measures; and

4.   Input measures.

Taken together, these measures provide deep insight into the performance, operation, and behaviour of a system. These measures provide a voice with which the system can speak about its behaviour, operation and performance. Importantly, these measures support analysis and prediction of future system behaviour and performance.

The four sets of system measures can be collected for the whole system as well as for subsystems within the system. In school systems, this means that data can be collected at the state, region/district, school, sub-school, classroom, and student levels.

> The four sets of system measures can be collected for the whole system as well as for subsystems within the system.

Table 5.1 illustrates a framework for measures for a school and classrooms. The aim of this table is not to provide a definitive list of measures for schools and classrooms, but rather to illustrate the concepts.

| | Performance | Process | Perception | Input |
|---|---|---|---|---|
| **School** | **Student**<br><br>**Academic**<br>State and National Testing<br>Pass rates/met standard<br>Graduation/completion<br>Pathways<br><br>**Character Development**<br>Attendance<br>Values and Behaviours<br>Confidence<br>Empathy<br><br>**Extra Curricular**<br>Programs<br>Health & Fitness<br><br>**System**<br><br>**Finance**<br>Expenditures to budget<br><br>**People**<br>Teacher attendance<br>Admin staff attendance<br>Staff turnover<br>Volunteering<br>Participation<br>Values and Behaviour | **Planning**<br>School Plan (long term)<br>Annual Operating Plan<br>School Self Assessment<br><br>**Improvement**<br>School Improvement Process<br>Professional Learning<br><br>**Communication**<br><br>**Risk and Compliance**<br><br>**Curriculum**<br>Curriculum planning<br>Unit planning<br><br>**Learning Programs**<br><br>**Assessment and Reporting**<br>Student self-assessment<br>Reporting to parents<br>Student-led conferences<br><br>**Learner Wellbeing**<br>Incidents<br>Suspensions and Expulsions<br><br>**Technology** | **Students**<br>Overall satisfaction<br>Joy in learning<br>Connectedness to<br>  school<br><br>**Staff**<br>Overall satisfaction<br>Joy in teaching<br>Connectendess to<br>  school<br>Communication<br><br>**Parents and**<br>**Community**<br>Overall satisfaction<br>Connectendess to<br>  school<br>Communication<br>Complaints | **Students**<br>Enrolments<br>Subgroups<br><br>**Staff**<br>Professional Teacher<br>  Standards<br>Education<br>Year of Experience<br>Professional Learning<br><br>**Parents and**<br>**Community**<br>Subgroups<br><br>**System**<br>Finance budget<br>Resources for special<br>  needs<br>Technology provision<br>Professional learning |
| **Classroom** | **Student**<br><br>**Academic**<br>State and National Testing<br>Pass rates/met standard<br>Growth in Student Achievement<br><br>**Character Development**<br>Attendance<br>Values and Behaviours<br>Confidence<br>Empathy<br>Participation/Engagement<br><br>**System**<br><br>**Finance**<br>Expenditures to budget<br><br>**People**<br>Teacher attendance<br>Parent and Community<br>  Participation<br>Volunteering | **Planning**<br>Curriculum programming<br>Unit Planning<br>Lesson planning<br><br>**Improvement**<br>Classroom Improvement<br>  Process<br><br>**Assessment and Reporting**<br>Student self-assessment<br>Reporting to parents<br>Student-led conferences<br><br>**Learner wellbeing**<br>Incidents<br>Suspensions and Expulsions<br><br>**Technology** | **Students**<br>Overall satisfaction<br>Joy in learning<br><br>**Parents and**<br>**Community**<br>Overall satisfaction<br>Connectendess to<br>  school<br>Communication | **Students**<br>Enrolments<br>Subgroups<br><br>**Parents and**<br>**Community**<br>Subgroups<br><br>**System**<br>Finance budget<br>Resources for special<br>  needs<br>Technology provision<br>Professional learning |
| **Student** | **Student**<br><br>**Academic**<br>State and National Testing<br>Pass rates/met standard<br><br>**Character Development**<br>Attendance<br>Values and Behaviours<br>Confidence<br>Empathy<br>Participation/Engagement | **Improvement**<br>Classroom Improvement<br>  Process<br>Learning improvement<br>  strategies<br><br>**Learning**<br>Goal setting<br>Class activities and<br>  assessments<br>Portfolio/Capacity Matrices | **Student**<br>Overall satisfaction<br>Joy in learning | |

Table 5.1 Measures for a school: a starting point

Specific measures are likely to be different for each district, school and classroom. Performance measures are strongly tied to the aims of the school and classroom, which vary from school to school, from district to district, and from state to state. As these aims adapt to specific contexts, so too must performance measures.

Process measures, perception measures and input measures will also need to be different, to some degree, from school to school, to reflect different aims and school contexts. The measures suggested in Table 5.1, therefore, can only be a starting point, a framework for discussion within schools and school systems.

Video Clip 5.1: School district performance data
http://www.qla.com.au/Videos/3

Source: Leander Independent School District, Texas.

## Measures on a system map

The system map was introduced in Chapter Three as an effective way to reach agreement about and document the key elements of a system. One of these key elements is results measures: the indicators of success for the organisation.

The results measures identified on a system map list the most significant performance measures and perception measures, and provide an overview of how the system is performing and the perceptions of key stakeholders in the system. Results measures summarise the key indicators of success: performance and stakeholder perceptions.

Figure 5.2 shows an example of a school system map with results measures.

*The results measures identified on a system map list the most significant performance measures and perception measures.*

# System Map
## Yarra Primary School

*Ratified by School Council on 26th May 2010*

**Who are the SUPPLIERS to the organisation?**

- Cleaning staff
- Volunteers
- Department of Education & Early Childhood Development & NMR
- Speech Pathologists
- Psychologists
- Music Teachers
- Department of Human Services
- Corporate Express
- Education Providers
- Federal Government
- Fundraising community groups
- Stephanie Alexander
- After school sports providers
- Bus companies
- Crossing Guards
- CRTs
- Childcare/Kindergartens/creches
- Artists in Schools

**What are the INPUTS required by the organisation?**

- Policy, strategy & guidelines
- Expertise & support
- Funding
- Social welfare & health support
- Media information
- Community support
- ICT, books & stationery
- Existing learning of future students
- Teacher replacement support
- Maintenance & cleaning services
- Professional development

**Who are the OTHER STAKEHOLDERS of the organisation?**

- Future parents
- Union
- Inner North Network
- Local members of parliament
- Local business sponsors
- Siblings
- Other local businesses and shop owners
- Student Teachers
- Community Groups
- Rotary
- Playgroups
- Police
- Neighbours
- Friends of the Wurrundjeri
- City of Yarra
- Other local schools
- Local sporting groups and clubs
- Broader community

**What is the PURPOSE of the organisation?**

The purpose of Yarra Primary School is to deliver a quality education which prepares our children for the future and creates a love of learning. Our school encourages friendship, respect, independence, community, and celebrates diversity

**What is the VISION for the organisation?**

### At Yarra Primary School:

- Our curriculum is innovative, creative and challenging
- Together we create an encompassing education that prepares students for independence and success
- Our teachers are inspiring, enthusiastic and motivating people who work together to deliver a quality education
- We have a respectful, caring, fun and safe learning environment based on shared values
- We value and maximize our technology, resources and facilities to continuously improve
- Our community is valued, committed and engaged

**What are the VALUES of the organisation?**

Respect, Caring, Commitment

**What are the CRITICAL SUCCESS FACTORS?**

- Student learning (strategic professional learning, recruiting the right staff, working as a team, commitment to continuous improvement)
- Student engagement and wellbeing (engaging curriculum, safe, respectful, caring environment)
- Student pathways and transitions
- Strong and supportive leadership, sound management (including financial management) and effective and open communication
- Positive community relationships
- Increased enrolments

**Who are the PEOPLE (individuals and groups) working in the organisation?**

- Students
- Teachers
- Principal
- Specialists
- Administrative staff
- YOSH staff
- SSOs
- School Council
- Specialists
- YOSH providers
- Volunteers

**What are the PROCESSES (sequences of actions) that enable the organisation to achieve its purpose and serve its clients?**

- Budgeting and resourcing
- Safety & discipline, incident reporting
- School Planning
- Curriculum Planning
- Fundraising
- Program Development
- Transition – K to P, 6 to 7
- Professional development
- Welfare and well-being
- Assessment and reporting
- Meetings (staff, Team, Class Liaison, School Council)
- Recruitment (Staff, Principal)
- Task allocation
- Junior School Council
- Excursions & Camps
- Enrolments
- Staff Induction
- Networks
- Policy Development
- Financial (purchasing, Cash Books)
- Rolls

**Who are the CLIENTS of the organisation?**

- Parents, carers and families
- High schools

**What are the OUTPUTS and OUTCOMES from the activities of the organisation?**

**Our Graduate Students:**

- Are confident, responsible, self-motivated learners who operate independently or as a member of a team
- Are critical thinkers who are resourceful and inquisitive. They take on challenges, solve problems and adapt to change
- Are accomplished in numeracy and literacy
- Are community minded and environmentally aware global citizens
- Are creative lifelong learners who are confident with technology, history, science, language, the arts and the natural world
- Are resilient, socially capable and have a foundation to live a healthy and happy life

**What are the RESULT MEASURES for the organisation?**

- Student achievement (NAPLAN, feedback and AusVELS teacher assessment)
- Student Satisfaction (attitudes to School Survey)
- Parent Satisfaction (Parent Opinion Survey)
- Number of Enrolments
- Attendance (staff and students)
- Staff satisfaction (including teacher support to improve practice) (Staff Opinion Survey)
- Access to and quality of resources
- Punctuality
- Teaching performance reviews
- School appearance
- Financial performance

© Copyright Quality Learning Australia
Version 3.0 13-Feb-09 Used with permission    www.qla.com.au    Canberra: PO Box 897, Belconnen, ACT 2616  Phone 02 6251 3870 Fax 02 6251 3871
Melbourne: PO Box 624, North Melbourne, Victoria 3051  Phone 03 9370 9944 Fax 03 9370 9955

**Figure 5.2 An example of a school system map showing results measures**

Source: Yarra Primary School, Victoria.

# Deciding what data to collect

Schools and education systems are typically drowning in data. It can be hard to know what data to collect, what way to collect it, how to use the data to achieve desired outcomes, and to identify what additional data might be required to better understand the current situation and/or identify potential problems.

Data are typically required for one of three main purposes:

1. **Monitoring performance**: Data are required to measure system performance, to monitor progress over time. These data measure the degree of improvement over time and can be used to make comparisons with the performance of similar systems. This is most commonly achieved using performance measures and some perception measures.

2. **Adjusting system operation**: Data are required to adjust the operation of key processes within the system, based on changes within the system, its inputs and its environment. This most commonly calls upon process measures, some perception measures, and key input measures.

3. **Understanding system operation and behaviour**: Data are also required to understand the context, inputs, relationships, actions and interactions that exist within and among systems. These data are used for analysis and diagnosis, and can be drawn from performance measures, process measures, perception measures, and input measures.

Each of these purposes is discussed in turn.

## Monitoring performance

Measures used to monitor performance are quantitative in nature. They provide numbers against a range of system characteristics linked to the aim of the system.

Schools, like other organisations, need a suite of performance measures. These can include measures to monitor:

- **Student learning**: these are measures of the outcomes of the core business of the school. They are typically an aggregation of individual student performances that is reported to parents and families;

- **Financial performance** to ensure their financial viability over time; and

> Measures used to monitor performance are quantitative in nature.

- **Perception Measures**: parent and community perceptions, staff perceptions and student perceptions. Each stakeholder group (or representatives from each group) is canvassed regarding their perceptions on key issues, particularly related to the purpose, vision and outcomes of the school.

## Adjusting system operation

Input measures and process measures are used to make adjustments to the operation of the system. In schools, for example, an increase in enrolments (input) usually precipitates adjustments to budgets, class sizes, number of classes, teaching loads and relief arrangements. This key input variable is monitored carefully, as it impacts heavily on a range of school structures and processes.

Input measures and process measures are used to make adjustments to the operation of the system.

At a classroom level, the prior learning of students is a key input variable to teaching and learning programs. Teachers need these data in order to plan learning units to effectively meet the needs of each of their students.

## Understanding system behaviour

We have previously shown that the interactions within a system and its containing systems govern performance much more than the actions of individuals or individual elements within the system. For this reason, data are required to deepen understanding of the context in which a social system exists — the characteristics of containing systems.

Data inform working theories regarding how the system behaves and can allow diagnosis.

Data are also required to understand the nature of the relationships and interactions with the elements of the system and its processes. Collection of such data informs working theories regarding how the system behaves and can allow diagnosis regarding what might be behind unexpected or unsatisfactory performance. These data can also be used to diagnose suspected systemic dysfunction.

At a whole school level, these data will include regular collection and reporting of demographic (people) data, including enrolments, gender, family background, and attendance.

From time to time, it will be necessary to collect data with the specific purpose of analysis or diagnosing some aspect of system behaviour. This is frequently the case when working on improvement projects. Improvement teams or individuals using the Plan–Do–Study–Act cycle can be called upon to investigate specific aspects of a system and its performance. This can call for collecting data specific to an improvement project.

# Selecting the right data

A natural reaction to the need for data is to ask questions such as "Where can we get data on this?" Unfortunately, this is the wrong question. It focusses attention on to how to collect data, rather than on identifying which data will provide the greatest insight into what we are trying to understand.

A better first question is "What is our purpose in seeking this data?", followed by, "What, precisely, would we like to know?" Only when the purpose is crystal clear should the search for data begin.

Start by clarifying the question to be asked of the system so that when it is given voice it truly speaks to the question at hand.

> Managers who don't know how to measure what they want settle for wanting what they can measure.
>
> Russell L. Ackoff et al., 2006, *Management f-Laws: How organizations really work*, Triarchy Press, p. 101.

Only when the purpose is crystal clear should the search for data begin.

# Consistency in measurement: Operational definitions

We introduced the concept of operational definitions in Chapter Four. In creating a definition for a specific concept, we can devise a simple procedure to test for conformance with the definition. For example, we could agree the following definition of neat handwriting:

**Neat Handwriting:**
1. Letters sitting on the line
2. Small letters the same height
3. Tall letters touching the line above
4. No scribble
5. Finger spaces between the words

This definition allows us to test handwriting for conformance and to measure instances of conformance — for example, by counting how many students in a class have letters sitting on the line or how many pieces of writing meet all the criteria.

Operational definitions are also required for measures. Here the aim of preparing an operational definition is to agree a process by which to translate an abstract concept into a measurement.

The aim of preparing an operational definition is to agree a process by which to translate an abstract concept into a measurement.

A clear definition of the process by which the numbers will be assigned to observations is required.

In order to have consistency in measurements, consistency in the process by which numbers are assigned to observations is required. To achieve this, a clear definition of the process by which the numbers will be assigned to observations is required.

> An operational definition is a procedure agreed upon for translation of a concept into a measurement of some kind.
>
> W. Edwards Deming, 1994, *The New Economics: For industry, government and education*, MIT, Massachusetts, p. 108.

Operational definitions help to ensure that data are reliable — measurements will be consistent over time, across different places, and allowing for different people collecting data.

Operational definitions are also cast with the aim of providing data that are valid — well founded and measure what they are supposed to measure (and not something else instead).

 Reliable: the data are consistent when collected in different places, at different times, and by different people.

 Valid: the data are well founded and measure what they are supposed to measure.

Changes to the operational definition will result in different numbers.

Operational definitions are critical to knowing precisely what is being measured and how it is being measured. Changes to the operational definition will result in different numbers.

Some examples of numbers in schools that can require precise operational definitions include:

- School income and expenditure;

- The number of students enrolled on census day;

- Special needs (funded) students;

- The number of students with learning difficulties;

- The number of children living in poverty;

- Test scores; and

- The entry score required for admission to a university course.

Notice that with each of these measures, if the definition or procedure changes, so too will the numbers. For example, change the questions on a test and student results will vary; change the definition of poverty and the number of students living in poverty will change. In each case, making changes to the procedure results in different numbers.

This leads to an interesting and important philosophical point:

> There is no true value of any characteristic, state or condition that is defined in terms of measurement or observation.
>
> W. Edwards Deming, 1994, *The New Economics: For industry, government and education*, MIT, Massachusetts, p. 107.

We cannot know the true value of a child's performance in reading, for example. There is no such thing. We can carry out a procedure (follow an operational definition) to create a measurement, but this only provides an indicator. Such a measurement is not the true value. Change the procedure (change the operational definition) and a new number will be produced.

Similarly, it is not possible to know the true value of a school's performance. Nor can anyone know the true value of the number of students requiring special needs funding. There is no true value of anything derived from observations. All anyone can ever have is an operational definition that results in a number.

*There is no true value of anything derived from observations.*

Another benefit of preparing an operational definition for each measure is to clarify procedures and responsibilities regarding the collection, collation, reporting and use of data. Table 5.2 illustrates the characteristics that can be included in an operational definition for a measure.

A copy of an operational definition template can be found on the QLA web site: www.qla.com.au.

| Operational Definition | |
|---|---|
| **Name** of the Measure | |
| **Purpose**<br>(Why do we measure this?<br>How will the data be used?<br>What decisions and actions will it inform?) | |
| What **type of measure** is it? (Circle one) | Performance / Perception/ Process / Input |
| Who is the **Custodian** of this measure?<br>(Who is accountable for the effective definition<br>and use of this measure?) | |
| **What, precisely, is to be measured?** | |
| Is **sampling** required?<br>If so, what sampling plan is to be used? | |
| **Who will collect** the data? | |
| **When** will the data be collected? | |
| **Where** will the data be collected? | |
| **How** will the data be collected? | |
| Where will the data be **recorded and stored**? | |
| **Who will collate** and present/report the data? | |
| **How** will the data be presented /reported.<br>(Which tool?) | |
| **To whom** will the data be presented /reported. | |
| **Who will analyse** the data? | |
| **Who will take action** on the analysis? | |

Table 5.2 Operational definition template for measures

# Fear and the misuse of data

In order to improve performance, organisations need to develop an understanding of their systems and processes in a way that is as objective and free of personal bias as possible. Subjective data can provide insights into the views, opinions and perceptions of stakeholders in the systems, and measurement enables monitoring of defined characteristics of performance.

Myron Tribus points out that the only legitimate reason to collect data is to inform decision making about what to do next. Taxable income is measured in order to establish how much income tax is to be paid. The number of students enrolled on census day is measured to determine how much money to allocate to a school. Students' prior learning is determined in order to optimise learning programs. Collecting staff feedback on a process guides improvement planning. All these data are used to determine what to do next.

> The only legitimate reason to collect data is to inform decision making about what to do next.

The same principle should be applied to student test scores. Myron Tribus expressed it in this way:

> The only legitimate purpose of an examination is to permit the teacher and learner to work together to decide how to improve the learning process of the student. In other words, the purpose should be for teacher and student to decide what to do next.
>
> Myron Tribus, 1993, "The Transformation of American Education to a System for Continuously Improved Learning", p. 17. Available at http://www.qla.com.au/Papers/5.

Unfortunately, data are frequently misused to rate, rank, humiliate, and demoralise people.

Collecting data is not, of itself, beneficial or harmful. It is what is done with data that really matters. Data can be used to increase understanding and inform decision making; it can also be misused to threaten, intimidate, blame, punish, and create fear in an organisation.

> Data can be misused to threaten, intimidate, blame and punish.

> Figures, like fear, have in many cases become a *weapon* of conventional management. Indeed, figures are often used to *generate* fear.
>
> Henry R. Neave, 1990, *The Deming Dimension*, SPC Press, Knoxville, p. 153. (Emphasis in original).

Deming was adamant that management must drive out fear. Where fear is generated due to the misuse of data, people will be tempted to manipulate data and the true performance of the system will not be understood.

Where there is fear, there will be wrong figures.

W. Edwards Deming, 1982, *Out of the Crisis*, MIT, Massachusetts, p. 266.

There are two dominant weapons to instil fear by misusing numbers: numerical goals (or targets), and rating/ranking.

## Numerical goals (targets)

Numerical goals or targets are used as a driver of improvement by many organisations. Sales targets, production targets, and safety targets are all examples of numerical goals.

In schools, targets are a feature of many planning processes. Schools are required to document targets against the key strategies in their strategic and/or operational plans. These targets may be created using a prescribed formula (for example, five per cent above what was achieved last year), or by the schools themselves establishing the numerical goal.

Numerical goals or targets are only beneficial when all of the following four conditions are met:

1.  The system or process is statistically stable (this is discussed later in this chapter);

2.  The system, including its cause and effect relationships, is clearly understood;

3.  There is a plan (theory) by which it is confidently predicted that the numerical goal will be achieved; and

4.  The plan has the active support of everyone required to take action as part of the plan.

If any one of these conditions is not met, setting numerical goals or targets as a strategy for improvement is simply management by wishing. If the above conditions are met, then there is a theory with methods by which the proposed performance level can be achieved. As the plan is enacted, the theory can be tested.

Numerical goals that do not meet above conditions usually drive dysfunctional behaviour. Some years ago, Brian Joiner identified three ways to proceed when it appears that a numerical goal is unlikely to be met:

1.  Distort the data;

2.  Distort the system; and

3.  Work to improve the system.

---

*Sidenote:* Numerical goals or targets are used as a driver of improvement by many organisations.

*Sidenote:* If certain conditions are not met, setting numerical goals or targets as a strategy for improvement is simply management by wishing.

Distorting the data can be done in many ways: move funds from one account to another; falsify the figures; change the operational definitions; work around the system so that certain data are not collected.

Distorting the system is also easy: encourage low achieving students to stay home on the day of the national or state test; teach to the test — focus only on literacy or numeracy in the classroom, as these are the skills that will be tested, rather than providing a more balanced approach to development of the child.

Clearly, the first two of the options above will result in wrong figures. Where there is fear, people can feel so pressured that they sacrifice their personal integrity in order to present the required numbers.

> Where there is fear, people can feel so pressured that they sacrifice their personal integrity in order to present the required numbers.

This is not to suggest that numerical goals should never be used. They can provide focus and inspiration. However, they should not be used to threaten, intimidate or punish people.

There is a bigger reason to approach numerical goals with caution: sub-optimisation. Setting numerical goals to optimise one part of the system is likely to result in sub-optimisation of the system as a whole. Myron Tribus summarised the problem of numerical goals in his perversity principle:

> Setting numerical goals to optimise one part of the system is likely to result in sub-optimisation of the system as a whole.

> If you try to improve the performance
> of a system of people, machines and procedures
> by setting numerical goals for the
> improvement of individual parts of the system
> the system will defeat you and
> you will pay a price
> where you least expected to.

Myron Tribus, 1992, "The Germ Theory of Management", p. 16. Available at http://www.qla.com.au/Papers/5.

## Rating and ranking

Sometimes the concepts of rating and ranking are not clearly understood. For the purpose of this discussion, we propose the following definitions.

 Rate: to appraise or estimate something's worth or value.

 Rank: to assign something to a particular position or classification relative to other things of the same type.

The rating and ranking of performance are dysfunctional approaches to driving improvement. Proponents of these approaches are of the belief that such approaches will motivate people to use improvement methods, which they must currently be withholding.

Rating and ranking performance is widespread within and among education systems. Schools frequently rate student performance based on numbers that have been assigned, usually by some form of assessment or test. The score is used as a numerical estimate or indicator of student achievement.

Rating can be useful, but only if used to decide what to do next. A test score of 67 per cent is relatively meaningless on its own. What does a student do with such a rating? They usually do nothing; they just move on. What does a teacher do with this rating? Teachers usually record the ratings in their mark books and move on. Knowing which areas have been mastered and which require further attention is far more useful as it allows learner and teacher to decide what to do next.

Ratings are frequently converted to rankings. If every student in a class is rated, then they can be classified as A, B, C, D or E (or according to some other classification system). They can also be placed, or ranked, in order from best performance to worst performance. The results (and, frequently, teacher perceptions of the students) can be placed in rank order, from the top of the class to the bottom. In this way, students are assigned to a particular position on the class list. Such rank ordered lists are sometimes called league tables.

Ranking performance is easy. Most seven-year-olds have learned to put numbers in order from largest to smallest. There are much better ways to analyse and report system performance, some of which will be explored in the second half of this chapter. For now, it is sufficient to make the point that it is not possible to manage and improve a system by applying the mathematics of seven-year-olds. More sophisticated thinking is required.

Ranking is an inadequate and destructive approach to performance reporting for the following reasons:

1. **No true value**: No true value is derived from measurement or observation. At best, a measurement is a form of estimate of a chosen characteristic — in this case, performance. The estimate may be a good one, or it may be quite inadequate. Ranking is of estimates, not of true values;

2. **Measures are reflective of system performance, not the performance of individuals**: The stronger influence on performance in any system is the performance of the system itself, not the individuals within the system. Any attempt to rate the performance of elements of a system, including the individuals within it, is really an exercise in rating the performance of the system. It is almost impossible to separate the performance of the elements from the systemic factors impacting upon them. (Most teachers know, in their hearts, that when they grade student tests they are really grading their systems of learning rather than student achievement);

3. **There is variation in all systems and measurements**: Systems abound with causes of variation. Every measurement is subject to variation, within the system and within the measurement process. This means that any method of rating and then ranking performance will be subject to variation. If the measurement upon which the ranking is based was repeated, the numbers would be different to those first collected and the rank order would consequently be different. The degree of difference in the ranking will be dependent on the amount of variation in the system and in the measurement process;

4. **Focussing on the top or bottom performers diverts attention away from improving the system**: Once items are placed in rank order, the natural tendency is to focus on those at the bottom and the top of the rank-ordered list. Effort is diverted from improving performance of the system as a whole and towards chasing deficiencies in the most poorly ranked and, sometimes, praising the efforts of the most highly ranked. Poor performers can be stigmatised while high performers are applauded and unhealthy dynamics between people are encouraged; and

5. **Ranking does not improve the system**: Placing students in rank order of performance does nothing to improve performance of the students or the systems in which they operate. Similarly, rank-ordering of schools does nothing to improve those schools or the school system as a whole.

Even if a method were developed to rank people with precision and certainty, distinct from the process that they work in, why would anyone suppose that this would improve people or the process?

Source: W. Edwards Deming, 1993, *The New Economics: For industry, government and education*, MIT, Cambridge, p. 118.

## RATING SCHOOL PERFORMANCE

The My School web site was launched in Australia in early 2010. It provides profiles of all Australian schools — nearly 10,000 in total — and reports their performance based on the Australian National Assessment Program – Literacy and Numeracy (NAPLAN). NAPLAN tests students in five areas: reading, writing, spelling, grammar and punctuation, and numeracy. Students in years 3, 5, 7 and 9 are tested each year.

The day after the My School web site was launched, various newspapers around Australia published the performance of schools as a series of league tables: listing schools in order from highest to lowest score in the learning areas. The political, media and community debate resulting from this was heated, and continues to this day.

An Australian Government Parliamentary Inquiry was established into "the conflicting claims made by Government, educational experts and peak bodies in relation to publication of the NAPLAN results". The committee received over 250 submissions and submitted its report in November 2010, making 12 recommendations.

The first recommendation relates to "ways in which to use below-average NAPLAN test results as a trigger for immediate assistance at helping individual schools and students perform at appropriate levels". We hope that policy makers realise that this has implications for half the students and half the schools in the country (a good estimate of the proportion that will be below average). As we shall see later in this chapter, targeting below average schools and students will do nothing to improve the system.

Recommendation seven relates to the need to prevent cheating by more strongly "enforcing security protocols". Evidence of cheating is evidence that there is fear about not achieving numerical goals. Individuals can feel compelled to sacrifice their personal integrity in order to avoid negative consequences. It's disappointing that the response was focussed on increasing policing in such a way, rather than acting to reduce fear.

Recommendation nine addressed "ways to mitigate the harm caused by simplistic and often distorted information published in newspaper league tables". Fortunately, the committee has recognised that publishing league tables is harmful. According to the revised terms of use of the site, publishing league tables is no longer lawful.

# The unknown and unknowable

Education systems around the world pay a great deal of attention to figures and numbers. Deming was fond of quoting Lloyd Nelson, another prominent statistician:

> The most important figures needed for management of any organisation are unknown and unknowable.
>
> Cited in W. Edwards Deming, 1982, *Out of the Crisis*, MIT, Massachusetts, p. 20.

It is not possible to measure everything that is important.

It is not possible to measure everything that is important. This may seem a peculiar concept, particularly coming from statisticians. Perhaps a few examples may illustrate the point. How could anyone possibly quantify:

- The benefits to a child and society that come from a teacher who truly cares about the development and learning of a child and who demonstrates this care to the child;

- The benefits to children and society that comes from a school that does whatever it takes to ensure that all children learn at school;

- The impact on enrolments and school revenue from unhappy parents telling others of their dissatisfaction with the school;

- The improvements in student learning and teacher capacity that come from effective professional learning;

- The impact on community perceptions of the school that are derived from the manner in which school administrators answer the telephone and greet visitors;

- The impact on a student when a teacher makes an off-hand, caustic remark;

- The impact on a teacher when a principal makes an off-hand, caustic remark;

- The loss to an individual teacher and society at large when a teacher burns out or leaves the profession;

- The loss to a student and society at large when a school does not have effective processes to intervene when a child begins to disengage with formal schooling;

- The missed opportunity from badly run meetings; or

- The missed opportunity from unclear purpose or lack of vision?

An organisation cannot be managed on numbers alone.

While numbers are needed to inform decision making, an organisation cannot be managed on numbers alone.

It is wrong to suppose that if you can't measure it, you can't manage it — a costly myth.

W. Edwards Deming, 1993, *The New Economics: For industry, government and education,* MIT, Cambridge, p. 36.

We can manage what we cannot measure.

Each of the examples given above is impossible to quantify. While it may be possible to estimate a numerical value, such estimates are unlikely to be reliable. This does not prevent managers seeking to minimise negative impacts and maximise the positive. It is possible to manage what cannot be measured by attentively managing systems; we can manage what we cannot measure.

As an example, in order to address off-hand, caustic remarks made about students or members of staff, leaders can model positive interactions and create leadership systems that make it culturally unacceptable for this to occur.

# Reflection questions

**?** What do you understand by the expression "data are the voice of the system?" What are the implications of this?

**?** Which of the following measures are used by your organisation? Can you give specific examples of: performance measures, process measures, perception measures, and input measures?

**?** How are these types of measures used across your whole organisation and within sub-systems?

**?** What examples of important characteristics of your system that cannot be measured — are unknown and unknowable — can you think of? How might each of these be managed?

**?** How does your organisation manage operational definitions for measures?

**?** Where are targets or numerical goals used in your organisation? Can you think of where they have resulted in distortion of data or of the system?

**?** What do you observe to be the effects of rating and ranking? Why?

# Quality learning tools for data

Each of the following tools can be used to support the use of data to better understand and improve systems.

 Radar chart

A radar chart, sometimes called a web diagram, is a way to display data from many measures on one chart over time.

The radar chart is comprised of spokes, or radii, each representing one performance measure. Data are plotted on each radii and connected with adjacent data points by a line.

A radar chart can be used to report the key performance measures for a system.

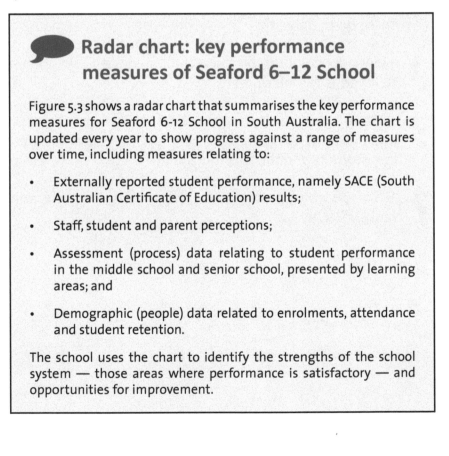

## Radar chart: key performance measures of Seaford 6–12 School

Figure 5.3 shows a radar chart that summarises the key performance measures for Seaford 6-12 School in South Australia. The chart is updated every year to show progress against a range of measures over time, including measures relating to:

- Externally reported student performance, namely SACE (South Australian Certificate of Education) results;

- Staff, student and parent perceptions;

- Assessment (process) data relating to student performance in the middle school and senior school, presented by learning areas; and

- Demographic (people) data related to enrolments, attendance and student retention.

The school uses the chart to identify the strengths of the school system — those areas where performance is satisfactory — and opportunities for improvement.

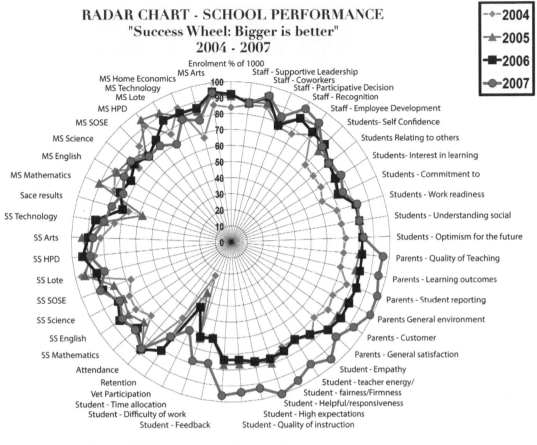

**Figure 5.3 Radar chart: school performance**

Source: Seaford 6–12 School, SA.

 **Structured brainstorming**

Structured brainstorming can be used to collect qualitative data.

Most people have participated in some form of brainstorming activity: an idea or question is posed and individuals contribute ideas.

Structured brainstorming is a little different. While it begins with an idea or question to be explored, before any ideas are shared, each participant individually and silently collects their thoughts and creates a list of the ideas they would like to contribute. Once the individual reflection is completed, each individual in the group contributes one — and only one — idea in turn until everyone has had their turn to contribute. An individual can choose not to contribute an idea by saying "pass".

Once everyone has had a turn, the cycle commences again, and each person is given another opportunity to contribute an idea, and so on, until all ideas have been recorded. If someone chooses to pass at any time, they still have a later opportunity to contribute when it is their turn.

A useful addition to the process is to have everyone write down each idea as they are submitted. When the brainstorming session is completed, everyone has the same list in front of them.

As with more common forms of brainstorming, criticism or discussion of others' ideas is not permitted. Only clarification can be sought — for example, "what do you mean by … ?"

Structured brainstorming is an effective tool for quickly gathering a comprehensive set of qualitative data. It has several advantages over traditional brainstorming:

- People who need time to get their ideas together before being asked to contribute are given this time, free of distractions;

- The period of individual reflection prior to sharing ideas can increase the diversity of ideas, ideas that might otherwise not arise or might be lost through the brainstorming process;

- Everyone has a chance to contribute; and

- Everyone has a chance to be heard.

Structured brainstorming is a tool that can give voice to the silent majority, while giving perspective to a vocal minority.

**Figure 5.4 Students using structured brainstorming to input to their vision for a perfect school**

Source: Hallett Cove R-12 School, SA.

# ✂ Affinity diagram

An affinity diagram is a practical tool for organising qualitative data.

Each idea is recorded on a separate card or sticky note. These can be collected using structured brainstorming.

The cards or sticky notes are laid out so that everyone can read them, often on large pieces of flip chart paper. They are then sorted into groups, with the ideas clustered according to common themes. We agree with David Langford's recommendation that the sorting be completed in silence, which prevents individuals dominating the group.

Once the cards or sticky notes are sorted into groups, a heading can be placed on each group that describes the key theme of that group. We sometimes find it helpful to have the team also write a phrase or sentence that summarises the key messages of that group of sticky notes.

**Figure 5.5 Students create an affinity diagram from the ideas of students, staff and parents**

Source: A primary school in NSW.

# ⚒ Measures selection matrix

A measures selection matrix provides a structured approach for determining what to measure when considering a specific topic or concept. The measures selection matrix can be used to determine measures of any type: performance, process, perception, and input measures.

In the first column of the matrix, a list of possible measures is brainstormed in response to the following question:

If we could measure anything we wanted, what would we like to be able to measure that would enable us to:

- Monitor performance of … now and into the future?

- Plot the perceptions of … on the issue of … over time?

- Track the frequency of occurrence of the most significant potential problems in the … process?

- Track the most important characteristics of … (key input variable) over time?

The choice of which specific question to ask will depend upon the type of measures to be selected: performance, perception, process, or input measures.

Once the list of possible measures has been created, these are prioritised (using the second column of the matrix), frequently using a multi-voting or hot dot tool (see Chapter Four). The aim is to identify the smallest possible number of measures that will provide an answer for the question.

For each of the selected measures, consideration is then given to determining how, when and where the data might be collected. This (third) column provides the beginning of the operational definition for the measure.

| WHAT to measure? (What would you like to be able to measure that will allow you to determine performance now and in the future?) | Prioritise (Hot Dot) | HOW to Measure? (What methods will you use to collect and how will you display the data?) | Comments (e.g. What do you predict the data will show?) |
|---|---|---|---|
| | | | |
| | | | |
| | | | |
| | | | |
| | | | |
| | | | |
| | | | |
| | | | |

**Measures Selection Matrix**

© Copyright 2015 QLA. Issue 2.0

New Zealand:  PO Box 1850, Wellington, 6140  Phone +64 273 021 747

Australia: PO Box 624, North Melbourne, Victoria 3051  Phone +61 3 9370 9944 Fax +61 3 9370 9955

learning • improvement

www.qla.com.au

**Figure 5.6 Measures selection matrix template**

A copy of this measures selection matrix template is available at www.qla.com.au

# Variation

Variation relates to the following principle of the theory of improvement:

Systems and processes are subject to variation that affects predictability and performance.

As has been discussed, taking measurements is a process of assigning numbers to observations. Observations relate to system characteristics and numbers are assigned to represent these characteristics. Any measurements taken from a system will be different from one to another. For example, a bank balance will usually change from day to day or week to week; test scores will be different for different students and will change with each test. These differences are referred to as system variation. They can make the interpretation of data difficult, and can lead to common traps.

System variation is observed within groups, between groups, and over time.

- **Within groups**: such as the students within a class, or schools within a district. For any items within a group, there are differences in the measurement of any characteristic.

- **Between groups**: such as between classes or between districts. For any group of items, there are differences in the measurements of the characteristics of the group.

- **Over time**: such as changes in perceptions or performance from year to year. Measurements of any characteristic of an item or group will change with time.

The challenge lies in understanding what these observations reveal about system behaviour and performance. This understanding can provide more useful insight than trying to explain differences from one single measurement to another. An important first step to achieve this understanding is to examine system performance with the aid of graphs and charts.

To do so, we turn to statistical thinking, which stresses the use of data as the voice of a system. Listening to this voice and responding accordingly to the variation it reveals is essential for the system to be optimised and improved.

Any measurements taken from a system will be different from one to another.

System variation is observed within groups, between groups and over time.

# What is statistical thinking?

The following definition of statistical thinking is based upon the work of the American Society for Quality.

> Statistical thinking: a philosophy of learning and action based on the following fundamental principles: all work occurs in a system of interconnected processes; variation exists in all processes; understanding and responding appropriately to variation are keys to success.

At the heart of statistical thinking is recognition that there is more benefit to be derived from seeking to understand the behaviour of a system than from seeking to attach a meaning to each and every data point.

In the absence of statistical thinking, people commonly fall into the following traps:

- Relying on averages to make comparisons and ignoring the variation behind the averages;

- Comparing individual results against a group average, thereby failing to acknowledge that about half the results will be above average and half will be below average;

- Comparing one single value against another single value, drawing conclusions about trends from only two data points and ignoring natural variation;

- Blaming individuals for poor performance and not recognising that most of the performance is driven by the system itself, not the individuals within the system; and

- Setting arbitrary numerical goals or targets.

These traps can be avoided with a proper understanding of the nature and impact of variation on system and processes.

> There is more benefit to be derived from seeking to understand the behaviour of a system than from seeking to attach meaning to each and every data point.

**RELYING ON AVERAGES IS AVERAGE ... AND SOMETIMES MEAN**

The problem with relying on averages is that they can mask or hide extremes that might lie within the data that, if seen, would lead to very different action. My feet may be in the freezer and my head in the oven but, on average, I can be a healthy temperature.

While we often use the term "average" when we add together all of our results and divide it by the sum of the total number of marks, statistically this is correctly known as the "arithmetic mean", or simply the "mean".

The "median" is the central point of a data set. To find the median, you would list all data points in order from largest to smallest, and then pick the entry in the middle of the list.

# Revealing the variation in systems: Preparing graphs or charts

The use of graphs and charts can help us to visualise the variation in a set of data.

The use of graphs and charts can help us to visualise the variation in a set of data.

Consider the following example. The data in Table 5.3 show test scores for a class of students, presented in alphabetical order like a teacher's mark book.

| Name | Test Score | Name | Test Score |
|------|-----------|------|-----------|
| Alejandro | 49 | Leonida | 13 |
| Bradford | 49 | Lyndon | 53 |
| Buena | 58 | Many | 33 |
| Charissa | 82 | Mitzi | 83 |
| Claude | 94 | Monnie | 39 |
| Delmar | 58 | Obdulia | 64 |
| Delmer | 28 | Regena | 59 |
| Derick | 43 | Selma | 62 |
| Echo | 54 | Shanae | 43 |
| Edythe | 48 | Solange | 49 |
| Elizebeth | 59 | Somer | 80 |

| Name | Test Score | Name | Test Score |
|---|---|---|---|
| Faustino | 77 | Stephaine | 54 |
| Grazyna | 48 | Sterling | 59 |
| Jaquelyn | 53 | Ta | 28 |
| Jeniffer | 54 | Tasha | 28 |
| Jose | 74 | Willodean | 19 |
| Kam | 28 | Yulanda | 53 |
| Kathline | 49 | Zachery | 43 |
| Latashia | 39 | | |

Table 5.3 Student individual test scores

A traditional response to such a set of data would be to seek out the largest and smallest numbers: What was the highest score? What was the lowest score?

Having found these extremes, the next step is to check the names to see if the good and bad results have come from the students (or schools) expected. This approach reinforces a focus on individual observations rather than consideration of the output of the system as a whole — potentially blaming individuals rather than the system for the outcomes or performance observed.

> A traditional response to such a set of data would be to seek out the largest and smallest numbers.

What if these test scores are plotted as a dot plot?

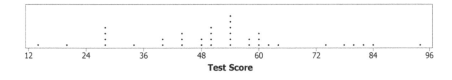

Figure 5.7 Dot plot of test scores

The range of values — the variation in the data — is now immediately apparent, as is the middle value. It is also apparent that the data are spread fairly evenly across the range, there are no large clusters of results. Finally, there are no apparent outliers: results that are significantly different to the rest.

These data can also be plotted as a histogram or frequency chart.

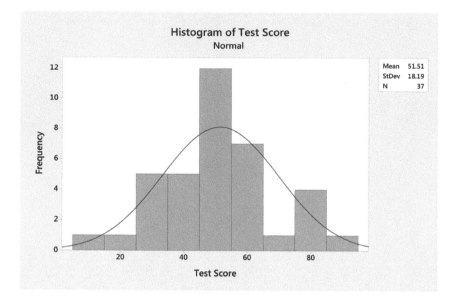

**Figure 5.8 Histogram of test scores**

A histogram or frequency chart makes variation in the data clearly visible. Like the dot plot, the histogram shows the range of data, the way in which the test scores are distributed across this range, any tight clustering, and any outliers.

In this instance, the test score data appear to have more points clustered around the middle than the edges, and there do not appear to be any outliers.

Both of these graphs offer significantly more rapid insight into the performance of the system than the column of figures presented in Table 5.1, including:

- The range of the data is immediately apparent without needing to look through the list of figures to find the largest and smallest values;

- The middle point can be quickly identified; and

- The nature of the spread from smallest to largest value is evident — there are no clusters of similar numbers, the spread is even, and there are no outliers.

Graphs and charts make interpretation of data much easier. For this reason, it is always advisable to plot data rather than examine tables of numbers.

Once the data have been displayed in this way, knowledge is required to interpret it and respond appropriately to the system variation present.

# Special and common cause variation

Variation is evident in all systems. No two things are exactly identical.

Consider, for example, the standard AA size battery, which has been around for over a century. AA size batteries are 50 mm long and 14 mm in diameter, as defined by international standards. They all look the same and are perfectly interchangeable. Yet each individual battery cannot be exactly 50 mm long and exactly 14 mm in diameter. Most people don't care that one battery is 50.013 mm long and another is 49.957 mm long; both will fit perfectly well in their flash light or remote control. To detect these differences, precise measuring equipment is required. Yet the variation remains.

The length of any AA battery is determined by the manufacturing process. A factory will produce batteries with a length that has a calculable mean, an observable spread, and a clustering of lengths around the mean, all of which are determined by the manufacturing process.

## 📌 NO TWO REAL THINGS ARE IDENTICAL

While two real things are never identical, we may think of them as being identical when our measurement system is unable to detect difference, or when any differences are of no practical significance.

For other measures, variation is more evident. The average height of an Australian 13-year-old boy is approximately 156 cm. Very few 13-year-old boys are precisely 156 cm tall, but nearly all will be within about three cm of this average height. These are the natural limits of variation; a normal 13 year old boy's height falls naturally within a range of heights centered at 156 cm and varying up to about three cm above and below this value.

All processes and systems exhibit natural variation. In both these examples, a battery's dimensions and the height of a 13-year-old boy, the characteristic being measured is different from observation to observation. Yet, as a set of observations they conform to a defined distribution, in this case the normal distribution.

## WHAT'S NORMAL ABOUT "NORMAL" DISTRIBUTION AND NATURAL ABOUT "NATURAL" LIMITS OF VARIATION?

A normal distribution reveals the natural limits of variation for the system under study: the expected range that any of the data points will fall within under normal circumstances.

For example, if we were asked to bet on whether a 13-year-old boy's height would fall within the range of heights centred at 156 cm and varying up to about three cm above and below this value, we would be 99.9 per cent sure we would win.

It is the system that produces natural variation.

The factors that cause this variation, from observation to observation, come from the system. In the case of AA batteries, it is the system of manufacturing; variation in the height of 13-year-old boys comes from genetic, societal and environmental factors. Either way, it is the system that produces natural variation.

To understand this variation, it is necessary to understand the system. No examination of individual examples can explain the system.

## Common cause variation

Variation observed in any system comes from a diverse and multitudinous number of possible causes. The fishbone diagram (introduced in Chapter Three) can be used to document the many possible causes of variation. The fishbone diagram in Figure 5.9, for example, lists possible causes of variation in student performance.

Causes that affect every observation, to greater or lesser degrees, are called common causes.

Each of the causes shown in Figure 5.9 affects every student to a greater or lesser degree. Students respond to each cause in different ways, so the impact is different for each student. For example, some students may be sensitive to background noise while others are not. Some students may struggle to balance family responsibilities, work and school, while for others this not an issue. All students will be affected to some degree by their prior learning and their attitude towards the subject matter. The key point, however, is that every student may be affected to some degree by every cause. It is how all of the causes come together for each individual student that results in the variation in student achievement observed across the class. Causes that affect every observation, to greater or lesser degrees, are called common causes.

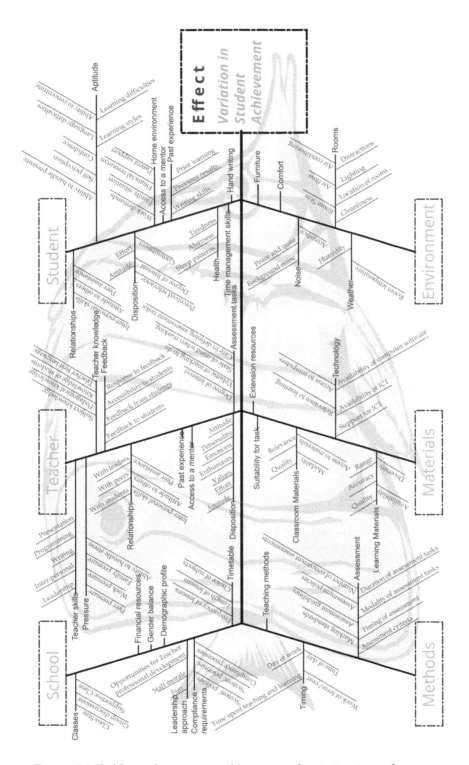

Figure 5.9 Fishbone diagram: possible causes of variation in student performance

Common cause variation: the variation inherent in a system, which is always present as the net result of many influences, most of which are unknown.

In general, it is the combination of the common causes of variation coming together uniquely for each observation that results in the distribution in the set of data points. Not surprisingly, this distribution is frequently a normal distribution. That is, the set of observations conform to a defined distribution.

For any single data point — for example a single student's test result — it is not possible to identify a single cause that led to the result achieved. Importantly, it is not worth trying to identify any such single cause.

This system of common causes determines the behaviour and performance of the system. In this case, it is a system of learning — the classroom. These causes include the actions and interactions among the elements of the system as well as features of the structure of the system and those of the containing systems.

Student effort is only one of the many causes of variation in student achievement.

## Special cause variation

The other type of variation is special cause variation.

When a cause can be identified as having an outstanding and isolated effect on any individual observation — such as a student being late to school on the morning of the assessment — this is called special cause variation or assignable cause variation. A specific reason can be assigned to the observed variation.

Special cause variation: variation that is unusual and unpredictable, which can be the result of a unique event or circumstance, and which can be attributed to some knowable influence. Also known as assignable cause variation.

Special causes of variation are identifiable events or situations that produce specific results that are out of the ordinary.

Special causes of variation are identifiable events or situations that produce specific results that are out of the ordinary. These out of the ordinary results may be single points of data beyond the natural limits of variation of the system, or they may be observable patterns or trends in the data.

Where there is evidence of special cause variation in a set of data, it is always worth investigating. The impact of a special cause may be detrimental, in which case it may be appropriate to seek to prevent occurrence of this cause within the system. The impact of a special cause may also be positive, in which case it may be worth pursuing how this cause can be harnessed to improve system performance.

Special causes provide opportunities to learn. The lesson might be as mundane as "that batch of electrolyte was contaminated", or it might be as exciting as the discovery of penicillin, or a new strategy for learning.

There are two key concepts that are fundamental to responding to system variation appropriately: stability and capability. Where these concepts are not understood, attempts to improve performance frequently make things worse.

# System stability

System stability relates to the degree to which the performance of any system is predictable — that the next data point will fall randomly within the natural limits of variation.

A formal definition can provide a useful starting point for exploring this important concept.

> Stability: a system is said to be stable when the observations fall randomly within the natural limits of variation for that system and conform to a defined distribution, frequently a normal distribution.

## System stability and variation within groups

All systems exhibit variation in all types of data: results, perceptions, processes, and inputs.

Consider, for example, the student results in Figure 5.10, which show the reading scores for 103 students attending an Australian high school. Each student was tested as part of NAPLAN when they were in Year 7.

System stability relates to the degree to which the performance of any system is predictable.

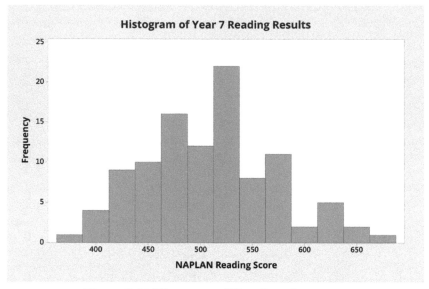

**Figure 5.10 Histogram of Year 7 reading scores**

Source: Prepared by QLA from NAPLAN individual student scores provided by an Australian high school.

The histogram shows the variation in student performance, from which we can see:

- The mean score is approximately 510 points; and

- the data seem to be roughly normally distributed, as there is a stronger cluster of scores around the mean score, and the curve appears roughly bell shaped.

## How do I know if my data are normal?

A statistical test can be used to consider if a set of data is normally distributed: a normal probability plot (see Figure 5.11). If all the data points on the plot fall in a straight line and appear within the two outer lines (confidence intervals), then we can be fairly confident that the data are normally distributed. (More correctly, when the data points remain within the confidence intervals, we have no grounds to suggest that the data are not normally distributed). When a statistical test, known as the Anderson-Darling test, produces a "p-value" greater than 0.005 we can accept that the data are normally distributed, which is the case in Figure 5.11.

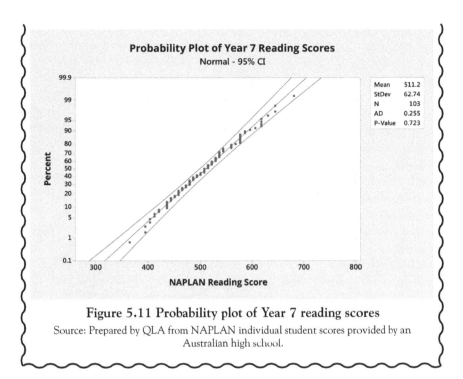

**Figure 5.11 Probability plot of Year 7 reading scores**
Source: Prepared by QLA from NAPLAN individual student scores provided by an
Australian high school.

A stable system produces predictable results within the natural limits of variation for that system.

If we use the histogram to study the variation in student NAPLAN results, we can assume that, if there were additional students in that group, their results would very likely fall within the distribution shown.

Furthermore, if nothing is done to change a stable system, it is rational to predict that future NAPLAN reading performances will be similar, both in the mean or average performance and in the range of variation evident in the results.

The histogram in Figure 5.12 shows the grammar scores of the same group of Year 7 students. Here the mean score is about 500 points.

However, notice here the presence of a single student with a score of approximately 100. This data point appears to be an outlier: it is noticeably different to the other data points.

A stable system produces predictable results.

If nothing is done to change a stable system, future performance will be similar.

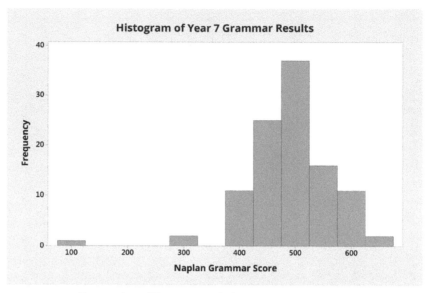

**Figure 5.12 Histogram of Year 7 grammar scores**

Source: Prepared by QLA from NAPLAN individual student scores provided by an Australian high school.

One could reasonably assume that this data point represents something out of the ordinary, that the causes that led to this result are different to those experienced by the remainder of the system.

Where specific causes can be identified they are called special causes or assignable causes.

Given that this data point is so different to the others, investigation is called for, and is likely to reveal a specific reason, an assignable cause. Where specific causes can be identified, they are called special causes or assignable causes. In this instance, investigation revealed that this student had scored about 200 points below expectation due to illness on the day of the test.

These examples of system stability, within groups, relate to measures of student learning at a particular point in time. Variation within a group of schools can also be examined.

Figure 5.13 shows a histogram of the mean Year 3 student NAPLAN reading score of each school in the Australian Capital Territory in 2009.

Figure 5.13 suggests that schools' performance of Year 3 reading in the ACT is stable. There do not appear to be any schools that are performing outside the natural limits of variation for this system of schools.

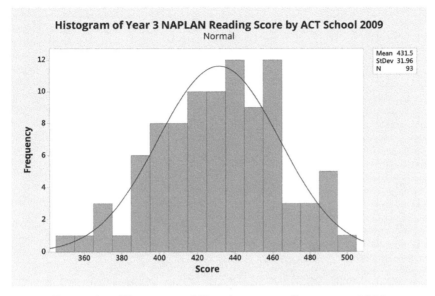

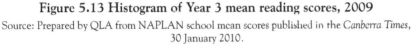

**Figure 5.13 Histogram of Year 3 mean reading scores, 2009**

Source: Prepared by QLA from NAPLAN school mean scores published in the *Canberra Times*, 30 January 2010.

Using the same logic as before, we can also conclude that, just as the Australian population raises 13-year-old boys with a height of approximately 156 cm, give or take about 3 cm, the current ACT school system produces schools with a Year 3 average reading scores of approximately 430, give or take about 100.

## System stability and variation between groups

The variation that is evident between groups is often of great interest. For example, we may be interested in variation between classes of the same grade or year, or between schools in different districts or states.

In these instances, the focus is no longer on variation within a set of data points, but upon differences in variation that is evident between groups (multiple sets) of data points.

Consider, for example, the sets of histograms presented in Figures 5.14 and 5.15. Both come from the same primary school, and both represent the growth in students' scores in key learning areas, as measured by NAPLAN, over the two-year period from Year 3 to Year 5.

> The variation that is evident between groups is often of great interest.

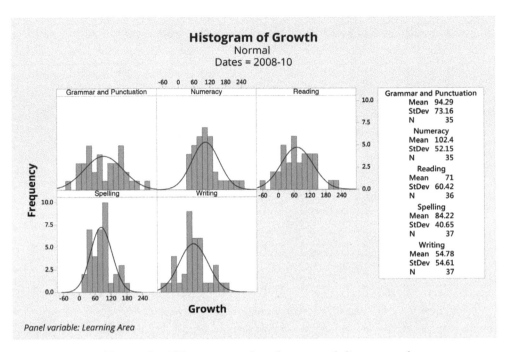

**Figure 5.14 Histograms of student growth literacy and numeracy,
Year 3–5, 2008–2010**

Source: Prepared by QLA from NAPLAN individual student scores provided by an Australian
primary school.

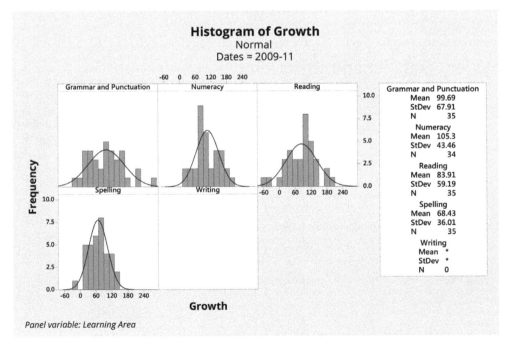

**Figure 5.15 Histograms of growth, Year 3–5, 2009–2011**

Source: Prepared by QLA from NAPLAN individual student scores provided by an Australian
primary school.

The first group of students (Figure 5.14) was initially tested in 2008, when the students were in Year 3. This same group of students was tested again in 2010, when they were in Year 5. The histograms show the difference, or growth, in scores over that two-year period.

The second group of students (Figure 5.15) is a year younger. These students were tested in 2009, when they were in Year 3, and again in 2011, when they were in Year 5. (Due to differences in the testing of writing between 2009 and 2011, growth in this area was not evaluated for the second group).

Has one group of students performed better than the other? These data look very similar. Analysis fails to show any significant difference between these two groups of students in either the mean score or variation for each of the four learning areas.

With two different groups of students, this school produced essentially the same results in terms of student growth over the two two-year periods. The data are practically the same for each group, only the names of the students are different.

Consider the scores for grammar and punctuation, for example. For both groups of students, the system produced a mean score of about 95 and a range from approximately -70 to 250. It appears the system produced consistent results with a mean growth of approximately 95 points and natural limits of variation plus or minus approximately 160. The story is similar for the other three learning areas.

We can reasonably predict that, unless something changes significantly at this school, the next group of students will again produce almost identical results. The system is thus said to be stable — the points fall predictably between the natural limits of variation for the system.

This is further evidence that it is the system that produces behaviour and performance, not the individuals in the system. In this example, the system produced the same growth results with two different groups of students. If the school wishes to see changes in performance, then it must set about improving the systems of learning.

> The system is said to be stable when the points fall predictably between the natural limits of variation for the system.

## System stability and variation over time

### Variation in single measures over time

Outliers, trends and unusual observations in time-series data can indicate the presence of special cause variation. Where these exist, the system is not stable.

So far we have used the histogram to help us to study variation in a system. We can also study system variation by plotting data as a time series using a run chart (or line graph) as in Figure 5.16. Here student attendance is plotted over weekly intervals for 22 weeks.

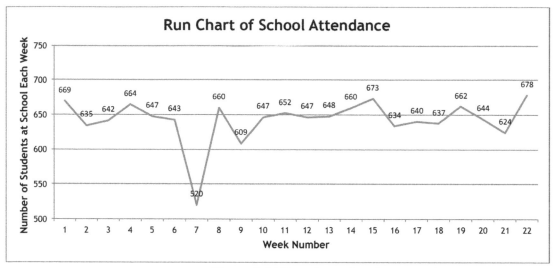

**Figure 5.16 Run chart of student attendance**

Notice the dip in attendance at week seven. One could reasonably seek an explanation and learn that it was, for example, the week of the Year 8 school camp, or an outbreak of influenza that lead to a decrease in student attendance. These would be examples of special cause variation.

Instances of special cause variation in time series data can be revealed by patterns or trends in the data, including:

- A series of consecutive data points that sequentially improve or deteriorate; and

- An uncommonly high number of data points above or below the average.

If there is an unexplained pattern in the data, this is evidence of special cause variation and investigation is justified. Such a system is said to be unstable.

If special cause variation is absent, future performance can be predicted with confidence. This performance will fall within the natural limits of variation for that process. If special cause variation is absent, or the presence of any special causes is explained, and system performance can be confidently predicted, the system is said to be stable.

If there is an unexplained pattern in the data, this is evidence of special cause variation and investigation is justified. Such a system is said to be unstable.

Where unusual data points or trends have not been explained, any predictions of future performance will be less reliable. In such cases, the system is said to be unstable. Confident prediction is not possible for an unstable system.

Confident prediction is not possible for an unstable system.

Consider again the example of school attendance shown in Figure 5.16. Allowing for the special cause (the occurrence of the school camp) for the anomalous data for week seven, the attendance appears to vary between about 600 and 680 students. These appear to be the natural limits of variation for this system over this period. There are no apparent trends or patterns in the data, so one can be confident that this system is stable. Next week, the attendance is highly likely to be between these natural limits of variation, 600 and 680.

### How many data points constitute a trend?

A trend is a pattern observed in the variation of data over time that suggests a drift or change of course. We frequently look for trends in data as evidence of improvement.

As a rule of thumb, eight or more data points are required to see a trend.

If we compare two data points, all we can observe is a difference. One will be higher than the other. This change usually does not signal improvement or degradation, only change. This change is quite likely to be as a result of natural or routine variation in the system.

In a stable system, the likelihood of the next data point being higher than the previous data point is 50 per cent, the same likelihood of it being lower. With three data points the likelihood that the second will be higher than the first and that the third will be higher than the second is 0.5 x 0.5, which is 0.25, or one in four. By the time we have eight data points falling in an increasing pattern, each higher than the last, the likelihood of this occurring by chance is one in 128. So, if we assume a trend of improvement based on these data, there is a one in 128 chance that there is no real improvement.

How many data points we require depends on how confident we wish to be that a trend really exists.

The main point is that two or three points of data can only indicate change, which is most likely due to common cause variation. The same can probably be said for four or five data points. Eight or more points are needed if we are to be confident that a trend in data is due to a change in the system rather than natural variation within the system.

An important corollary of this observation is the need to collect regular data to allow time to see trends. If data is reported annually, one must wait eight years to see a trend.

When looking for trends in multiple measures of performance, as opposed to looking for a trend in a single measurement over time, similar logic can be applied. If there are, for example, eight measures of system performance, and if the performance of the system is stable, the likelihood of any single measure showing improvement is 50 per cent. If all eight measures show improvement, by the same logic as above, there is only a one in 128 chance that there is, in fact, no improvement. In short, trends can be evident across multiple measures in shorter time frames than it takes for trends to become evident in a single measure.

## Variation in sets of data over time

Frequently it is changes in the variation within groups, occurring over time, which is of interest.

To return to the earlier example of NAPLAN performance in school mean reading scores shown in Figure 5.13, when the data for the following year was published, the system performance was nearly identical, as Figure 5.17 suggests.

The system remained stable, with no evidence of special cause variation, and the mean and standard deviation of the distribution were remarkably similar to those of the previous year.

This histogram, when compared with the data from the previous year (Figure 5.13), suggests that not only are the schools all performing within the natural limits of variation for this system of school, but also that the system is producing predictable results from year to year. (Further statistical testing failed to find evidence of special cause variation or any significant differences in mean or standard deviation.) It would be reasonable to conclude that the school system being studied produced similar results from one year to the next. It would also be reasonable to predict that, unless significant changes are made to the school system, the results in the future will be similar to those past.

Unless significant changes are made to the school system, the results in the future will be similar to those past.

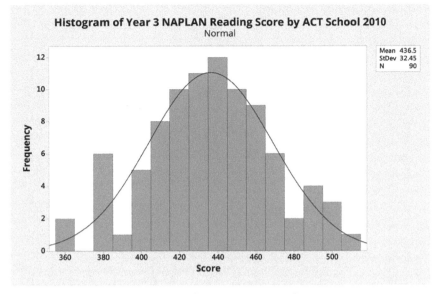

**Figure 5.17 Histogram of Year 3 mean reading scores, 2010**
Source: Prepared by QLA from NAPLAN school mean scores as published in the *Canberra Times*, 5 March 2011.

It is certainly true that the mean score in some schools will have increased and others will have decreased, such is the nature of variation in systems. However, the evidence suggests that the system of schools is producing predictable results that are free of special cause variation and that performance is not changing over time; the performance of this system of schools appears to be stable.

## Control charts and control limits

In 1931, Walter Shewhart published his groundbreaking text *Economic Control of Quality of Manufactured Product*, in which he provided a detailed rationale for the use of control charts to guide action for system improvement.

The control chart is based on the use of standard deviations. A standard deviation is a statistic that indicates the spread, width, or range of a set of data. A small standard deviation indicates a narrow range of values, whereas a larger standard deviation indicates a more broad range of values. Standard deviation, like an average, is a statistic derived from the data using a mathematical formula.

A control chart is an extension of the run chart, but is different in that it includes lines for the average or mean, and the natural limits of variation.

A control chart is an extension of the run chart, and includes lines for the average or mean, and the natural limits of variation.

The natural limits of variation are referred to as control limits on a control chart.

The natural limits of variation are referred to as control limits. Figure 5.18 shows a control chart that details both an upper control limit (UCL) and a lower control limit (LCL).

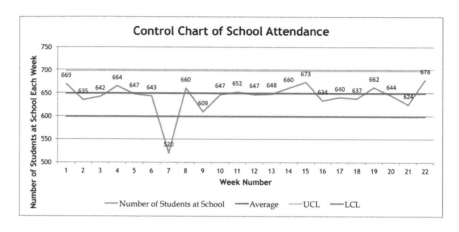

**Figure 5.18 Control chart of school attendance**

In the school attendance example first introduced in Figure 5.16, the actual range of values, from smallest to largest, is 609 to 678. The mean number of days all students can be present per week is thus calculated to be 648.

The standard deviation is calculated to be 16.5.

To calculate the control limits, we multiply the standard deviation by three:

3 x 16.5 = 49.5.

To define the control limits we then take the mean, plus or minus three times the standard deviation:

648 + 49.5 = 698 is the upper control limit

648 - 49.5 = 599 is the lower control limit

Points falling outside the control limits suggest the presence of special cause variation and are worthy of further investigation.

If we insert these into the run chart, we create the control chart in Figure 5.18.

Notice that in Figure 5.18 all the data points, with the exception of the dip at week seven, fall within the upper and lower control limits. Points falling outside the control limits suggest the presence of special cause variation and are worthy of further investigation.

Once the presence of special causes has been confirmed, these data are excluded from the calculations of the control limits. In this case, because the dip at week seven was a due to an identified special cause, this data point is excluded from the calculation of the mean and from calculation of the natural limits of variation.

Note also that the control limits, which quantify the natural limits of variation, are derived directly from the data. It is customary to define the control limits to be three standard deviations from the mean. In the same way that the mean, or average, is derived directly from the data, so too are the control limits.

Control limits indicate nothing about whether the performance of a system is desirable or acceptable, they simply indicate the variation or natural range of performance of the system.

Deming pointed out that the application of control charts to manufacturing represents only a very small fraction of their potential application and he emphasised the value of control charts across industry, education, and government.

> The most important application of Shewhart's contribution is in the management of people.

W. Edwards Deming, 1993, *The New Economics: For industry, government and education*, MIT, Cambridge, p. 182.

*Control limits are derived directly from the data.*

*Control limits indicate nothing about whether the performance of a system is desirable or acceptable.*

## WHY THREE STANDARD DEVIATIONS?

The convention that control limits be set three standard deviations either side of the mean value was established by Walter Shewhart.

Shewhart's efforts were focussed on the economic control of quality. He was seeking a practical and economic method to determine when effort should be expended to identify assignable causes of variation — also known as special causes — and deal with them individually, and when attention should be paid to changing the system as a whole in order to improve overall performance.

To set the control limits too close to the mean increases the risk of reacting to an outcome as if it came from a special cause, when in fact it is the result of the many common causes of variation — a form of overreaction.

To set the control limits too far from the mean increases the risk of treating an outcome as if it came from a common cause, when it was the actually result of a special cause. This would result in missing a special cause — a form of under-reaction.

To make either mistake results in loss. Overreaction wastes effort by seeking to identify assignable causes where none exist and taking unnecessary action trying to address an issue that is simply part of the common causal system. Under-reaction results in losses associated with failing to learn from and take action on assignable causes.

Shewhart's empirical studies identified the general rule that three standard deviations provide for minimum economic loss. When control limits are set at three standard deviations and a system is subject only to common cause variation, we can roughly predict that only one in 400 points would be wrongly attributed to a special cause. If we set the control limits to two standard deviations, then roughly one in 20 points would be wrongly attributed to a special cause.

In education, some Australian jurisdictions use two standard deviations to determine which students with intellectual disabilities are eligible for support; others use three. If we consider the need to allocate support resources to students who are identified as exhibiting an intellectual disability:

- If the control limits are set too close to the mean, the risk of overreaction is increased and students will be wrongly identified as requiring support for intellectual disability, resulting in increased costs; and

- If the limits are set too far from the mean, the likelihood of under-reaction is increased and students who are in real and genuine need of support services will not be identified. This will result in costs that are less tangible but just as real: costs to teachers having to bear the load of supporting the children without additional help, costs to the students' classmates resulting from teachers being less available to support them, and costs to the students that result from lost opportunities stemming from potentially diminished learning without special assistance.

In this case, the system will be optimised when the total costs are minimised. Obviously, this is not an easy equation.

# System capability

Just because a system is stable does not mean that it is producing satisfactory results. For example, if a school demonstrates average growth in spelling of about 70 points from Years  w3 to 5, is this acceptable? Should parents be satisfied with school scores that range from 350 to 500? These are questions of system capability.

Capability relates to the degree to which a system consistently delivers results that are acceptable — within specification, and thus within acceptable limits of variation.

> Capability: the degree to which a system consistently delivers results that are within acceptable limits of variation.

Note that stability relates to the natural variation that is exhibited by a system, capability relates to the acceptable limits of variation for a system. Stability is defined by system performance. Capability is defined by stakeholder needs and expectations.

It is not uncommon to find systems that are both stable and incapable; systems that consistently and predictably produce results that are beyond acceptable limits of variation and are therefore unsatisfactory. No doubt, you can think of many examples.

Cries for school systems to "raise the bar" or "close the gap" are evidence that stakeholders believe school systems to be incapable (in this statistical sense) because the results they are producing are not within acceptable limits of variation. However, the results are totally predictable, the system is stable, but the results are unsatisfactory; the system is incapable.

In Australia, NAPLAN defines standards for student performance. National minimum standards are defined to reflect a "basic level of knowledge and understanding needed to function in that year level".

Proficiency standards, which are set higher than the national minimum standards, "refer to what is expected of a student at the year level". Depending on the year level and learning area, between two per cent and 14 per cent of students fail to reach national minimum standards. By definition, then, the Australian education system is incapable. It fails to consistently produce performance that is within acceptable limits of variation, because a known proportion of students fails to meet minimum standards, let alone perform at or better than the expected proficiency.

---

*Sidebar notes:*

Capability relates to the degree to which a system consistently delivers results that are acceptable.

Stability is defined by system performance. Capability is defined by stakeholder needs and expectations.

The Australian education system is incapable. It fails to consistently produce performance that is within acceptable limits of variation.

Figure 5.19 shows the spelling results for 161 Year 9 students at an Australian high school, as measured by NAPLAN. These results fall between the upper and lower control limits, which have been found to be at 297 and 794 respectively. Careful analysis failed to reveal evidence of special cause variation. This system appears to be stable.

The national minimum standard for Year 9 students is 478. In this set of data, there are 33 students performing below this standard. Thus we can conclude that the system which produced these spelling results is stable but incapable.

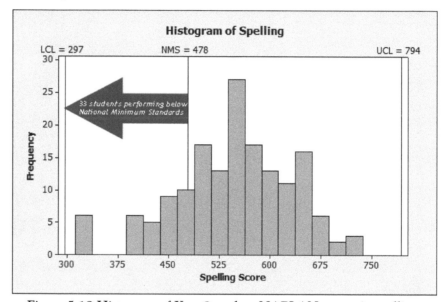

**Figure 5.19 Histogram of Year 9 student NAPLAN scores in spelling, indicating a system that is stable but incapable**

Source: Prepared by QLA from NAPLAN individual student scores provided by an Australian high school.

# Taking effective action: Responding appropriately to system variation

With an understanding of the concepts of common cause and special cause variation, responding to system data becomes more effective.

The flowchart in Figure 5.20 summarises an appropriate response to system data.

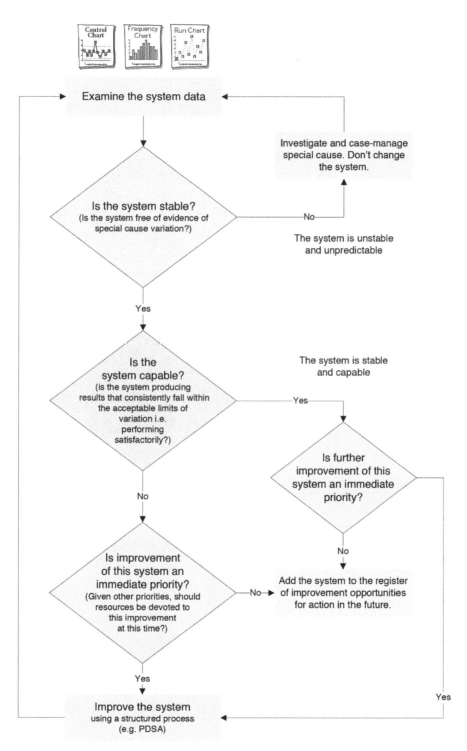

**Figure 5.20 Flowchart: responding appropriately to system variation**
Source: QLA and David Langford.

## Is the system stable?

The first thing to do when examining system data is to ask if the system is stable. Is there any evidence of special cause variation? Is the system producing consistent and predictable results, within its natural limits of variation? Are there outliers or trends?

If there is evidence of special cause variation, then the system is unstable, not predictable. The special causes of variation should be investigated. Most commonly, there will be clear explanations for observed trends and out of the ordinary results, whether these be good or bad. These can be responded to on a case-by-case basis.

Occasionally, special causes are identified that highlight opportunities for system improvement by making changes that minimise or maximise the occurrence of damaging or helpful circumstances.

Failing to seek to identify the causes behind an out of the ordinary observation or a pattern in the data is called under-reacting. To under-react is to miss an opportunity to investigate and learn about special causes affecting the system. Overreaction is making changes to a system in the absence of understanding the nature and impact of variation upon that system. It is also called tampering, and will be discussed shortly.

If the system is free of evidence of special cause variation, then it is said to be stable. It is predictable.

## Is the system capable?

Once the system is stable, the next question to ask is whether the system is capable. Is the system producing results that consistently fall within the acceptable limits of variation? Is the system performing satisfactorily? Is it performing as well as our customers would like it to perform?

If the answer is no, then the system is incapable and improvement is required.

If the answer is yes, then the system is capable. Improvement may still be desirable, as it is always possible to further improve any system and reduce variation.

Consideration needs to be given to the immediate priorities of the organisation before any further action is taken.

---

*If there is evidence of special cause variation, then the system is unstable, not predictable. The special causes of variation should be investigated.*

*To under-react is to miss an opportunity to investigate and learn about special causes affecting the system.*

*Once the system is stable, the next question is whether the system is capable.*

# Is improvement of this system an immediate priority?

All systems can be improved, but they cannot all be improved at once. Prioritisation is required. An organisation also has to decide if each improvement opportunity is an immediate priority to which resources will be allocated.

If improvement of the system is an immediate priority, then a structured improvement process, such as Plan–Do–Study–Act (see Chapter Four) can be applied.

To highlight some key points about the process:

- The key to system improvement is to examine the cause and effect relationships affecting the system and identify the few dominant (root) causes that have the greatest impact on system performance.

- Common causes of variation affect every data point, to a greater or lesser degree. It is usually the case that most of the variation comes from a minority of causes. The challenge is to identify which causes have the greatest impact.

- In practice, a list of potentially dominant causes can be identified though conversations with those individuals who know the process most intimately, usually the process users. There may also be experts who can provide valuable input.

- Care needs to be exercised to separate causes from symptoms. Frequently, symptoms will be identified because these are felt more strongly than causes.

- Once the dominant causes are identified, a theory can be formed as to how the system might be changed to improve performance. This theory can then be tested, preferably on a small scale.

If improvement of the system is not a sufficiently high priority the system can be added to the organisation's register of improvement opportunities. This register provides a list of all the opportunities for improvement that have been identified for an organisation. On a regular basis, usually tied to the planning cycle, the register is reviewed, prioritised, and improvement projects planned.

*All systems can be improved, but they cannot all be improved at once. Prioritisation is required.*

*If improvement of the system is not a sufficiently high priority the system can be added to the organisation's register of improvement opportunities.*

> ### 📌 A QUESTIONABLE ATTITUDE TO STUDENT ATTITUDE
>
> We have lost count of the number of times that school improvement teams have identified "student attitude" as a major cause of variation and unsatisfactory student results.
>
> Further (root cause) analysis nearly always identifies that student attitude is a symptom of a range of other more dominant causes, such as boring lessons or lack of relevance of curriculum.

# Stop tampering

When we fail to follow the procedure outlined in Figure 5.20, we risk taking action that will make things worse. This is what Deming called tampering.

📖 Tampering: making changes to a system in the absence of an understanding of the nature and impact of variation affecting the system.

The most common forms of tampering are:

- Overreacting to evidence of special cause variation;

- Overreacting to individual data points that are subject only to common cause variation, usually because these data are deemed to be unacceptable;

- Chopping the tails of the distribution (working on the individuals at the extreme ends of the distribution without addressing the system itself); and

- Failing to address root causes.

Tampering with a system will not lead to improvement. If we examine the performance of the education system over the last decade, we find evidence of persistent tampering. The result has been a predictable failure to improve.

*Tampering with a system will not lead to improvement.*

Let us look more closely at each of these forms of tampering and their impact.

# Tampering by overreacting to special cause variation

Consider the true story of the young teacher who observed a student in the class struggling under the high expectations of her parents. The teacher thought that the student's parents were placing too much pressure on the child to achieve high grades, which the teacher believed to be beyond the student. The young and inexperienced teacher wrote a letter to the parents suggesting they lower their expectations and lessen the pressure on their daughter. Receipt of this letter did not please the parents, who demanded to see the school Principal. Following this event, the Principal required all correspondence from teachers to parents to come via her office. Faculty heads within the school, not wanting to have their faculties make the same mistake, required that correspondence come through them before going to the Principal.

The end result was a more cumbersome communication process for everyone, which required more work from more people and introduced additional delays. The principal overreacted to a special cause. A more appropriate response would have been for the principal to work one-on-one with the young teacher to help them learn from the situation. Making changes to a system in response to an isolated event is nearly always tampering.

> Making changes to a system in response to an isolated event is nearly always tampering.

A more mundane example of this type of tampering is when a single person reports that they are cold and the thermostat in the room is changed to increase the temperature. This action usually results in others becoming hot and another adjustment being made. If any individual in the room can make changes to the thermostat setting, the temperature will fluctuate wildly, variation will be increased and more people will become uncomfortable, either too hot or too cold.

Most people can think of other examples where systems or processes have been changed inappropriately in response to isolated cases.

The appropriate response to evidence of special cause variation is to seek to understand the specific causes at play and have situations dealt with on a case-by-case basis, without necessarily changing the system.

Occasionally, investigation of a special cause may reveal a breakthrough. The breakthrough may be so significant that changes to the system are called for in order to capitalise on the possibilities. This is, however, rare and easily identified when it is the case.

---

### 💬 TAMPERING WITH ARRIVAL TIME

A staff member was arriving late for school on a regular basis. The Principal decided to introduce a process whereby everyone would sign in when they arrived at school in the morning. At 8.30 am (the expected arrival time) the Principal would walk out of his office and draw a line in the sign on book. Anyone arriving late would now be prominently displayed by having to sign below the line. The Principal overreacted to a special cause.

Other staff that had previously been generous with their time, arriving early and leaving late, regarded this as unreasonable. They began clock watching: arriving just in time in the morning and leaving at 3.45 pm each day. The person who had always arrived late continued to do so. Tampering with the system instead of managing the source of the special cause sub-optimises the system.

---

## Tampering by overreacting to individual data points

Another common form of tampering comes from overreacting to individual data points.

Another common form of tampering comes from overreacting to individual data points. Such tampering is very common and very costly.

Figure 5.21 is a dot plot of mean Year 3 school results, measured across five key learning areas by NAPLAN in 2009. These results are from an Australian jurisdiction and include government-run schools and non-government schools. For the purpose of the argument that follows, these data are representative of results from any set of schools, at any level, anywhere.

The first thing to notice is that there is variation in the school mean scores. Normal probability plots suggest the data appear to be normally distributed, as one would expect. The system is stable and is not subject to special causes (outliers).

The policy response to variation such as this is frequently a form of tampering. Underperforming schools are identified at the lower ends of the distribution and are subjected to expectations of improvement, with punishments and rewards attached.

This response fails to take into account the fact that data points within the natural limits of variation are only subject to common cause variation. To single out individual schools (classes, students, principals or teachers) fails to address the common causes and fails to improve the system in any way.

When this approach is extended to all low performing elements, it becomes an even more systematic problem: attempting to chop the tail of the distribution.

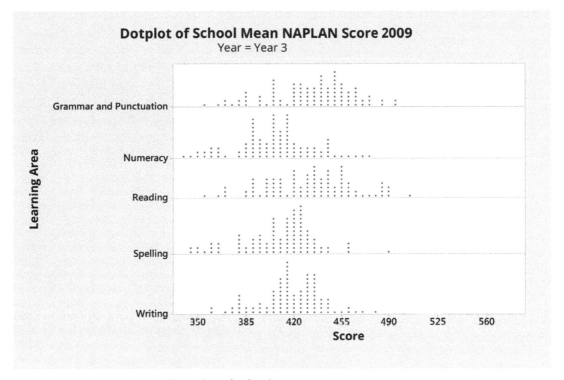

**Figure 5.21 Dot plot of school mean scores**

Source: Prepared by QLA from NAPLAN school mean scores as published in the *Canberra Times*,
30 January 2010.

## Tampering by chopping the tails of the distribution

Working on the individuals performing most poorly in a system is sometimes known as trying to chop the tail of the distribution. This is also tampering.

There are three main reasons why this is bad policy, all of which have to do with not understanding the nature and impact of variation within the system.

Firstly, it is not uncommon to base interventions on mean scores. Yet it is well known within the education community that there is much greater variation within schools than there is between schools. Similarly, there is much greater variation within classes than between classes within the same school. Averages mask variation.

Consider two schools. School A (Figure 5.22) is performing at the lower end of the distribution for reading scores — with a mean reading score of approximately 390. School B (Figure 5.23) has a mean reading score approximately 30 points higher.

> Working on the individuals performing most poorly in a system is sometimes known as trying to chop the tail of the distribution. This is also tampering.

The proportion of students in each school that is performing below any defined acceptable level is fairly similar. School A, for example, has 12 students with results below 350. School B has seven. In some systems, resources are allocated based on mean scores. Those with mean scores beyond a defined threshold are entitled to resources not available to those with mean scores within certain limits. If School A and School B were in such a system and the resourcing threshold was set at 400, for example, School B could be denied resources made available to School A, simply because its mean score is above some defined cut-off point.

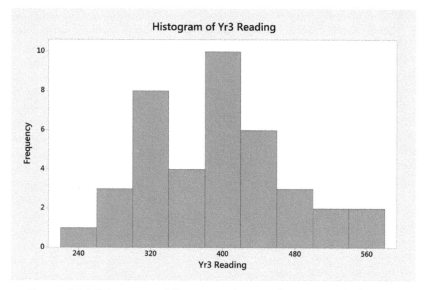

Figure 5.22 Histogram of Year 3 student reading scores (School A)

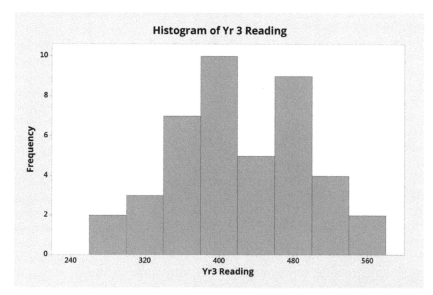

Figure 5.23 Histogram of Year 3 student reading scores (School B)

Where schools or classes are identified to be in need of intervention based on mean scores, the nature and impact of the variation behind these mean scores is masked and ignored. If the 12 students in School A receive support, why is it denied to those equally deserving seven students in School B?

Secondly, the distribution of these results fails to show evidence of special cause variation. The variation that is observed among the performance of these schools is caused by a myriad of common causes that affect all schools in the system. Singling out underperforming schools for special treatment each year does nothing to address the causes common to every school in the system, and fails to improve the system as a whole.

Even if the intervention is successful for the selected schools, the common causal system will ensure that, in time, the distribution is restored, with schools once again occupying similar places at the lower end of the curve. The system will not be improved by this approach.

Thirdly, this approach consumes scarce resources that could be used to examine the cause and effect relationships operating within the system as a whole and taking action to improve performance of the system as a whole.

In education, working on the individuals performing most poorly in a system is a disturbingly common approach to improvement. It never works. A near identical strategy is used within classes to identify students who require remediation. The "bottom" — underachieving — kids are given a special program; they are singled out. Sometimes the "top" — gifted and talented — kids are also singled out for an extension program.

This is not so say that we should not intervene when a school is struggling or when a student is falling behind. Nor are we suggesting that students and schools who are progressing well should not be challenged to achieve even more. It is appropriate to provide this support and extension to those who need it. The problem is that doing so does not improve the system. Such actions, when they become as entrenched as they currently are, are merely part of the current system.

It should be noted that focussing upon poor performers also shifts the blame away from those responsible for the system as a whole and onto the poor performers. The mantra becomes one of "if only we could fix these schools/students/families". The responsibility lies not with the poor performers, but with those responsible for managing the system: senior leaders and administrators. It is a convenient, but costly diversion to shift the blame in this way.

---

*Where schools or classes are identified to be in need of intervention based on mean scores, the nature and impact of the variation behind these mean scores is masked and ignored.*

*Singling out underperforming schools for special treatment does nothing to address the causes common to every school in the system.*

*It is appropriate to provide support and extension to those who need it, but doing so does nothing to improve the system.*

*Focussing upon poor performers also shifts the blame away from those responsible for the system as a whole.*

Unless action is taken to improve the system as a whole, the data will be the same again next year; only the names will have changed.

If targeting the tails of the distribution is the primary strategy for improvement, it is tampering and it will fail. Unless action is taken to improve the system as a whole, the data will be the same again next year, only the names will have changed.

Over time, targeting the tails of the distribution also increases the variation in the system. This increasing variation is evident in Australian Year 2 to Year 7 student mathematics learning data presented by Geoff Masters (Figure 5.24).

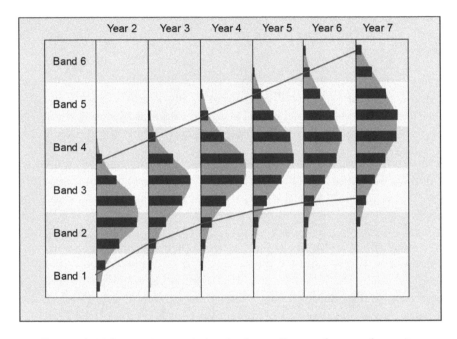

**Figure 5.24 Increasing variation in Australian student mathematics achievement over the years of schooling**

Source: Geoff Masters, 2007, "Realising the Promise of Education in the 21st Century", Keynote Presentation at the ACEL National Conference, October 2007.

This sort of tampering is not restricted to schools and school systems. It is very common, and equally ineffective, in corporate and government organisations. It is quite common that the top performers are rewarded with large bonuses, while poor performers are identified and fired or transferred. Sales teams compete against each other for reward and to avoid humiliation. Such approaches do not improve the system; they tamper with it. These approaches can also inflict suffering and psychological damage to the individuals involved, as will be discussed in the next chapter.

## Tampering by failing to address root causes

Tampering commonly occurs when systems or processes are changed in response to a common cause of variation that is not a root cause or dominant driver of performance. People tamper with a system when they make changes to it in response to symptoms rather than causes.

It is easy to miss root causes by failing to ask those who really know. Who can identify the biggest barriers to learning in a classroom? The students. Teachers can be quick to identify student work ethic as a problem in high schools. It is a rare teacher who identifies boring and meaningless lessons as a possible cause. Work ethic is a symptom, not a cause. It is not productive to tackle the issue of work ethic directly. One must find the causes of good and poor work ethics and address these in order to bring about a change in behaviour.

There has been a concerted effort in recent years in Australia to decrease class sizes, particularly in primary schools. Teachers are pleased because it appears to reduce their work load and provides more time to attend to each student. Students like it because they may receive more teacher attention. Parents are pleased because they expect their child to receive more individualised attention. Unions are happy because it means more teachers and therefore more members. Politicians back it because parents, teachers and unions love it. Unfortunately, the evidence indicates that these changes in class size have very little impact on student learning. (See John Hattie, 2009, *Visible Learning*, Routledge, London and New York.) This policy is an example of tampering on a grand and expensive scale. Class size is not a root cause of performance in student learning.

Managers need to study the cause and effect relationships within their system and be confident that they are addressing the true root causes. Symptoms are not causes.

Every time changes are made to a system in an absence of understanding the cause and effect relationships affecting that system, it is tampering. Tampering will not improve the system; it has the opposite effect.

> People tamper with a system when they make changes to it in response to symptoms not causes.

> Every time changes are made to a system in an absence of understanding the cause and effect relationships affecting that system, it is tampering.

# Reflection questions

**?** What graphs and charts are in regular use in your organisation? How do these charts help (or hinder) interpretation of system variation?

**?** Consider the fishbone diagram in Figure 5.9. What additional common causes of variation in student performance can you identify? How might you identify which are dominant causes? How might you determine which are the root causes?

**?** What are the common causes affecting behaviour and performance in your organisation? What are examples of special causes? How do you know?

**?** What are some examples of stable and unstable systems? How do you know?

**?** What are some examples of capable and incapable systems? How do you know?

**?** From your experience, what are some common examples of under-reaction and overreaction to special causes, failing to address root causes, overreacting to individual data points, and chopping the tails?

# Quality learning tools to examine variation

Each of the following tools can be used to examine variation in system and process data.

 ## Dot plot

A dot plot is a simple tool for showing the central tendency and variation among a set of data. Each data point is plotted as a dot on a continuum across a range of results.

**Figure 5.25 Dot plot of Year 12 student test results**

 ## Histogram

A histogram is a useful tool for visualising the distribution of a set of data. It enables easy examination of the central tendency, variation and overall shape of the distribution.

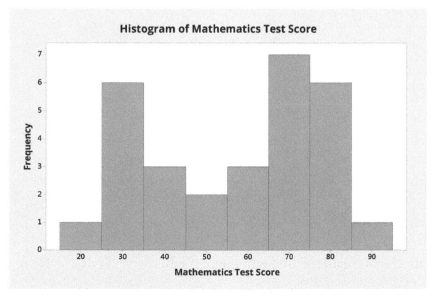

**Figure 5.26 Histogram of Year 9 mathematics test scores**

The data in Figure 5.26 suggests two distinct groups within this collection of students: one centred around 30, the other around 70. Such a distribution is said to be bimodal and is suggestive of the data representing two different underlying situations.

# Box and whisker plot

A box and whisker plot, also known as a box plot, displays the variation within a set of data and makes it easy to compare two or more sets of data.

The box represents the 25th to the 75th percentile: the middle 50 per cent of the ranked data. The median, or middle value, is represented by a line within the box. The lines — whiskers — represent the upper and lower 25 per cent of the distribution, excluding outliers (special causes).

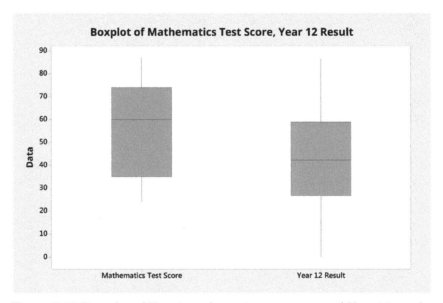

**Figure 5.27 Box plot of Year 9 mathematics test scores and Year 12 results**

Figure 5.27 shows same data from the dot plot and histogram examples above, presented as two box and whisker plots on the same vertical axis. It is immediately evident that the mathematics scores were, for the most part, higher than the Year 12 test results, and that the Year 12 test results exhibited wider variation.

Figure 5.28 represents one school's NAPLAN student scores over four years in the five learning areas for Years 3, 5 and 7. Outliers — special causes — are clearly indicated by stars beyond the whiskers in each case.

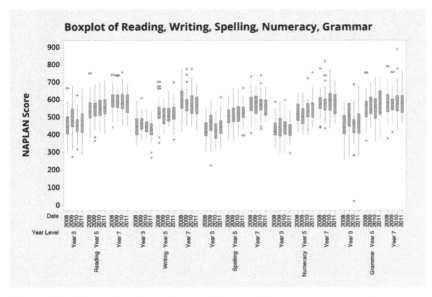

**Figure 5.28 Box plot of reading, writing, spelling, numeracy and grammar**

Source: Prepared by QLA from NAPLAN individual student scores provided by an Australian primary school.

 **Run chart**

A run chart, or time series chart, can be used to visualise variation over time. Each point is plotted in time order on a line graph.

Figure 5.29 shows a run chart from a Year 2 class that tracked the time it took them to be ready to learn each morning. The data show a general trend of improvement, reduced preparation time, over the three terms.

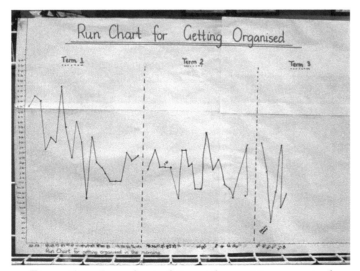

**Figure 5.29 Run chart of time taken getting organised**

Source: Roxburgh Homestead Primary School, Victoria.

# ⚒ Control chart

Control charts track data over time in order to detect the presence of special causes of variation, and are based on the use of standard deviations (a statistic that indicates the spread, width or range of a set of data). A small standard deviation indicates a narrow range of values, while a larger standard deviation indicates a broader range of values. Standard deviation, like an average, is a statistic derived from the data using a mathematical formula.

Upper and lower control limits — which are placed three standard deviations above and below the mean — can indicate the presence of out of the ordinary data points that may provide evidence of special causes of variation. Once the presence of special causes has been identified, these data are excluded from the calculations of the control limits.

Figure 5.30 is a control chart showing a Year 5 class weekly spelling test results for the forty weeks of a school year. Each week, students completed a weekly spelling test of ten words chosen from the weekly spelling list. Students recorded how many words they spelt correctly and the teacher added the student totals to determine the weekly total number of words spelled correctly. The middle line represents the mean (which was 163), the lines above and below the mean represent the upper and lower control limits respectively (214 and 112).

There are two points outside the control limits, one at week nine (87) and one at week 29 (54). These points are evidence of special cause variation. Upon investigation, the reason these points are below the lower control limit could be determined; on both occasions, approximately half the class was absent during the spelling test as these students were involved in a choir rehearsal at that time. Consequently, these two weeks of data have been omitted from calculation of the mean, upper and lower control limits.

It can be observed that the spelling process, with the exception of weeks when many students were absent at the choir rehearsals, is stable; the class of students can confidently expect to spell between 112 and 214 words correctly each week. There are no trends, thus there are no signs of improvement over time. Without change, this spelling process can be expected to continue to deliver similar results.

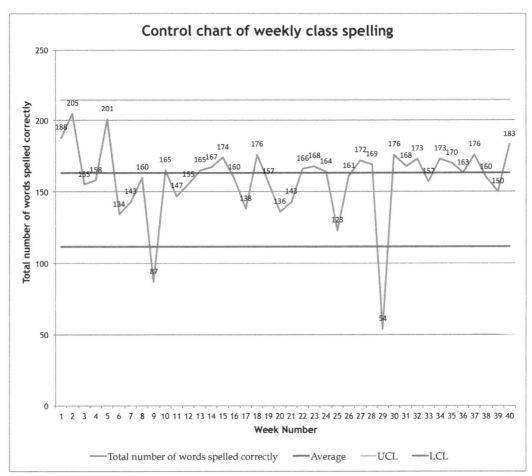

Figure 5.30 Control chart showing Year 5 class weekly spelling test results

 A control chart template is available on the QLA web site: www.qla.com.au.

# ✗ Pareto chart

A Pareto chart is a column chart in which the plotted values are arranged from largest to smallest. It is used to highlight the most frequently occurring events, ideas, causes, etc.

The Pareto chart is named after Vilfredo Pareto, an Italian economist, who over a century ago observed that 80 per cent of the land was owned by 20 per cent of the population. This observation was generalised to become the 80-20 rule, or the Pareto principle.

This general principle suggests that 80 per cent of the variation comes from 20 per cent of the causes. For example, most school principals know that 80 per cent of student behaviour problems in a school come from 20 per cent of the teachers.

The Pareto chart shown in Figure 5.31 details what participants wanted to learn about at a Quality Learning Conference held in Wallaroo, South Australia in 2014. Learning these things would make it a perfect conference in participants' eyes.

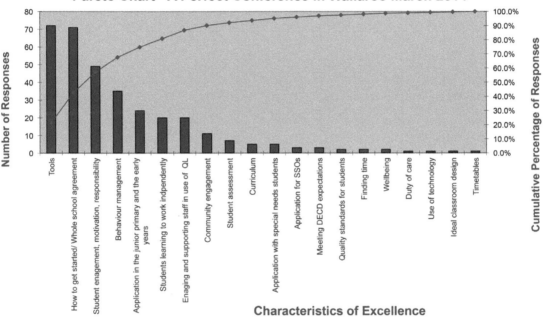

Figure 5.31 Pareto chart: A perfect conference

A Pareto chart template is available on the QLA web site: www.qla.com.au.

# Chapter summary

In this chapter we have explored the principles relating to the third area of Deming's system of profound knowledge, knowledge about variation:

**Data:**  Facts and data are needed to measure progress and improve decision making

**Variation:**  Systems and processes are subject to variation that affects predictability and performance.

In doing so, we have explained that:

- Data are the voice of a system — performance, process, perception and input measures give the system a voice;

- Some figures are unknown and unknowable;

- Data can be used for three main purposes: to monitor performance, to adjust system operations, and to understand the system operation and behaviour;

- Operational definitions are essential for creating shared meaning and to ensure consistency in the collection and use of data;

- Data can be misused. Numerical goals or targets, rating and ranking are prime examples of misuse of data;

- Variation exists in all systems;

- Variation can be observed within groups, between groups and over time;

- Common cause variation is always present and is built into the system. It establishes the natural limits of variation for a system;

- Special cause variation is the result of unique events or situations;

- A stable system is predictable, within the natural limits of variation;

- A capable system consistently and predictably produces satisfactory results;

- Management need to respond differently to special cause variation than to common cause variation. Special cause variation needs to be case managed, while common cause variation can only be reduced by changing the system;

- Tampering with a system — making changes in the absence of an understanding of the variation impacting upon the system — is a common practice that makes things worse. Forms of tampering include: overreacting to special causes, failing to address root causes, overreacting to individual data points, and seeking to chop the tails of a distribution; and

- There are quality learning tools that provide practical strategies to take action, including: radar chart; structured brainstorming; affinity diagram; measures selection matrix; dot plot; histogram; box and whisker plot; run chart or time series chart; control chart; and Pareto chart.

# Further reading

Donald J. Wheeler, 1993, *Understanding Variation: The key to managing chaos*, SPC Press, Tennessee.

Quality Learning Australasia, 2012, *Understanding variation: Using data to improve*, QLA.

# Chapter 6:
# Improving Relationships

All the people that work within a system can contribute to improvement, and thus enhance their joy in work.

Dr. W Edwards Deming (1989), *The Essential Deming* (2013) Joyce Orsini (Ed.), p72

# Chapter contents

# Introduction

This chapter is about people. It discusses the fourth and final area of Deming's system of profound knowledge — psychology. The three principles that encapsulate this fourth key concept underpinning organisational improvement are:

**Motivation:**    Removing barriers to intrinsic motivation improves performance.

**Relationships:**    Strong human relationships are built through caring, communication, trust and respect.

**Leadership:**    It is everybody's job to improve the systems and processes for which they are responsible by working with their people and role modelling these principles.

In exploring these principles, we will examine intrinsic motivation, which comes from within the individual, and extrinsic motivation, which comes from sources external to the individual. While use of extrinsic motivators, such as rewards and punishments, is deeply rooted within education systems, extrinsic motivation rarely leads to emotional engagement; only intrinsic motivation can produce engagement. As we will show, there are factors that can enhance intrinsic motivation — purpose, choice, mastery and belonging — that can be designed into learning systems.

This chapter also demonstrates how relationships are critical to the success and functioning of an organisation. Dependent relationships, which are characterised by dominance and compliance, are common in organisations, including schools. In a dependent student-teacher relationship, students are deprived the opportunity to build capacity for self-management. It is only through the development of truly interdependent relationships that students, teachers and administrators can collaborate in a way that continually improves the systems of learning for the benefit of everyone.

This chapter also discusses how many of the practices of the prevailing system of management and leadership (such as extrinsic rewards and punishments, praise, empowerment, competition, artificial scarcity, and fear) are toxic to interdependent relationships. We argue that leadership is about inspiring others to follow, not telling others what to do. Everybody is a leader of systems and processes and to improve performance, everyone needs to be engaged in improving systems, processes and relationships, with the support of those working in the system.

The following flowchart provides a summary of the chapter and its contents.

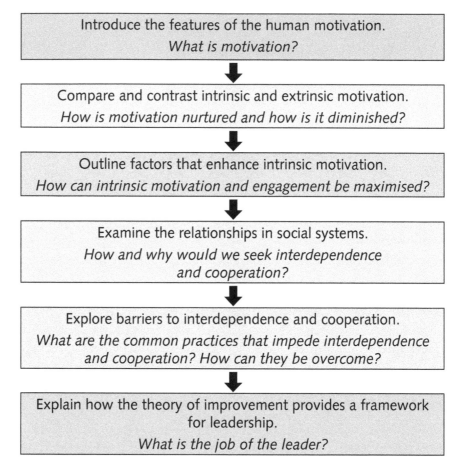

# Motivation

This section of the chapter expands on the following principle of quality learning:

Removing barriers to intrinsic motivation improves performance.

The topic of human motivation is fascinating, complex and controversial. Research on the subject is voluminous, publications are innumerable, and theories abound. Authors gain currency for a time, only to have their work questioned when counter examples are found, or when the original research methodology is questioned or cannot be replicated. This is particularly true of contemporary research into intrinsic motivation, extrinsic motivation and the interaction between the two.

In our discussion of motivation, it is not our goal to contribute to this controversy, but to identify areas where there is broad agreement. This includes important theory underpinning human motivation, extrinsic and intrinsic motivation. We are most interested in intrinsic motivation, as it is a key to engagement and learning. As will be shown, there are many systemic barriers to be removed from school education before intrinsic motivation, engagement and learning can flourish.

> The topic of human motivation is fascinating, complex and controversial.

> We are most interested in intrinsic motivation, as it is a key to engagement and learning.

## What is motivation?

The work of three pioneering American psychologists, Maslow, Herzberg and McGregor, established a sound basis for thinking about human motivation.

### Maslow's hierarchy of needs

Abraham Maslow proposed the hierarchy of needs as a psychological theory of motivation in 1943.

Maslow's hierarchy is usually portrayed as a pyramid, as shown in Figure 6.1, with the fundamental and basic human needs at the bottom.

Maslow argued that human needs progress in a hierarchical fashion, and that, in a general sense, the lower level needs must be satisfied in order to move to higher level needs. He referred to the lower four levels as "deficiency" needs. These needs must be satisfied in order for people to focus upon the highest level "being" needs, which he referred to as "self-actualisation".

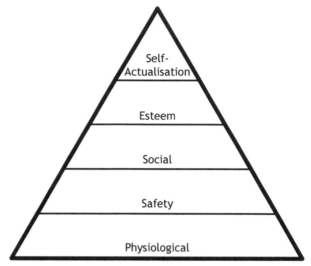

**Figure 6.1 Maslow's hierarchy of needs**

Source: Abraham Maslow, 1943, "A Theory of Human Motivation", 50:4, pp. 370–396.

The needs represented in the hierarchy are:

- **Physiological**: the basic requirements for human survival — air, water, food, clothing, and shelter;

- **Safety**: freedom from danger and harm, a sense of security, including needs for economic and psychological security, and the need for physical safety;

- **Social**: the need to feel acceptance, love and belonging in social groups;

- **Esteem**: the need to feel respect-worthy, needed, capable and self-confident; and

- **Self-actualisation**: the drive to achieve one's personal potential — a desire for self-fulfilment, presence and being.

Maslow's theory identifies human needs which, if not satisfied, directly impact upon a person's desire and capacity to strive to be their best. There is little doubt that the need for a sense of security, social acceptance, belonging, capability and self-esteem impacts upon an individual's passion for learning.

If basic human needs are not satisfied, people are inhibited from striving to be their best. Many schools have breakfast clubs, free school lunch and other programs to ensure that children are not distracted from their learning by hunger. School welfare policies and programs usually address the physiological and safety needs of students. Disadvantaged students

> If basic human needs are not satisfied, people are inhibited from striving to be their best.

can be supplied with clothing or school uniforms at reduced or no cost. These are all programs and actions aimed at ensuring students' lower level needs are met so that they can focus upon learning and being their best.

There is growing agreement that the relationships among human needs are more complex and systemic than a simple hierarchy. Critics also suggest that Maslow's model is ethnocentric, having been developed in the individualistic environment of American society. In time, Maslow's model may be replaced by a more universally accepted model of human motivation. Research continues, but there is general acceptance that people are subject to a system of interdependent human needs.

> There is general acceptance that people are subject to a system of interdependent human needs.

Even with its weaknesses, Maslow's hierarchy of needs has practical relevance for school education. Schools frequently claim that their aim is to support students to learn and develop into well rounded and productive members of society. These statements express a desire to move students beyond just doing well in tests, and to equip them to fulfil a more complete and human state of being.

If a school system is to optimise learning and help students become wonderful young people, then it must pay attention to the factors that directly affect individual drive. Sadly, this is not always a sincere focus in many school systems.

> If a school system is to optimise learning and help students become wonderful young people, then it must pay attention to the factors that directly affect individual drive.

## REACHING OUR FULL POTENTIAL?

We have struggled with the notion of schools and teachers setting their sights on helping students "reach their full potential". While this appears to be a laudable objective, our uneasiness stems from the inability to determine if the objective has been met. Firstly, some argue that human potential is infinite, and secondly, how can one human being predict the potential of another?

We frequently observe that establishing an objective for students to "reach their full potential" can lead to low expectations for those students who are deemed to have lower potential than others. Lower expectations usually lead to lower achievement. Thus, with the kindest of intentions, some teachers are unwittingly constraining the potential of students when their stated aim is to do just the opposite.

We believe a more desirable and pragmatic goal for schools would be to equip students to become capable young people prepared for the future. Such a goal would lead into an exploration of the meaning of "capable young people", and what they might need to be ready for their future.

We have asked a similar question of many school communities in Australia: "What do we seek as the characteristics of a graduate of this school?" The process of creating such an operational definition leads the community into exciting and meaningful dialogue. The debate rapidly moves beyond test scores into characteristics such as humility, generosity, compassion, courage, and cooperation.

## Herzberg's two factor theory

Frederick Herzberg first published his highly influential theory of job satisfaction in 1959. He proposed that there are two distinct sets of factors that influence people's motivation: motivation factors and hygiene factors.

- **Motivation factors** include achievement, recognition and responsibility. Motivation factors increase an individual's job satisfaction.

- **Hygiene factors** include pay, supervision, and company policy and administration. While hygiene factors do not, of themselves, increase job satisfaction, when absent or handled badly they can lead to dissatisfaction.

*There are factors that can motivate and factors that can demotivate.*

In other words, there are factors that can motivate and factors that can demotivate. Herzberg argued that these factors could act independently of one another.

Herzberg's theory was based upon studies across many different workplaces that took place over many years. In each case, the results were remarkably similar. Certain factors enhance job satisfaction and other factors diminish it.

*In order to increase motivation, attention must be paid to the systemic factors that affect motivation.*

Herzberg's work explicitly explores the relationship between factors in the workplace — a social system — and the motivation of individuals working within that system. Herzberg highlights that systemic factors — those factors that relate to the design, structures, processes and operation of the system — have a direct impact on motivation. A key implication of this is that in order to increase motivation, attention must be paid to the systemic factors that affect motivation. Motivation is affected by the system, not just the individual.

A second implication of Herzberg's work is that if we are to increase motivation, we must pay attention to:

1.  Ensuring provision of those factors that enhance motivation; and

2.  Identifying and diminishing those factors that demotivate.

## McGregor's Theory X and Theory Y

Douglas McGregor was an American social scientist who published *The Human Side of Enterprise* in 1960. This book stimulated widespread and ongoing discussion and research into the nature of human motivation.

McGregor challenged managers to question the assumptions (theories) underpinning their actions, particularly with respect to methods of direction and control. He proposed two theories based on competing assumptions, which he called Theory X and Theory Y.

Theory X represents a dominant traditional view, based on three assumptions derived from the management literature of the time:

1.  The average human being has an inherent dislike for work and will avoid it if he can.

2.  Because of this human characteristic of dislike for work, most people must be coerced, controlled, directed, threatened with punishment to get them to put forth adequate effort toward the achievement of organisational objectives.

3.  The average human being prefers to be directed, wishes to avoid responsibility, has relatively little ambition, wants security above all.

Douglas McGregor, 2006, *The Human Side of Enterprise*, annotated edition, McGraw Hill, New York, pp. 44–45.

Theory Y was proposed by McGregor as a contrasting view and as a starting point for dialogue about an alternative theory for the management of people. Theory Y is based upon very different assumptions:

1.  The expenditure of physical and mental effort is as natural as play or rest.

2.  External control and the threat of punishment are not the only means for bringing about effort toward organizational objectives. Man will exercise self-direction and self-control in the service of objectives to which he is committed.

3.  Commitment to objectives is a function of the rewards associated with their achievement.

4.  The average human being learns, under proper conditions, not only to accept but to seek responsibility

5.  The capacity to exercise a relatively high degree of imagination, ingenuity, and creativity in the solution of organizational problems is widely, not narrowly, distributed in the population.

6.  Under the conditions of modern industrial life, the intellectual potentialities of the average human being are only partially utilized.

Douglas McGregor, 2006, *The Human Side of Enterprise,* annotated edition, McGraw Hill, New York, pp. 65–66.

Theory X and Theory Y represent profoundly different views of human motivation. The assumptions of Theory X lead to a command and control management style, while those of Theory Y promote a collaborative and capacity-building management style.

Debate continues around McGregor's theories. Which is most relevant today? Under what circumstances does each theory apply? Which is most dominant in management practices today?

Regardless of how one chooses to answer these questions, McGregor makes a significant contribution by highlighting the importance of being aware of one's assumptions in dealing with others.

> McGregor was focussed upon encouraging managers to reflect upon their own assumptions about people and motivation.

Some people have interpreted McGregor as advocating Theory Y as a superior approach. In fact, McGregor was focussed upon encouraging managers to reflect upon their own assumptions about people and motivation, which frequently operate at a subconscious level, and the behavioural implications of these assumptions.

Another important contribution McGregor made is to highlight the distinction between intrinsic and extrinsic motivation.

# What are intrinsic and extrinsic motivation?

Motivation is what drives people to do what they do, those things that provide the stimulus for action.

 Motivation: stimuli or drive for action.

The distinction between intrinsic and extrinsic motivation hinges on the origins of the stimulus or drive for action. If an individual's behaviour is attributed to an internal stimulus or drive for action, then it is the result of intrinsic motivation. If an individual's behaviour is attributed to some external stimulus or drive for action, on the other hand, then it is the result of extrinsic motivation.

 Intrinsic motivation: stimuli or drive for action coming from within an individual.

Extrinsic motivation: stimuli or drive for action coming from sources external to an individual.

Intrinsic motivation originates within an individual and stems from the inherent interest and enjoyment to be found in undertaking a task or activity. The pleasure to be derived from the activity can be sufficient motivation to do it. A child will play, sing, dance, or run, purely for the joy of it. This is intrinsic motivation. Some adults can play computer games, ride a bicycle, or paint for hours at a time. This is intrinsic motivation.

> A child will play, sing, dance, or run, purely for the joy of it. This is intrinsic motivation.

Extrinsic motivation stems from something that is separate from the activity or task being undertaken. Someone goes to work at a job they dislike just to get paid. This is extrinsic motivation. Commonly the thing being sought is some form of reward, as is the case of working only for the money. People can also undertake activities in order to avoid punishment. There are very few people, for example, who find pleasure in paying an income tax bill. Most people pay taxes because they see it as an obligation and because they wish to avoid fines or other forms of punishment.

In short, intrinsic motivation stems from sources within the individual; extrinsic motivation stems from sources external to the individual.

> Intrinsic motivation stems from sources within the individual; extrinsic motivation stems from sources external to the individual.

In essence, the stimuli or drives behind extrinsic motivation are either rewards or punishments.

Behaviour is rarely driven exclusively by either intrinsic motivation or extrinsic motivation. More commonly, tasks are subject to both intrinsic and extrinsic motivation factors. While most people go to work to earn money, for example, many find aspects of their jobs that are inherently appealing and are intrinsically motivated to do them. Athletes are intrinsically motivated to achieve a personal best, but also enjoy the rewards that come with winning a contest.

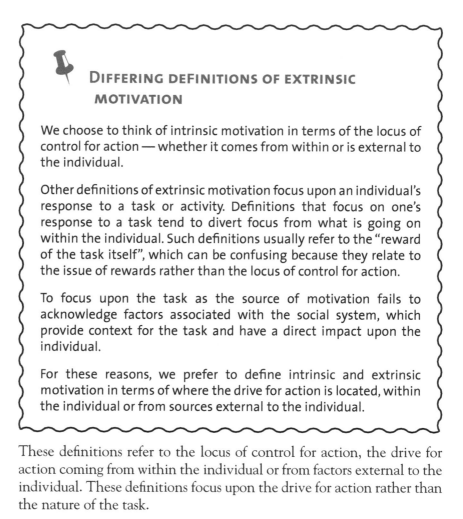

**DIFFERING DEFINITIONS OF EXTRINSIC MOTIVATION**

We choose to think of intrinsic motivation in terms of the locus of control for action — whether it comes from within or is external to the individual.

Other definitions of extrinsic motivation focus upon an individual's response to a task or activity. Definitions that focus on one's response to a task tend to divert focus from what is going on within the individual. Such definitions usually refer to the "reward of the task itself", which can be confusing because they relate to the issue of rewards rather than the locus of control for action.

To focus upon the task as the source of motivation fails to acknowledge factors associated with the social system, which provide context for the task and have a direct impact upon the individual.

For these reasons, we prefer to define intrinsic and extrinsic motivation in terms of where the drive for action is located, within the individual or from sources external to the individual.

These definitions refer to the locus of control for action, the drive for action coming from within the individual or from factors external to the individual. These definitions focus upon the drive for action rather than the nature of the task.

Unfortunately, in Australia and elsewhere most attempts to improve schools and schooling continue to focus on extrinsic motivators. The accountability movement —which holds that by using a set of assessments, good schools can be recognised and rewarded, while bad schools can be identified for assistance (or closure) — is based on extrinsic motivators.

In the USA, the *No Child Left Behind Act* ties federal funding to state achievement standards. Similarly, the USA Race to the Top grant scheme provides federal funding for schools based upon specific performance criteria.

In the United Kingdom, "schools causing concern" and "underperforming schools" are identified and subject to external interventions.

In Australia, National Partnership Agreements provide a framework by which federal funding is provided to lift the performance of schools that are identified as being in particular need of improvement. Extrinsic motivators are applied regularly in the name of school improvement.

Extrinsic motivators are applied regularly in the name of school improvement.

## Rewards

Any discussion of motivation would not be complete without some reference to rewards. It is the topic of rewards that appears most complex and controversial in the motivation literature.

> Reward: a desired object or experience that is conferred upon an individual or group contingent upon certain criteria being met.

A reward is conditional. If specific conditions are met the reward is given; if they are not met the reward is not conferred. Others refer to these as contingent rewards or "if-then" rewards.

A reward is conditional.

A reward may be a tangible object. Students can be rewarded with a sticker, stamp or lollipop issued by their teacher. Employees are paid for their efforts. A manager who meets performance targets may be rewarded with a cash bonus.

A reward may be a tangible experience. Parents may promise their children a trip to the movies on the condition that they are good during the week. Primary classroom teachers may plan a pizza party contingent on students achieving certain goals during the term. If the sales team exceeds their targets they may be rewarded with a trip to the Gold Coast or Hawaii.

A reward may also be a positive physiological or psychological experience. Pleasure can be found in the sensations that come from physical exercise. Most people experience a sense of joy from achieving challenging and meaningful goals. Human beings experience a sense of wellbeing when we connect deeply and meaningfully with others. These are all desirable experiences that can serve as rewards.

Rewards can be intrinsic or extrinsic.

Rewards can be intrinsic or extrinsic.

> Intrinsic reward: a desired object or experience that is conferred upon an individual or group, contingent upon having satisfied certain criteria, the conference of which is independent of the influence of others.

Intrinsic rewards derive directly from meeting the criteria associated with the task itself. The act of creating a magnificent image can be intrinsically rewarding for a photographer — the criteria relate to achieving a superb image. The pleasant sensations of physical exercise derive directly from the exercise itself. Helping others is intrinsically rewarding for most people. The criteria relate directly to the task itself.

> Intrinsic rewards come directly from undertaking the task or activity.

Intrinsic rewards come directly from undertaking a task or activity, independent of the influence of factors beyond the individual and the task. The intrinsic reward enjoyed by a photographer is independent of the reactions of others to the image. The joy that comes from solving a challenging puzzle or mastering a new skill is a personal experience, an intrinsic reward, which has little or nothing to do with what others think or how they behave. Others' responses can have an impact on the individual, but this is separate from the intrinsic reward derived from the task itself.

Extrinsic reward: a desired object or experience that is bestowed by sources external to the individual or group, contingent upon the individual or group having satisfied certain criteria.

Extrinsic rewards are objects and experiences that are separate to meeting the criteria associated with the task. A visit to the cinema is only related to good children's behaviour in that it is the offered reward. The desirability of a visit to the Gold Coast or Hawaii is quite separate from a team's capacity to exceed a sales target.

> Extrinsic rewards are separate from the task and are bestowed by others.

Another key feature of extrinsic rewards is that they are offered by someone external to the individual being rewarded. Intrinsic rewards are bestowed upon an individual directly from their engagement in the task itself, while extrinsic rewards are bestowed upon the individual by others.

Thus, extrinsic rewards are separate from the task and are bestowed by others. Here there is an implicit extension of the simple "if-then" notion to the more involved "if you do this, then I will do that", which has significant implication for relationships, which will be discussed later in this chapter.

In the presence of extrinsic rewards, an individual's focus is drawn to the reward. By definition, extrinsic rewards are offered to drive individuals to take action. The desirable nature of the reward captures the attention of the individual and elicits action. The greater the reward, the greater the focus.

Unfortunately, an unintended consequence of using an extrinsic reward is that the focus is more on gaining the reward than it is on the task. Extrinsic rewards divert attention from the task to the reward.

## Rewards in schools

The use of extrinsic rewards in schools and school systems is deeply ingrained.

Many classroom teachers offer extrinsic rewards regularly as part of their behaviour management approach. From an early age, students learn to please the teacher in order to be rewarded. Gold stars, lolly jars, student of the week, bonus points and free choice activities are offered as incentives. Teachers have been taught to do this; it is common practice. It diminishes the important intrinsic reward that comes from learning. Learning soon becomes more about work to please the teacher than personal growth and achievement.

When teachers are asked why they use extrinsic rewards — such as stickers, lollies, bonus points, or classroom parties — the answer is always the same: "The kids like them, and they work."

This response reflects a few assumptions about efficacy and motivation that can be questioned:

- "The kids like rewards." Just because someone likes something does not mean it is good for them, or that it helps them to learn. The more important question is whether rewards aid learning, and whether they offer a superior approach when compared to alternatives;

- Which kids like rewards? Obviously, the kids getting the rewards like them. There are few people who don't enjoy recognition, acknowledgement and being treated as a bit special. But what of those students who miss out? What of those students who are just as deserving but are not rewarded? How do they feel? Teachers are busy watching the faces of the rewarded students and rarely notice the faces of those who are disappointed. Being repeatedly disappointed can be extremely demotivating;

- The kids like rewards compared to what? Certainly, they could be expected to like getting rewards when compared to the option of not getting rewards. Who wouldn't? But what about the option of getting rewards when compared to the option of discovering and experiencing the true joy of learning? Do the students have a reference point for this comparison? Even very young students have the capacity to distinguish between rewards and learning, if given the opportunity;

> Extrinsic rewards divert attention from the task to the reward.

> The use of extrinsic rewards in schools and school systems is deeply ingrained.

- What does it mean to say that the rewards work? Does this mean that student learning is enhanced by rewards, or does it mean that rewards encourage compliance? Most importantly, how do rewards improve learning compared to other approaches? As John Hattie is at pains to point out, nearly everything works in education, the real question is how well particular approaches enhance learning when compared to their alternatives;

- Rewards create energy for more rewards. In an environment where rewards are common, so is the question "What do we get for doing this?" In some cases, rewards can actually lower achievement, as students who are motivated by extrinsic rewards will do just enough to get a reward, but won't go any further, artificially limiting their potential and motivation to achieve; and

- Why are rewards necessary anyway? Do we really need to bribe people to do the right thing? Do people deliberately withhold their best efforts and better methods waiting for the offer of a reward? Do students or teacher fail to try because they are waiting for reward to be offered? Of course not.

An implicit assumption behind an offer of rewards is that people need rewards because they won't do their best without them.

Myron Tribus makes explicit reference to the damage done by extrinsic motivators:

> Quality is what makes learning a pleasure and a joy.
>
> You can increase some measures of performance by using strong external motivators, such as grades, prizes, threats and punishments, but the attachment to learning will be unhealthy.
>
> It takes a joyful experience with learning to attach a student to education for life. Where there is joy in learning, the effort required does not seem like work.
>
> Myron Tribus, "When Quality Goes to School", p. 4. Available at http://www.qla.com.au/ Papers/5.

An implicit
assumption
behind an offer
of rewards is
that people need
rewards because
they won't
do their best
without them.

### 💬 LEARNING OR FISH AND CHIPS?

Rachelle Hedger, a teacher at Roxburgh Homestead Primary School, spent much of the first part of the year focussing her Year 2 class on their learning. The class developed a system map to clarify their values, vision and key processes (shown in Figure 3.8). They agreed that their purpose was learning. They developed processes and systems to support student learning: flowcharts, capacity matrices, quality criteria, and more. They became very focussed upon their learning.

Across the corridor, a more traditional teacher decided that his Year 2 class could have a class party if they completed their work. The class party would include fish and chips as a reward.

News of the proposed party spread to Rachelle's class. Could they have one too?

Rachelle didn't want to engage with extrinsic motivators such as this. She knows that they interfere with learning. After a lengthy discussion with the students, the students agreed that they didn't want the class party; they preferred to have real learning. They were genuinely happy that they would have real learning rather than fish and chips.

**Figure 6.2 Year 2 students discussing their learning**
Source: Roxburgh Homestead Primary School, Victoria.

## STUDENT OF THE WEEK CERTIFICATES

Some schools reward students with a certificate for being student of the week. The certificate is often presented at a school assembly in front of the whole school. It's a big deal.

This is Tom with his pupil of the week award. Tom's teacher, like many others, keeps a record of the winner each week. As the year progresses, each student in her class will take turns to be awarded pupil of the week. Everyone needs to be pupil of the week sometime; imagine the disappointment if a child were to miss out.

The students in Tom's class all know they will get a turn, so why bother? Rather than manipulating the children's emotions and wasting time doing so, wouldn't the effort be better spent on processes that really add value, like building strong relationships and improving learning?

Figure 6.3 Tom with his pupil of the week award

# Punishment

Another source of extrinsic motivation is punishment.

> 📖 Punishment: a negative or unpleasant experience imposed upon an individual or group in response to behaviour that is deemed to be unacceptable.

Punishments, like extrinsic rewards, are conferred upon an individual or group by other individuals or groups. They are frequently imposed by some form of authority, be it a court of law, a government official, a parent, guardian or teacher.

Like extrinsic rewards, punishment is contingent on certain criteria being met. Unacceptable behaviour is nearly always the criterion to be satisfied in order for the punishment to be imposed.

*Punishment is contingent on certain criteria being met.*

In contrast to extrinsic rewards, which are desirable to the recipients, punishments are undesirable. But the threat of punishment is used in a manner similar to extrinsic rewards: to modify behaviour.

A key feature of punishments and rewards is that they are bestowed or imposed upon the individual by other individuals or groups. This has profound implications for the nature of the relationship between the individual being punished or rewarded and those dishing out the treatment. Offering punishments and rewards reinforces dominance in a relationship, which can promote an unhelpful dynamic in social systems.

*Offering punishments and rewards reinforces dominance in the relationship.*

---

📌 **AN IRONY OF PUNISHMENT AND REWARDS IN SCHOOLS**

A common form of punishment in schools is to spend more time there. Being held in class during a break, for example, or staying after school for detention.

Similarly, a common form of reward is to escape from the routine tasks of learning: free time, playing games on the computer, or getting out early.

In such instances, teachers and school administrators are really saying, "We all know this is a horrible place to be: if you mess up, you have to spend more time here; if you behave well, you can escape."

---

# Consequences

Most schools are explicit that if behavioural guidelines or rules are broken there will be consequences. Unfortunately, some schools use the word consequences as a euphemism for punishments: "If you continue to misbehave, there will be consequences."

 Consequence: an outcome that follows as a result of something occurring earlier.

A key feature of consequences, like extrinsic rewards and punishments, is that the outcome is contingent on particular conditions being met.

There are natural consequences. Failing to water the garden during dry weather causes plants to wither and die. If you stand in the rain, you will get wet. If he stops breathing he dies. A glass falls from the bench and breaks. These are all examples of consequences. Plants need water to survive, animals need to breathe, gravity causes objects to fall, and glass is fragile. Interestingly, these are all examples of natural consequence, in which cause and effect relationships are based on laws of the natural world. Natural laws dictate natural consequences.

*Natural laws dictate natural consequences.*

 Natural consequence: an outcome that follows predictably from the laws of the natural world as a result of something occurring earlier.

There are also legal consequences. Governments pass laws and make regulations spelling out the consequences of failing to abide by the laws of the land. In Australia, for example, if you are caught speeding, you will be subject to a fine and demerit points or the loss of your driver's license. If you fail to pay your taxes, you will be fined and you can be sent to prison. In a democracy, such consequences are based upon community consensus. These consequences are laws of the community rather than laws of the natural world.

Other consequences are determined by unilateral decree. Parents can set clear expectations regarding the behaviour for their children and what will happen in the event of a breach of behavioural guidelines. Such decrees set boundaries for children and provide a clear basis for parent and child to understand what will follow as a result of boundaries being crossed. This can be helpful, as children need structure and boundaries in order to help them learn to self-regulate behaviour.

Dictators impose behavioural expectations and define consequences. These consequences are laws of the ruler and can have little to do with community consensus or laws of the natural world.

Laws, regulations and decrees are intended as extrinsic motivators. They intend to affect behaviour and, in this respect, are similar to rewards and punishments.

Schools and teachers frequently make rules and set consequences. These may be established in consultation with the school community, with the classroom community, or they may be unilaterally decreed. In the same way that parents set boundaries, it can be helpful for everyone to have clear understanding of the antecedents and the consequences. Making rules and consequences clear can ensure that there are well defined boundaries regarding what is acceptable and what is not.

Unfortunately, the discussion of consequences within schools frequently stops with definition of the rules and exposition of the consequences of breaking them.

If schools are truly charged with the task of preparing young people for greatness, then more attention needs to be paid to natural consequences. Individuals who truly understand and can anticipate the natural consequences of their actions will be more effective than those who cannot. Running out of time is a natural consequence of leaving things until the last minute. Falling over and hurting yourself is a natural consequence of running through the playground. Disciplined practice naturally develops enhanced skills. Young people would benefit from learning more about natural consequences than rules and punishments.

> Young people would benefit from learning more about natural consequences than rules and punishments.

Like all extrinsic motivators, consequences can distort individuals' intrinsic motivation. Where rules, regulations and consequences are strongly reinforced in a school culture, the focus naturally shifts to compliance with rules and regulations. This can be at the expense of accepting personal responsibility to get along with one another and do the right thing. The consequences can become the focus, rather than building capacity for desirable behaviour.

## 📌 PRINCIPLES AND CONSEQUENCES

In Chapter Two we introduced the quality improvement philosophy as a set of principles. We have attempted to define the philosophy as a set of principles that represent natural laws of social systems.

As such, failure to behave in a manner consistent with these principles has natural consequences. Our aim through these chapters has been to expand on the principles and describe the sub-optimisation that occurs when the principles are not understood or are ignored.

## Compliance versus engagement

Consider the logical extremes of pure extrinsic motivation and pure intrinsic motivation. While it is likely that nearly all motivation is the result of a combination of intrinsic and extrinsic factors, examination of the further reaches of such a continuum can provide valuable insight.

At one end of the continuum is compliance.

📖 Compliance: submission to the will of others.

Handing your money to an armed bandit is an act of compliance. Paying a speeding fine is an act of compliance. Meeting the obligations of an organisational policy with which you disagree is an act of compliance. Submitting assignments and doing homework can be acts of compliance. The key feature of compliance is that the stimuli and drive for action come from sources external to the individual — the individual is extrinsically motivated to comply. Extrinsic motivation can thus lead to compliance.

Individuals can also choose not to comply. They may, for whatever reason, decide that they will not submit. Such behaviour occurs from time to time. For the most part, this is done after careful consideration of the consequences. Extrinsic motivation can also lead to defiance.

Defiance is frequently met with an increase in extrinsic motivation factors. If we fail to pay our taxes in time, a penalty is applied. If we still refuse to pay, we can be taken to court and be required to pay court costs as well as the fine and penalty. If we continue to defy the law, we can be sent to jail. Students can be subjected to detention, suspension and expulsion.

Compliance is the best we can hope for if we rely solely upon extrinsic motivation. Inherent in seeking compliance is the risk of defiance. In short, extrinsic motivation factors lead to either compliance or defiance.

At the other end of the continuum is engagement.

📖 Engagement: enthusiastic commitment of attention, effort and care.

The keen gardener who spends numerous hours each week tending to plants and flowers demonstrates engagement. The adult who persists with a Sudoku puzzle until it is solved demonstrates engagement.

---

Compliance is the best we can hope for if we rely solely upon extrinsic motivation.

The musician who practices regularly to perfect their performance demonstrates engagement. Students with a love for learning also demonstrate engagement.

Engaged people are willing, passionate, and persistent.

Intrinsic motivation can lead to engagement.

Clearly, there are degrees of engagement. A Sudoku puzzle may be captivating, while weeding the garden is somewhat less inspiring. The degree of enthusiasm and commitment varies from person to person.

It is impossible to compel someone to become highly engaged. The enthusiasm to commit to a task or activity and the choice to devote care, attention and effort to it can only come from within. It may be possible to force compliance to complete a task or activity; it is not possible to force engagement. High degrees of engagement can only come from intrinsic motivation, from the drive within each individual.

> It may be possible to force compliance to complete a task or activity; it is not possible to force engagement.

There is a wealth of evidence that intrinsic motivation and engagement with learning typically declines with a child's progress through the current schooling system. It also seems that many fail to reclaim their intrinsic motivation after it has been suppressed through schooling. A large global study of nearly 11,000 workers world-wide, undertaken by Blessing White in 2011, found that fewer than one in three employees world-wide are engaged. It would seem that the diminishing engagement that teachers observe through the school years extends into work life.

What is causing this decline in engagement over time? The prevailing system of management.

> The prevailing system of management is driving the loss of engagement in organisations and communities.

The prevailing system of management is driving the loss of engagement in organisations and communities. It pays insufficient attention to factors that enhance intrinsic motivation and engages in practices that systematically deprive individuals of joy in work and learning. This point was constantly emphasised by Deming:

> One is born with intrinsic motivation, self-esteem, dignity, cooperation, curiosity, joy in learning. These attributes are high at the beginning of life, but are gradually crushed by the forces of destruction.
>
> W. Edwards Deming, 1993, *The New Economics: For industry, government and education*, MIT, Cambridge, p. 125.

Myron Tribus was fond of using the diagram shown in Figure 6.4 to illustrate the hidden assumption in managers' heads: workers have no heads, cannot think, and must therefore be directed and coerced into action.

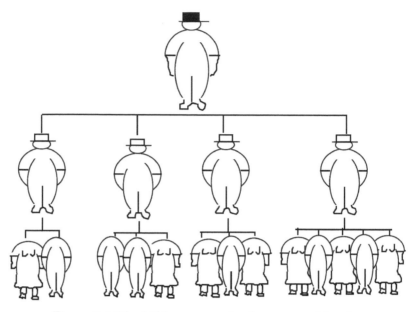

**Figure 6.4 The hidden assumption in managers' heads**
Source: Myron Tribus, 1992, "The Germ Theory of Management".
Available at http://www.qla.com.au/Papers/5.

Sadly, this assumption appears to remain to this day. It applies within schooling systems in which administrators make decisions for their principals and teachers. Many principals similarly hold this assumption in making decisions for teachers, and many teachers hold this assumption about their students.

As has been stated, compliance is no substitute for engagement.

The factors that can enhance engagement will be discussed shortly, but first the interactions among intrinsic and extrinsic motivation factors are worthy of a brief exploration.

*Compliance is no substitute for engagement.*

## Interaction among intrinsic and extrinsic motivation factors

Research into the interaction among motivation factors, particularly the impact of extrinsic rewards on intrinsic factors, is contentious and ongoing.

One phenomenon that demonstrates how the use of extrinsic rewards can negatively impact on intrinsic motivation is overjustification. Overjustification occurs when an extrinsic reward diminishes the intrinsic motivation towards an activity. Where offering an incentive to complete homework is found to reduce individuals' intrinsic motivation for home learning, for example, then the incentives are a form of overjustification. Some argue that even the presence of extrinsic rewards undermines pre-existing intrinsic factors.

Overjustification can be explained by the shift in the locus of control from within the individual to an externally provided reward, which brings with it a degree of submission and compliance. This in turn diminishes the individual's perceptions of self-determination and their intrinsic motivation.

> Extrinsic motivation factors can diminish intrinsic motivation.

Research on the phenomenon of overjustification is contentious and inconclusive. It is widely agreed that overjustification can occur, for example, when a previously administered reward is withdrawn. In such cases intrinsic motivation has been shown to be diminished (see the story below for an example from personal experience). Overjustification is an unintended consequence of the use of extrinsic motivation factors.

For the most part, researchers agree there are interactions among extrinsic motivation factors and intrinsic motivation factors. They do not agree, however, on the circumstances in which extrinsic and intrinsic factors reinforce each other or oppose one another.

It is sufficient to recognise that overjustification can occur and that it is possible to diminish intrinsic motivation with extrinsic factors. This is a key reason that care must be exercised in the use of extrinsic motivation factors.

 **WHAT WILL THEY OFFER NEXT?**

I used to travel regularly to Sydney on business. During my initial visits I tried a number of hotels to find one that best met my needs within the available budget.

I found a hotel that met my requirements. It had clean rooms, acceptable food, easy access to transport, and was located in an interesting area in which I could take a walk in the evening. After a few visits, the hotel invited me to join their frequent guest program. I accepted the offer.

When I entered my room at the commencement of my next visit, there was a small box of chocolates awaiting me, thanking me for being a frequent guest.

During the following visit, I was greeted with a large bowl of fruit.

The rewards escalated: a half bottle of wine, a full bottle of wine, a bottle of port wine.

I began to look forward to my visits to Sydney, wondering what I would be rewarded with next. Then ... nothing. There was no tangible reward. Nor was I rewarded during my next visit. For some reason, the hotel had cancelled the reward program. Perhaps it was costing too much, I do not know.

I distinctly remember being both disappointed and resentful that they took away my reward.

Downplaying my reasons for selecting the hotel in the first place, I moved to a different hotel. This was a lose–lose outcome: the hotel that had offered and then cancelled the reward program lost my custom, and I lost sight of why I chose the hotel in the first place, putting myself through the task of finding a new one.

# Enhancing intrinsic motivation and engagement

## Motivation: it's personal

One of the biggest challenges in coming to understand human motivation is its highly personal nature. Something that you find compelling, others may find tedious. Your intrinsic motivation towards an activity may be weak, while the same activity may have strong appeal to someone else. The factors that enhance my motivation can be very different to those that enhance yours. Factors that demotivate me may have little effect on you.

The rewards and threats of punishments needed to stimulate action vary enormously from person to person. The factors that drive deep engagement also vary.

Given this, how can teachers be expected to motivate their students? How can principals be expected to motivate their teachers? How can anyone be expected to motivate another individual? In short, they cannot.

Despite this fact, most of us have been taught that a key aspect of a leader's job is to motivate others. This is particularly true of teachers, which is unfortunate. Teachers can certainly inspire, support, encourage and mediate the learning of their students, but they cannot motivate them. However, the systems and processes they put into place in their classrooms can demotivate them.

> The factors that enhance my motivation can be very different to those that enhance yours.

> Teachers can certainly inspire, support, encourage and mediate the learning of their students, but they cannot motivate them.

Teachers manage systems of learning, the most notable of which is the classroom. In order to maximise motivation and learning, teachers need to work with students to identify and remove the demotivators — the barriers to learning — and create a systemic environment that maximises the factors that unlock intrinsic motivation and enhance learning. But how can this be achieved when the impact of the various factors on students' motivation varies so widely from one student to the next?

Teachers can do three things to manage the systems that impact so strongly on the motivation of each individual student. Teachers can:

1. Build caring, respectful and productive relationships with their students so that they learn, along with their students, the factors that enhance and detract from their motivation;

2. Share the generic factors that enhance intrinsic motivation for most people with their students and use these factors as the basis for the design, operation and continual improvement of the systems of learning; and

3. Work with their students to identify and remove the barriers to students' intrinsic motivation and learning.

These factors, outlined in Table 6.1, form the corner-stone of a theory for action for teachers. The resulting theory and practices can be modified and adapted in the light of what is learned with individual students and groups of students from year to year.

## Intrinsic motivation: building influencing factors into systems

High degrees of engagement and intrinsic motivation come from the drive within each individual. We build extrinsic motivation factors, such as rewards and punishments, into the structure and operation of our systems and, in so doing, damage intrinsic motivation. It is not possible to compel others to become engaged, so how can we maximise engagement and intrinsic motivation?

Over the past decade we have drawn upon a wide range of research, as well as our own experience, to develop the following model of the factors that can enhance intrinsic motivation and engagement: purpose, choice, mastery, and belonging.

> In order to maximise motivation and learning, teachers need to work with students to identify and remove the demotivators — the barriers to learning.

> We have developed the following model of the factors that can enhance intrinsic motivation and engagement: purpose, choice, mastery, and belonging.

| Purpose | Meaning | Advancing my interests and passions. Making a positive difference to me or others. |
|---|---|---|
| | Relevance | Pertinent to me, my situation and my future. |
| | Possibility | Accepting what is to be accomplished and uncovering the potential of what could be achieved. |
| Choice | Responsibility | Committing to the task. Experiencing a sense of authority. Being relied upon by others. |
| | Autonomy | Selecting methods and resources, defining quality standards and determining time-lines and milestones. |
| | Creativity | Exploring and expressing thoughts, skills, imagination and individuality. |
| Mastery | Challenge | Finding the task interesting, compelling and achievable. |
| | Achievement | Monitoring one's own progress and performance. Celebrating learning and success. |
| | Learning | Trying things, making mistakes, developing new skills and finding different ways of thinking. |
| Belonging | Collaboration | Enjoying interdependence, working towards shared goals and experiencing authentic teamwork. |
| | Feedback | Giving and receiving constructive feedback and encouragement. |
| | Support | Recognising skills and abilities in one's self and others. Sharing, helping, learning together. Being free of fear. |

**Table 6.1 Factors that can enhance intrinsic motivation and engagement**

The factors identified in this model are generic, in that they apply, to varying degrees, to everyone. It is a model of common causes. By building these into our systems we tap into intrinsic motivation.

Let's look more closely at each of the factors.

## Create purpose

Of the four groups of factors that can enhance motivation and engagement, purpose is perhaps the most personal. Purpose relates to the nature of a task. Things that abound with meaning, relevance and possibility for one person can be totally devoid of purpose for another.

## Meaning

Activities that tap into an individual's interests and passions result in greater drive than activities that do not. Our brains are designed to "select in" information that has meaning to us — it is easier to learn what is meaningful to us. Most people are driven to do things that will make a positive difference for themselves and in their own lives. Most individuals also derive meaning from making a positive difference for others. Finding a sense of meaning in a task or activity can be a strong motivator. Meaning inspires passion and commitment. Meaning unlocks intrinsic motivation.

## Relevance

To be driven to action, that action needs to bear some relation to the life of the individual. Actions that accord to the circumstance and needs of the individual provide greater intrinsic motivation than those that do not. Lack of relevance is a demotivator, just ask any teenager (or teacher who is a participant of a professional learning workshop).

## Possibility

Possibility relates to the extent to which an individual uncovers and buys into a vision of what might be possible. As a first step, the potential of an activity must be clearly understood and accepted. What could be the benefit of this? What would it look like to do this superbly well? Failing to see the possibility in a task is usually demotivating.

Collectively, these three factors — meaning, relevance and possibility — help the individual understand what is to be done, why it should be done, how it relates to the individual and the individual's future, what can be achieved, and how pursuit of the activity matters in the larger scheme of things.

## Provide choice

These factors relate to the extent to which an individual has a sense of control over tasks. These factors consider the degree to which the task offers the opportunity to practice responsibility, enhance skills of self-management, and exercise creativity and self-expression. Not feeling in control leads to anxiety, which is a major barrier to intrinsic motivation and learning.

## Responsibility

Being given the authority to get the job done and doing what it takes to do the job well is what responsibility is all about.

Following someone else's directive is very different to accepting responsibility. Some managers complain that their employees don't accept responsibility. Parents and teachers make the same complaint about children. Some principals complain about teachers. Often what they are saying is that people will not do as they are told, rather than failing to exercise responsibility.

Being afforded the authority to engage with a whole task, not just a bit of it, and developing a sense of being needed by others can enhance motivation. Not being given the authority necessary to take responsibility is demotivating.

### Autonomy

While responsibility is about accepting one's role in the completion of an activity, autonomy is about exercising choice regarding the activity itself and how the activity is handled.

To act autonomously is to make choices about the activities, methods and resources to be used, which include establishing a schedule and self-managing that schedule. To act autonomously is also to participate in defining quality standards — the criteria by which the quality of the activity will be measured.

With autonomy comes a sense of control. Exercising autonomy can unlock intrinsic motivation.

### Creativity

Creativity goes beyond taking on a task and choosing how it will be managed, into the realm of individual expression. The freedom to explore one's own imagination, thoughts and skills, and then applying them to a task can be highly motivating.

## Promote mastery

Mastery is about building capacity, capability and competence. In order to develop mastery an individual needs to be challenged (just the right amount, not too much, not too little), to monitor and celebrate their achievements, and to learn as they go.

### Challenge

For an activity to pose a challenge, it must be interesting to those doing it. Without interest there can be no challenge. (Note that interest is different to relevance and meaning).

Activities that place too much demand on the skills and abilities of an individual can lead to a loss of interest because they are deemed to be too difficult and the outcome unachievable. Activities that place insufficient demand, on the other hand, are deemed boring.

Getting the level of challenge just right can make a task compelling, unlocking high levels of intrinsic motivation. (Vygotsky referred to this as the zone of proximal development).

The right degree of challenge, with interest, can be a motivator. Too much challenge or too little challenge can be a demotivator.

**Achievement**

Monitoring one's own performance, and celebrating growth and accomplishments along the way, is what achievement is all about. Seeing progress can be highly motivating; to fail to see progress can be demotivating.

**Learning**

Everyone is born with a passion for learning. Learning is as natural as breathing. Humans find great joy in trying new things, developing new skills, building on existing capabilities, and exploring new ways of thinking. Learning contributes greatly to one's sense of mastery and can be a powerful intrinsic motivator.

## Foster a sense of belonging

The factors that comprise belonging are different in nature to the three previous groups of purpose, choice and mastery. These all relate in some way to the relationship between the individual and the activity. Can the individual see purpose in the activity, are they afforded choice as they approach the activity, and does the activity build mastery?

This set of factors recognises that humans are social beings and that a good deal of learning goes on in a social context — in a social system — and that we have a deeply felt need to belong and feel connected to others. There are factors within social systems that can enhance motivation and others that can suppress motivation which relate to a sense of belonging.

**Collaboration**

The joy that comes from working closely and effectively with others towards a shared goal can be highly motivating. It takes time, skill and effort to learn to work with others in a truly cooperative manner.

When this is achieved, the results can be spectacular and the experience highly memorable. There is little doubt that much more can be achieved working in collaboration with others than can be achieved working alone.

### Feedback

Feedback is an essential feature of every self-regulating system. Comparing our knowledge of where we are and where we prefer to be in order to decide what to do next is critical to our sense of wellbeing.

In a social system, individuals give each other feedback that can be used to adapt behaviour and performance. Where this is done in a caring, constructive and encouraging manner, it can fan the flame of intrinsic motivation. Where feedback is given in a critical, malicious or spiteful way, it can be dispiriting and deeply demotivating.

Learning can be accelerated with feedback. When a teacher works with a learner to help them reflect upon a task, their learning processes and their metacognitive approaches, this feedback can significantly improve learning. It also enhances the learner's capacity to manage their learning, which is highly motivating. This was established as a highly significant factor in the influence of learning through the research of John Hattie (see John Hattie, 2009, *Visible Learning: A synthesis of over 800 meta-analyses relating to achievement*, Routledge, New York).

### Support

Recognising the contribution, progress and abilities of others is a first step in offering support to them. Offering to share, help and learn together can significantly boost an individual's motivation.

Intrinsic motivation can be enhanced by paying attention to these factors and working with students to design these factors into our systems of learning.

The following video clip presents Daniel Pink's discussion of the factors that influence intrinsic motivation and the research behind these findings.

Video Clip: Daniel Pink on YouTube
http://www.youtube.com/watch?v=u6XAPnuFjJc

**FEEDBACK TO CONTROL SYSTEMS**

Feedback is necessary for any system to remain on track. A feedback loop involves measuring the output of a system, and then comparing it to a reference value in order to generate an error signal that is fed back into the system as an input. The aim is to regulate the system output to match the desired reference.

As individuals, we constantly monitor others' reactions to our own actions. (Some people do this better than others, of course.) This observation of their reaction (measurement of the output) is evaluated against the reaction we expect and would like to see (our reference value), and we note any difference (the error signal) and use it (as an input) to adapt our behaviour. We do this spontaneously.

We also do this with task performance. We monitor our progress on a task (measure the output), compare it to where we would like to be (the reference), and if the two don't match (an error signal) we use this as an input in order to decide what to do next.

Every system needs feedback loops if it is to self-regulate. This applies equally to: the air conditioner requiring a thermostat; checking the bank balance before (or, sadly, after) we go on a spending spree; and to students and teachers needing feedback to evaluate the efficacy of their actions.

## Intrinsic motivation: removing barriers

It is far more productive to identify and remove the barriers — demotivating factors — to learning and improvement than to push harder. For example, it is far more effective to identify the reasons people have not implemented a new program and then take action on those reasons, than to exhort those individuals to get on with it.

Intrinsic motivation plays a part as people make their own choices regarding purpose and methods. By understanding these choices, leaders are able to adapt in such a way that effort aligns. Trying to force a change may bring only compliance.

> It is far more productive to identify and remove the barriers to learning and improvement than to push harder.

## FORCES AFFECTING CHANGE

This principle of managing change in social organisations is attributed to the work of Kurt Lewin, a German-American social psychologist, regarded as one of the founders of modern psychology, who lived during the first half of last century. Lewin is well known for his contribution to the study of group dynamics, action research and the development of force field analysis.

Force field analysis is the study of the driving and restraining forces of social systems. Lewin recognised that social systems exist in equilibrium. Forces drive social systems toward a goal while other forces restrain movement toward the goal. These forces are not static, but are changing within the system and its environment.

Force field analysis helps to identify restraining forces — barriers. Strategies can then be developed to limit the impact of the most significant restraining forces, or to remove them altogether. With system change, it is generally more effective to address restraining forces than it is to increase driving forces.

The force field analysis tool is discussed and its use illustrated in Chapter Three. It remains one of the most powerful tools in the quality learning toolbox.

## Intrinsic motivation in the classroom

Traditional didactic approaches to teaching do not promote intrinsic motivation. Some teachers churn through endless cycles of plan–teach–assess in the hope that students may learn. If educators truly take to heart the need to unlock intrinsic motivation in learners, then a different approach is required. A more collaborative approach is needed.

Every learner is different, which adds enormously to both the joy and the complexity of teaching. The breadth and depth of prior knowledge varies, interests vary from student to student, as does the sense of belonging within a class or school.

The home environment varies enormously too. Some families support and strongly encourage learning while others are less committed.

How are teachers supposed to manage this variation? It can be extremely difficult to teach a class where the variation in knowledge and skills is measured in years of development.

The most common response seems to be sorting students into similar capability groupings. This is frequently called streaming or tracking. Teachers are expected to design separate programs for each group or, as a minimum, establish different assessment criteria.

There are three main problems with this approach. Firstly, how can we be certain that a student has been assigned to the correct group? How can they move between groups when their progress calls for it? Secondly, this approach demands yet more work for teachers already struggling to do all that is required of them. Finally, students in the lower performing groups can become known as "the dummies" group, identified by themselves and others as losers, which creates a very demotivating learning environment. Capability grouping is also a form of chopping the tail, the disadvantages of which were discussed earlier in Chapter Five. It does not improve the system.

Enhancing intrinsic motivation in students is not more work, nor is it something teachers can do alone. The factors that enhance intrinsic motivation, identified earlier in this chapter, may be seen as requiring teachers to do even more than they do currently. How can teachers be expected to assess each factor on the model for each student for each learning activity and then respond to the findings? They cannot, it is too much to ask, even with small class sizes. However, it can be done if teachers equip students to take greater responsibility for their learning and if they work with the students to adapt classroom processes.

Teachers and students can learn to work together in a manner that is more interdependent than the traditional dependent student-teacher relationship. This is not additional work for teachers, rather it is a different way of approaching the role. The key is to work with the students, which requires different relationships and the use of tools to support the collaboration. A capacity matrix, for example, is a profoundly useful tool to help learners understand what is to be learned, and to allow them to set goals and track progress. There is more to be said regarding the student-teacher relationship in the next section of this chapter.

> Teachers and students can learn to work together in a manner that is more interdependent than the traditional dependent student-teacher relationship.

The capacity matrix becomes an individual learning plan for every learner. Being clear what is to be learned, setting goals and monitoring progress accelerates learning.

Learning plans are currently used for students exhibiting special needs, but more recently there have been calls for all students to have individualised learning plans. Requiring teachers to develop the traditional individual learning plan for each of their students and then managing each plan is a practical impossibility. In the current system, teachers simply do not have the time to do this well for large numbers of students. To adapt the system to make it possible for teachers to develop individual learning plans for every student would not be beneficial either. Firstly, to require teachers to develop individual learning plans for every student would be prohibitively expensive. More teaching resources would need to be devoted to this activity than are currently available. Secondly, to do so would deprive students of yet another opportunity to take responsibility for their learning. There is nothing stopping students from learning how to develop and monitor their own individual learning plans.

The capacity matrix is an effective and efficient way for students to take responsibility for their learning, to create individual learning plans in the classroom, and to significantly enhance intrinsic motivation.

> The capacity matrix is an effective and efficient way for students to take responsibility for their learning.

## GIVING STUDENTS VOICE

In recent times there has been a push to give students voice in the school, the classroom and their learning.

Unfortunately, in many schools this extends only to the election of representative student leaders who occasionally meet as a Student Representative Council to discuss student related issues after consulting with classmates. The matters they discuss are restricted in terms of their impact on school operations and improvement.

Alternatively, some schools have embraced an all-inclusive approach where every student is given a voice. This proves to be highly motivating, building student ownership and pride in the school, and most importantly, breeding responsibility for learning.

The use of quality learning tools provides a means for all students to have input to school and classroom operations. At the school level, they can contribute to direction-setting and planning, the agreement of school values and behaviours (which can replace imposed school rules), and the development of school policy and processes. They are part of all continual improvement efforts.

School and classroom Plan–Do–Study–Act activities include students as team members. There are very few improvements to be made in a school or classroom where students are not a key stakeholder. Their input is invaluable.

Tools like the parking lot can be used to frame the agenda for class meetings in order to continually improve the learning environment, while the correlation chart and plus delta can provide a vehicle for every student to provide feedback and input to improve learning and teaching processes.

# Reflection questions

**?** How are rewards and punishments used in your organisation? To what effect?

**?** To what degree is the focus on natural consequences at your school, in contrast to rules-based consequences? What are the students learning as a result?

**?** Under what circumstances do students exhibit compliance? Under what circumstances do they exhibit genuine engagement? How do you know?

**?** Think of learning experiences where you were truly engaged. How did the factors that influence intrinsic motivation, as outlined in Table 6.1, apply for you in those experiences? What about experiences that were disengaging?

**?** How well do the activities set for students at your school reflect the factors that influence intrinsic motivation?

**?** Can you think of examples of extrinsic motivation (rewards) negatively affecting learning and/or performance?

# Quality learning tools to enhance motivation

The following tools, along with many others throughout this book, can play a role in enhancing motivation.

The inclusive nature of the tools contributes to a sense of belonging by fostering collaboration and a culture of feedback. Others help with clarifying purpose and provide choice to each individual.

# ✖ Capacity matrix

The capacity matrix, developed by Myron Tribus and David Langford, is probably the most important motivation and learning tool among the suite of quality learning tools. An example is shown in Figure 6.5

Its importance comes from the manner in which it puts the learner in control of their learning. The capacity matrix enables many of the factors that enhance intrinsic motivation, particularly those to do with choice. The capacity matrix goes a long way to supporting the development of mastery, a key factor in enhancing intrinsic motivation.

## Being clear about what is being learned

The capacity matrix is a visual learning and charting technique. It makes explicit what the learner is working towards knowing, understanding and being able to do as a result of their learning efforts.

Capacity matrices enable learners to take greater responsibility for their learning by making it explicit and visible. Each row of the matrix defines a learning outcome. Desired outcomes and curriculum requirements are broken down into specific and manageable elements, row by row. Learners track their progress against these elements.

The matrix makes explicit the breadth and depth of learning. It expresses learning intentions explicitly and in a manner that is meaningful to the learner. Learning outcomes are expressed in a clear language that the learner can understand, not in abstract curriculum-speak.

With the aid of a capacity matrix, learners can plan their learning, monitor their progress and track their learning over time.

Note that a capacity matrix documents what is being learned. It does not include reference to how it is being learned. It does not include activities or tasks. Nor does it dictate the order in which it is to be learned. These factors can be left for the learner to decide.

## Levels of learning

The columns in the capacity matrix are used by the learner to track their progress through different levels of learning.

Typically, four levels of learning are used. These four levels are related to Bloom's Taxonomy (L. W. Anderson, D. R. Krathwohl, et al. (eds.) 2001, *A Taxonomy for Learning, Teaching, and Assessing: A revision of Bloom's Taxonomy of educational objectives*, Allyn and Bacon, Boston). They are:

1. **Information**: factual knowledge, being able to recall facts and data;

2. **Knowledge**: conceptual knowledge, being able to understand, interpret and explain;

3. **Know-how**: procedural knowledge, being able to use knowledge in a practical way across different situations; and

4. **Wisdom**: metacognitive knowledge, being able to synthesise creative new solutions, to recognise new problems and possible solutions.

The learner shades, ticks or dates their progress through these levels of learning and the capacity matrix reflects their journey.

The final column in a capacity matrix is used by the learner to record evidence of their learning in order to demonstrate, document and defend their self-assessment.

## Evidence of learning

Evidence of the learning progress demonstrated in the capacity matrix is captured by the learner in a learning portfolio. Along the way, each learner creates a portfolio of evidence to demonstrate his or her progress.

This portfolio is not a folder of their best work, but rather provides evidence to demonstrate, document and defend their self-assessment of learning. It contains work samples and other artefacts that illustrate mastery to the levels claimed in the matrix. Periodically, the learner confers with their teacher to verify their self-assessment and records of progress.

Video Clip 6.1: Capacity matrices in high school
http://www.qla.com.au/Videos/3

Source: Mordialloc College, Victoria

Video Clip 6.1 shows secondary school students explain how their use of project based, integrated curriculum capacity matrices help them to take responsibility for their learning.

Video Clip 6.2: Capacity matrices in primary school
http://www.qla.com.au/Videos/3

Source: Hackham East Primary School, SA.

In Video Clip 6.2, we see highly motivated Year 2 students explaining the use of capacity matrices to accelerate their learning and enhance their engagement with spelling.

There are examples of capacity matrices in Appendix 1, and there are many more on the QLA web site: www.qla.com.au.

Templates to develop a capacity matrix can also be found on the QLA web site.

# Capacity Matrix

| AIM | Capacity | Capacity Breakdown | Information | Knowledge | Know-how | Wisdom | Evidence of Learning 3-D Portfolio |
|---|---|---|---|---|---|---|---|
| First Area | | | | | | | |
| Second Area | | | | | | | |
| Third Area | | | | | | | |

Learners Name: _____

Date Updated: _____

Figure 6.5 Capacity matrix template

# Mathematics. Stage 5: Measurement

Name: James Wright

Date Updated: 10 June

| AIM | Capacity | Capacity Breakdown | Learning Process | | | | Evidence of Learning: 3-D Portfolio |
|---|---|---|---|---|---|---|---|
| | | | I have heard of this (Information) | I can explain this in my own words (Knowledge) | I can apply this on my own (Know-how) | I relate this to new situations and teach others. (Wisdom) | Portfolio, Activity, Presentation, Worksheet, Assignment, etc. |
| Length (MS2.1 & MS3.1) | Units of Measure | Metre (m) | | | | | I led a workshop on this |
| | | Centimetre (cm) | | | | | I led a workshop on this |
| | | Millimetre (mm) | | | | | I led a workshop on this |
| | | Kilometre (km) | | | | | Poster project |
| | | Converting between mm, cm, m and km | | | | | Poster project |
| | | Speed (km/h) | | | | | Activity 6.2 - workbook |
| | | Decimal notation (2 decimal places) | | | | | Activity 6.3 –workbook |
| | | Decimal notation (3 decimal places) | | | | | Activity 6.3 – workbook |
| | Estimating length | Strategies for estimation | | | | | |
| | | Length | | | | | |
| | | Distance | | | | | |
| | | Perimeter of a square | | | | | Activity 6.6 - workbook |
| | | Perimeter of a rectangle | | | | | Activity 6.6- workbook |
| | | Perimeter of an equilateral triangle | | | | | |
| | | Perimeter of an isosceles triangle | | | | | |
| | | In different units of measure | | | | | Notes in maths note book |
| | Measure and record | Length | | | | | Measurement project |
| | | Distance | | | | | Measurement project |
| | | Perimeter of a square | | | | | Measurement project |
| | | Perimeter of a rectangle | | | | | Measurement project |
| | | Perimeter of an equilateral triangle | | | | | |
| | | Perimeter of an isosceles triangle | | | | | |
| | | Features of objects associated with length that can be measured (e.g. Height, width, etc.) | | | | | Notes in maths note book |
| | Comparisons | Referred to a known length (e.g. 1m) | | | | | Measurement project |
| | | Differing measurements of same item | | | | | |
| | | In different units of measure | | | | | Measurement project |
| | Measurement devices | Ruler | | | | | Measurement project |
| | | Tape measure | | | | | Measurement project |
| | | Wheel | | | | | |
| | | Scales on a map | | | | | |

**Figure 6.6 Completed mathematics capacity matrix**

Name: _____    Date started: _____

Completed: _____

## Talking and Listening Matrix – Stage 3

Syllabus Outcome TES 1.1, 1.3, 1.4 TS 1.1, 1.3, 1.4, 2.1, 2.3, 2.4, 3.1, 3.3, 3.4

| Capacity | Capacity Breakdown | Information I know something about this. | Knowledge I can do this with help | Know-how I can do this on my own all the time | Wisdom I can teach others | Do I have proof? Separate evidence required for each criteria. |
|---|---|---|---|---|---|---|
| Social Purpose | Speaks on a range of topics for different purposes. | | | | | |
| | Listens to gather information, follow instructions and share ideas. | | | | | |
| | Communicates ideas and information in classroom, school and social situations independently with peers and in groups. | | | | | |
| Presentation Skills | Uses various skills to give an oral presentation: Tone | | | | | |
| | Volume | | | | | |
| | Pace | | | | | |
| | Eye contact | | | | | |
| | Expression | | | | | |
| | Asks and responds to a range of questions (who, what, when, why, how). | | | | | |
| Language structures and features | Recognises different types of, and purposes for spoken language | | | | | |
| | Identify features and organisational patterns of spoken texts. | | | | | |
| | Plans and sequences own presentation | | | | | |
| | Uses visual prompts to give a presentation | | | | | |
| | Evaluates own performance using criteria | | | | | |

**Figure 6.7 Talking and listening capacity matrix for Year 5 and 6 students**

Source: Developed by the Armidale Catholic Schools Office, NSW.

## Activities and resource matrices

In addition to the capacity matrix, it is sometimes helpful to create two additional matrices: one for recommended learning activities, and another for associated resources. For these additional matrices, the rows are identical to that of the capacity matrix while the columns refer to activities and resources. The cells in each matrix identify the degree to which each activity or resource contributes to learning against a specific capacity.

| Aim | Capacity | Capacity Breakdown | | Learning Activity | | | | Learning Resource | | | |
|---|---|---|---|---|---|---|---|---|---|---|---|
| | | | | System Mapping | Improvement Team Project | Classroom Project | School Document Activity | System Map Guide Book | PDSA Guide Book | Classroom Manual | School Documentation DVD |
| SYSTEMS – Understand your systems | Systems | Creating System Maps | Creating System Maps | | | | | | | | |
| | | | School System Maps | | | | | | | | |
| | | | Classroom System Maps | | | | | | | | |
| | | Documenting Systems | Documenting systems: policies, processes and forms | | | | | | | | |
| | | | Document control | | | | | | | | |
| | | Determining Cause and Effect | Determining Cause and Effect | | | | | | | | |
| | | | Fishbone Diagram | | | | | | | | |
| | | | Five Whys | | | | | | | | |
| | | Understanding Interrelationships | Understanding system interrelationships | | | | | | | | |
| | | | Optimising systems | | | | | | | | |
| | | | Interrelationship Diagraph | | | | | | | | |
| | | | Correlation Chart | | | | | | | | |
| | Purpose | Building Shared Purpose | Establishing purpose | | | | | | | | |
| | | | P²T | | | | | | | | |
| | | Creating Visions of Excellence | Developing shared vision | | | | | | | | |
| | | | Quality Criteria | | | | | | | | |
| | | | Problem Statement | | | | | | | | |
| | | | Imagineering | | | | | | | | |
| | Processes | Process Thinking | Identifying and documenting processes, training and coaching | | | | | | | | |
| | | | Deployment Flowchart | | | | | | | | |
| | | | Fixing processes, removing blame | | | | | | | | |
| | Clients | Understanding Clients' Needs | Identifying system/process Clients | | | | | | | | |
| | | | Obtaining Client input to understand needs | | | | | | | | |
| | | | Using Client needs to drive planning and improvement | | | | | | | | |
| | | | Perception Analysis | | | | | | | | |
| | Stakeholders | Managing Stakeholder Relationships | Identifying stakeholders of the system | | | | | | | | |
| | | | Managing key stakeholder relationships | | | | | | | | |
| | | Developing Shared Values | Establishing shared values | | | | | | | | |
| | | | Expressing values and behaviours | | | | | | | | |
| | | | Self/peer assessment of behaviours | | | | | | | | |
| | | | Values in use | | | | | | | | |
| | | | Code of Cooperation | | | | | | | | |
| | | | **Totals** | 13 | 16 | 8 | 12 | 14 | 14 | 9 | 13 |

**Figure 6.8 Resources and activity capacity matrix for systems thinking**

# ✗ Consensogram

A consensogram is a tool developed by David Langford as a means to quickly determine and display the degree of consensus on a topic, question, or proposal.

Each member of the group writes a number on a sticky note — usually a number between zero and ten, or a percentage from zero to one hundred — representing their response to a statement or question. No names or commentary are required, just the number representing one's perspective.

When the sticky notes are collected and laid out as a bar chart, the degree of consensus is clearly visible to all.

The consensogram can be used to determine what to do next. Where the degree of consensus is consistently high, greater than 70 per cent, for example, little resistance to the proposal is expected. Where consensus is not high or is subject to significant variation, then further development of the proposal is probably in order. Attempting to implement a proposal that lacks strong consensus is likely to result in significant resistance.

The consensogram enables everybody to express their view. Everyone can see their sticky and know that their perspective is being taken into account and that they are being taken seriously. The consensogram also enables each individual to see, in a non-threatening way, where their views sit with those of the rest of the group.

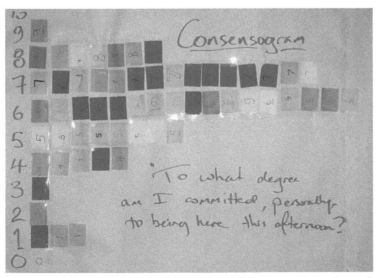

**Figure 6.9 Consensogram taken at the commencement of an after-school professional learning workshop to determine the degree to which people were favourably disposed to attending the session**

Source: QLA workshop at an ACT high school.

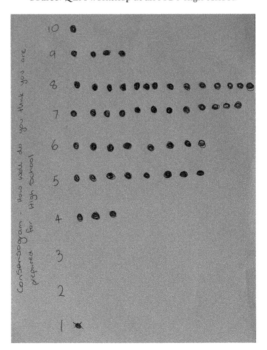

**Figure 6.10 Consensogram used to determine staff perceptions of the degree to which their students were fully engaged with their learning**

Source: QLA workshop at an ACT high school.

**Figure 6.11 Consensogram used to determine student perceptions of the degree to which they feel they are prepared for high school**

Source: Sunraysia Schools Network, NSW.

A template to develop a consensogram can be found on the QLA web site: www.qla.com.au.

# ✖ Loss function

The loss function tool is a practical method for determining the optimum value for a process. It is based upon the work of Genichi Taguchi, a Japanese statistician, who identified that losses progressively increase as process settings move away from their optimum, rather than rising instantly when a specification is exceeded.

A loss function can be prepared for any situation where the optimum numerical value of a process variable is sought. Examples include:

- How many pages to read for home learning each night;

- How many minutes to spend solving mathematics problems each lesson;

- The duration of a meeting;

- The starting time for a meeting;

- Which week during the term teachers should complete reports for parents; and

- How many lessons or weeks to spend on a project.

The example in Figure 6.12 illustrates a loss function used to determine the preferred length of a lunch break at a seminar.

To construct a loss function, each participant is provided with three small sticky notes of different colours, in Figure 6.12 these are pink, yellow and orange.

Firstly, participants note their ideal value. In Figure 6.12, the preferred length of lunch has been noted on yellow sticky notes.

Secondly, each participant is asked to note the value that would be too small for them on a different coloured sticky note (in this case, pink). This is achieved by thinking back from their ideal value in defined increments (in this case, five minutes) to find the value at which they would be dissatisfied. The first value at which they would be dissatisfied is recorded on a sticky note.

Thirdly, each participant then identifies the value that for them would be too great (in this case, on orange sticky notes). In a similar fashion, each individual thinks forward from their ideal value, in defined increments, until they reach a value that for them would be too great.

Finally, beginning with the ideal values, three histograms are created on the same sheet. Losses are calculated for each value by determining the number of people that would think that value was too great plus the number of people who find that value too small. The total losses are then added and the point of minimum loss determined.

Note that this approach is used to determine the point at which the least number of people will be dissatisfied, not the point at which the most people will be satisfied. This is an important distinction, as the aim of the approach is to minimise loss.

This minimum loss point is sometimes different from the most preferred value. The ideal values (shown in yellow in this example) are only used if there is more than one value representing minimum loss. Where the loss is at a minimum across more than one value, the ideal value can be used to determine which value to choose.

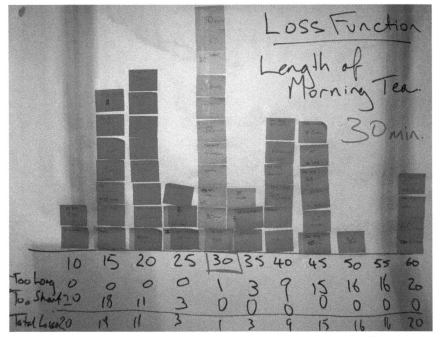

**Figure 6.12 Loss function used with workshop participants to determine that the optimum length for the morning break is 30 minutes (as there is minimum total loss at this time)**

Video Clip 6.3: Loss function tool
http://www.qla.com.au/Videos/3
Source: Sherbourne Primary School, Victoria.

In Video Clip 6.3 a Year 6 student discusses how her classroom used a loss function to agree the amount of time spent each day on reading.

 An Excel template to develop a loss function can also be found on the QLA web site: www.qla.com.au.

#  Plus delta

The plus delta tool is a quick and inclusive way to gather feedback about what is going well and what could be improved.

The topic for investigation is agreed among the group. This could include: English lessons, preparation for major assessments, staff meetings, the planning process, and so on.

Each individual identifies things that are going well. These are listed under the heading of "Plus". Identifying the positives promotes recognition and celebration of the good things, including identification of things to be sustained through any proposed changes.

They also identify things that could be improved. These are listed under the heading of "Delta" or "Δ", the Greek symbol for change.

A plus delta can be prepared with each individual using a simple T chart with two columns: plus and delta. It can also be prepared using sticky notes followed by affinity diagrams, one for each side, to sort ideas into themes.

With a plus delta, as with the other tools in this section, each participant's ideas are collected, collated, and valued. When action is taken on the findings, participants appreciate that their views are being respected; intrinsic motivation increases as a result.

| + | Δ |
|---|---|
| • Good range of logical structured activities<br>• Excellent tools, scaffolds, charts, etc.<br>• Love the Mind Maps!<br>• Time to plan and discuss forward planning<br>• Systems to analyse direction<br>• Strategies to identify priorities<br>• Very practical<br>• Allowed clear time to focus on and discuss priorities<br>• Bone diagram was very helpful in determining what the real issue was/were<br>• Time to have professional discussion<br>• Well balanced program talk – action<br>• Given time to think and to learn<br>• Specific to our school (remained our business – didn't have to waste time reporting back to Michael and Jane)<br>• Facilitated well<br>• Productive<br>• Worked as a team<br>• Minimal talk at us<br>• Strategies are fabulous<br>• Gave clear process overview<br>• Fantastic support from the presenters<br>• Kept us on track | • Opportunity to work on lap tops<br>• Possibly last session could be streamlined<br>• Ensure that system initiatives are clearly articulated to all schools<br>• Ran out of water<br>• We now know how much work we are in for<br>• Unsure of the value of the interrelationship digraph |

**Figure 6.13 Plus Delta from participants in a recent workshop**

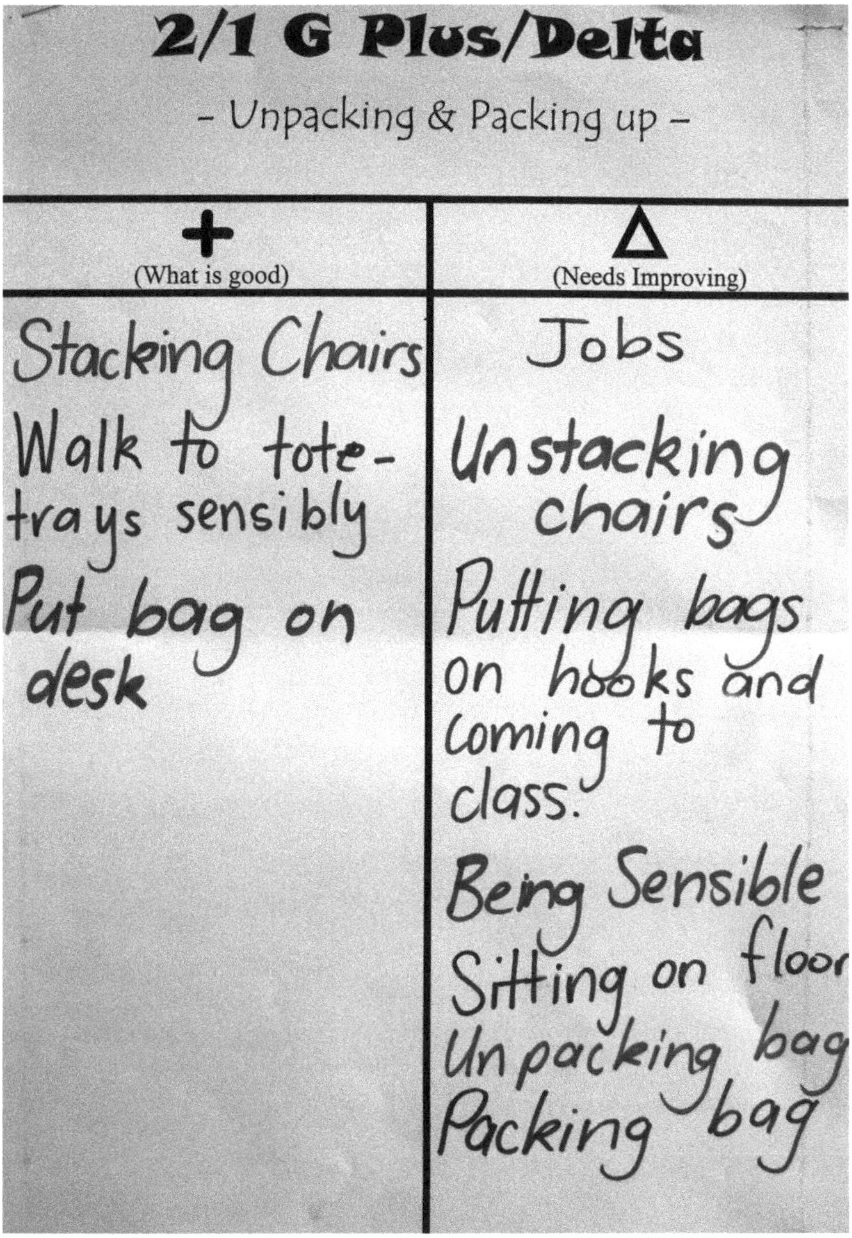

## 2/1 G Plus/Delta

### – Unpacking & Packing up –

| **+**<br>(What is good) | **△**<br>(Needs Improving) |
|---|---|
| Stacking Chairs<br>Walk to tote-trays sensibly<br>Put bag on desk | Jobs<br>Unstacking chairs<br>Putting bags on hooks and coming to class.<br>Being Sensible<br>Sitting on floor<br>Unpacking bag<br>Packing bag |

**Figure 6.14 Plus Delta from a Year 1/2 class examining the unpacking and packing up process**

Source: Calwell Primary School, ACT.

A template to write a plus delta can be found on the QLA web site: www.qla.com.au.

# Relationships

This section of the chapter expands on the following principle of quality learning:

> Strong human relationships are built through caring, communication, trust and respect

## What are relationships?

Organisations as social systems are unique in two ways.

Firstly, individuals within a social system, as an element of that system, have the capacity to choose their own purposes and methods. We are free to choose how we respond to other elements in the system, and how we respond to the structures of the system.

Secondly, it is not the individual elements of the system that dominate the behaviour and performance of the system, it is the interactions among the elements of the system and the containing system.

In other words, people are in a constant and complex state of action and interaction with those around them, and with the structures and processes of the systems they inhabit. These interactions may have a positive effect upon the system, or they may detract from the efficacy of the system. The behaviour and performance of the system is a product of these actions and interactions.

Relationships are central to the behaviour and performance of all social systems, including schools and classrooms. People interact or relate to one another continually within these systems. These interactions dominate system behaviour and performance.

*Relationships have a profound effect on the performance of schools and classrooms.*

There are many types of relationships: student to student, teacher to student, teacher to teacher, principal to student, teacher to principal, parent to teacher, and so on. As any educator knows, relationships have a profound effect on the performance of schools and classrooms.

### Interactions, relationships and conversations

The nature of the actions and interactions that people have with one another define the nature of the relationships between them. Where actions and interactions are positive and supportive, we say there is a good relationship. Where actions and interactions are tense, destructive or spiteful, we say there is a bad relationship.

People can choose how they respond to stimuli. We can choose our purposes, methods and responses. Sometimes, particularly when emotions are involved, it can be hard to remember that we have the freedom to choose our responses. Recognising that we have this freedom and consciously seeking to exercise it is an important step in reflecting upon and improving the interactions we have with others. Unless we learn to exercise our choice of response to others, we are likely to remain locked in habitual patterns of behaviour, which may not always serve us well.

New knowledge can provide cause for new responses. The concepts described in this book may be new for some readers. They call for different behaviours to those exhibited under the prevailing system of management. By reflecting upon new knowledge, and considering the questions that it raises, one can begin to adapt and behave differently towards others. If the discussion on intrinsic motivation has you wondering about the impact of rewards and punishments on individuals' behaviour, for example, you may consider trialing alternative approaches to engaging your children or students. In this way, new knowledge can bring new responses and new interactions with others.

*New knowledge can bring new responses and new interactions with others.*

Changing the questions we ask of others, based on new knowledge, also changes the interactions with them. Asking different questions elicits different responses.

*Changing the questions we ask of others, based on new knowledge, also changes the interactions with them.*

The nature of any relationship is directly observable in the conversations of the individuals concerned. Warm and loving relationships exhibit connected and caring conversations. More casual conversations are commonplace among mere acquaintances. Off-hand and sometimes callous interactions occur among individuals with varying degrees of dislike for one another. Being unwilling to converse with another person and ignoring them can signal contempt. The state of the relationship is evident in the interactions and the conversations.

*As we seek to change the nature of relationships, we will change the nature of conversations.*

It is not possible to build good interpersonal relationships without good conversations. In this way, conversations are pivotal in building relationships. It follows that, as we seek to change the nature of relationships, we will change the nature of conversations.

## Relationships in social systems

Relationships are strongly influenced by systemic factors.

Relationships are strongly influenced by systemic factors. Where key processes are poorly defined, ineffective or misunderstood, confusion and frustration usually follow, frequently resulting in tense and sometimes resentful relationships. Bad processes are toxic to relationships.

Similarly, factors outside the school have a direct impact on relationships. The regulatory environment, for example, imposes certain requirements and processes on schools and classrooms that can have a significant impact upon relationships.

While it is true that systemic factors dominate relationships, there is plenty we can do to actively encourage healthy and productive relationships in schools. Usually this involves changing structures and processes within the system with a view to changing the interactions among those within the system.

The first step is to create a vision of what relationships could look like if they were to be exemplary. In creating a vision of excellence for relationships in organisations, the spectrum from dependence to independence to interdependence provides a sound starting point.

# Dependence, independence and interdependence

To achieve high performing social systems, our aim must be to develop relationships that are highly interdependent.

To achieve high performing social systems, our aim must be to develop relationships that are highly interdependent. This is especially the case in schools and classrooms, where students need to develop the capacities and attitudes of relationship interdependency in order to make the most of their learning. Unfortunately, in schools and classrooms, dependent relationships tend to dominate the learning landscape.

## Dependence

In a dependent relationship, one party dominates another. We are born dependent. Incapable of looking after themselves, infants willingly submit to the domination of their parents or carers who take the lead in providing for, and giving direction and support.

 Dependent relationship: one party exerts a dominant position over another.

In a dependent student-teacher relationship, a student is continually seeking direction from the teacher and looking to comply with his or her requirements. There is little room for conflict, provided everyone does as they are directed. Dependent relationships are all about compliance.

Dependent relationships are all about compliance.

Signs of a dependent student-teacher relationship in a classroom include:

- Students asking "What are we doing today?" at the start of a class;

- Students waiting for the next worksheet;

- Students not knowing what to do when they finish a task or activity;

- Students waiting for teacher instructions;

- Teachers feeling under pressure to have all the answers;

- Teachers providing all the feedback; and

- Teachers doing things students are capable of doing for themselves — depriving students of opportunities to learn, help someone else, or practice a skill.

There are similar signs in dependent teacher-leader relationships.

## Independence

In recent years, there has been a shift in the rhetoric across schooling systems, recognising the need to move away from dependent teacher-student relationships towards the creation of independent learners. Students need to learn how to learn for themselves and by themselves (as well as how to learn with others).

As children, we soon learn that we have the capacity to recognise our needs and desires, and to choose methods to achieve them. Before long, we begin to try to manipulate our environment and to act independently in order to achieve our goals. While this often requires acknowledgement of the reactions of others around us, we learn to make our own choices; we learn to act independently.

The focus of independence is meeting one's own needs.

The focus of independence is meeting one's own needs.

Independent relationship: each party acts with autonomy towards their individual goals.

Recognising and celebrating one's uniqueness finds expression in the capacity to create one's own dreams, set goals and make choices about how to pursue them. Everyone needs to discover and celebrate his or her individuality. Students also need to experience multiple ways of learning to see how they learn best in different situations. Students need to learn how to learn. These are critical skills of independence, but they are not enough.

Independence creates the potential for conflict. Once people begin acting independently, the chosen goals and methods of each individual can come into conflict with those of others. The goals and methods of individuals can also come into conflict with those of the social systems to which the people contribute. This misalignment of goals can quickly lead to rivalry and competition. Individuals may seek to achieve their own goals, even at the expense of others.

## Interdependence

To transcend rivalry and competition, individuals need to learn how to develop and sustain productive interdependent relationships.

 Interdependent relationship: parties willingly collaborate to achieve individual and shared goals.

Interdependence in relationships is more than just interactions among elements within a system. All elements within a system interact with one another; the performance of the system is governed by these interactions. Interdependence in relationships moves beyond acknowledging interactions and towards recognising reliance upon others and accepting one's personal responsibility to the whole as well as to oneself. To simply acknowledge and tolerate other students in the room or other teachers in the school is not interdependence. Interdependence calls on each individual to act on the knowledge that we are mutually dependent upon each other and therefore responsible to one another.

> Interdependence calls for individuals to act in the interest of the system as a whole.

Interdependence calls for individuals to act in the interest of the system as a whole, not merely in self-interest.

As a society, we are habituated to attributing success or failure to the individual. Heroes are worshiped. Individuals are singled out for recognition or humiliation. People are seen to succeed or fail by their own efforts alone. Individualism is the doctrine de jour. These beliefs appear to be a defining characteristic of contemporary western society. In reality, we are much more interconnected with one another than such an individualistic perspective would suggest.

If we are truly interconnected with others, and if our fates are intertwined, then surely we have a moral obligation to accept that we are, in many ways, responsible for and responsible to others. Interdependence requires acknowledgement of mutual dependence and an acceptance of responsibility to others. We need to learn to develop healthy interdependent relationships.

In an interdependent relationship, parties are free to act independently, but choose to work together. The choice to work together is driven by an acknowledgement that more can be achieved by working collaboratively than by working alone. Working together can meet individual needs while contributing to the needs of the whole.

Signs of an interdependent student-teacher relationship include:

- Students working productively together in self-managing teams;

- Students seeking a teacher's advice on alternative learning strategies;

- Students who have demonstrated mastery of a topic supporting other students' learning;

- Students seeking feedback about their progress, processes and approaches to learning;

- Teachers acknowledging they don't have all the answers, but feeling confident they can work things out with the help of their students;

- Teachers seeking and welcoming feedback from students about the efficacy of their teaching strategies;

- Teachers working with students to develop in them the skills necessary for goal setting, planning and self-evaluation;

- Teachers working with students to identify processes and approaches that maximise learning; and

- Students and teachers working together to:

    - Clarify and document the aim or purpose of classroom activities;

    - Define and improve key classroom processes;

    - Agree criteria by which levels of learning will be evaluated; and

    - Explore and agree alternative methods by which mastery of a topic may be demonstrated.

## Preconditions for interdependent relationships

There are four preconditions for interdependent relationships: shared purpose, respect, trust, and open and honest communication.

There are four preconditions for interdependent relationships: shared purpose, respect, trust, and open and honest communication.

## Shared purpose

The first precondition for interdependence in a relationship is shared purpose.

Parties can agree they have purposes in common and that by coming together they will be able to achieve their individual purposes as well as their shared purposes.

Common purpose frequently benefits others too.

A classroom of students, who realise that the true purpose of their classroom is learning for all, is encouraged to work together in such a way that all students can learn. This shared purpose reflects individuals' need to learn and connects these individual needs to those of the group.

Shared purpose aligns effort.

As was discussed in Chapter Three, shared purpose aligns effort.

## Respect

The second precondition for interdependence is recognition of and respect for individuals.

At the core of respect is an acceptance of the right of all individuals to be treated with dignity.

Most people recognise that everyone is different, but for some it can be a challenge to move from tolerance, through acceptance, to respect. At the core of respect is an acceptance of the right of all individuals to be treated with dignity.

One cannot demand the respect of others; one can only demonstrate respect towards them.

People have much more in common with those they see as being different than they have in difference. People are hard-wired to look for differences in the things around them. Identifying changes in the immediate environment or detecting the presence of a predator has been a survival skill through the ages. However, when considering differences in people, there is a tendency to over-emphasise what is different and under-recognise the multitude of things people have in common with one another. The most significant commonality is simply being human.

The desire to be respected is ubiquitous. The authors of this book have worked with scores of schools to help them clarify their purpose, vision and values. Every time, without exception, the theme of respect has been high on the list of desirable attributes for the school community.

Everyone needs to be shown respect and to be taken seriously. Listening attentively demonstrates respect. Providing encouragement demonstrates respect. Offering support demonstrates respect. All these things send signals that people are valued and cared about. When one individual actively engages with another human being, they are demonstrating that they take them seriously; they are also showing respect towards them.

## Trust

The third precondition for interdependence is trust.

Trust is about the expectations of others. To trust someone is to have a confident expectation they will not let you down. To have trust in another person requires confident expectation in two dimensions: their intentions and their abilities. To trust someone is to believe they care and they are capable.

> To trust someone is to believe they care and they are capable.

To care, in the context of trust, is to take someone seriously and to demonstrate goodwill towards them. You are more likely to trust someone if you believe they have your wellbeing at heart. In essence, caring is about their intentions. Do they demonstrate caring intentions? Are their motives genuine, straightforward and supportive of one's wellbeing, or are they more inclined towards self-interest? To develop and sustain an interdependent relationship, there must be a confident expectation that the other cares about our wellbeing. There must be trust in their intentions.

Good intentions are not enough. There must also be a confident expectation of their abilities. It is all very well to believe that a surgeon cares about a patient, but if the patient is not satisfied that the surgeon has what it takes to perform the procedure successfully, the patient is unlikely to submit to the scalpel. In order to trust someone, a confident expectation must be developed that they have the skills, knowledge, ability, attitude and resources to do what they undertake to do — a confident expectation of their capabilities is required. This includes confidence in their ability to consistently demonstrate integrity. Are their words and deeds congruent? Do they say what they will do and do what they say? Do they say one thing to a person's face and something altogether different in their absence?

To develop and sustain interdependent relationships requires a confident expectation that others have what it takes to do what is required, including the integrity to follow through. They must be seen as trustworthy.

## Open and honest communication

The final precondition for interdependent relationships is open and honest communication.

> It is only through regular, open, honest and productive interactions that interdependence can be created and sustained.

It is only through regular, open, honest and productive interactions that interdependence can be created and sustained. Communication provides the vehicle for ongoing reflection on shared purpose, for the reinforcement of individuals' uniqueness and value, for the clarification of individuals' intentions, and for understanding one anothers' capabilities.

Communication is a two-way street. One does not communicate to others, one communicates with others. A proclamation is not communication, nor is a directive, announcement, newsletter or email — these are transmissions. Unless transmitted messages are received and acknowledged, there is no communication.

Real communication is about creating shared understanding.

Open and honest communication includes:

- Being available for one another;
- Keeping one another informed of developments;
- Sharing relevant feelings, concerns, uncertainties and wonderings;
- Acknowledging one another;
- Sharing information in an accurate and timely fashion;
- Telling the truth;
- Recognising that communication is a two-way process;
- Feeding back to confirm understanding; and
- Accepting responsibility to ask, not just waiting to be told.

Open and honest communication is the lubricant that minimises friction in interdependent relationships. In the absence of communication, tensions can build, tempers become frayed, issues over-heat and individuals are tempted to slide back into independence.

We are grateful to the work of Ron Crosling in providing the foundations for this discussion. To find out more, read Ron's paper, "Building Highly Effective Relationships" on the QLA web site: www.qla.com.au.

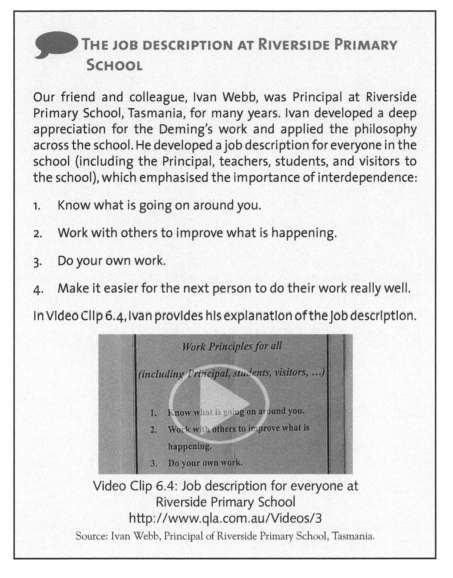

## THE JOB DESCRIPTION AT RIVERSIDE PRIMARY SCHOOL

Our friend and colleague, Ivan Webb, was Principal at Riverside Primary School, Tasmania, for many years. Ivan developed a deep appreciation for the Deming's work and applied the philosophy across the school. He developed a job description for everyone in the school (including the Principal, teachers, students, and visitors to the school), which emphasised the importance of interdependence:

1.   Know what is going on around you.

2.   Work with others to improve what is happening.

3.   Do your own work.

4.   Make it easier for the next person to do their work really well.

In Video Clip 6.4, Ivan provides his explanation of the job description.

Video Clip 6.4: Job description for everyone at Riverside Primary School
http://www.qla.com.au/Videos/3

Source: Ivan Webb, Principal of Riverside Primary School, Tasmania.

# Student-teacher relationship continuum

While he was teaching in Alaska, David Langford collaborated with his students to create a model that illustrates the range of relationships that exist between teacher and student. This model has been adapted into Figure 6.15.

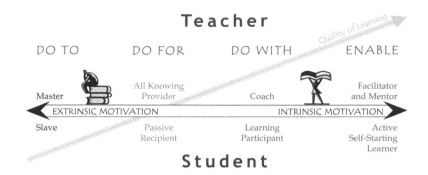

**Figure 6.15 A student–teacher relationship continuum**
Source: Adapted by QLA from David Langford's *Quality Learning Training Manual*,
Version 12.1, Motivation, p. 6.

On the left hand side is an extrinsically-driven dependent relationship, in which students submit to the will of the teacher. To the right of the continuum, motivation is more intrinsic and the relationship more interdependent — students are actively enabled to work with one another and take responsibility for their learning.

In order to move from left to right, students need to be equipped with the capacity to operate with greater levels of responsibility through independence and interdependence. Just as we need to learn strategies and methods to be independent, we must learn strategies and methods to be interdependent.

> Just as we need to learn strategies and methods to be independent, we must learn strategies and methods to be interdependent.

This takes time. For some students it can take months, sometimes years, to develop the skills and discipline necessary to plan and monitor their own learning.

In reflecting upon this model, it is worth keeping in mind that variation will also affect the journey to interdependence:

- Within any class, students can have significantly different self-management skills. Some students may be ready to self-manage, others may need more support;

- Over time, the same student can exhibit variation in capacity for self-management. Everyone has good days and bad days. Students may need more "do for" or "do with" on some days; and

- Students will vary in the level of support they need across different areas of learning in order to move to interdependence. New topics may require significantly more support or "do for" than where existing skills are to be practiced or refined.

Most importantly, if teachers desire to see students act interdependently, then equipping them to act interdependently must become a conscious educational objective. The desired outcome of productive, interdependent learners who take responsibility for their learning cannot happen by chance. Teachers need to work with their students to progressively create the capacity in the students to learn in this way. Constancy of purpose and perseverance are required.

Students can learn to manage their own learning. Quality learning tools such as the capacity matrix, force field analysis, system map, inter-relationship digraph, Gantt chart, flowchart, and lotus diagram all provide methods that enable students to plan, monitor and reflect upon their learning. Even young children can learn to use these tools to enhance their learning.

If we want students to accept responsibility for their learning, then we need to equip them with the capacity to do so. As Myron Tribus was fond of saying:

> If we want students to be more responsible we must teach them to be more response-able.

Myron Tribus, 1993, "The Transformation of American Education to a System for Continuously Improved Learning", p. 13. Available at http://www.qla.com.au/Papers/5.

# Building healthy interdependent relationships

If productive interdependent relationships are to be created and sustained, care and attention must be paid to the preconditions for interdependence.

Productive interdependent relationships are fragile.

There are many practices in organisations that are counterproductive to interdependency in relationships. Many of these have become habits, handed down through generations of managers and teachers. These habits can be hard to break. The current system of schooling imposes barriers to interdependence. These barriers are entrenched in the systems of management and schooling that dominate today. Let us examine a few of the more prevalent dysfunctional practices that rob our schools and classrooms of the highly productive interdependent relationships that we seek.

> If teachers desire to see students act interdependently, then equipping them to act interdependently must become a conscious educational objective.

> The current system of schooling imposes barriers to interdependence.

## Recognition, not rewards or praise

Not only do extrinsic rewards and punishments interfere with intrinsic motivation, they are toxic to relationships. Dominance and a desire to obtain compliance are implicit in the use of extrinsic motivation. By definition, a compliant relationship is one where one party submits to the will of another. This is a dependent relationship.

Extrinsic rewards can also be used to manipulate behaviour. Manipulating behaviour does not build capacity for self-regulation in those being manipulated. Where a teacher, principal or system leader resorts to practices that rely upon extrinsic motivation factors, such as rewards and punishments, they diminish their capacity to develop interdependent relationships. It can be difficult to respect people who threaten us with punishment or attempt to bribe us with rewards. Where punishment and rewards are used, trust in intentions can be diminished as people grow suspicious as to why such extrinsic motivators are required. Similarly, trust in a person's ability to lead is diminished when extrinsic motivators are used.

It is rare to see open and honest communication in a climate of potential punishments and rewards. A focus on avoiding the punishments and gaining the rewards tends to distort communication. Leaders sell themselves short when they resort to punishments and rewards. In so doing, they close conversations and suppress the potential to develop truly interdependent relationships.

Rewards are not the same as recognition. Interdependence withers under extrinsic rewards, but it thrives on recognition.

*Interdependence withers under extrinsic rewards, but it thrives on recognition.*

 Recognition: respectful acknowledgement of an individual.

Recognition, particularly when given sincerely, regularly and in a low key manner, is the life-blood of interdependence.

Recognition is an expression of respect for another individual. Recognition highlights that a person is being taken seriously and that their skills and contribution are noticed and valued. Unlike extrinsic rewards, recognition is not contingent on particular criteria being met. People are recognised for who they are. Recognition is unconditional. A smile, a greeting, a compliment, a friendly wave, this is recognition.

Recognition reinforces shared purposes. It is a demonstration of respect for the individual. It reinforces that one's intentions acknowledge the wellbeing of that individual. It is a necessary starting point for open and honest communication.

Recognition is a demonstration of respect for the individual.

Recognition is required among all relationships if an interdependent community is to be created. Not only do teachers need to recognise students, but students need to learn to recognise teachers. Students recognise students, teachers recognise teachers, leaders recognise teachers, teachers and leaders recognise parents, and so on.

People sometimes confuse praise with recognition.

📖 Praise: the act of expressing approval or commendation.

To give praise is to pass judgement upon someone. To praise presumes a position of power or superiority over them. Praise can be detrimental to interdependence when it promotes dependence or subordination.

To give praise is to pass judgement upon someone. Praise is a form of extrinsic reward.

Praise is a form of extrinsic reward. Those being praised can become hungry for praise. "What do you think of my painting, Miss?" Those from whom the praise is sought can be seduced into providing it freely and reinforcing their position of dominance over the individual seeking praise.

It can be challenging to break the habit of praise-giving. Many teachers find it difficult to resist the spontaneous exclamation of excitement on seeing an impressive student display. "What a wonderful painting!"

Asking a student how they think they have done can provide great insight and enhance learning far more than spontaneous praise. Praising a student in the absence of knowledge of their view is risky. Imagine a student who throws together an assignment at the last minute with minimal effort or care. The student happens to be quite capable and is quite knowledgeable on the topic. The teacher may be impressed with the product of the student's limited efforts. What will be the impact of praise at that point? At best, the teacher may encourage the student to achieve more next time. More likely, however, the teacher will diminish the student's trust in the teacher's knowledge of them and their ability. The student may learn that minimal effort is acceptable.

## Fabulous feedback

Teachers support learners with feedback. Learners support teachers with feedback.

In a truly interdependent student-teacher relationship, both parties are working together towards capacity development of each other. The teacher offers support, not from a position of superiority or dominance, but from a position of being a caring and highly skilled individual.

The teacher's role is to mediate the student's learning — to help the student learn most effectively. For this to happen, the teacher can provide feedback across a number of levels: the task level, the degree to which the task has met agreed quality criteria; the process level, the range and efficacy of strategies and approaches employed by the student; and the meta-cognitive level, the degree to which the learner was self-monitoring and reflecting upon their learning process.

Learners support teachers with feedback on the efficacy of the teacher's approaches and methods in helping the student to learn.

Both teacher and learner provide feedback to one another in order for each of them to learn from the experience. Such feedback is very different to praise.

---
*Teacher and learner provide feedback to one another in order for each of them to learn from the experience.*

---

### EMPOWERED STUDENTS

It is common to hear teachers make assertions such as "We need to empower our students to take control of their learning."

This could mean one of three things: authorising students to take control, giving them permission to take control, or equipping them to take control.

Any suggestion that students need to be authorised or given permission implies a dependent or dominant relationship. How can we assert that students need to be given the authority to control their learning? Who are we to give permission? Only the students can have this authority, and they don't need permission.

What is really needed is for students to be equipped with the information, knowledge and know-how to take responsibility for their learning. We need to guide students to build their capacity for self-management. Capacity building — actively enabling — is what is needed, not empowerment.

# Cooperation not competition

The aim of any competition is to separate winners from losers. A competition may be for a prize, such as a sporting trophy. Among corporations, competition can be for market share, investment funds, or qualified employees. Competition among animals can be for dominance of the pack. At the end of any competitive contest there are winners and losers. Frequently, there is one winner and many losers.

Some competitions are designed for spectator enjoyment, particularly sports competitions with large television audiences. Rules are carefully refined over decades to even out the competition, enhance the contest and heighten the entertainment.

The purpose of school education should not be to create losers, nor should it be to provide entertainment. It is fairly common, however, for teachers to promote competition among students under the guise of encouraging them to do better.

Every parent wants the best for their child. Yet, every time a school promotes rivalry and competition among students (or teachers, for that matter), the outcome will be winners and losers.

The promotion of competition in learning is usually subtle and implicit, such as having a "student of the week", asking "let's see who can sit up straight and listen", remarking that "Johanna did the best essay in the class", or saying "let's vote on this curriculum proposal". Competition creates losers. It is not the job of a school to create losers.

> Competition creates losers. It is not the job of a school to create losers.

Such competition, whether it is subtle or overt, can be entertaining. Other students along with the teacher can find pleasure in observing individuals striving to be or do better than one another. While it can be fascinating to observe competitive struggles, there can be a fine line between fascination and schadenfreude — harm-joy: deriving pleasure from the misfortunes of others.

The goal for any classroom should be that everybody learns to a high standard. Achievement of this goal brings a healthy joy to all involved.

Setting a goal such as "By the end of this lesson, let's see if we can have everyone with a perfect looking poster," will result in very different behaviour and outcomes than a goal such as "Let's see who can create the best poster." With the first goal, the aim is for everyone to work collaboratively — interdependently — to achieve a positive outcome individually and as a class. The second goal sets students against one another to compete for the prize. A likely unintended consequence is that some students will not even begin the activity and that few will see it through. The aim of those who complete the task will be to win the prize, not to learn how to create a great poster. Very few members of the class will learn how to create a perfect looking poster, which was the primary intention.

Behaviour management in each case will be very different too. In the first instance, students will be supported in working together. In the second, many students will soon become distracted, having given up on the task, and their resulting behaviour is likely to be disruptive.

> Cooperation in schooling achieves far more than competition.

Cooperation in schooling achieves far more than competition. Helping students learn to act interdependently not only improves learning outcomes for all, but it significantly enhances the quality of school life.

Competition in learning is frequently used to allocate scarce resources. Students in Australia compete for university places. In New South Wales, for example, each student is provided with an Australian Tertiary Admission Rank (ATAR) score, which is a number between zero and 99.95. This number quantifies students' rankings against other Higher School Certificate students in that year. An ATAR score of 75, for example, means that a student has performed at the upper 25th percentile of the state. (As an added incentive, there are regional and subject bonuses to consider.) ATARs are used as a key factor in selecting students for admission into university courses. Frequently, conversations with students approaching this competition reveal that they are able to clearly explain the points they need to enter the university course of their choice. They can also clearly articulate why some subjects should be chosen over others, not because they will be more useful in the future, but because they can result in a higher ATAR score. These students recognise that they are playing a game, they understand the rules, and they are playing to win.

Each year when the ATAR scores are published, newspapers, radio and television are filled with stories of the handful of people that topped the state — almost as if it is a miracle that any individuals could be placed at the top of the rankings of all students. The media is silent on the impact upon those who were below average — half the population.

> ### 💬 COMPETITION IN LEARNING AT UNIVERSITY
>
> Michael completed a Master of Business Administration before learning about quality improvement. The business school he attended was reputed to be among the best in Australia. Entry to the course was extremely competitive. Once admitted, it was made clear to everyone that those deemed to be the best in class were guaranteed great jobs and would earn piles of money. The subtext to this was that if you didn't make the top ten per cent, your prospects were still okay, but that the real winnings are reserved for the special few.
>
> This competitive approach crippled any chance of interdependence. There were many examples of this, the most memorable of which relates to the behaviour of one syndicate and their use of library resources. This syndicate of high flyers established a process whereby at the first lecture of a new topic, when the topic outline and resource list was distributed, they would send one or two members of their syndicate to the library to borrow all the listed resources. They later admitted that they did this not only to get first access to the resources, but also to prevent others from having them.
>
> Other examples of our academic experience of competition in learning driving dysfunctional behaviour include pages being removed from text books; "out of order" signs being placed on fully functional laboratory equipment; and instances of physical and emotional violence during the creation of syndicate groups.

Another way that competition is created within learning environments is through artificial scarcity. This forces competition and rivalry where it need not exist.

Grading to a curve — requiring, for example, only ten per cent of students to receive an A, 20 per cent a B, and so on — forces artificial scarcity. Why should only ten per cent receive an A? Is it not desirable for all students to do well? It makes no sense to prevent them from doing well. When students are graded on a curve, rivalry and competition are an inevitable consequence.

*When students are graded on a curve, rivalry and competition are an inevitable consequence.*

Setting out to do well is very different to setting out to do better than someone else. To do well, a student will usually be happy to collaborate with fellow students. Students compare answers and learn with one another. Everyone wins when this happens. When competing, the goal is to do better than others. One way to do better than others is to prevent others from doing well.

At times there is true scarcity of resources. For example, there are frequently insufficient university places for the students wishing to be admitted to some courses. In Australia this is addressed by only opening places to students with high exam scores. An alternative approach can always be found. In this case it could be to identify all those students who meet the entry criteria, and then run a ballot for places.

The key message here is that in learning, interdependent relationships cannot exist in an environment of competition.

## Drive out fear!

Fear inhibits intrinsic motivation.

Deming was adamant the people have a right to enjoy their work, and to be treated with dignity and respect. Yet many organisation's processes increase fear and anxiety. These include:

- Blaming and punishing individuals for deficiencies in the system;

- Leaving people out of decision-making;

- Criticising people in front of others;

- Failing to give people access to the information or resources needed to do a job well;

- Ignoring suggestions or treating them as criticism;

- Offering critical feedback on performance without a simultaneous, genuine offer of support; and

- Requiring people to undertake tasks that are unlikely to be completed successfully.

The challenge is to drive out fear in order to create an environment where people feel safe and secure.

Fear has a way of creeping into organisations, even those that seek to expunge it. Vigilance and effort are required to constantly drive out fear.

The challenge is to drive out fear in order to create an environment where people feel safe and secure. This is not to suggest creating an environment free from responsibility or accountability, rather an environment of respect, dignity and professionalism.

> ### 💬 REHABILITATING TEACHERS
>
> Some years ago, we visited Riverside Primary School in Tasmania, which at that time was deep in the application of quality improvement philosophy.
>
> The principal explained to us that several of the teachers were "refugees" from other schools. They had come to Riverside on their last chance. Previous schools had labelled them as "failing" and "dead wood". If it didn't work out at Riverside, they were going to have to leave teaching.
>
> We met them. They were delightful individuals who were doing a great job.
>
> At Riverside there was a strong focus on providing everyone with a safe and secure environment that was free of fear. Abundant support enabled these teachers to regain their confidence, pride and dignity.
>
> Usually, when we ask teachers, "What gets in the way of you doing a good job?" they have many suggestions. When we asked this at Riverside, we received blank stares; such was the level of safety, security and support.

Video Clip 6.5: Drive out fear!
http://www.qla.com.au/Videos/3
Source: Leander Independent Schools District, Texas, USA.

## Interactions, conversations and questions

Interactions within social systems directly affect behaviour and performance. As the number of elements in the system increases, the number and significance of interactions increases exponentially. By the time there are 20 people in a system, there are over one million possible interaction combinations among them. These interactions dominate performance of the system. In short, how people relate to one another impacts significantly on the behaviour and performance of any organisation.

The actions and interactions between any two individuals reflect the state of the relationship between them. As we have seen, the relationship may be one of dependence, independence, or interdependence. Interactions can demonstrate respect, indifference, or disrespect. They may be underscored by trust or mistrust. Communication may be open, honest and two-way, or it may be incomplete and one-sided. Interactions between people can be positive, supportive and productive, but they can also be toxic, manipulative and destructive.

## Conversations

The state of a relationship is reflected in communication, and communication affects the state of the relationship. The communication between two individuals who know, love and care deeply for one another is very different to communication between neighbours who don't get along. An offhand comment or snide remark will detract from a relationship, whereas a kind word can strengthen it.

As we seek to promote healthy and productive relationships in organisations, we have found it to be of practical benefit to focus on conversations rather than communication. In this context, conversations are taken to mean more than just one-on-one spoken interactions. Conversations include all interactions among people. For example, people who choose not to speak to one another can be seen as having a silent, but quite meaningful, conversation. A presentation at a staff meeting is part of an ongoing conversation. A smile across the classroom is part of an ongoing conversation.

Conversations provide a practical surrogate for communication because they represent an easily identifiable and tangible activity to which people readily relate. For example, there is more practical meaning to the statement "observe the conversations around you" than "observe the communication around you". Communication can seem esoteric and theoretical, whereas conversations are real and practical.

This insight enables us to reframe an earlier assertion: the state of a relationship is reflected in conversations, and conversations affect the state of the relationship.

*How people relate to one another impacts significantly on the behaviour and performance of any organisation.*

*The state of a relationship is reflected in conversations, and conversations affect the state of the relationship.*

We can readily observe the nature and content of conversations in a classroom and use this evidence to form a view of the state of relationships within the classroom. This is useful for developing an understanding of the behaviour within a social system and how we might respond to it.

Even more useful, perhaps, is our ability to use this data to frame questions we might ask of ourselves and others. But first, we need to consider the systemic effects.

## Systemic effects

As we have seen, individuals' behaviour is a function of the interactions they have with others. Yet, an individual's behaviour is also a function of the interactions she or he has with an organisation's processes and with elements of the containing systems and environment. Note that processes, in this context, include policies, procedures, infrastructure, technology, and so on. The most kind-hearted and skillful individuals can become dispirited and despondent when subjected to dysfunctional processes and external influences. Bad processes are toxic to relationships. So are bad systems.

> Bad processes are toxic to relationships. So are bad systems.

Organisations' processes evolve over time. In organisations such as schools, many processes were first developed decades ago, based upon old assumptions about the world and how it worked — assumptions that may no longer hold.

In the chapters of this book we have challenged many of the traditional assumptions that underpin leadership and management in the western world. We have discussed in detail an approach to organisational improvement that is significantly different to that in common practice.

Not surprisingly, many organisations find themselves with approaches and processes that contradict the principles discussed in this book. Individuals find themselves butting up against processes that cause frustration, wasted effort, and loss of enthusiasm. On a daily basis, an organisation's way of doing things can rob individuals of joy in their work.

## Asking different questions, engaging in different conversations

We hope you will have discovered, in the pages of this book, concepts, ideas and tools that resonate and interest you. Hopefully you will have already started questioning your assumptions and those of your organisation. New questions can stimulate new and helpful conversations in your organisation.

Firstly, we can ask ourselves questions about our interactions with others. Am I being respectful in my conversations with others? Am I truly listening? Am I being understanding? Am I being supportive? Am I being open and honest? Remember, we have the power to choose different responses, to engage in different conversations.

Secondly, we can ask questions about the systems in which we operate. Open and honest conversations about how the social system operates and how everyone collaborates to get better are vital for system improvement. These conversations can be stimulated by questions based upon improvement theory. Questions derived from the principles in this book can provide a powerful catalyst for reflection, learning and improvement.

In Appendix 3, we have distilled a selection of questions about schools and the school system. These are generic questions that can be asked at any level of the system, from the classroom to the national system of schooling. These questions are structured under the following themes:

- School direction;
- Leading improvement;
- Student learning;
- Teacher professional learning;
- Process management; and
- Performance management.

These themes were chosen because they represent areas where there is frequently a significant gap between current practice and what might be derived from improvement theory. They are derived from the theory, practices and experiences described in this book.

We encourage you to reflect upon these questions from your own perspective and engage others in conversations about them. These questions can provide a great starting point for new conversations. But they are only a starting point. No doubt you will be able to think of additional questions, probably better ones that suit your specific context.

New questions will stimulate new responses. The better the questions, the greater the potential impact on improving your organisation.

---

*Sidebar notes:*

Questions derived from the principles in this book can provide a powerful catalyst for reflection, learning and improvement.

New questions will stimulate new responses.

# Reflection questions

**?** Are relationships in your organisations predominantly dependent, independent, or interdependent in nature? What drives them to be that way?

**?** In what ways does the student–teacher relationship continuum have meaning for you? To which other relationships might it apply?

**?** How do you make the distinction between recognition, praise, and feedback? Which is most common in your organisation? How do you know?

**?** What has been your experience with competition on and off the sporting field?

**?** What systems, processes and practices in your workplace give rise to fear? How they get in the way of your ability to do a good job? What practices do you participate in that could promote fear in others? What can be done to drive out fear from organisations?

**?** How is the nature of the relationships in your organisation reflected in the conversations you hear? What can you do to improve the quality of interactions and relationships within your organisation?

# Quality learning tools to enhance relationships

All of the tools introduced in this book so far can enhance relationships. They do this through a combination of the following:

- Developing or clarifying shared purpose;
- Promoting respect for individuals;
- Clarifying expectations and building trust; and
- Promoting open and honest communication.

The following tools assist relationship building in the following ways:

| Tool | Benefit to relationships |
|---|---|
| Consensogram | Captures and displays the degree of consensus among a group regarding a specific topic. |
| Flowcharts | Provides clarity regarding the steps to be followed and responsibility for taking action. |
| Hot dot | Enables everyone to contribute to prioritisation of issues affecting the group. |
| Operational definition | Provides clarity of meaning preventing miscommunication. |
| Parking lot | Enables all individuals to have input about how a team/project/system/class is operating. |
| Plus delta | Provides an opportunity for individuals to identify what is good about a situation and what can be improved. |
| Process accountability matrix | Ensures clarity of responsibilities for agreed processes. |
| Purpose, outcomes, process, evaluation (POPE) | Promotes agreement among individuals regarding how a meeting or activity is to be handled. |
| Structured brainstorming | Includes everyone in idea generation. |
| System map | Clarifies purpose and direction, which aligns the efforts of individuals. |

**Table 6.2 Tools that assist relationship building**

Two additional tools that can enhance relationships are the code of cooperation and the decision and action (meeting) record.

# ⚒ Code of cooperation

The code of cooperation was developed by David Langford as a means for teams to identify, acknowledge, and record the factors they believe necessary for a high degree of cooperation.

A code of cooperation is developed collaboratively. It is not to be confused with a code of conduct, which is frequently developed by one individual or small group and then imposed upon others.

Structured brainstorming is used to allow each individual to contribute his or her ideas about what is needed for the team to ensure a high degree of cooperation. "How do we need to behave to all get along?" Frequently, this provides an opportunity for team members to identify the things that they need, personally, from other team members.

The code of cooperation is used as an ongoing reference to guide team behaviour. It gives license to discuss behaviour if the behaviour of one or more members of the team is not appropriate.

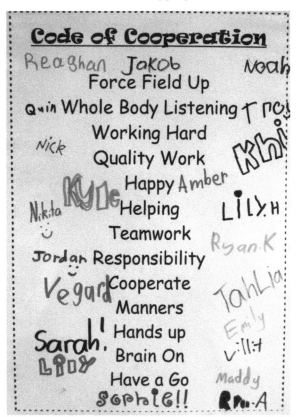

**Figure 6.16 Year 1/2 class code of cooperation**
Source: Calwell Primary School, ACT.

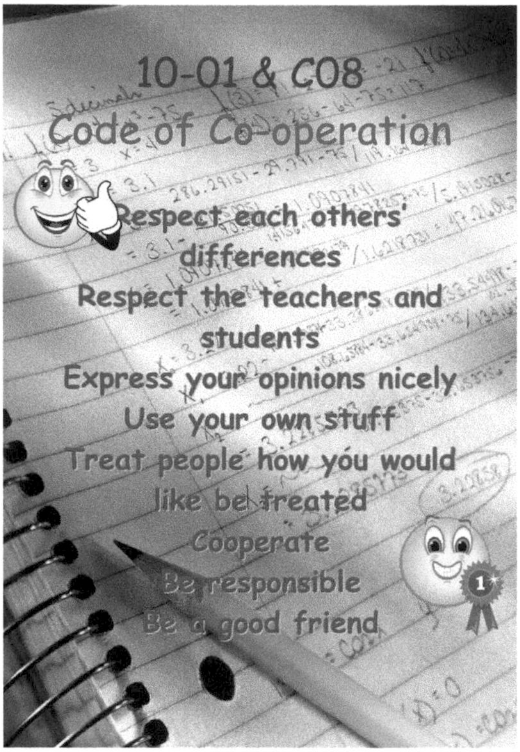

**Figure 6.17 Year 10 class code of cooperation**
Source: Seaford 6–12 School, SA.

# ⚒ Decision and action record

A decision and action record is used in the place of meeting minutes. It captures the agreements reached by the team in the form of decisions and actions. It also records the purpose of the meeting, the date, time, duration, and location of the meeting.

The record is brief and captures in table form:

*   What was agreed at the meeting;

*   Who is taking responsibility to complete that action (note only one name);

*   When this is to be completed by; and

*   Whether the item has been completed (noted at future meetings).

A decision and action record is preferable to meeting minutes because the record of the meeting is captured at the time of the meeting by a pre-agreed scribe. No one has to go away after the meeting and write up copious pages of minutes (which usually no one has time to read). For those who miss the meeting and where further clarity is needed as to the context of the decisions and agreements made, they can ask. Many organisations use the template in electronic form. At the end of the meeting, the record is emailed to each of the attendees. Where a handwritten hardcopy is generated, it can be photocopied and distributed to each participant before the meeting ends.

## Decision and Action Record

Date: _____          Attendees: _____

Time: _____

Duration: _____          _____

Location: _____

                                _____

                                Apologies: _____

Purpose of Meeting: _____

## Decisions and Actions

| Decisions and Actions | Who | When | Done? |
|---|---|---|---|
|  |  |  |  |
|  |  |  |  |
|  |  |  |  |

Figure 6.18 Decision and action record template

A meeting record template is available to download from the QLA web site: www.qla.com.au. This template combines the POPE tool and the decision and action record into a single meeting record template.

# Leadership

In these final pages of this chapter we examine the notion of leadership by expanding on the last principle of quality learning:

> It is everybody's job to improve the systems and processes for which they are responsible by working with their people and role modelling these principles.

Key to continual improvement is a relentless focus upon the improvement of processes and relationships. This calls for leaders and workers to collaborate for improvement. At all levels of an enterprise, individuals will be working together and engaging in productive conversations in order to improve processes and relationships.

The quality learning philosophy provides a proven and robust theory that gives confidence to everyone that their efforts towards continual improvement will be effective and valued by others.

The quality learning principles provide a compassionate and insightful lens through which to view our roles as leaders. They encapsulate a guide to more effective action than the prevailing system of management. They provide a proven and more productive way of thinking and leading.

> The quality learning principles provide a compassionate and insightful lens through which to view our roles as leaders.

## What is leadership?

The literature on leadership is abundant. Much of it focuses on characterisations of leaders: the charismatic leader, the authoritarian leader, the intercultural leader, the pedagogical leader, and so on. There are also innumerable models and frameworks for leadership: autocratic leadership, transformational leadership, bureaucratic leadership, participative leadership, distributed leadership, and so on, ad infinitum.

These models essentially describe the characteristics or features of a particular type of leader or style of leadership. They generally do not describe what leaders do, even fewer explain how.

Before we explore leadership, let's briefly discuss the concepts of management and leadership, which are used interchangeably within many organisational settings, including schools. This is necessary because management and leadership are very different.

Both management and leadership are required for organisational improvement. However, to manage is not necessarily to lead.

📖 Management: the ability to organise resources and coordinate the execution of tasks necessary to reach a goal in a timely and cost effective manner.

Management relates to goals, tasks, resources, systems and processes. It involves the resources of an organisation, including time, money and effort, and completing tasks effectively and on time.

Leadership is not management. Leadership is about the relationship between those guiding the way and those choosing to follow.

📖 Leadership: the ability to articulate a vision that causes others to move with a passion.

The defining feature of leadership is followership. Leaders inspire others to follow. To follow is to move along a path of the leader's choosing. True leaders inspire their followers; they do not coerce them. Leaders work with their people to create a shared vision, and then they guide the way towards it.

Myron Tribus crystallised the distinction between leadership and management when he said:

> You lead people. You manage things.

Myron Tribus, presentation, Telstra management group, Melbourne, 1994.

# It's everybody's job

Everyone is a manager. Everyone has tasks to complete. Everyone is engaged in enacting the processes of their organisation.

Teachers have many processes to enact and must manage their resources carefully. Students have learning tasks to be completed; in this, they are managers too.

Everyone has processes and systems for which they are individually and uniquely responsible. Students are responsible for a wide range of processes, from managing their pens and pencils to managing their system for home-learning. School executives have systems and processes to manage too, such as school planning, budgeting, and acquitting regulatory requirements.

To manage is to take responsibility for one's systems and processes.

*Management relates to goals, tasks, resources, systems and processes.*

*Leadership is about the relationship between those guiding the way and those choosing to follow.*

*Everyone has processes and systems for which they are individually and uniquely responsible.*

Everyone can be a leader. Anyone can exercise leadership. Leadership is not the exclusive domain of those with great authority. As Myron Tribus was fond of saying:

> Leadership belongs to those who assert it.

Myron Tribus, "Eleven Links in the Transformation of an Enterprise to Make Quality the Strategy for Success", p. 2. Available at http://www.qla.com.au/Papers/5.

Teachers can lead their students or colleagues with a vision of learning that inspires them to engage with passion.

Individual students can lead. A student may have a vision for a learning project so enticing that the whole class follows, including the teacher. Ironically, some of the most disruptive students can be the most remarkable leaders.

Everyone is a manager and anyone can exercise leadership. Continual improvement requires both.

> Everyone is a manager and anyone can exercise leadership. Continual improvement requires both.

# Improving processes and relationships

It was Myron Tribus who first asserted that the manager's job has been redefined.

> People work <u>in</u> a system. The job of a manager is to work <u>on</u> the system, to improve it, continuously, with their help.

Myron Tribus, "Quality Management in Education", p. 5. Available at http://www.qla.com.au/Papers/5.

Only the manager has the authority to change the system.

Only the manager has the authority to change the system. The manager of a system is the one person who is responsible for that system. The people working in the system cannot make changes, only the manager can do so by working on the system.

So if the manager, the individual responsible for a system, does not take steps to improve that system, who will? Nobody.

This has profound implications. If everyone is a manager, then everyone needs to be engaged in improvement activities; everyone needs to engage in improving processes and relationships.

Everyone needs to know how to prioritise their improvement opportunities and apply a process of rigorous improvement to the processes for which they are responsible. Everyone needs to be working to improve conversations, thereby improving relationships. Everyone: not just senior management, not just the school improvement committee. Everyone: administrators, teachers, assistants, bus drivers, and students.

> A leader, by virtue of his authority, has obligation to make changes to the system of management that will bring improvement.

W. Edwards Deming, 2012, *The Essential Deming: Leadership Principles from the Father of Quality*, edited by Joyce Orsini, McGraw-Hill, New York, p. 81.

For continual improvement to become a reality across an organisation, everyone must set to work to continually improve the processes for which they are responsible and the relationships they have with others. It is not sufficient to limit improvement efforts to the priorities listed on the school improvement plan.

Certainly, it is helpful to have identified and resourced school-wide improvement priorities, but these alone will not be sufficient to engage everyone in improvement of the things that matter. If improvement efforts are limited to the priorities outlined in the district or school plan, people will be confined to routine activities, waiting to be told what to improve. Improvement becomes the domain of senior management. Opportunities are missed. Relationships stagnate.

Everyone must work on the system, to improve it, continually.

*Everyone must set to work to continually improve the processes for which they are responsible and the relationships they have with others.*

# Working with people

Managers working on the system need to engage with their people working in that system in order to improve it (as discussed at length in Chapter Three). Only those working in the system truly understand the detailed workings of the system and the barriers to improvement.

Only students knows which aspects of classroom processes help them learn and which ones hinder learning. Only the teachers preparing reports know the barriers to completing them on time and with high quality.

Managers must work with the people in the system to bring about improvement in both processes and relationships.

*Managers working on the system will need to engage with their people working in that system in order to improve it.*

# Role modelling

It is unreasonable to expect of others what we are not doing ourselves. If we seek to be a leader — causing others to follow — we must develop a profound understanding of these principles, and seek to role model them in everything we do.

The principles and concepts of quality learning form a coherent and comprehensive management philosophy. This philosophy (as you will have realised by now) is quite different to the prevailing system of management. It is a different paradigm.

For followers to be inspired, leaders must become the best example of this philosophy they possibly can. They must continually learn, apply and refine their understanding of the principles, concepts, tools and methods.

Leaders must role model the principles.

This was expressed by Sarasohn over sixty years ago:

> A leader's main obligation is to secure the faith and respect of his followers. To do so he must be the best example of what he would like to see in his followers. In a democratic sense a leader does not drive his people, nor does he make his people advance by kicking them in the back.
>
> Rather he goes ahead of the others, as if he were lighting their way through a dark tunnel, showing them the path to take and forging ahead so that others can come after, having full confidence that they are treading a firm safe path that will ultimately lead to the desired goal.
>
> Homer M. Sarasohn and Charles A. Protzman, 1949, *The Fundamentals of Industrial Management: CCS management course.* Available at http://www.valuemetrics.com.au/.

These principles not only provide guidance about how leaders relate to their people, they also provide guidance about how to organise goals, tasks and resources that are the domain of management.

The principles apply to everyone. Leaders who embody these principles inspire others to follow. Individuals who manage by these principles demonstrate continual improvement.

That these principles represent a new and different paradigm to the prevailing system of management is a major challenge. Adopting a new paradigm is no simple matter. As Thomas Kuhn wrote about changing scientific problem solving paradigms:

*For followers to be inspired, leaders must become the best example of this philosophy they possibly can.*

The man who embraces a new paradigm at an early stage must often do so in defiance of the evidence provided by problem-solving.

He must, that is, have faith that the new paradigm will succeed with the many large problems that confront it, knowing only that the older paradigm has failed with a few.

A decision of that kind can only be made on faith.

Thomas S. Kuhn, 1962, *The Structure of Scientific Revolutions*, University of Chicago Press, Chicago, p. 158.

By their actions, the most senior leaders in any organisation play a pivotal role in the future performance of the organisation. Those wedded to the prevailing system of management — characterised by competition over cooperation, by objectives rather than by process, and the use of extrinsic motivators over the fostering of intrinsic motivation — can find it difficult to adopt the new philosophy.

Senior leaders, through their questioning, conversations and action, can create outstanding organisations. They can also rapidly and seriously damage the processes and relationships developed by predecessors who had been seeking to role model these principles. Organisational approaches that have taken years to develop and nurture can be quickly destroyed. This is bad news. Individuals who come to develop a deep and profound understanding of the philosophy of quality learning nearly always find that they cannot willingly return to the old way. That is good news.

> Organisational approaches that have taken years to develop and nurture can be quickly destroyed. This is bad news. Individuals who come to develop a deep and profound understanding of the philosophy of quality learning nearly always find that they cannot willingly return to the old way. That is good news.

## Don't wait for others

Given the power and influence of senior leaders, it can be tempting to wait for the people who occupy these roles in our organisations to adopt a new approach before we follow their lead.

Such an approach does not lead to change.

For transformation to be achieved, everyone will need to learn to role model these principles. The change can start with you.

> The change can start with you.

If you are not personally learning about these principles, developing your capacity to apply them, and working with your people to improve processes and relationships, then you have no right to complain about the inactivity of your superiors.

Become the change you wish to see in others.

# Reflection questions

**?** Where do you manage in your organisation? Where do you lead?

**?** What leadership models have you used in the past to guide the way you lead? How have these been effective or ineffective?

**?** How do other leadership models you know of differ from the quality learning principles? In what way do these distinctions make you approach leadership in a different way?

**?** What might you do differently to more fully role model the principles of quality learning?

# Chapter summary

In this chapter, we have examined the three principles relating to the fourth and final area of Deming's system of profound knowledge, psychology:

**Motivation:**   Removing barriers to intrinsic motivation improves performance.

**Relationships:**   Strong human relationships are built through caring, communication, trust and respect.

**Leadership:**   It is everybody's job to improve the systems and processes for which they are responsible by working with their people and role modelling these principles.

Through this chapter, we have explained the following ideas:

- Intrinsic motivation comes from within the individual, extrinsic motivation comes from sources external to the individual. Punishments and rewards are common examples of extrinsic motivation factors;

- Extrinsic motivation can lead to compliance or defiance;

- Engagement can only come from tapping into intrinsic motivation;

- Purpose, choice, mastery and belonging can enhance intrinsic motivation;

- The key to enhancing intrinsic motivation is to work with others to remove barriers from systems and processes;

- Relationships in social systems are interdependent. For relationships to flourish, they require shared purpose, respect, trust, and open and honest communication;

- Many of the practices of the prevailing system of management are toxic to interdependent relationships, including the use of: extrinsic rewards and punishments, praise, empowerment, competition, artificial scarcity, and fear;

- Everybody is a manager of systems and processes. To improve performance, everyone needs to be engaged in improving systems, processes and relationships, with the support of those working in the system;

- Leadership is about inspiring others to follow, not telling others what to do;

- Individuals can lead a transformation by learning about and role modelling the principles described in this book; and

- The quality learning tools detailed throughout this book provide invaluable ways to apply these principles. Additional tools include: capacity matrix; consensogram; loss function; plus delta; code of cooperation; and decision and action record.

# Further reading

We recommend the following references.

Ron Crosling, 2008, "Building Highly Effective Relationships". Available from http://www.qla.com.au/papers/building-highly-effective-relationships/2112870989 — Ron Crosling's paper provides a practical approach to the theory and practice of building great relationships in social systems.

Tony Miller and Gordon Hall, 2013, *Letting go: Breathing new life into organisations*, Argyle Publishing, Glendaruel — A beautifully written discussion of the need to let go of the command and control management paradigm.

Daniel H. Pink, 2009, *Drive: The surprising truths about what motivates us*, Riverhead Books, New York — Daniel Pink's book on motivation provides an accessible reference on the research into human motivation.

Peter R. Scholtes, 1998, *The Leader's Handbook*, McGraw-Hill, New York — A comprehensive and easy to read work on leading organisations towards continual improvement.

Additional references can be found in the annotated bibliography.

# Chapter 7:
# Making Improvement Happen

One need not be eminent in any part of profound knowledge in order to understand and apply it.

W. Edwards Deming, 2012, *The Essential Deming: Leadership principles from the father of quality*, edited by Joyce Orsini, McGraw-Hill, New York, p. 56.

# Chapter contents

# Introduction

In this final chapter we share what we have learned as we have applied the improvement principles described in this book across many organisations, particularly schools.

In this chapter we help you strengthen your improvement efforts. For those just beginning, we show you how to get started.

In this chapter
we help you
strengthen your
improvement
efforts.

We begin with an exploration of the lessons applicable to schools and school systems seeking to apply the principles and practices of continual improvement. We emphasise those aspects of improvement that are less evident in the current literature, policy and practice, but which are critical to the transformation that is needed.

We describe an approach to implementation we have found to be effective across many sectors and organisations, including schools. It is a simple approach that provides a reference point for anyone serious about improving learning and learning how to improve.

We also include suggestions for those working outside the system of school education who want to contribute to its transformation.

Some of the key lessons learned along the way include:

- Everyone has a role in leading organisational transformation by personally improving systems, processes and relationships;

- Constancy of purpose and a relentless focus on continual improvement is essential. Continual improvement is never ending, by definition;

- Within schools, the focus needs to be upon developing ever improving systems of learning and establishing processes that support continual learning; and

- There is great variation in students' prior knowledge and learning speed. Systems of learning can only be successful if students are engaged in planning, managing and monitoring their own learning.

The following flowchart provides a summary of the flow of the chapter.

| Outline key lessons from application. |
|---|
| *What have we learned over the past decades?* |

⬇

| Describe an implementation approach. |
|---|
| *What can you do to make improvement happen?* |

# Lessons from application

In the pages that follow we share key lessons from the past two decades of our experiences working with schools, school systems and other organisations that have been seeking to apply the principles and practices outlined in this book.

Our aim is to use this learning to provide guidance for readers seeking to lead the transformation of the prevailing system of management to one focussed upon improvement.

This is not a summary of the key messages presented earlier in the book. The concepts and practices described earlier speak for themselves. They need to be explored, learned and applied.

The emphasis here is on what you need to do to make improvement happen. The focus is less on theory and more on application. We pay particular attention to the approaches that are least evident in organisations we have observed.

While our emphasis here is on schools and school systems, it should be noted that the lessons and theory apply equally to any organisation. After all, it is one system, and we need to work together to bring about transformation of the prevailing system of management.

> Our aim is to provide guidance for readers seeking to lead the transformation.

> The lessons and theory apply equally to any organisation.

## Lead improvement

The responsibility to lead improvement is not limited to senior management. Everyone needs to be actively engaged working on the system to improve it. It is not sufficient to merely work in the system.

Everyone has a responsibility to lead improvement of processes and relationships. Within our individual spheres of influence, we can each make a major contribution to improvement within our organisation. Everyone has the opportunity to contribute to improvement and experience the satisfaction that arises from doing so.

The obligation to lead improvement cannot be delegated. For improvement to be sustained, the leader of the system must be personally and continually engaged in leading the improvement effort.

School principals, for example, must personally lead the school's improvement efforts. Classroom teachers must personally lead the improvement of processes and relationships in their classrooms. Each leader personally and actively participates and guides the improvement planning and implementation.

> Everyone has the opportunity to contribute to improvement and experience the satisfaction that arises from doing so.

Leaders must actively champion the strategy for two reasons. Firstly, active participation accelerates the leader's learning about the improvement approach, making them even more effective as leaders. Secondly, the active engagement of a leader in improvement demonstrates the importance being placed upon improvement.

## Improve processes using PDSA

We all have responsibility for processes. Senior leaders have a wider span of influence than junior staff, but everyone has processes for which they are responsible. Teachers lead classroom processes. Students are responsible for their learning processes. All processes can be improved, and the person responsible for a process must lead its improvement. If the person responsible doesn't lead this improvement, nobody will.

Processes deliver outcomes. To improve the outcome, one must improve the processes that deliver the outcomes.

Undertaking improvement projects using a structured process such as Plan–Do–Study–Act is the method by which processes can be improved. Everyone can use Plan–Do–Study–Act to improve the processes for which they are responsible.

> Everyone can use PDSA to improve the processes for which they are responsible.

## Remove barriers

In Chapter Three we explained that it is better to remove barriers than to push harder when seeking to bring about change in a social system. It follows that one of the keys to continual improvement is systematically identifying and removing the barriers to learning and improvement. Every leader can engage in conversations with their people to identify barriers to learning and improvement, and initiate actions to address them systemically and systematically.

> Every leader can engage in conversations with their people to identify barriers to learning and improvement, and initiate actions to address them systemically and systematically.

## Improve relationships

Everyone works in relationship with others. The interactions we have with others are the lifeblood for our experiences within an organisation. Positive interactions can raise our spirits, just as negative interactions can be draining.

Strong and productive relationships have their foundations in interactions among people. It is only through productive conversations that mutual agreement can be reached. It is through these conversations that shared understanding is created and trust is strengthened or diminished. We are an integral part of every interaction in which we engage, and we have the capacity to enhance or diminish the value of each interaction with others. Are we engaging with others such that they welcome our contribution? Are we genuine, supportive and constructive?

Conversations change when leaders ask different questions. To change responses, change the questions. As we ask new and better questions, we can engage in better conversations.

How can we learn to ask better questions? The answer lies in aligning our questions with principles. The principles outlined in this book represent a body of knowledge that has been developed, tested and proven over time. They are our current best understanding of the theory of quality improvement. The principles can lead to new and better questions than those asked under the prevailing system of management.

Principles derived from rigorously tested theory and practices provide a sound basis for leaders' questions.

Everyone has an opportunity to lead. Every individual can lead improvement of the processes for which they are responsible. We can all lead improvement in our interactions and conversations with others by aligning our behaviour and questioning with proven principles. What's more, you don't need permission to lead improvement. Begin!

> Conversations change when leaders ask different questions. To change responses, change the questions.

> You don't need permission to lead.

# Maintain constancy of purpose

There are no quick fixes. Quality improvement is neither a quick fix nor a fad. When it comes to continual improvement, persistence is required.

## Ensure a relentless focus on improvement

A relentless focus on learning and improvement is essential. In the absence of such a commitment to an explicit improvement agenda, approaches to improvement will come and go like the tides. Without constancy of purpose for continual improvement, opportunities to learn and build capacity for improvement will be lost.

> Without constancy of purpose for continual improvement, opportunities to learn and build capacity for improvement will be lost.

Learning and improvement are opposite sides of the same coin. When a theory for improvement (hypothesis) is created and tested, benefits flow: learning and improvement. If a hypothesis is proven, you learn. If a hypothesis is disproven, you learn. If proven, the hypothesis improves your ability to predict, and knowledge is created. If disproven, you have the opportunity to revise the hypothesis. You learn either way. What's more, when hypotheses aimed at improvement are tested and proven, performance improves.

# Recognise that improvement is not a program

Schools are well accustomed to implementing programs. Planning and programming is a core competence for all educators. Teachers are very skilled at developing programs and implementing them. In particular, teachers are highly skilled in the development and implementation of curriculum programs. Reviewing curricula, adapting scope and sequences, developing new units of work, learning activities and assessment tasks — these are all routine activities for teachers. Districts and departments also implement programs. Many government policies result in programs being rolled out across states and territories.

Continual improvement is not a program, it is a set of principles and practices that define a system of management. Programs have a defined start. People expect programs to have a defined finish too. Some chose to wait for them to go away. Not so with continual improvement.

There will be curriculum implications arising from adopting the approach outlined in this book. School leaders, teachers and students will need to learn the theory, and they will need to use the Plan–Do–Study–Act cycle and tools. It is important to note that emphasis must be placed upon using the tools and methods, not teaching the tools and methods. Even though there are learning requirements, continual improvement is not a curriculum program. The concepts described in this book define a system of management, not a program.

> The concepts described in this book define a system of management, not a program.

This system of management provides a unifying approach to improvement across the organisation: there is one approach to be applied by everyone. It provides commonality in principles, language, tools and application. It provides a unifying theory for leadership and management at all levels. No longer are innovation and improvement the domain of senior management, they belong to everybody.

# Make it your own

Organisations need to make this approach their own. For example, the Leander Independent School District in Leander, Texas, has "The Leander Way", as illustrated in Figure 7.1, which describes their approach to management and continual improvement. While their approach is based on Deming's ideas, it is their way. It is not "The Deming Program".

If you attach a specific name to your approach to continual improvement, you risk having it perceived as a program. Programs have a finite life. Programs can be criticised, and programs can be terminated.

> Use the principles, tools and methods to inform the development of your own theory for improvement.

Use the principles, tools and methods to inform the development of your own theory for improvement.

**Figure 7.1 The Leander way**
Source: Leander Independent School District, Texas.

# Build a critical mass of volunteers

The capacity for ongoing organisational improvement resides largely in the individual and collective minds of those working in the organisation. In order to develop organisational capacity, we must develop individual capacity. Organisations need to build capacity to understand and apply the improvement philosophy and methods.

Successful organisations begin by seeking to build a critical mass of volunteers who can lead the change. If only a few individuals understand and apply the principles and practices, it will be difficult for them to sustain application. The pressure to return to the prevailing system of management will be immense. A critical mass of individuals is needed to support one another, lead, sustain and extend the transformation.

A critical mass of individuals is needed to support one another, lead, sustain and extend the transformation.

Deming suggested a good rule of thumb: a critical mass requires the square root of the number of people in the organisation. For an organisation of 100, a critical mass becomes evident with about ten people. For a staff of 36, a critical mass is approximately half a dozen. Our experience supports this suggestion.

A critical mass requires the square root of the number of people in the organisation.

We have found the volunteer rule an effective approach to identifying individuals to establish and extend the critical mass. The volunteer rule requires management to:

- Clarify purpose and seek to develop a shared understanding of what is possible, involving everyone in the organisation;

- Encourage people to volunteer;

- Work with everybody who does volunteer;

- Vigorously support the volunteers to ensure they are successful;

- Celebrate success; and

- Repeat the cycle.

Through this approach, people leading the change have chosen to participate. They work as a team and can support one another as they learn and apply the principles and practices. Over time, a critical mass is created and extended. Don't waste time or energy with those who don't volunteer. Give them time to observe, reflect, and then choose to join in. Ultimately, when a majority is behind the transformation, those who still don't wish to contribute can seek more suitable options elsewhere. From our experience, it is a very small minority of people who don't want to be part of a continually improving organisation.

Those who commence early and see the benefits tend to learn quickly and become advocates for transformation.

As things get moving, early adopters can become coaches for others. Those who commence early and see the benefits tend to learn quickly and become advocates for transformation. They act as guides and coaches for others.

It is important to publically celebrate the successes of these early pioneers. These celebrations not only recognise the pioneering efforts, they also make a clear statement to others about the importance placed on improvement work. Seeing success provides drive to continue.

# Engage everyone in improvement

Everyone can and should be engaged in improvement.

## All key stakeholders

When key stakeholder groups are not engaged in improvement, the system will be suboptimised. If students, for example, are not consulted, let alone actively leading improvement projects, the system cannot be optimised for learning. Only students truly know the barriers to their learning. Similarly, teachers know the barriers that affect them. All key stakeholders need to be actively engaged in improvement, continually.

## Right across the organisation

When key areas of the organisation are not engaged in improvement, the system will be suboptimised. If only some classrooms are seeking to apply the concepts identified in this book, the system will not be optimised for learning. It should be an explicit objective to include all areas of the organisation in continual improvement. Over time, continual improvement of processes and relationships becomes "how we do things around here", across all parts of the organisation.

## Top down and bottom up

It has been our experience that transformation is best achieved when approached top-down and bottom-up. Senior leadership has the authority and responsibility to enact organisation-wide systems and processes that support and drive transformation. Senior leaders also lead with new questions that challenge old practices and behaviour. Those with less positional power and authority can still achieve significant local breakthroughs, which serve as powerful examples for others. Middle managers quickly see that the new way is being adopted at the top and delivering success at that bottom. This can accelerate their engagement with the change process.

# Engage the students

In most schools, students are merely passive observers of the school's improvement efforts. This is a shameful waste of talent and potential.

## Engage students in managing their learning

All students can learn. Some take longer than others, but all students can learn. Most can learn to a deep level and produce remarkable evidence of their learning. Students need mediation and support, not grades and artificial deadlines.

Students can learn to manage their own learning. Even very young students can learn to plan, monitor and assess their learning. They can also learn to manage their time in order to achieve their goals for the day, week and term. Some take longer to learn this than others, but with appropriate guidance, encouragement and support they can learn to manage their time well.

*Students can learn to manage their own learning.*

## Engage students in improvement projects

Students can learn to lead improvement. Our experience has been that students pick up the tools rapidly. They can also lead improvement teams working through the Plan–Do–Study–Act improvement cycle. In doing so, students can play an important role in making improvement happen in classrooms and across the school. Students have an enormous contribution to make to improvement teams working on classroom processes and whole school improvement projects.

Students are key to making improvement happen in schools. Engaging all students in improvement projects across all levels of the school unleashes enormous energy, creativity and drive towards school improvement. Too many schools ignore this diamond mine of potential.

*Students are key to making improvement happen in schools.*

## Engage students as advocates

Students become the advocates for transformation. Students tell their families, friends and relatives of the great improvements at their school, and the part they played in them. They also describe, with excitement, their progress in learning, the evidence upon which they base that assessment, and their goals for the coming period. Conversations change for the better.

*Students become the advocates for transformation.*

Students are critical stakeholders in the adoption of the new management philosophy and realisation of continual school improvement. They can play a crucial and productive role. All that is required is to ask them, and show them how.

# Sustain continual learning

Improvement and learning are like the two sides of a coin. They present different faces, but they are one with each other. To sustain continual improvement, one must sustain continual learning. What follows are observations of how this might be encouraged across organisations.

*To sustain continual improvement, one must sustain continual learning.*

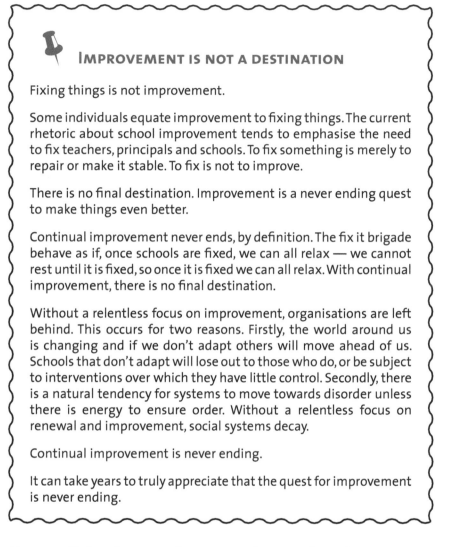

### IMPROVEMENT IS NOT A DESTINATION

Fixing things is not improvement.

Some individuals equate improvement to fixing things. The current rhetoric about school improvement tends to emphasise the need to fix teachers, principals and schools. To fix something is merely to repair or make it stable. To fix is not to improve.

There is no final destination. Improvement is a never ending quest to make things even better.

Continual improvement never ends, by definition. The fix it brigade behave as if, once schools are fixed, we can all relax — we cannot rest until it is fixed, so once it is fixed we can all relax. With continual improvement, there is no final destination.

Without a relentless focus on improvement, organisations are left behind. This occurs for two reasons. Firstly, the world around us is changing and if we don't adapt others will move ahead of us. Schools that don't adapt will lose out to those who do, or be subject to interventions over which they have little control. Secondly, there is a natural tendency for systems to move towards disorder unless there is energy to ensure order. Without a relentless focus on renewal and improvement, social systems decay.

Continual improvement is never ending.

It can take years to truly appreciate that the quest for improvement is never ending.

## Be explicit about what people need to know, understand, and be able to do

This book has described the principles and practices that represent the quality improvement philosophy.

In order to transform the prevailing system of management, we must develop a critical mass of people who understand the principles and practices, and know how to apply them.

Organisations can make explicit what people are expected to know, understand and be able to do. Capacity matrices are a good method for expressing this knowledge and skills (see Chapter Six). Capacity matrices enable learners to plan, monitor and manage their learning.

Appendix 1 provides capacity matrices based upon the principles and practices discussed in this book. It can provide a starting point for you and your colleagues to review and systematically develop your understanding of the principles and practices of improvement.

Copies of these capacity matrices can be downloaded from the QLA web site: qla.com.au

## Encourage learning from experiments and mistakes

Encourage experimentation and learning. People can be encouraged to use the Plan–Do–Study–Act cycle in order to form and test hypotheses aimed at improvement. This facilitates learning both about the area of focus and about the improvement processes itself.

People must not be fearful of making mistakes, as fear stifles creativity and learning. As Deming said, "Drive out fear!"

## Ensure that professional learning role-models the philosophy

People can be provided access to opportunities to learn about the philosophy and its implementation. Both education and training will be required. (If you are unsure of the difference, think of the difference between sex education and sex training.) Whatever learning opportunities are created, it is important that they are conducted in a manner that is consistent with the principles and practices.

Professional learning seminars and workshops need to model the approach. These interventions will be most effective when they are designed in such a way that they maximise intrinsic motivation (see Chapter Six), role model the principles in action, and use the tools effectively.

Make explicit what people are expected to know, understand and be able to do.

People must not be fearful of making mistakes, as fear stifles creativity and learning.

Professional learning seminars and workshops need to model the approach.

## Ensure constancy of message

Organisations benefit from finding a master teacher and sticking with them. As an organisation commences the transformation, this single teacher provides a consistent message for everyone in the organisation. A single teacher can sustain the same message over time as more people are trained and new ones join the organisation. As individuals learn more and gain experience in the application of the methods, this teacher can support the organisation in making the approach its own. The master teacher provides consistent training to the whole organisation while guiding the senior leader in planning the improvement strategy. This should be the aim — learn from the master teacher and create the organisation's own approach.

> Organisations benefit from finding a master teacher and sticking with them.

This is in contrast to the common approach in schools where one or two teachers attend a professional development workshop and are then expected to teach everyone else what they have learned. The absurdity of this approach is particularly evident when the original course ran for a day or two, and the teachers are expected to teach everyone else during a one-hour staff meeting. Find a master teacher and offer their training to everyone.

Over time, it becomes beneficial to learn from others, beyond your master teacher, who are expert in particular aspects of the principles and practices. In the initial stages, however, our experience suggests that having a single voice and reference point ensures constancy of language and consistency of message.

## Provide in context coaching

The principles and practices described in this book have application across a wide range of sectors and individuals' roles in organisations, including corporations, government departments, districts, schools and classrooms. Every organisation is different, but the same theory of management applies. Similarly, within each organisation, the concepts and methods apply to everyone, from the most senior leaders to those who mop the floors.

> People need to understand the relevance to them, personally, in order to make meaning.

Individuals need help to contextualise the philosophy to their world. Individuals will seek to make sense of these ideas as they apply to them. They need help to do this. Examples from other sectors or job roles are of limited benefit for this purpose. People always want to know "What does this mean for me?" People need to understand the relevance to them, personally, in order to make meaning and new neural connections.

As organisations apply these ideas to their unique contexts, individuals will need support to understand how the ideas apply to them personally and in their roles. Organisations need to plan to provide this in-context coaching.

## Celebrate successes

The journey of improvement has many ups and downs. There will be times when progress is good, and times where things seem to be regressing. Throughout the journey, it is often easier to see how far there is to go than to see how far one has come. The road ahead is endless, and it can certainly feel like it at times.

A paradox of continual improvement is that as things improve, you find even more that can be improved. As you identify and eliminate loss and waste across the organisation, you become even more aware of loss and waste. It is not that there is suddenly more waste, only that you become more aware, conscious and intolerant of it.

For these reasons, it is important to celebrate successes as they occur. Take time to acknowledge the progress that has been made and to recognise the contributions of those that made it happen. Celebrations build commitment and intrinsic motivation.

> Celebrations build commitment and intrinsic motivation.

Recognise the efforts of individuals and teams along the way.

## Develop systems for ever improving learning in the classroom

Most people consider the role of teachers is to teach. This is unfortunate, unhelpful and limiting. A teacher's job is to manage and continually improve systems of learning. Let us explain.

> A teacher's job is to manage and continually improve systems of learning.

### Build systems of learning

Education is created through student learning. Without learning there is no education. Without students creating and rewiring their neural pathways, there is no learning and no education. Learning is the primary focus of education. Teaching is a critical support process for learning, but learning is the aim of the system.

Teachers are responsible for setting the learning agenda, hopefully with the aid of their students. They also establish the processes of the classroom. As such, teachers are the managers of the classroom learning processes — they establish systems of learning. These systems of learning

> Teachers are responsible for the systems of learning at the classroom level.

can be top-down and directive, or they can be enabling. They can be established with or without the support of the students. Teachers are responsible for systems of learning at the classroom level.

As teachers are responsible for systems of learning, they must also be responsible for improving those systems. If they don't continually improve the systems for which they are responsible, nobody can.

In short, a teacher's job is to manage and continually improve the systems of learning for which they are responsible. This will include teaching, of course. But to limit the role of teachers to simply teaching is to ignore their wider responsibilities for improving systems.

Assisting students to learn is not improvement work, it is daily work.

It is worth reiterating that assisting students to learn is not improvement work, it is daily work. Teaching and learning are the daily work of schools — working in the system. To work on the system is to improve the systems of learning and teaching.

In an environment where the systems of learning are continually improving, student performance improves year on year. Each successive cohort of students benefit from the lessons learned from those that preceded them. The capability of the system gets better each year; teachers manage systems that result in deeper, richer more rapid learning. Key performance indicators show improvement, year in, year out.

## Focus on quality teaching

Teaching is traditionally seen as providing instruction to impart knowledge and skills — delivery of curricula. We prefer to see teaching as the mediation of student learning. The teacher works with students in a highly interactive way, each providing feedback to the other as the teacher actively mediates student learning. Teacher and students work together to maximise the creation of neural pathways in the brain (learning) in the students. This is a good deal more involved than simply instructing students.

Teaching is the most critical support process for learning.

While most students can learn on their own, the support of a skilled teacher accelerates learning enormously. Teaching is therefore the most critical support process for learning. Without teaching, without feedback, learning is stunted. Not surprisingly, improving the quality of teaching has been shown to improve the quality of learning.

What is needed is quality teaching.

In recent times, the educational debate has shifted to suggest that schools need quality teachers. This is unfortunate, as it promotes the blame game by suggesting that the quality of teachers is the problem. What is needed is quality teaching, which is quite different to quality teachers.

To improve the outcome, improve the process; don't try and "fix" the people. Policy makers have a responsibility to support improvements in the quality of teaching; they do not need to fix the teachers.

What does it mean to improve the quality of teaching? Teachers learning to manage and improve systems that help more and more students to learn, more broadly, deeply and rapidly than those that went before them.

This is achieved by managing and improving systems of learning, which is the job of teachers, administrators, and policymakers.

## Seek mastery in learning

Traditional teaching is based on a cycle of plan–teach–assess. In line with the curriculum, the teacher plans a unit of work, teaches the unit, and then assesses the students' learning. The cycle is repeated unit to unit, semester to semester, year to year.

For many students, this cycle is cram–test–forget.

Students come to learn that after they sit a test, they may never refer to the material again. Once a unit has been taught and tested, it is done, and students are frequently given permission to forget it.

> Once a unit has been taught and tested, it is done, and students are frequently given permission to forget it.

Learning can occur at progressively deeper levels:

- **Information**: I have heard of this and can answer simple questions about it;

- **Knowledge**: I can explain this in my own words and relate it to other things;

- **Know-how**: I can apply this and know when to do so; and

- **Wisdom**: I know why this is so, can apply it in new situations, and can teach others.

The cram–test–forget approach to learning does not produce mastery. It frequently fails to generate understanding. Students benefit a lot more from learning experiences that produce deep and permanent levels of learning: wisdom.

> The cram–test–forget approach to learning does not produce mastery.

We have had the opportunity to ask many school communities what they think students should learn at school. We have asked this question of students, staff and families across scores of Australian schools. While there is some local variation in responses, there are themes that are very common. Students, families and staff certainly want students to become literate and numerate. But they also want students to learn to be confident, resilient, respectful, independent, motivated, and caring.

They want students to be equipped with skills for problem solving, life, relationships with others, and active citizenship. Families are looking to schools to help equip their children to address the challenges of the future. Not surprisingly, these attributes extend beyond what is evaluated in most state and national standardised tests. Communities are looking to schools to help students gain wisdom.

Communities can identify and agree what students need to learn at school. A process of consultation, such as we have undertaken with these schools, can determine the desired exit outcomes for students. The graduate profile for the Leander Independent School District (see Chapter Three) illustrates this and has been used to guide progress in their district over the past two decades.

Having identified what students need to learn at school, the challenge is to manage the curriculum and learning processes in order to ensure that the desired learning takes place. This can only be achieved through thoughtful and compounding deep learning experiences.

Cram–test–forget simply isn't good enough.

## Respond appropriately to variation in learning

Progression through school is currently based on serving the time, not demonstrating learning. Students are put into batches, with students of the same age grouped together. At the end of the year, the batch progresses to the next year level. Sometimes individual students are held back to repeat a year and, very rarely, students may skip a year level. But for the vast majority, progress is time-based. Students serve their time and move on in much the same manner in which prisoners serve their time while waiting for freedom. The vast majority of students need not demonstrate acceptable learning in order to move on, and they learn this very quickly.

In such systems, time is fixed and learning is variable. Students spend the same amount of time in a class, but the learning of each individual student is highly variable. Students learn at different rates, and this learning varies by curriculum areas. Some students may learn a great deal of mathematics, for example, in a year in which other students learn very little. It could take one student only minutes to master a concept, while others may take weeks.

> Families are looking to schools to help equip their children to address the challenges of the future.

> Progression through school is currently based on serving the time, not demonstrating learning.

The challenge for the current system of schooling is that it approaches time inflexibly. Assessment measures the degree to which students can master a subject within a given time frame, which implies that being able to master something within a constrained time is more important than mastering it at all.

Students are expected to adapt to the school system and to thrive in a system with rigid timelines. All students cannot demonstrate excellence when time is constrained. Where time is seen to be more critical than learning, work of any quality is accepted, provided it is handed in on time. Students see this and respond accordingly: "What do I have to do to pass?" Under these conditions, learning is not required and mediocrity is accepted.

The school system needs to be flexible to the learning needs of each student. The systems of learning that the school is managing must seek to minimise this input variation and be robust to it. Systems and processes must support every student to achieve deep learning while recognising that learning is variable from student to student. For learning to become fixed, time must become variable. Students must be given the time they need to develop deep learning.

> For learning to become fixed, time must become variable.

Recognising the importance of this, the only way for learning to become assured is for students to be put in charge of their own learning. There must be a clear, explicit and viable curriculum put in the hands of the students, not just teachers' programs. Students need the skills and tools to plan, monitor, evaluate and demonstrate their learning. They need to be able to work at their own pace, moving on only after they have mastered the requisite skills. They need to be enabled to learn with their colleagues, support others, and learn from them. Teachers need to learn how to establish, manage and continually improve such a system of learning.

> The only way for learning to become assured is for students to be put in charge of their own learning.

This system of student-led learning can support individual learning, progress and growth. Such a system only works when teachers see themselves as mediators of learning who are responsible for managing and improving systems of learning. It will not be achieved by teachers who believe their job is teaching in the traditional sense. It cannot be achieved by batching students according to birth date.

# What can I do?

In this section, we discuss what individuals and organisations can do to apply the ideas in this book to improve the system of school education.

We outline an approach to adoption of the philosophy, which can apply to any organisation or individual. This approach is as applicable to a classroom as it is to a whole school, district, work-group or department. If you work in the system, this is what you can do.

If you work outside the system of school education, there are also things you can do. You can begin asking new questions — based on the principles outlined in this book — of those who have responsibilities within the system of school education. Given what you have learned about the principles of improvement, you are well placed to ask questions that can change conversations within schools and about school improvement. Appendix 3 suggests some questions you may like to ask school leaders, including classroom teachers. These questions explore the themes of school direction, leading improvement, student learning, teacher learning, process management, and performance management.

If you are serious about adopting the improvement philosophy, you will plan to address each of these six areas in a systematic manner.

If you work in the system, there are six key areas of activity that, when taken together and applied with integrity, lead to a sustainable transformation to a culture of innovation and continual improvement. If you are serious about adopting the improvement philosophy, you can address each of these six areas in a systematic manner:

- Agree and apply the principles;

- Think and act systemically;

- Use data effectively;

- Conduct regular self-assessment;

- Apply tools and the PDSA cycle; and

- Capture and share the learning.

Figure 7.2 illustrates these six areas of activity and the relationships among them. Note that the principles apply to all activities undertaken by the organisation. Similarly, effective use of data also applies to all areas of activity. The improvement cycle involves:

- Thinking systemically;

- Conducting regular self-assessment of the system;

- Applying the tools and PDSA to improve processes and relationships, based upon the findings of the self-assessment; and

- Capturing the learning as new processes and approaches.

These six areas of activity can form the basis of an organisation-wide plan to learn about, apply and embed a culture of continual improvement. The plan can be developed and documented as a Gantt chart in a program of activity. Each of these areas is described in turn.

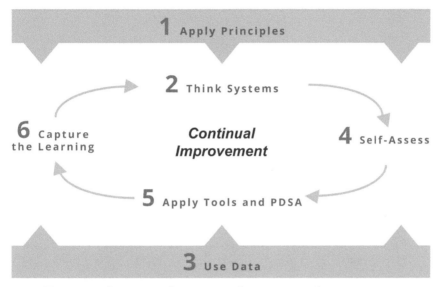

**Figure 7.2 Six areas of activity to drive continual improvement**

# Agree and apply the principles

The first requirement is to commit to developing an individual and collective understanding of the principles and practices. As Deming said, "There is no substitute for knowledge."

## Agree and apply the principles in your context

This book explains the 12 principles that encapsulate the key concepts underpinning quality learning and improvement. This book — including the references listed at the end of each chapter and those in the bibliography — can provide a foundation for learning about these principles. The 12 statements in Figure 7.3 represent our best expression of Deming's theory as a set of principles for organisational improvement.

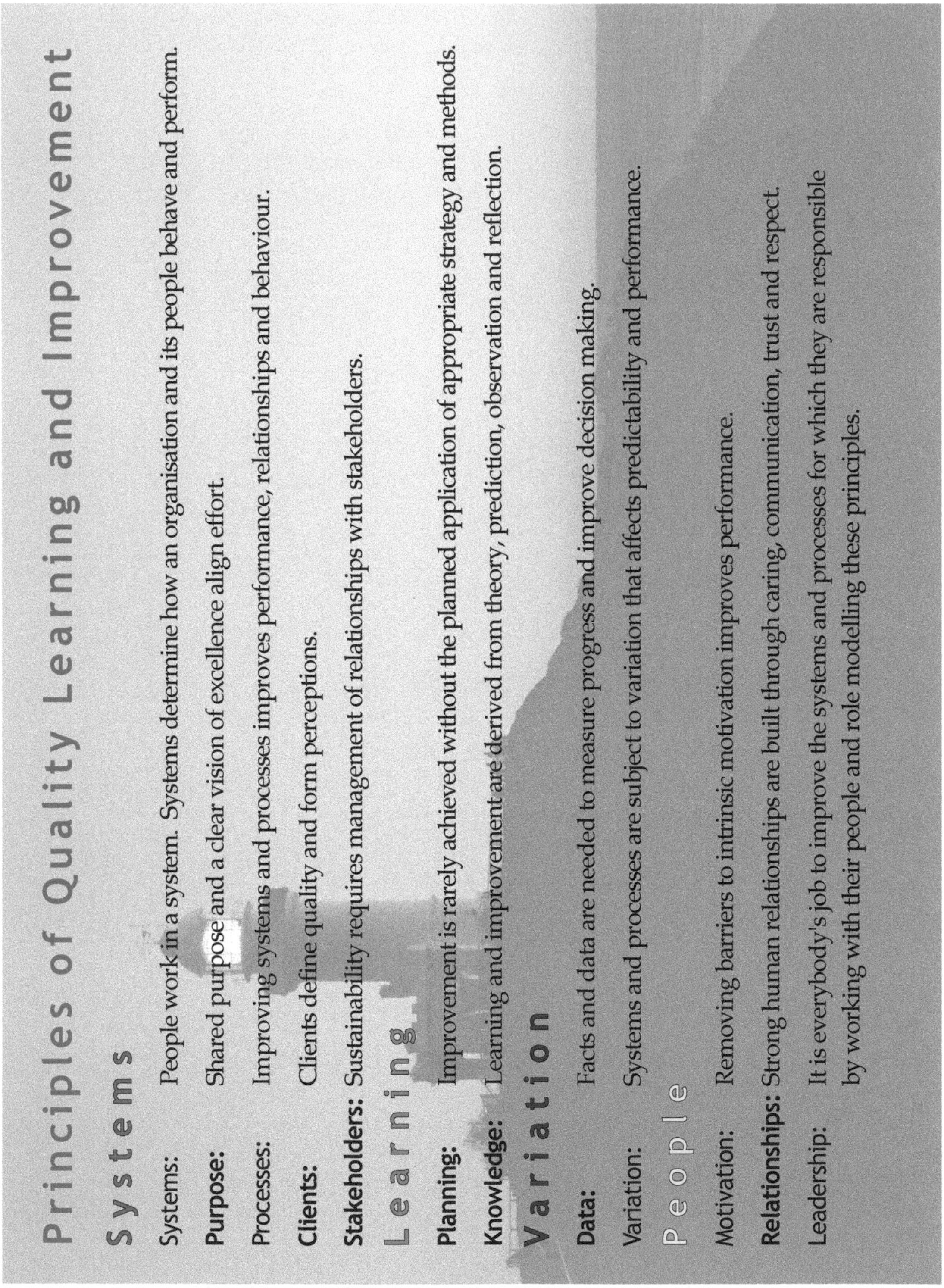

# Principles of Quality Learning and Improvement

## Systems

**Systems:** People work in a system. Systems determine how an organisation and its people behave and perform.

**Purpose:** Shared purpose and a clear vision of excellence align effort.

**Processes:** Improving systems and processes improves performance, relationships and behaviour.

**Clients:** Clients define quality and form perceptions.

**Stakeholders:** Sustainability requires management of relationships with stakeholders.

## Learning

**Planning:** Improvement is rarely achieved without the planned application of appropriate strategy and methods.

**Knowledge:** Learning and improvement are derived from theory, prediction, observation and reflection.

## Variation

**Data:** Facts and data are needed to measure progress and improve decision making.

**Variation:** Systems and processes are subject to variation that affects predictability and performance.

## People

**Motivation:** Removing barriers to intrinsic motivation improves performance.

**Relationships:** Strong human relationships are built through caring, communication, trust and respect.

**Leadership:** It is everybody's job to improve the systems and processes for which they are responsible by working with their people and role modelling these principles.

**Figure 7.3 The principles of quality learning and improvement**

These principles can be used for two purposes:

1. **As a basis for self-assessment**, the principles enable you to learn about the philosophy, its relevance to your organisation, and the degree to which your organisation's processes and behaviour are aligned to the principles. Self-assessment identifies strengths to be celebrated and sustained, and opportunities for improvement to be prioritised and acted upon.

2. **To form the basis of new questions** that can change interactions and improve relationships and performance.

The principles are one way in which the theory may be expressed. As you read, learn and experience more, you will probably find other ways to express the concepts, ways that may be more appropriate and meaningful in your context. We encourage you to adapt these principles to become your own. Express the principles in language that suits your context and resonates with your stakeholders. Make it your theory for improvement. Learn and adapt. Take care, however, not to lose any of the key concepts. It is easy to omit what you don't see or don't understand. For this reason, we encourage ongoing conversations among all key stakeholders about quality improvement philosophy, its underpinnings and expression. Through these ongoing conversations, you can agree the best expression of the principles for you and your organisation.

> Express the principles in language that suits your context and resonates with your stakeholders. Make it your theory for improvement

Just as these principles apply to organisations, there are also principles for individuals, principles that encapsulate what it is to be a decent, collaborative and productive human being. Many authors have written on this topic and there are plenty of good references from which principles can be drawn. Stephen Covey's *7 Habits of Highly Effective People* is one such example. The principles for individuals are used for the same two purposes — self-assessment and new questions — although the focus is upon individual behavior rather than organisational behavior.

We encourage you to be explicit about the principles your organisation is using. Agree the principles you are operating by, both at an organisational level and at an individual level. Publish, promote and hold yourselves accountable to them.

Remember, this is a journey of never ending learning and improvement. Learning about the principles and learning to apply them is a life-long endeavour.

### LEANDER INDEPENDENT SCHOOL DISTRICT'S TEN ETHICAL PRINCIPLES

Over a decade ago, the Leander Independent School District in Leander, Texas, USA, identified ten ethical principles (shown in Figure 7.3). In compiling these principles, the district considered many different cultures that survived and thrived, and they examined how people behaved in those cultures. The aim was to create a cross-cultural framework that could be used to guide behaviour and decision making across the district. The district's ten ethical principles were the result of this effort and have been guiding decision making across the district ever since. They are used for self-assessment and as the basis for questions.

Whereas the 12 principles of organisational improvement are used to guide organisational practices and behavior, the ethical principles guide individual practice and behaviour. Taken together, these principles represent the organisation's agreement regarding how people behave as they go about improving and working in the organisation.

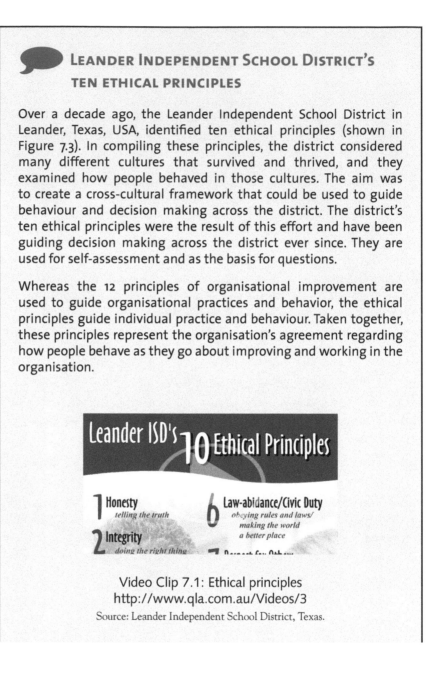

Video Clip 7.1: Ethical principles
http://www.qla.com.au/Videos/3
Source: Leander Independent School District, Texas.

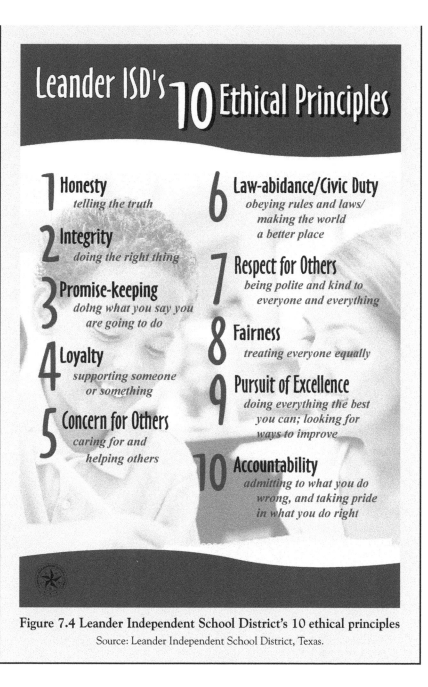

**Figure 7.4 Leander Independent School District's 10 ethical principles**
Source: Leander Independent School District, Texas.

## Ask principle-based questions

To bring about a transformation in social systems, it is usually necessary to change the way people think, talk and act. There are key processes that organisations can adapt to support the desired changes in behaviour. At an individual level, however, you can have a significant influence on others through the interactions you have with them. To achieve a change in these interactions, you will probably need to change the nature of the questions you ask yourself, the questions you ask of others, and the questions you ask of the system itself.

### Questions to ask ourselves

The way in which we relate to ourselves, our self-talk, strongly influences how we relate to others. There is enormous variation in how people view and relate to themselves. In a work context, for example, people often view the same job quite differently. Consider two receptionists: one considers himself to be "just the receptionist", while the other thinks of himself as "the director of first impressions". This concept of self and associated self-talk will have a profound impact upon how these individuals relate to others throughout the organisation.

We have the freedom to choose our responses. Early in life we try different responses to situations, and based upon what seems to work for us we begin to develop preferred responses to situations. Before long, these responses become habits. As adults it can be very difficult to understand why we respond in the way we do, and even harder to remember that we can choose to respond differently.

We can change the conversations we have with ourselves. By reflecting upon principles for individuals and organisations we can ask ourselves different questions, we can consider new responses, and we can change our self-talk.

Consider the following questions:

- Am I being truly objective in my assessment of this situation? Am I seeking to understand?

- Am I being proactive? Am I making a conscious choice?

- Am I emotionally present and engaged? Why/why not?

- Am I acting in the best interests of the system? Am I acting in the best interests of others? Am I seeking a win–win solution?

- Is this the truth?

- Is this fair to all concerned?

- How does this fit with my personal belief system?

These questions, and questions like them, have the potential to change the conversations we have with ourselves.

As a leader, you can reflect upon your self-talk and the questions you ask of yourself. Importantly, you can also support others to consider how they relate to themselves and the nature of their internal conversations.

## Questions to ask others

A powerful way to change your interactions with others is to change the questions you ask of them. This is particularly true for leaders. To adopt a system of management that is focused on learning and improvement, one must ask questions that promote learning and improvement.

> A powerful way to change our interactions with others is to change the questions we ask of them.

Consider the following questions, which could be asked when a problem is encountered in an organisation:

- What is the system we are talking about? Do we have an agreed system map (see Chapter Three) for it?

- Which process in particular is causing this issue? Do we have a flowchart of the process? At which steps in the process do we seem to be having difficulty?

- What data do we have regarding performance of the process? Do we have a control chart or histogram?

- What is the variation in process performance telling us about the process? Is the process stable? Is it capable?

- Based upon this evidence, what should we do next? What is our theory for improvement? How shall we go about testing that theory?

This is an example of a line of questioning based upon the improvement principles, which is quite different to the typical line of questioning derived from the prevailing system of management. The principles provide a rich source of inspiration for new questions that can bring about change for the better in the interactions among people.

Other conversation changing questions could include the following:

- What is the system for which I am responsible?
- Who are the clients of that system?
- What do they require? How do we know?
- What is our clients' vision of excellence for this system? How do we know?
- How is this system performing in their eyes? How do we know?

- What are we working to improve right now? By what method are we seeking to improve it?

- How did we set the improvement priorities?

Using the principles outlined in this book, you will be able to create your own questions to improve relationships and performance.

There is another powerful idea for changing your interactions with others. Give explicit permission for others to tell you when you are not behaving in a manner consistent with the agreed principles, and then accept and respond to that feedback with gratitude, contemplation and good grace. It can be remarkably liberating to have others provide direct and constructive feedback on one's own behaviour. Other people can help us see aspects of our behaviour to which we are blind. It can also be confronting. Feedback given and received with compassion, care and grace strengthens both individuals and the relationship between them.

> Feedback given and received with compassion, care and grace strengthens both individuals and the relationship between them.

## Questions to ask the system

Most organisations have performance measures of some kind. The principles require us to interpret and respond to these measures in a manner that is somewhat different to the traditional response in most organisations. In particular, we need to pay careful attention to the degree to which our processes are stable and capable. This is necessary if we are to stop tampering. As we discussed at length in Chapter Five, we need to respond appropriately to common cause and special cause variation.

> Paying careful attention and responding appropriately to variation in system performance is how we listen to the voice of the system.

Measures give voice to the system. Paying careful attention and responding appropriately to variation in system performance is how we listen to the voice of the system. The system can tell us if it is producing consistent and predictable results, it is our responsibility to ask.

We can ask the system about its wellbeing. Performance measures answer the question, "how did we go?" Process measures ask the question, "how are we going?" As was discussed in Chapter Five, we need more than just performance measures; we need process measures to monitor progress and predict performance.

We can ask new questions of the system by:

- Identifying appropriate measures, particularly process and performance measures;

- Collecting, collating and charting the data in order to see the variation;

- Listening to the voice of the system, expressed as variation in the data; and

- Responding appropriately to common cause and special cause variation, not tampering.

An examination of the wellbeing of the system in this manner leads to new questions that can change conversations within the organisation. These questions include:

- What are the most appropriate process measures for this process? How will we know how this process is performing?

- How do we operationally define this measure?

- How do we best display the data to see variation in performance?

- Do we have sufficient data to reliably interpret the variation?

- Is the process stable? How do we know?

- Is the process capable? How do we know?

- What are the highest priorities for improvement?

## Be prepared for new questions and conversations

New questions can prompt new ways of thinking and new responses. The questions outlined above provide a basis for new conversations within systems of education, the schools and classrooms. Those working within the system are encouraged to ask these new questions of one another and to engage in the new conversations.

Over the past couple of decades, the conversations about school education have been gradually changing. There is greater acknowledgement of the systemic nature of school education and the interconnectedness of its component parts. There is a growing acceptance that student learning is the aim, not teachers teaching. Recently, there has been recognition that the performance of school education systems in the western world has been largely stable but incapable, in spite of significant increases in funding. This evolution of understanding is stimulating new questions and new conversations.

*Over the past couple of decades, the conversations about school education have been gradually changing.*

The conversations about school improvement will continue to evolve. For example, at the moment there is little discussion about the role of students and parents in school improvement. What little discussion that takes place is usually limited to the role of students and parents in learning, not improvement. There is little discussion of the use of a structured improvement process, such as Plan–Do–Study–Act. There is far too much discussion of what excellent schools might look like, at the expense of how schools might achieve excellence. We hope that this book can, in some way, make a positive contribution to the debate about school improvement.

Appendix 3 discusses what those who do not work within the system of school education can do to support school improvement. In essence, people can ask new questions based upon the principles and practices outlined in this book. Educational leaders at all levels can benefit from examining these questions and carefully considering their responses to them. The questions and conversations are changing; leaders have an opportunity to prepare for their future conversations.

> Leaders have an opportunity to prepare for their future conversations.

# Think and act systemically

The second area of activity to lead the transformation relates to adopting a practical systems thinking mind-set.

## Understand, agree and document your systems

One of the keys to thinking and acting systemically is to identify, understand and document the systems of which you are part. This begins with identifying and documenting the systems for which you are responsible. The challenge then is to work with stakeholders to reach a mutual agreement regarding the key elements comprising the system within which, and upon which, you will work together.

The system map provides a structure for such documentation. A system map represents a mutual agreement regarding the elements that must work together for the benefit of all stakeholders.

A system map needs to be agreed among all key stakeholders. This requires ongoing conversations as the system evolves and adapts to changes in its environment. To this end, the system map becomes a living, evolving document, which is never cast in stone.

> A system map captures today's learning, providing a basis for tomorrow's conversations.

A system map captures today's learning, providing a basis for tomorrow's conversations. As such, it forms the basis for a learning organisation. New conversations emerge from new questions. Which system are we discussing? Do we have a system map for it? Which process is of concern? Do we have a flowchart of the process?

The system map template shown in Figure 7.5 was first introduced in Chapter Three.

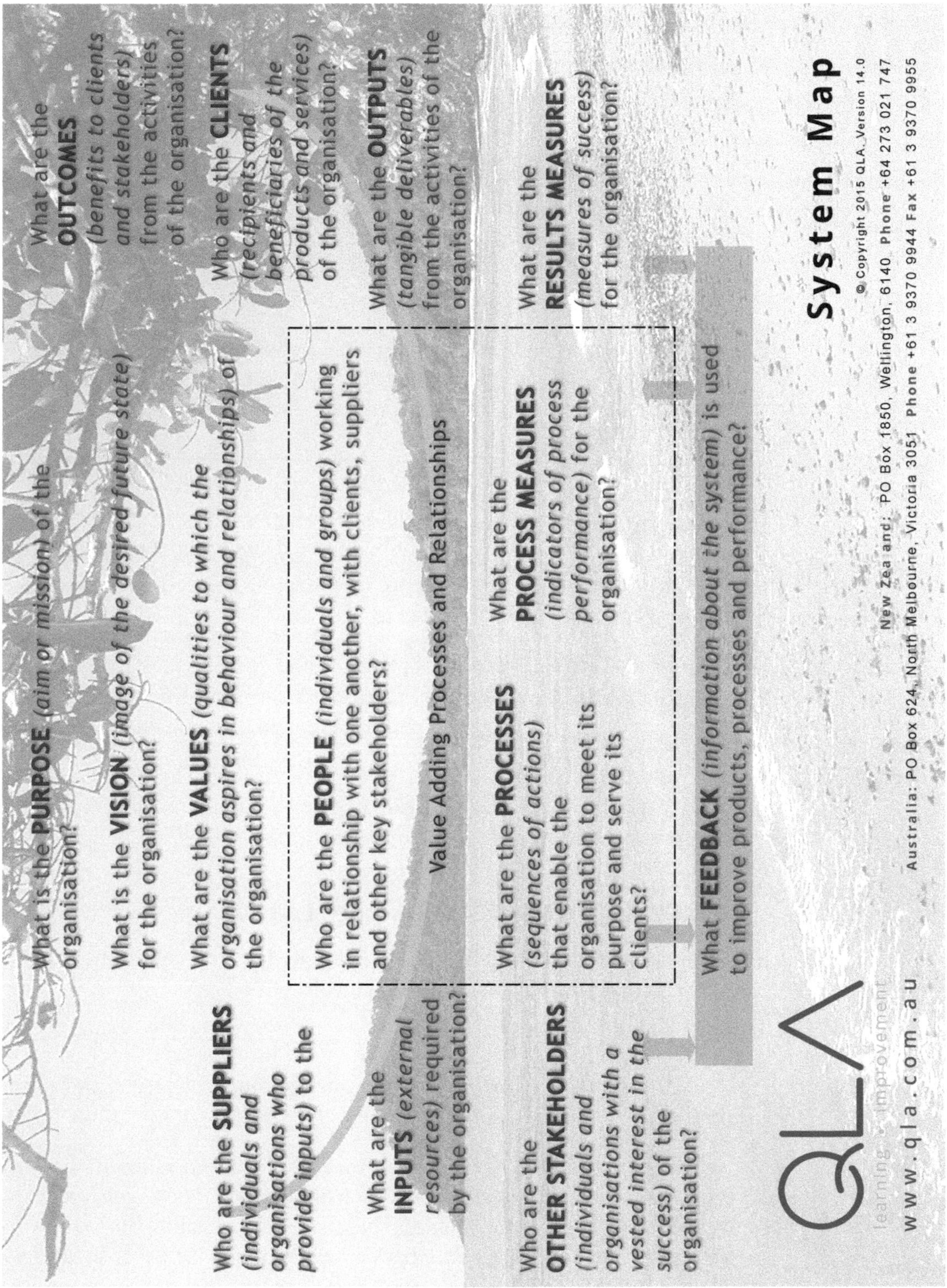

The following text appears within the system map figure:

What is the **PURPOSE** (aim or mission) of the organisation?

What is the **VISION** (image of the desired future state) for the organisation?

What are the **VALUES** (qualities to which the organisation aspires in behaviour and relationships) of the organisation?

Who are the **PEOPLE** (individuals and groups) working in relationship with one another, with clients, suppliers and other key stakeholders?

Value Adding Processes and Relationships

What are the **PROCESSES** (sequences of actions) that enable the organisation to meet its purpose and serve its clients?

What are the **PROCESS MEASURES** (indicators of process performance) for the organisation?

What **FEEDBACK** (information about the system) is used to improve products, processes and performance?

What are the **OUTCOMES** (benefits to clients and stakeholders) from the activities of the organisation?

Who are the **CLIENTS** (recipients and beneficiaries of the products and services) of the organisation?

What are the **OUTPUTS** (tangible deliverables) from the activities of the organisation?

What are the **RESULTS MEASURES** (measures of success) for the organisation?

Who are the **SUPPLIERS** (individuals and organisations who provide inputs) to the

What are the **INPUTS** (external resources) required by the organisation?

Who are the **OTHER STAKEHOLDERS** (individuals and organisations with a vested interest in the success) of the organisation?

**System Map**

© Copyright 2015 QLA, Version 14.0

New Zealand: PO Box 1850, Wellington, 6140  Phone +64 273 021 747

Australia: PO Box 624, North Melbourne, Victoria 3051  Phone +61 3 9370 9944 Fax +61 3 9370 9955

QLA

learning . improvement

w w w . q l a . c o m . a u

Figure 7.5 System map template

## Optimise the system

Everyone's efforts need to be aligned to the aim of the system. Without an aim, there is no basis for alignment and optimisation. Without such alignment of efforts, there will be frustration, waste and loss.

Everyone needs to act in the interest of the whole system if the aim of the system is to be achieved. This means that individuals and groups within the organisation may need to sacrifice some of their own goals in order to support those of the system as a whole. To optimise the whole will be to sub-optimise the parts.

The organisation's processes for personal performance and development may need to be modified to promote action that is in the interest of the system as a whole, rather than promote the actions of individuals or parts of the organisation.

# Use data effectively

The third area of activity relates to the effective use of data as the voice of the system. This was discussed in detail in Chapter Five.

Firstly, to use data effectively for planning and decision making, processes are required to collect, collate, report and act upon suitable measures. These measures will relate to performance, processes, perceptions, and inputs.

Secondly, interpretation and action on these measures must be informed by statistical thinking in order to prevent tampering.

## Establish measurement processes

Measurement and monitoring will be required at all levels of the system, particularly at school and classroom levels.

### Whole school

As a school, processes are needed to ensure ongoing collection, collation, reporting and action upon school data.

School performance needs to be measured and monitored. Ideally, measures will be identified against each of the desired outcomes, perhaps expressed as a graduate profile. These measures enable the school to determine the degree to which it is improving over time, as well as identifying areas of priority for improvement. School performance measures can include:

- Student performance on state and national tests;

- Pass rates/met standard;

- Student learning expressed as growth per semester or year; and

- Student exit outcomes measured against the school graduate profile.

Key school processes will also have measures associated with them. These measures enable the school to initiate process adjustments to ensure the school processes remain both stable and capable. School process measures could include:

- Staff professional learning needs;

- Student and staff attendance;

- Critical incidents, suspensions and expulsions;

- Curriculum delivery against plan;

- Parent participation in key school activities, including student-led conferences;

- Improvement project milestones met and project achievements; and

- Indicators related to staff personal performance and development.

Stakeholder perceptions need to be monitored regularly and action taken where required. This will include regular monitoring of:

- Staff perceptions;

- Student perceptions;

- Parent perceptions; and

- Other key stakeholder perceptions.

Some key inputs will also need to be monitored, again to make process adjustments as required to ensure processes remain stable and capable. Input measures could include:

- Projected enrolments by year level;

- Numbers and types of students with identified or special needs; and

- Staff qualifications, experience and expertise.

## Classroom

For each classroom system, similar measures will be required.

Class performance needs to be measured. This will include rates of student learning as well as summative assessment outcomes.

Key classroom processes also need to be measured, the primary process being learning. Learning can be measured using formative assessments as well as student self-assessments. These learning process measures will be predictive of the summative performance measures and enable learner and teacher to make adjustments to the learning processes in order to maximise learning.

Stakeholder perceptions are just as relevant at the classroom level as the school level and can be monitored regularly with tools such as the consensogram and correlation chart.

Input measures for a class typically relate to students' prior learning and are used to adjust classroom processes to maximise learning.

## An integrated set of processes

As schools set about developing processes to regularly collect, collate, report and act upon system measures, they soon discover that coordination is required. There can be overlap between the data required at the school level, and those required at the classroom level. There are opportunities to aggregate data from classes to provide a whole school picture, as there are also opportunities to stratify school data by class, gender, minority groups, and so on.

Before long, schools identify the need to develop an integrated set of processes for data collection, collation, reporting, and action. These processes will include development and management of operational definitions for the key measures.

# Apply statistical thinking

Data need to be interpreted with the aid of statistical thinking.

Once data are collected, collated and reported, the data need to be interpreted with the aid of statistical thinking.

Importantly, evidence of special cause variation must be responded to differently than that of common cause variation. Don't immediately change the system in response to evidence of special cause variation — investigate and learn. Similarly, don't risk tampering by overreacting to common cause variation. The primary questions here relate to system stability and capability, and how these might be improving over time.

These concepts were discussed in detail in Chapter Five.

# Conduct regular self-assessment

Self-assessment provides a method to understand the current state of a system and to identify next steps.

Self-assessment provides a method to understand the current state of a system and to identify next steps.

## The self-assessment process

There are six steps to any self-assessment process, as shown in Figure 7.6. Each of these steps is discussed in turn. As we shall see, there are many options with self-assessment.

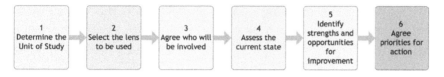

**Figure 7.6 The self-assessment process**

1.  What are we self-assessing? Clarify the system upon which the self-assessment will be focused:

    •   The whole organisation, such as a school or district; or

    •   Sub-systems within the organisation, such as work groups, classrooms or an individual's learning system.

2.  What is the vision of excellence against which the system will be compared? The chosen lens provides a description of excellence against which the system can be compared and evaluated. For an organisation this could be:

    •   The principles; or

    •   One of many excellence frameworks, such as the Australian Business Excellence Framework, the Baldrige Education Criteria for Performance Excellence in the USA, Quality Teaching model, or the Australian National School Improvement Tool.

    At an individual level, the lens could be:

    •   The principles for individuals;

    •   The organisation's values (expressed as "I" statements, as discussed in Chapter Three);

    •   Statements of professional standards for teachers and school leaders; or

    •   Learning against a given area of curriculum, expressed as a capacity matrix.

3. Who really knows what is going on? Who will be directly involved in the self-assessment?

- Individual self-assessment — Clearly, at an individual level, individuals undertake their own self-assessment; or

- Organisational self-assessment — Within an organisation, a choice has to be made. In general, self-assessment is most productive when a small team is formed comprising leaders of the system (the unit of study) along with people working within that system. Leaders are most likely to be informed about the thinking and planning behind the organisation's activities. Those working within the system will understand what's actually happening on the ground. This is a powerful combination.

4. How is the system currently performing? Compare the activities and results of the system against each of the dimensions of the vision of excellence:

- These dimensions will be the elements of the chosen lens — for example, each of the guiding principles, the categories and items of a business excellence framework, or each item of the capacity breakdown on a capacity matrix;

- The assessment usually results in either a description of the current state, some rating of the current state, or both;

- The evidence upon which the assessment has been based is also noted.

5. What is going well? What can we improve? Identify and document strengths and opportunities for improvement. These flow quite naturally from step four.

6. What do we need to do next? Self-assessment usually identifies many opportunities for improvement:

- It is neither practical nor desirable to address all of these at once, so prioritisation is required; and

- Those items with the greatest strategic impact can be carried forward into the planning process as improvement projects.

## Benefits of self-assessment

Self-assessment enhances learning. During the process of self-assessment, individuals and teams actively engage with both a vision of excellence for the system and evidence of the system's current processes and performance. This engagement promotes learning about:

Self-assessment enhances learning.

- The lens, or framework, being used as the basis for the self-assessment;

- The vision of excellence being described by the lens; and

- The performance of the unit of study.

Where the self-assessment is against the principles, those participating in the self-assessment will firstly need to think deeply about the meaning of each principle. Secondly, they will need to reflect upon the relevance of the principle to the system or sub-system they are studying, including how the principle translates to this context. Thirdly, they will reflect upon the current system and how it performs in respect to the principles.

It is also worth emphasising that where a team is conducting self-assessment, team members will need to work together to achieve consensus on the findings, which also promotes learning.

Similar learning occurs when self-assessment is undertaken at an individual level. Consider a student undertaking self-assessment using a capacity matrix, for example. Here the student will reflect upon the capacities to be developed — "What am I seeking to learn?" Secondly, they will reflect upon the relevance of the use of a capacity matrix to evaluate and monitor this learning — "How do I best use this capacity matrix?" Thirdly, they will evaluate the current state of their learning — "How am I going?" Finally, this leads to identification of strengths to be celebrated and opportunities for improvement to be acted upon — "What do I need to do next?"

In short, self-assessment requires individuals and teams to develop a common understanding of:

- The meaning of each dimension of the lens;

- The relevance of the lens to their context; and

- The current processes and outcomes of the system.

This is rich learning indeed.

Self-assessment identifies strengths and opportunities for improvement. A key finding of a self-assessment process is identification of the things that are going well in the system — strengths — and those things that could be improved — opportunities for improvement. Strengths are to be celebrated, sustained and extended. Opportunities for improvement can be prioritised for action. In this way, self-assessment provides a structured approach to identifying and prioritising what should be the focus for improvement projects.

Self-assessment identifies strengths and opportunities for improvement.

Self-assessment can also be used to monitor progress. Self-assessment can be undertaken on a regular basis, as part of the planning cycle. When conducted regularly, the findings of self-assessment can be compared from one cycle to the next in order to determine progress. Over time, these findings provide an evidence-based assessment and record of progress.

> Self-assessment can be used to monitor progress.

## Self-assess individual learning and behaviour

At the individual level, there are two basic forms of self-assessment:

1. Levels of learning — using a capacity matrix; and

2. Individual behavior — using a statement of values and behaviours, ethical principles or principles for individuals.

Capacity matrices were introduced in Chapter Six. Appendix 1 provides a capacity matrix based on the content of this book. It can provide a starting point for individual self-assessment regarding knowledge of continual improvement. Organisations can also develop capacity matrices for specific roles. These capacity matrices will make explicit what people need to know, understand, and be able to do to fulfill their roles. Regular self-assessment identifies progress in learning as well as gaps where further development may be required. Self-assessment using capacity matrices can be integrated into the personal performance and development process (discussed shortly) to ensure development needs are identified and action taken where necessary.

> Regular self-assessment identifies progress in learning as well as gaps where further development may be required.

Individual behaviour can also be self-assessed. The lens for this self-assessment might be agreed values expressed as directly observable behaviours, as discussed in Chapter Three. It could also be the agreed organisational principles for individuals, such as Leander ISD's 10 Ethical Principles (above). In any case, individuals can self-assess their behavioural alignment on a scale — such as "rarely" to "nearly always". This self-assessment can also be integrated with the personal performance and development process to ensure individuals are required to reflect formally upon their behaviour, and to take action should improvement be required.

## Self-assess system learning and behaviour

At the system or organisation level, there are two basic forms of self-assessment:

1. Processes and performance, using the principles for organisations; and

2. Processes and performance, using a recognised framework of excellence.

Self-assessment can be undertaken against the principles described in this book. This is an excellent process for learning about the principles and how they apply to an organisation. Self-assessment against the principles provides a good starting point.

Appendix 2 provides details of a process for school self-assessment against the principles of quality learning, using a matrix approach. Any school can use the process to reflect upon the current state of learning and application of the principles across the school. From the self-assessment, current strengths and opportunities for improvement can be identified and prioritised for action.

Self-assessment can also be undertaken using recognised frameworks of excellence. As previously mentioned, frameworks such as Australian Business Excellence Framework, the Baldrige Education Criteria for Performance Excellence in the USA, and the Australian National School Improvement Tool provide evidence-based visions of excellence against which the processes and performance of an organisation can be compared.

In some cases, it may be appropriate to examine the activities and results of the organisation using the assessment dimensions of Approach, Deployment, Results and Improvement (ADRI). These dimensions enable an analysis regarding how the organisation goes about: thinking and planning (Approach); implementing and doing (Deployment); monitoring and evaluating (Results); and reviewing and improving (Improvement). ADRI is a feature of the Australian Business Excellence framework and underpins many performance excellence frameworks around the world. Figure 7.7 illustrates how ADRI can be used as part of a self-assessment process.

An annual cycle of self-assessment, integrated with the organisation's planning process, provides a powerful approach to focussing an organisations' improvement efforts.

> Self-assessment against the principles provides a good starting point.

# ADRI - Review Process

Version 5.0

## Approach

**1. Clarifying Purpose**
> What, specifically, are we reviewing? Which program or system?
> To what extent has its purpose been identified and documented?
> How does this purpose relate to that of our organisation?
> How have our clients and key stakeholders been identified and their needs determined?
> To what extent have our desired outcomes and goals been defined and articulated?

**2. Designing**
> How explicitly have we considered and designed strategies, structures and processes to achieve our objectives?

**3. Measuring Success**
> How do we measure performance and progress? What are our Measures of Success, quantitative and qualitative?
> What processes have we designed to collect and collate the required data?

**To achieve this:** consider how purpose, outcomes and goals have been designed and specified. Check for alignment with those of the overall organisation. Consider the methods by which these objectives will be achieved and how success will be measured. Focus on the thinking and planning, not the doing.

Our aims, goals, strategies, structures and processes are well considered, articulated and focussed on improvement. Appropriate performance measures have been specified.

We have articulated our purpose, outcomes and goals. The design of our strategies, structures and processes has been explicitly considered.

We have considered our purpose and outcomes. We have some strategies, structures and processes in place.

We have not yet planned our activity in this area. Our approach is ad-hoc or reactive.

*How do we rate our Approach for this program or system?*

## Deployment

**4. Implementing**
> To what extent are our strategies, structures and processes being implemented in line with the Approach?
> How widely are people involved as planned?

**5. Accepting and Integrating**
> How well has the Approach been embraced by staff?
> How widely and well have the strategies, structures and processes been integrated into normal operations?

**To achieve this:** examine the relationship between the Approach and what is actually being done. Consider the processes used to communicate and implement the Approach across the organisation. Consider the extent to which it has become part of the 'way we all do things around here'.

Our strategies, structures and processes have been implemented widely and deeply as planned. They are well accepted and are now part of our normal operations.

Our Approach has been implemented in most areas and is becoming part of normal operations.

We have implemented our Approach in some areas but this is not yet part of how we normally do things.

Our actions are ad-hoc and show little relationship to our Approach.

*How do we rate our Deployment of this program or system?*

## Results

**6. Monitoring**
> How do we monitor performance of this program or system?
> How are the data we identified as part of our Approach being collected and collated?
> How do we report and monitor our Measures of Success?

**7. Evaluating**
> To what extent are our Measures of Success showing positive trends?

**To achieve this:** Examine how performance of your program or system is tracked. Consider the processes used to monitor and evaluate performance on an ongoing basis.

We have reliable Measures of Success that are reviewed regularly. We can demonstrate that we are improving.

We have data of performance that is reviewed periodically. There is some evidence of improvement.

We collect some data but rarely consider its significance.

Our knowledge of performance is limited to anecdote and opinion.

*How do we rate our Results of this program or system?*

## Improvement

**8. Reviewing**
> How do we review the appropriateness and effectiveness of our Approach and its Deployment? What processes do we use?

**9. Improving**
> How are the findings of these reviews prioritised and translated into a program of improvement?
> How do we capture and share what is learned?

**To achieve this:** examine the processes used to review and improve the program or system, not just the improvements that have been achieved. Consider the extent to which the desired goals are being met. Consider the extent to which both the Approach and Deployment are contributing to the observed performance. Examine the extent to which these reviews are part of the organisation's plans for improvement?

We conduct regular reviews as part of a structured improvement cycle that has delivered demonstrable and continuous improvement.

We conduct periodic reviews and have the beginnings of a structured improvement cycle.

We undertake ad-hoc reviews from which improvements sometimes follow.

We have not reviewed or improved the program or system.

*How do we rate our Improvement on this program or system?*

## The Review Process

Assemble a small team, including representatives of key stakeholders, to conduct the review. Consider the program or system as it currently is (not as you would like it to be). Identify things that are going well (strengths) and opportunities for improvement. Generate questions, ideas and identify issues. Document these as you proceed.
Use the scoring grids to rate your program or system in each assessment dimension, giving each a score out of 10. Use the discussion to clarify your thoughts on the strengths and opportunities for improvement.
Use the **Parking Lot** tool to provide structure to document the findings of your review.
Prioritise your findings into a plan for action.
Use the PDSA **Improvement Process** to take action on the high priority opportunities.

Parking Lot

What is going well?

What are the questions?

QLA
learning • improvement

© 2015 Quality Learning Australasia Pty Ltd    **New Zealand:** PO Box 1859, Wellington, 6140 **Phone** +64 273 021 747    E-mail office@qla.com.au
**Australia:** PO Box 624, North Melbourne, Victoria 3051 **Phone** +61 3 9370 9944 **Fax** +61 3 9370 9955    Web www.qla.com.au

**Figure 7.7 ADRI — Review Process**

Source: Adapted by QLA from the *Australian Business Excellence Framework*, the *Malcolm Baldrige National Quality Awards Criteria*, and the *European Foundation for Quality Management Excellence Model*.

# Using ADRI during self-assessment

The assessment dimensions of Approach-Deployment-Results-Improvement (ADRI) can be very helpful for self-assessment. ADRI provides a structure under which the activities and results of an organisation can be broken down to identify, quite specifically, where the strengths and opportunities for improvement may lie.

## The ADRI assessment dimensions

**Approach** relates to the thinking and planning behind the area of endeavour – how it has been designed. Considering an Approach leads to an examination of:

- Clarity of purpose;
- Clients, key stakeholders and their respective needs;
- Desired outcomes — the vision of excellence;
- Design of strategies, structures and processes to meet the desired outcomes; and
- Identification of measures of success.

In most organisations the senior leaders, sometimes with the support of content specialists, determine the approach. For example, senior leaders of a school, frequently with the help of a specialist curriculum committee, usually lead the approach to curriculum. It is the responsibility of these leaders to be clear on the purpose of curriculum in the school, to understand the needs of key stakeholders (including teachers, families and curriculum regulatory bodies), and the desired curriculum outcomes for the school. Armed with this understanding, the structures and processes (including documentation) necessary to meet the intentions of the school can be designed. It is during the design stage that the measures of success are also determined from the desired outcomes (the vision of excellence): what data will be used to monitor progress over time? Senior leaders do the thinking and planning – the design.

**Deployment** relates to implementing and doing — how the design is put into effect. Considering Deployment leads to an examination of:

- The degree to which the designed strategies, structures and processes have been implemented across the organisation and down through the organisation;

- The extent to which staff have embraced the organisation's approach; and
- How well the strategies, structures and processes have been integrated into the day-to-day operation of the organisation.

Those doing the daily work know most about how the daily work is done. Those that are expected to implement an organisation's approach know most about it has been deployed. The school curriculum committee may have designed an excellent approach, but it is up to each classroom teacher to implement it. If classroom teachers are not adhering to the agreed school curriculum approach, it has not been deployed well.

**Results** relates to monitoring and evaluating — how success is gauged. Considering the Results dimension leads to an examination of:

- How performance is monitored;
- How the data relating to the measures of success (determined as part of the Approach) are collected, collated and reported; and
- The degree to which trends of improvement are evident in these data.

Monitoring and evaluating is a management responsibility. School leaders are responsible for monitoring and evaluating the data used as measures of success for their approach to curriculum. Unless these data are collected, collated and reported, the effectiveness of the approach and its deployment will be unknown.

**Improvement** relates to the processes of reviewing and improving the approach and its deployment. Considering the Improvement dimension leads to an examination of:

- The process by which the appropriateness and effectiveness of the approach and its deployment are reviewed;
- How these reviews have led to improvement; and
- How the lessons learned are captured and shared.

Improvement is a management responsibility. Continuing the school curriculum example, a school's senior leaders are expected to regularly review and refine the school's curriculum. This assessment dimension examines the process by which that is undertaken, the improvements that have resulted and how these improvements are documented and shared with staff and other key stakeholders.

## Why ADRI is useful

The assessment dimensions are useful for two purposes: diagnosis and design.

**Diagnosis**

When something is not working well in an organisation, ADRI provides a lens for examining activities and results to determine why it isn't working and then to determine what to do about it. When things aren't going well, it could be because:

1. The Approach is weak; or
2. The Deployment is poor.

If the approach is weak, attention must be paid to reviewing and improving the design. Deploying a poor approach will not deliver good results.

A sound approach, poorly deployed, will not deliver good results either. If the approach is well thought through but is not being applied, then attention needs to be paid to ensuring people know about and implement the agreed approach.

Note that these two causes — a weak approach and poor deployment — have the same effect: disappointing results. ADRI can assist in determining which cause is more significant.

For example, a school may identify parent dissatisfaction with student reports. Firstly, knowledge of ADRI would lead the school leadership team to seek clarity and reflect upon the school's design for assessment and reporting. Which assessments are to be undertaken? What is the schedule? What is the agreed process for reporting? Is the approach appropriate? These are questions regarding the approach. Secondly, they would explore the extent to which the approach is being applied in practice. Do staff understand and follow the agreed procedures? Are timelines being met? These are questions regarding deployment. Actions required to address parent dissatisfaction will be quite different depending where the opportunities for improvement lie: in the approach, or more to do with deployment.

**Design**

ADRI is also useful when designing organisation's systems, structures and processes. In thinking about how to pursue any area of endeavour, ADRI provides useful guidance to ensure key considerations are not overlooked. If you look back over the considerations associated with each of the dimensions, you can easily identify key questions to be answered when determining how to design processes that will achieve an organisation's goals. These questions could include:

- Have we clearly articulated our purpose, desired outcomes and a vision of excellence?
- What are the needs of our clients and key stakeholders?
- What strategies, structures and processes are required to achieve our aspirations?
- What data do we need to measure effectiveness and track progress over time? How will these data be collected, collated and regularly reported?
- How will we document, train and coach people to adopt the new approach?
- How will we monitor the acceptance and application of the new approach?
- How will ongoing performance data be monitored and evaluated?
- What is the cycle of review and improvement for this approach and its deployment?

## How to use ADRI

The assessment dimensions of ADRI can be used in many ways. Typically, they are used as

1. A checklist for reflecting upon the activities and results of an organisation;
2. A framework for describing the activities and results of an organisation; and
3. An assessment model to evaluate the activities and results of an organisation.

ADRI is commonly used as a checklist to think about what is happening in an organisation. For example, thinking about whether observed difficulties are due to a deficient approach or poor deployment is a common application.

ADRI can provide a structure for describing how an organisation goes about its business. This use of ADRI is common in performance excellence awards processes such as those based on the Australian Business Excellence Awards, the Malcolm Baldrige National Quality Awards in the USA, and those of the European Foundation for Quality Management. Organisations describe explicitly how they go about each assessment dimension for each area of endeavour. The areas described are usually the categories or items of these specific frameworks, but the use of ADRI in this way is applicable to any area of organisational activity. A school (or district) could use ADRI as a structure to describe any program, initiative, project or other area of endeavour. For example; a district could document its thinking and planning (approach) to community engagement, how that has been implemented across the district (deployment), how data demonstrate effectiveness in community engagement (results), and the process by which the district reviews and improves community engagement (improvement). The act of documenting the activities and results in this structure usually leads to the identification of strengths and areas of opportunity for improvement.

The assessment dimensions can also be used to evaluate or rate the organisation's activities and results. Figure 7.7 provides a structure for such an evaluation. Each of the four dimensions, ADRI, is evaluated, given a rating, which leads to identification of strengths and opportunities for improvement.

Download a copy of Figure 7.7 (ADRI – Review Process) from the QLA web site: qla.com.au

# Apply tools and the PDSA cycle

Improvement doesn't just happen; it must be made to happen. Use of the quality learning tools and a proven and structured process, such as the Plan–Do–Study–Act cycle illustrated in Figure 7.8, is the fifth area of activity.

Improvement doesn't just happen; it must be made to happen.

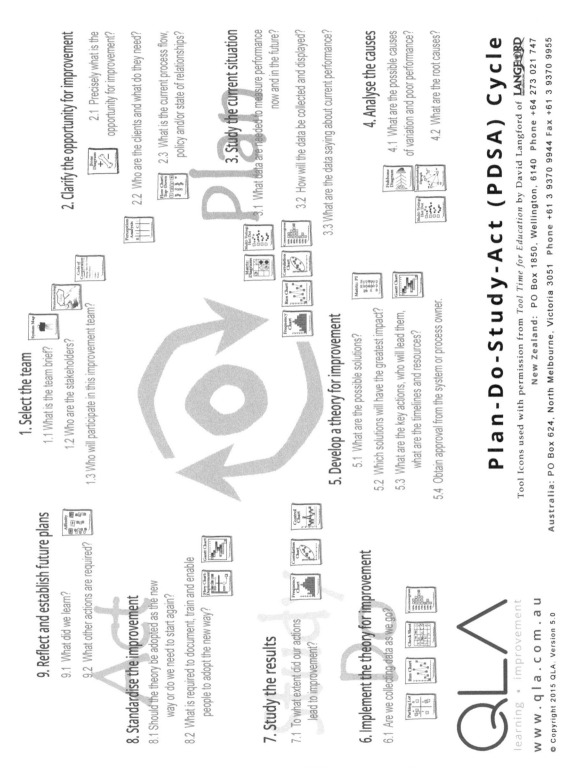

**Figure 7.8 A nine step PDSA learning and improvement cycle**

## Use the quality learning tools

The quality learning tools in this book provide methods for engaging people in the application of the quality improvement philosophy. The tools are all strongly aligned to the principles. They provide effective methods for harmonising behaviour with the principles, which can guide conversations and interactions.

Individuals and teams need to learn to use the tools. Most people learn best by doing, so it is beneficial to deliberately try new tools and to encourage others to do the same. If you are a teacher, you need to remember that it is more important to use the tools than it is to teach the tools.

At first, it can be challenging to know which tool to use. In the early days, questions tend to centre around which tools are best for which situation. The best way to answer these questions is to try a tool and see how it goes. What is the worst that can happen? You will have tried a new tool and discovered that a different tool may have been better.

It can be tempting to fall back on the tools we know best. While there are certainly benefits to having favourites, there are also advantages to continually expanding our repertoire of options.

The tools are not worksheets. They each have a clear purpose and can be used over and over to achieve that purpose. If you hear people exclaim, "We've already done that tool, we don't need to do it again," then they might not be aware that the tools are useful in a variety of different contexts.

There is no substitute for knowledge. Knowledge comes from theory, experience and reflection. You can only develop deep knowledge in the use of each tool though repeated application, experience and reflection.

Using the tools changes questions, conversations and relationships for the better.

> The quality learning tools are all strongly aligned to the principles.

> It is beneficial to deliberately try new tools and to encourage others to do the same.

> Documents need to be stored in a way that ensures they remain available to those who need to use them.

> Each tool has a clear purpose and can be used over and over to achieve that purpose.

> You can only develop deep knowledge in the use of each tool though repeated application, experience and reflection.

## Establish and train improvement project teams

We have discussed at length the importance of having a theory for improvement. The Plan–Do–Study–Act (PDSA) learning and improvement cycle was introduced in Chapter Four as the basis of a scientific approach to improvement.

Individuals and teams need such a structured approach if they are to maximise the likelihood of achieving improvement, not just change.

The PDSA cycle provides such an approach. If you are not using a structured approach to improvement, what approach are you using? How well is your current approach working? How do you know?

Learning to apply the PDSA cycle and tools can be challenging. The challenge arises from the need to be working and thinking simultaneously at three levels:

Learning to apply the PDSA cycle and tools can be challenging.

1.  **Task level**: Here the team is grappling with the mechanics of each task associated with the PDSA cycle — creating a storyboard, using the tools, and addressing the requirements of each step in the PDSA cycle.

2.  **Content level**: The team grapples with details associated with the issue being addressed. As team members are nearly always stakeholders, there is usually a great deal of detailed knowledge available to the team, and a great deal of passion about the current situation. Teams benefit from having at least one member who is new to the content of the improvement opportunity and who can thus challenge current assumptions and practices.

3.  **Process level**: At this level, the team is encouraged to step back and reflect upon the PDSA process itself and their application of it. This can be difficult. The task and content levels can consume team energies. A skillful facilitator can add significant value by helping the team disconnect from task and content to reflect on the process.

For these reasons, it is recommended that teams start with improvement projects that meet the following criteria:

*   The area is in need of improvement — there is an opportunity to deliver real benefits for stakeholders;

*   The project is of manageable size — in most instances, the opportunity for improvement will be a local one that affects a limited number of people. Large projects are complex to manage and not really suitable subjects for teams learning to apply the PDSA cycle; and

Careful selection of initial improvement projects can prevent some of the barriers to team success during the important learning phase.

*   The process is in regular use, such that at least 16 data points can be collected before and after the improvement — being able to collect sufficient data before and after improvement is essential to quantifying the impact of the improvement efforts.

Careful selection of initial improvement projects can minimise some of the barriers to team success during the important learning phase.

In time, priorities for improvement will be determined from self-assessments. Once a self-assessment process is in regular use, and is integrated with an organisation's planning process, improvement opportunities will be regularly identified, prioritised and improvement projects planned. The PDSA cycle then becomes the basis for the actions of improvement project teams.

Remember to capture the findings of the improvement projects as storyboards. This provides discipline for project teams and helps them remain focussed. It also provides a mechanism by which the activities and findings of the project team can be shared with stakeholders in the process. This provides important support for the learning of the team as well as for those yet to participate in a PDSA improvement project.

Share and celebrate the process and outcomes. The stories that emerge become powerful forces for positive change across the organisation.

### 📌 EARLY APPLICATION OF PDSA

It is quite common for organisations that are just beginning to use the Plan–Do–Study–Act cycle to select improvement projects that are not based on processes. For example, school teams sometimes pick "communication" as the opportunity for improvement, rather than a specific communication process, such as the school newsletter process or the reporting to parents process. Starting with a focus on a specific process can make the job easier as people learn to apply the PDSA cycle.

Where the opportunity for improvement is not a specific process, the PDSA cycle still applies. Early in the cycle, as root causes are being identified, the team can identify specific processes to be improved. Remember, to improve any outcome, we need to improve the processes that deliver that outcome.

# Capture and share the learning

The final area of activity to support adoption of a continual improvement approach relates to the documentation of key processes, associated policies, and supporting documents. Key processes must be identified, systematically documented and used. The aim is not to constrain people with rigid procedures that must be followed, but rather to ensure everyone is using the current best known and agreed processes.

*The aim is not to constrain people with rigid procedures that must be followed, but rather to ensure everyone is using the current best known and agreed processes.*

For most organisations, this is achieved in two phases:

- Identifying, documenting and agreeing upon key processes, along with their associated policies and supporting documents; and

- Establishing a system for managing the resulting documentation.

These two phases are interdependent. Where you choose to start will depend on the immediate and longer-term needs and priorities within your organisation.

## Identify, document and agree key processes

The key processes of the organisation can be identified, listed and documented. A useful starting point is to brainstorm, with key stakeholders, the processes that fall under each of the following three headings:

- Leadership or management;

- Core or learning; and

Identify and
list the key
processes of the
organisation.

- Support or administration.

Alternatively, the school process reference model (shown in Chapter Three) can be useful. In any case, developing an agreed list of key processes is the first step to capturing an organisation's current methods as a basis for consistency and improvement.

As improvement teams are established, they can use the PDSA cycle to improve processes, thus creating new best known standard processes for use in the organisation. They can also update the polices and supporting documents associated with these processes. It is important to capture this learning and ensure that the new approach becomes the new way of doing things. Otherwise, it will be all too easy to return to the more familiar old ways.

Other teams will have been charged with identification and documentation of the organisation's key processes. In doing so, they will also create the current best known standard processes to be adopted across the organisation.

Adopting the
best known
standard
processes
reduces variation
in process
operation
and process
performance.

Adopting the best known standard processes reduces variation in process operation and process performance. This in turn provides a platform for continually improving these processes.

To ensure the new methods become standard, organisations need to document, train, and coach.

## Document

The first step towards ensuring people stick to the best known standard process is to ensure that processes are documented and that this documentation is available to those expected to use it. Most commonly, processes are documented as flowcharts. Having a flowchart provides a reference point for process operators (and improvement teams) to understand how things are done, by whom, and when.

Associated policies are also documented, as are supporting documents, such as forms, letters, templates, presentations, and so on.

## Train

The second step is to train people in the agreed processes. Individuals need to be trained in how to enact the processes. They need to clearly understand what is required of them and they need the skills to undertake those actions. Training provides this.

## Coach

The final ingredient to ensuring everyone adopts the best known standard process is to ensure that individuals are coached and actively enabled to follow the agreed processes. People need to be encouraged and supported to use the agreed new process. Any barriers to adopting the new way can be identified and addressed. The personal performance and development process can support this coaching.

It is insufficient to rely solely on documentation, or training, or coaching (or even any pair of these). All three are required. Without documentation there is no clear and explicit description of what is required. Without training, there is limited knowledge and skills. Without coaching, it is easy to slip back into old habits.

> It is insufficient to rely on just documentation, or training, or coaching. All three are required.

To adopt the new way: document, train, and coach.

# Review core leadership processes

There are core leadership processes that drive the culture and behaviour of organisations. These processes are critical. They need to be aligned with the principles if they are to promote and reinforce the desired behaviour.

> There are core leadership processes that drive the culture and behaviour of organisations.

These processes are as follows:

- **Recruitment process:** ensuring that the organisation brings in people with the requisite mind-set, knowledge and skills for their position, and that recruits are aligned to and supportive of the vision, values and direction of the organisation.

- **Personal performance and development process**: ensuring every individual brings their unique talents to work in and on the system, and that their contributions are maximised, valued and recognised.

This process, which is undertaken at least twice per year, includes individual self-assessment against the principles for individuals, a review of progress against the agreed individual work plan (from the previous meeting), and agreement of the individual work plan for the coming period. The performance and development review meeting between each individual and their supervisor is structured around discussion of the following questions:

- What are we doing together to work in the system?

- What are we doing together to work on the system?

- What in my behaviour as your leader could I improve?

- What in your behaviour could you improve?

- What other barriers are in the way?

- What are you doing to improve your capacity to work in and on the system?

The output from each meeting is a revised individual work plan that details:

- the work being done together by the employee and the supervisor to work in the system;

- the work being done together to work on the system; and

- the learning to be undertaken to build individual capacity.

- **Education and training process**: ensuring that all staff have the capacities required to work in and on the system. Individual requirements are determined by mutual agreement through the personal performance and development process, and can be captured in a capacity matrix.

- **Planning processes**: ensuring that the organisation meets its purpose and achieves its vision through stakeholder engagement in the development of mutually agreed plans and clearly defined accountabilities. The improvement plan makes explicit the theory for improvement.

- **Review and corrective action process**: ensuring the objectives in the organisation's plan are met through regular progress reviews and corrective action as required.

- **Annual reporting process**: ensuring key stakeholders remain informed of the organisation's priorities, progress, and performance.

- **Continual improvement process**: ensuring improvement projects are identified, registered, prioritised, resourced and monitored using a structured approach such as Plan–Do–Study–Act.

These core leadership processes are highly interrelated and serve as the core of the leadership system of the organisation. For most organisations, these processes will need to be explicitly reviewed in order to ensure their alignment with quality learning and improvement principles.

> These core leadership processes will need to be explicitly reviewed to ensure their alignment with the quality learning and improvement principles.

## Establish system documentation

Having identified, documented and agreed your key processes, and having reviewed your core leadership processes, these documents need to be stored in a way that ensures they remain available to those who need to use them. This documentation will include process flowcharts, associated policies and supporting documents, such as templates, forms, letters and presentations. Establishing system documentation involves the following steps:

- Agree the structure of the system;

- Agree on document control arrangements;

- Populate the system; and

- Train and coach staff in use of the system.

Each is discussed in turn.

### Agree the structure of the system

There are structural considerations in establishing a system of documentation, including:

- **Will the system be hard copy or electronic format?** In many instances, school system documentation is likely to be electronic, whereas classroom system documentation may exist in hard copy.

- **What type of information management system will be used?** School networks sometimes support the use of applications such as MS SharePoint, Moodle, or other systems. Some schools may prefer simply to use specific folders on the school network drive, or physical folders in the front office. Others may choose more sophisticated cloud-based applications such as Promapp.

- **Will documents be hyperlinked?**

- **How will the documents be structured?** Documents can be grouped by type — process, policy, and supporting documents. Alternatively, they can be grouped by function or topic, such as suggested in the school process reference model presented in Chapter Three.

## Agree document control arrangements

Document control is essential if people are to have access to the latest version of the right document at the time they need it. Considerations for document control include:

- **How will each document be uniquely identified?** How might prefixes (such as "POL" for policies, "PRO" for processes, and "SD" for supporting documents) and meaningful titles be used to ensure that people can find the documents they need?

- **What format and structure will be used for each type of document?** Consistency can be promoted by the use of agreed templates for each type of document. These templates conform to an agreed structure for each type of document, including the use of specific fonts and styles.

- **How will version control fields be used?** Version control fields can be included in every document, including information such as the date the document was endorsed (to know you have the latest version) and 'Page x of y' (to know that you have all the pages).

- **Where is the process owner identified?** Specifying the process owner makes it clear who is responsible for the overall performance of the process and to whom suggestions for improvement can be sent.

- **Where does the document reside?** Including file names and paths can make it easy to find the original file.

## Populate the system

As processes are documented and improved, new documentation needs to make its way into the documentation system. As new documents are added or existing documents amended, the index will need to be updated.

## Train and coach staff in use of the system

Documentation alone is not enough to ensure that agreed processes are followed. Staff will require training in the use of the system documentation, and they will need to be coached to use it.

# Plan your improvement journey

This section has outlined the six key areas of activity which, when undertaken with discipline and integrity, lead to a culture of continual improvement. We conclude with a recommendation that you carefully plan how you will go about these six areas of activity.

You will need to decide, given the uniqueness of your context, how you propose to address these six areas. You cannot do it all at once. You will need to progress systematically, and a careful plan can be most useful. One effective method is to engage key stakeholders in the development of such a plan in the form of a Gantt chart.

> To progress systematically, a careful plan can be most useful.

Appendix 4 gives an example of what such a Gantt chart could look like for a school planning the first two years of the journey. If you are planning for your classroom, you can also develop a Gantt chart, which will be similar but more simple than that shown in Appendix 4.

## The principal must lead

You may have noticed that the principal features heavily in most of the steps in the suggested implementation Gantt chart in Appendix 4. This is no accident.

It should be abundantly clear by now that improvement must be actively led by the leader of the system. For a school, this is the principal. The principal must role model the principles. Responsibility for leading improvement cannot be delegated. The principal must commit to personally leading by taking an active role in each key step along the way. This includes participating in all key meetings, workshop and training sessions.

> The principal must commit to personally leading by taking an active role in each key step.

# Conclusion

We began this book by describing the characteristics of the current system of school education in the English-speaking western world. The system, which was designed at the beginning of the industrial revolution, was focussed on meeting the learning needs of the time. The world has changed; education has failed to keep up. The system is failing to meet the needs of a substantial proportion of students. Radical improvement is required.

W. Edwards Deming has provided a foundation for the practice of improvement. This has been known and practiced by many organisations for decades. Not all organisations apply these principles and practices. Very few schools do. Those that apply these ideas with persistence and integrity will benefit from continual improvement across all aspects of their organisations' activities. Everyone wins.

The philosophy of quality improvement has been developing for decades. There have been contributions from many disciplines, including psychology, statistics, epistemology and systems research, to name but a few. It calls for significant changes to individual and organisational behaviour. It is a philosophy that is at odds with many aspects of the prevailing system of management.

We have described in detail Deming's four areas of profound knowledge as they apply to improving school education. Our aim has been to explain this theory and its implications for school education as thoroughly as possible. We wrote this book in response to requests for a reference that explained this theory for educators. Through this explanation, we have sought to describe a new and proven approach to leadership, learning, and improvement.

In this final chapter we have outlined the lessons we have learned over the past two decades as we have supported schools and other organisations to adopt this philosophy. We have outlined an approach to implementation that can be used in any organisation. And we have offered suggestions regarding how everyone can contribute to refocussing efforts towards school improvement based on quality improvement philosophy.

School education is ready for major transformation. A management philosophy, based on quality improvement is known; it simply needs to be applied widely, with discipline and persistence.

We sincerely hope this book contributes to one of the most important challenges we face: improving learning. We trust what we have learned and shared will provide not just ideas, but practical how-to methods necessary to improve our schools and classrooms.

So don't wait. Get started!

We look forward to many more years of learning and improving with you.

# Reflection questions

**?** What are the processes for which I am responsible? What is my approach to improving these?

**?** What is the state of my relationships with my colleagues? What questions do we typically ask one another? How might these be improved? What new questions might I begin to ask?

**?** What do we call our approach to continual improvement? What might we call it?

**?** How might we build a critical mass in our organisation?

**?** What does "continual improvement is never ending" mean for me and for our organisation?

**?** How do we celebrate success?

**?** To what degree do teachers at my school see their role as managing and improving systems of learning? How do we know?

**?** To what degree does our school develop wisdom in students? How do we know?

**?** How well are our core leadership processes aligned with the principles outlined in this book?

**?** How am I using new questions to bring about changes in the conversations and practices of schooling?

# Chapter summary

In this chapter we have examined the following:

- Everyone has a role in leading organisational transformation by personally improving systems, processes, and relationships;

- Constancy of purpose and a relentless, never ending focus on continual improvement is essential. Continual improvement is never ending, by definition. It is a never ending adventure, not a destination or a program;

- Start by building a critical mass of individuals who understand and can apply the philosophy;

- Progressively engage everyone in improvement;

- Establish processes that support continual learning;

- Students benefit from deep learning and development of wisdom. This is not currently the focus in many schools;

- There is great variation in students' prior knowledge and the speed at which students learn. Systems of learning will be most successful when students are engaged in planning, managing, and monitoring their own learning;

- Students can learn and they can learn to manage their learning. They can learn to lead improvement of their own learning;

- Students can play a vital role in school improvement. This is currently not the case in most schools; and

- There are six key areas of activity in which organisations of any size can engage to bring about transformation to a system of management based upon these principles:

  1. Agree and apply the principles;
  2. Think and act systemically;
  3. Use data effectively;
  4. Conduct regular self-assessment;
  5. Apply the tools and the PDSA cycle; and
  6. Capture and share the learning.

# Appendices

# Appendix 1: Quality Learning Capacity Matrix

Capacity matrices can be used to plan and monitor your learning as you seek to apply the improvement philosophy outlined in this book to your own personal context. There are five matrices, one relating to each of the four areas of profound knowledge and one relating to the quality learning tools.

Each of the rows of the matrices detail specific capacities to developed.

The levels of learning are as follows:

- **Information**: I have heard of this and can answer simple questions about it;

- **Knowledge**: I can explain this in my own words and relate it to other things;

- **Know-how**: I can apply this and know when to do so; and

- **Wisdom**: I know why this is so, can apply it in new situations and can teach others.

The evidence column is for you to provide examples that verify your level of learning, which can be used to corroborate your self-assessment.

Copies of these capacity matrices can be downloaded from the QLA website: www.qla.com.au

# Chapter 3: Working on the System

| Aim | Capacity | Capacity Breakdown | Information | Knowledge | Know-how | Wisdom | Evidence |
|---|---|---|---|---|---|---|---|
| Working on the system | Systems | Different types of systems | | | | | |
| | | Nested systems | | | | | |
| | Social Systems | Key characteristics: choice of purpose and methods | | | | | |
| | | Interactions within social systems | | | | | |
| | | Direct and interaction effects | | | | | |
| | System behaviour and performance | Cause and effect | | | | | |
| | | Optimisation and sub-optimisation | | | | | |
| | Improving systems | The blame game | | | | | |
| | | Working in and on the system | | | | | |
| | | Daily routines | | | | | |
| | | Improving systems and processes | | | | | |
| | | Innovation projects | | | | | |
| | | Documenting systems | | | | | |
| | System mapping | Elements of the system map: Purpose, Vision, Values, People, Clients, Suppliers, Other Stakeholders, Inputs, Outputs, Outcomes, Processes, Results Measures, Feedback | | | | | |
| | | Creating system maps | | | | | |
| | Purpose | Individual | | | | | |
| | | Team | | | | | |
| | | Organisation | | | | | |
| | | Alignment | | | | | |
| | Vision | Shared vision | | | | | |
| | | Alignment | | | | | |
| | | Quality criteria | | | | | |
| | Values | Behaviours | | | | | |
| | | Alignment with guiding principles | | | | | |

| Aim | Capacity | Capacity Breakdown | Information | Knowledge | Know-how | Wisdom | Evidence |
|---|---|---|---|---|---|---|---|
| Working on the system | Processes | SIPOC | | | | | |
| | | Impact on relationships and behaviour | | | | | |
| | | Waste: Rework, Non-value adding activities, Unnecessary checking | | | | | |
| | | Mapping processes | | | | | |
| | | Types of processes: Management, Core and Support | | | | | |
| | | Roles: Accountable, Responsible and Consulted | | | | | |
| | Process improvement | Processes produce outputs and outcomes | | | | | |
| | | Use of a structured improvement process | | | | | |
| | Clients | Direct and indirect clients | | | | | |
| | | Perceptions: Basic, Performance-related, Delight | | | | | |
| | | Internal clients | | | | | |
| | Stakeholders | Types: Clients, People in the system, Suppliers, and Others | | | | | |
| | | Competing demands | | | | | |
| | | Emotional engagement | | | | | |

**Figure A1.1 Chapter 3: Working on the System capacity matrix**

# Chapter 4: Creating and Applying Theory

| Aim | Capacity | Capacity Breakdown | Information | Knowledge | Know-how | Wisdom | Evidence |
|---|---|---|---|---|---|---|---|
| Creating and applying theory | Planning | A process; Interrelated decisions; Desired future state | | | | | |
| | | Types of planning | | | | | |
| | | Characteristics of good planning | | | | | |
| | | Actions vs. strategies | | | | | |
| | | Improving systems vs. to do lists | | | | | |
| | | Improvement projects | | | | | |
| | Theory of Knowledge | Prediction | | | | | |
| | | Creating and testing hypothesis | | | | | |
| | | Operational definitions | | | | | |
| | | Learning, not copying | | | | | |
| | | Creating a theory for improvement | | | | | |
| | | Plan–Do–Study–Act learning and improvement cycle | | | | | |
| | | Storyboards for PDSA teams | | | | | |

Figure A1.2 Chapter 4: Creating and Applying Theory capacity matrix

# Chapter 5: Using Data to Improve

| Aim | Capacity | Capacity Breakdown | Information | Knowledge | Know-how | Wisdom | Evidence |
|-----|----------|--------------------|-------------|-----------|----------|--------|----------|
| Understanding and responding to variation | Data | Subjective and objective | | | | | |
| | | Qualitative and quantitative | | | | | |
| | | The voice of the system | | | | | |
| | | Reliability and validity | | | | | |
| | Measures | Measurement defined | | | | | |
| | | Performance measures | | | | | |
| | | Process measures | | | | | |
| | | Perception measures | | | | | |
| | | Input measures | | | | | |
| | | Operational definitions for measures | | | | | |
| | Use of data | Monitoring performance | | | | | |
| | | Adjusting system operations | | | | | |
| | | Understanding system behaviour | | | | | |
| | | Numerical goals (targets) | | | | | |
| | | Rating and ranking | | | | | |
| | | Fear and the misuse of data | | | | | |
| | | The unknown and the unknowable | | | | | |
| | Statistics | Statistic defined | | | | | |
| | | Mean, median, mode | | | | | |
| | | Range, standard deviation | | | | | |
| | Variation | Statistical thinking | | | | | |
| | | Displaying data: Graphs and Charts | | | | | |
| | | Variation: Within groups, Between groups, Over time | | | | | |
| | | Normal distribution | | | | | |
| | | Special cause variation | | | | | |
| | | Common cause variation | | | | | |
| | | Control charts and control limits | | | | | |
| | | System stability | | | | | |
| | | System capability | | | | | |
| | | Responding appropriately to system variation | | | | | |
| | Tampering | Overreacting to special cause variation | | | | | |
| | | Overreacting to individual data points | | | | | |
| | | Chopping the tail of the distributions | | | | | |
| | | Failing to address root causes | | | | | |

**Figure A1.3 Chapter 5: Using Data to Improve capacity matrix**

# Chapter 6: Improving Relationships

| Aim | Capacity | Capacity Breakdown | Information | Knowledge | Know-how | Wisdom | Evidence |
|---|---|---|---|---|---|---|---|
| Removing barriers to learning and improvement | Motivation | Maslow's hierarchy of needs | | | | | |
| | | Herzberg's two factor theory | | | | | |
| | | McGregor's X and Y theories | | | | | |
| | | Intrinsic motivation | | | | | |
| | | Extrinsic motivation | | | | | |
| | | Interactions between intrinsic and extrinsic factors | | | | | |
| | | Rewards, punishments and consequences | | | | | |
| | | Compliance vs. engagement | | | | | |
| | | Purpose: Meaning, Relevance, Possibility | | | | | |
| | | Choice: Responsibility, Autonomy, Creativity | | | | | |
| | | Mastery: Challenge, Achievement, Learning | | | | | |
| | | Belonging: Collaboration, Feedback, Support | | | | | |
| | | Removing barriers | | | | | |
| | Relationships | Dependence | | | | | |
| | | Independence | | | | | |
| | | Interdependence | | | | | |
| | | Preconditions for interdependence | | | | | |
| | | Student–teacher relationship continuum | | | | | |
| | | Recognition vs. rewards and praise | | | | | |
| | | Feedback | | | | | |
| | | Cooperation vs. competition | | | | | |
| | | Drive out fear | | | | | |
| | | Conversations and questions | | | | | |
| | Leadership | Management vs. leadership | | | | | |
| | | Followership | | | | | |
| | | Improving processes and relationships | | | | | |
| | | Role modelling | | | | | |

Figure A1.4 Chapter 6: Improving Relationships capacity matrix

# Chapter 7: Making Improvement Happen

| Aim | Capacity | Capacity Breakdown | Information | Knowledge | Know-how | Wisdom | Evidence |
|---|---|---|---|---|---|---|---|
| Applying the principles and practices to achieve continual improvement | Key considerations in application | Lead improvement | | | | | |
| | | Maintain constancy of purpose | | | | | |
| | | Build a critical mass of volunteers | | | | | |
| | | Engage everyone in improvement | | | | | |
| | | Sustain continual learning | | | | | |
| | Apply the principles | Agree the principles in your context | | | | | |
| | | Ask principle-based questions | | | | | |
| | Think and act systemically | Understand, agree and document your systems | | | | | |
| | | Act in the interest of the whole system: Optimise | | | | | |
| | Use data effectively | Establish measurement processes | | | | | |
| | | Apply statistical thinking | | | | | |
| | Conduct regular self-assessment | Self-assess invidual learning and behaviour | | | | | |
| | | Undertake system self assessment | | | | | |
| | Use tools and the PDSA cycle | Establish and train improvement project teams | | | | | |
| | | Use the quality learning tools | | | | | |
| | Capture and share the learning | Identify and document key processes | | | | | |
| | | Review core leadership processes | | | | | |
| | | Establish system documentation | | | | | |

**Figure A1.5 Chapter 7: Making Improvement Happen capacity matrix**

# Quality Learning Tools

| Aim | Capacity | Capacity Breakdown | Information | Knowledge | Know-how | Wisdom | Evidence |
|---|---|---|---|---|---|---|---|
| Increase collaboration and apply the guiding principles | System tools | Deployment flowchart | | | | | |
| | | Fishbone diagram | | | | | |
| | | Five whys | | | | | |
| | | Force field analysis | | | | | |
| | | Imagineering | | | | | |
| | | Interrelationship digraph | | | | | |
| | | Paper passing purpose tool (P³T) | | | | | |
| | | Parking lot | | | | | |
| | | Perception analysis | | | | | |
| | | Process accountability matrix | | | | | |
| | | Purpose, outcomes, process, evaluation (POPE) | | | | | |
| | | SIPOC modelling | | | | | |
| | | Standard flowchart | | | | | |
| | | System map | | | | | |
| | | System's progress | | | | | |
| | | Top-down flowchart | | | | | |
| | Planning and knowledge tools | Bone diagram | | | | | |
| | | Gantt chart | | | | | |
| | | Hot dot | | | | | |
| | | Lotus diagram | | | | | |
| | | Operational definition | | | | | |
| | | Potential improvement matrix | | | | | |
| | | Problem statement | | | | | |
| | Variation and data tools | Affinity diagram | | | | | |
| | | Box and whisker plots | | | | | |
| | | Control chart | | | | | |
| | | Dot plot | | | | | |
| | | Histogram | | | | | |
| | | Measures selection matrix | | | | | |
| | | Pareto chart | | | | | |
| | | Radar chart | | | | | |
| | | Run chart | | | | | |
| | | Structured brainstorming | | | | | |

| Aim | Capacity | Capacity Breakdown | Information | Knowledge | Know-how | Wisdom | Evidence |
|---|---|---|---|---|---|---|---|
| | Motivation and relationship enhancing tools | Decision and action record | | | | | |
| | | Capacity matrix | | | | | |
| | | Code of cooperation | | | | | |
| | | Consensogram | | | | | |
| | | Loss function | | | | | |
| | | Plus delta | | | | | |

**Figure A1.6 Quality Learning Tools capacity matrix**

# Appendix 2: Quality Learning School Self-assessment

Quality learning school self-assessment enables schools to:

- Engage in dialogue about student learning, school performance and the principles of quality learning;

- Evaluate school application of the quality learning philosophy to identify strengths and opportunities for improvement, inform planning, and set priorities;

- Measure progress in growth of organisational learning and application of the quality learning approach; and

- Identify where specific and additional support may be required.

The school self-assessment is structured around the 12 principles of quality learning.

A key aim of the self-assessment process is to encourage dialogue around school performance and the quality learning principles. Agreeing which statements best describe the school and which ratings are achieved are to be treated as a secondary objective.

The self-assessment can be repeated periodically to measure progress over time.

A key aim of the self-assessment process is to encourage dialogue around school performance and the quality learning principles.

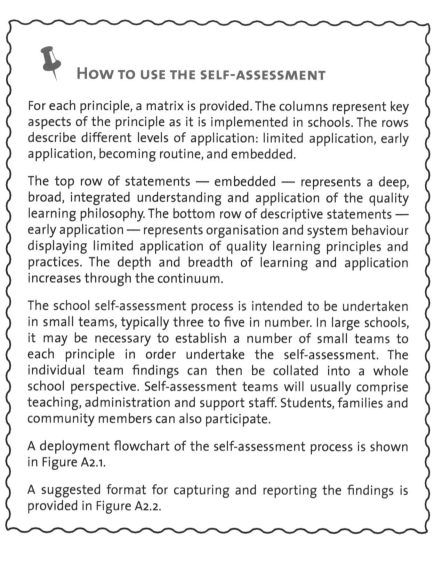

## How to use the self-assessment

For each principle, a matrix is provided. The columns represent key aspects of the principle as it is implemented in schools. The rows describe different levels of application: limited application, early application, becoming routine, and embedded.

The top row of statements — embedded — represents a deep, broad, integrated understanding and application of the quality learning philosophy. The bottom row of descriptive statements — early application — represents organisation and system behaviour displaying limited application of quality learning principles and practices. The depth and breadth of learning and application increases through the continuum.

The school self-assessment process is intended to be undertaken in small teams, typically three to five in number. In large schools, it may be necessary to establish a number of small teams to each principle in order undertake the self-assessment. The individual team findings can then be collated into a whole school perspective. Self-assessment teams will usually comprise teaching, administration and support staff. Students, families and community members can also participate.

A deployment flowchart of the self-assessment process is shown in Figure A2.1.

A suggested format for capturing and reporting the findings is provided in Figure A2.2.

 Templates are available from the QLA website: www.qla.com.au

# Quality Learning School Self-Assessment Process Deployment Flowchart

Process Intent: To reflect on and evaluate progress in the application of Quality Learning, engage in dialogue about progress and performance, and identify strengths and opportunities for improvement.

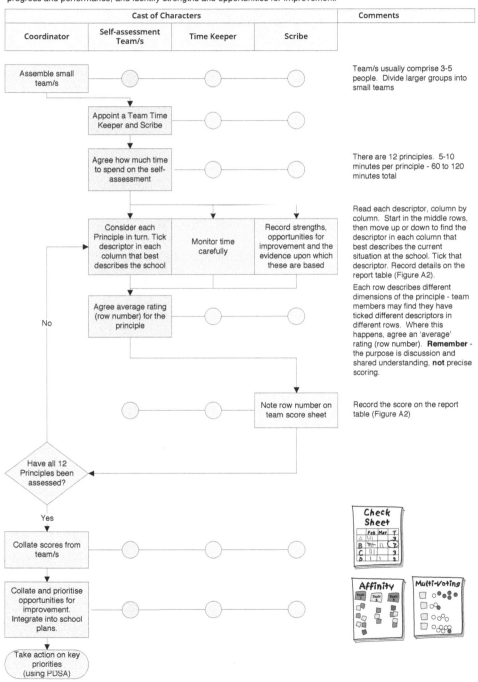

Figure A2.1 The quality learning self-assessment process

School _____

Date of self-assessment _____

| Principle | What is going well? | What can we improve? | Evidence | Score |
|---|---|---|---|---|
| Systems | | | | |
| Purpose | | | | |
| Processes | | | | |
| Clients | | | | |
| Stakeholders | | | | |
| Planning | | | | |
| Knowledge | | | | |
| Data | | | | |
| Variation | | | | |
| Motivation | | | | |
| Relationships | | | | |
| Leadership | | | | |

**Figure A2.2 Template for recording self-assessment discussion and findings**

Download a report template from the QLA website: www.qla.com.au

# Systems: People work in a system — systems determine how an organisation and its people perform

| | A. Map school systems | B. Map classroom systems | C. Work in and on the system | D. Optimise the system |
|---|---|---|---|---|
| **Embedded:** Everybody, always, everywhere | We have an agreed school system map that is regularly reviewed and is used as the basis for planning and decision-making. | Students and teachers agree and document the elements of their systems of learning. | All staff and students explicitly schedule and spend time working on improving their systems as well as working in them. | All systems within the school are optimised to the achievement of whole school goals, especially maximising student learning and success. Everyone puts whole school needs ahead of their own. |
| **Becoming routine:** Systems and structures in place and documented | Most elements comprising the school system have been discussed, analysed and documented as a system map. | A majority of teachers and students engage in discussion and documentation of the key elements of their systems of learning. Many have documented these as system maps. | A majority of staff and students allocate time to working on improving systems as well as completing the daily work of the school. | Most systems within the school have been reviewed and optimised to achieve the goals of the school as a whole. Most individuals and groups put the whole school needs ahead of their own. |
| **Early application:** Ad hoc, with some patterns | Key elements of the school as a system — such as stakeholders, purpose, vision, values and key processes — have been agreed and documented. | Some classes discuss and document key elements of their system of learning, such as stakeholders, purpose, vision, values and key processes. | Most staff and students spend the bulk of their time doing the daily work of the school, with a little time devoted to working on improving systems. | The goals of individuals and groups across the school are sometimes in conflict with those of the whole school. |
| **Limited application:** Event driven | No attempts have been made to analyse and document the school as a system. | No attempts have been made to analyse and document classrooms systems of learning. | We spend our time doing the daily work of the school with no time spent improving systems. | The goals of the school are unclear. |

# Purpose: Shared purpose and a clear vision of excellence align effort

| | A. Agree school purpose and vision | B. Agree class purpose and vision | C. Clarify purpose for activity | D. Use quality criteria |
|---|---|---|---|---|
| **Embedded:** Everybody, always, everywhere | We have clear and explicit statements of purpose (or mission) and vision, which were developed as the result of extensive dialogue among key stakeholders. The purpose and vision are current, used to guide planning and decision making, and are subject to periodic review. | It is routine for students and teachers to agree, document and regularly review the purpose and vision for their class. | All staff and students explicitly establish and reflect upon the purpose of their learning and other key activities. | Staff and students routinely establish and reflect upon a vision of excellence and document explicit quality criteria for important learning and other activities. |
| **Becoming routine:** Systems and structures in place and documented | We have a school purpose (or mission) and vision that were developed with input from many stakeholders. The purpose and vision are referred to from time to time. | Many teachers and students engage in discussion and documentation of the purpose and vision for their class. | Many staff and students routinely establish the purpose of their learning and other key activities. | Many staff and students routinely establish a vision of excellence and document explicit quality criteria for important learning and other activities. |
| **Early application:** Ad hoc, with some patterns | We have a school purpose (or mission) and vision that were developed by a small group with limited input from others. | Some classes discuss and document the purpose and vision for their class. | Some staff and students routinely establish the purpose of their learning and other key activities. | Some staff and students establish a vision of excellence and document explicit quality criteria for important learning and other activities. |
| **Limited application:** Event driven | If we have a school purpose (or mission) and vision, few people know it. | We rarely discuss the purpose or vision of our classes. | The purpose of our actions is rarely discussed. | We rarely consider the quality of what we do. |
| | **A.** Agree school purpose and vision | **B.** Agree class purpose and vision | **C.** Clarify purpose for activity | **D.** Use quality criteria |

# Processes: Improving systems and processes improves performance, relationships and behaviour

| | A. Identify and map key processes | B. Create and use system documentation | C. Ensure role clarity | D. Manage and improve processes |
|---|---|---|---|---|
| **Embedded:** Everybody, always, everywhere | A comprehensive system of training is in place for flowcharting. All key school and classroom processes have been identified and documented as flowcharts. | Everyone works together to agree, document and follow our key school processes along with their associated policies and supporting documents. Staff are trained, coached and supported in their use. | Responsibilities for the management and improvement of all key school processes have been agreed and documented. These responsibilities are subject to periodic review. | We have a comprehensive system for actively managing and improving key school and classroom processes. Waste is proactively minimised. |
| **Becoming routine:** Systems and structures in place and documented | Most staff and students are competent in process flowcharting. Key school and classroom processes have been identified. | Most key school processes, policies and supporting documents are agreed, systematically documented and available to all who need them. These processes are followed by the majority of staff. | Responsibilities for the management and improvement of most key school processes have been agreed and documented. | We have a system by which our key school and classroom processes are managed and improved. We explicitly seek to reduce waste: re-work, non value-adding activities and unnecessary checking. |
| **Early application:** Ad hoc, with some patterns | Some staff and students have been trained in process mapping. Some key school and classroom processes have been identified and documented as flowcharts. | Some school processes, policies and forms have been agreed and documented. Many people insist on doing things their own way rather than following these standard school processes. | Responsibilities for the management and improvement of some key school processes have been agreed. | We have the beginnings of a system to manage and improve our key school and classroom processes. We are beginning to reduce waste: re-work, non value-adding activities and unnecessary checking. |
| **Limited application:** Event driven | Neither staff nor students have been trained in process mapping. | Almost none of our school processes and related policies are documented. | There is confusion regarding who is responsible for key school processes. | We neither manage nor improve our key processes. We blame people when things go wrong. |
| | **A.** Identify and map key processes | **B.** Create and use system documentation | **C.** Ensure role clarity | **D.** Manage and improve processes |

# Clients: Clients define quality and form perceptions

| | | | | |
|---|---|---|---|---|
| **Embedded:** Everybody, always, everywhere | We regularly meet with parents and students to discuss their needs, expectation and preferences. This information drives planning, programming and improvement. | Robust processes are in place to manage, measure and continually improve parent and student relationships, building loyalty to the school. | The school has robust processes to regularly collect data on parent and student perceptions of the school. These data are used to drive planning and improvement efforts. | There are school wide processes for seeking, receiving and responding to feedback from internal clients (next person in the process) to improve performance. These processes are in constant use and are subject to regular review. |
| **Becoming routine:** Systems and structures in place and documented | We meet with many parents and students to discuss their needs, expectation and preferences. This information influences planning, programming and improvement. | Processes are being developed to manage, measure and improve relationships with parents and students. | The school collects some data on parent and student perceptions. These data influence planning and improvement efforts. | Many staff use agreed process to gather feedback from their internal clients (next person in the process) to better meet their needs. |
| **Early application:** Ad hoc, with some patterns | We only sometimes meet with parents and students to discuss their needs, expectation and preferences. | There are some agreed processes by which we manage parent and student relationships. | Few data are collected on parent and student perceptions of the school. We rely on anecdotal evidence. | Some staff seek feedback from their internal clients (next person in the process) to better meet their needs. |
| **Limited application:** Event driven | We only meet with parents when there is a problem, and rarely meet with parents and students at the same time. | We do not actively manage parent and student relationships, they just happen. | We don't pay attention to parent or student perceptions of the school. | Staff do not recognise the next person in a process as their client. |
| | **A.** **Understand parent and student needs** | **B.** **Manage relationships with parents and students** | **C.** **Monitor parent and student perceptions** | **D.** **Manage internal client relationships** |

# Stakeholders: Sustainability requires management of relationships with stakeholders

| | A. Identify and agree stakeholders | B. Actively engage stakeholders | C. Monitor stakeholder perceptions | D. Identify and engage internal stakeholders |
|---|---|---|---|---|
| **Embedded:** Everybody, always, everywhere | All stakeholders in the school have been identified, agreed and documented. This document is reviewed regularly. | Comprehensive and integrated processes are in place to actively engage all key stakeholders as partners in the school's activities. These processes are subject to regular review. | The school routinely measures key stakeholder perceptions of the school and acts upon these measures to improve school systems, processes and performance. | We have robust processes to ensure that the needs of internal stakeholders are carefully considered before changes are made to systems and processes. These stakeholder engagement processes are routinely followed. |
| **Becoming routine:** Systems and structures in place and documented | Key stakeholders in the school have been identified and agreed. | Some stakeholder engagement processes are in place. Key stakeholders play an active role in the school and support student learning. | Some key stakeholders' perceptions of the school are periodically measured and sometimes acted upon. | We have processes to ensure the needs of internal stakeholders are considered before changes are made, however, these processes are not always applied. |
| **Early application:** Ad hoc, with some patterns | Some stakeholders in the school have been identified. | Our processes for managing and engaging stakeholders are not well developed. | Perceptions of a few key stakeholders are measured infrequently. | The needs of internal stakeholders are sometimes considered as part of change and improvement activities. |
| **Limited application:** Event driven | We are unsure who are our stakeholders. | We pay little attention to our stakeholders. | We have limited data regarding stakeholder perceptions of the school. | Stakeholders in different parts of the school, including classrooms and the office, are not identified. |

# Planning: Improvement is rarely achieved without the planned application of appropriate strategy and methods

| | A.<br>Establish whole school planning | B.<br>Integrate individual planning | C.<br>Monitor progress | D.<br>Use quality learning tools |
|---|---|---|---|---|
| **Embedded:** Everybody, always, everywhere | We have a comprehensive and integrated whole school planning process to agree and align our priorities, goals and improvement projects among key stakeholders. The process is focussed upon achievement of our purpose and vision. Progress is regularly reviewed, reported and acted upon. | Students and staff have individual plans with priorities and goals that clearly support the achievement of whole school goals and priorities. Progress against the plans is regularly reviewed. | We have a robust process to ensure we systematically and regularly review progress towards goals for the whole school, all individual staff members and all students. | Quality learning tools are in routine use across all classrooms and in interactions among teams, leaders, staff, parents and school board. |
| **Becoming routine:** Systems and structures in place and documented | We have the beginning of a whole school planning process that engages many staff in setting consistent priorities, goals and improvement projects. Progress is reviewed. | Most staff and many students have individual plans with priorities and goals that are aligned to those of the school. Progress is reviewed. | We have the beginnings of a process to regularly review progress towards goals for the school, staff and students. | Most staff students and other stakeholders use quality learning tools to support collaboration and make decisions quickly and effectively. |
| **Early application:** Ad hoc, with some patterns | Our planning process engages some staff in establishing priorities, goals and improvement projects, though these seem to keep changing and are not well supported. | Some staff and a few students have individual plans with priorities and goals that are aligned to those of the school. | We sometimes review progress against the goals in our individual and school plans. | Some staff and students use quality learning tools to support collaboration and make decisions quickly and effectively. |
| **Limited application:** Event driven | We may have plans, but most of us never use them. | Few staff or students have individual plans. | We do not review progress against our goals. | We don't use tools. We prefer to talk, endlessly. |

# Knowledge: Learning and improvement are derived from theory, prediction, observation and reflection

| | A.<br>Conduct regular organisation self-assessment | B.<br>Conduct regular individual self-assessment | C.<br>Set and monitor learning goals | D.<br>Use a structured improvement process |
|---|---|---|---|---|
| **Embedded:**<br>Everybody, always, everywhere | Self-assessment of processes and performance is an integral part of school planning for improvement and monitoring school progress over time. | We have robust processes by which all students and staff regularly engage in self-assessment of their learning and achievement. | All staff and students participate in robust processes to establish, document, monitor progress and report against learning goals. | We have a structured and ongoing program of improvement projects at school, faculty, class, team and individual levels. All improvement projects use an agreed school-wide standard process that engages key stakeholders. The improvement process is subject to periodic review. |
| **Becoming routine:**<br>Systems and structures in place and documented | There is the beginning of a process for regular school self-assessment of processes and performance. | Most students and staff engage in self-assessment of their learning and achievement. | Most students and many staff engage in goal setting, which is monitored regularly. | We have the beginnings of a structured program of improvement projects across the school. Most projects use an agreed school-wide standard process (e.g. PDSA) |
| **Early application:**<br>Ad hoc, with some patterns | The school rarely undertakes self-assessment of its processes and performance. | Some students and staff self-assess their performance and achievements. | Some students and staff engage in goal setting for their learning. | Some staff and students are involved in improvement projects. |
| **Limited application:**<br>Event driven | We do not self-assess as a school. | Individuals do not undertake self-assessment. | Neither staff nor students set learning goals. | We rarely establish improvement projects. There is no agreed improvement process. |

# Data: Facts and data are needed to measure progress and improve decision making

| | A. Collect and use performance data | B. Collect and use process data | C. Collect and use input data | D. Build capacity to use data effectively |
|---|---|---|---|---|
| **Embedded:** Everybody, always, everywhere | Comprehensive and integrated performance measures are in place for students, classes, staff teams and the whole school. We use these measures to monitor progress toward the school purpose and vision. | We have a comprehensive and integrated set of process measures that are used to adjust processes as required and to predict performance. | We have a comprehensive set of processes to collect and use input measures (including formative assessments and records of prior learning) that are used effectively to adjust school and classroom processes to optimise learning. | All staff and students collect, display, interpret and act on data. They have access to the data they require, and use it effectively to monitor performance, diagnose problems and set priorities. |
| **Becoming routine:** Systems and structures in place and documented | We have many performance measures in place at the student, class, staff, team and school levels. These measures relate to our school purpose and vision. | Many of our key processes have measures that we use to adjust processes as required and to predict performance. | We have processes to collect and use input measures (including formative assessments and records of prior learning). These data are not always used effectively to improve learning. | Many staff and students collect, display, interpret and act on data. They use data to monitor performance, diagnose problems and set priorities. |
| **Early application:** Ad hoc, with some patterns | We seek performance data before making key decisions or setting priorities. We have some performance measures in place at the student, class, staff, team and school levels. | Some of our key processes have measures that enable us to adjust processes as required and to predict performance. | We collect and use some input measures (including formative assessments and records of prior learning) to adjust our teaching programs. | Some staff and students collect, display, interpret and act on data. They use data to monitor performance, diagnose problems and set priorities. |
| **Limited application:** Event driven | We have few performance measures in place. | We don't use process measures. | We don't use input measures. | We don't use data effectively, decisions are mostly made on gut feel. |

# Variation: Systems and processes are subject to variation that affects predictability and performance

|  | A. Clarify terms to minimise variation | B. Identify and address root causes of variation | C. Distinguish common cause from special cause variation | D. Respond appropriately to variation |
|---|---|---|---|---|
| **Embedded:** Everybody, always, everywhere | Staff and students routinely use operational definitions to ensure clarity, and to reduce confusion and variation in understanding. | We use agreed processes and tools to ensure we understand the root causes and impact of variation in our systems and processes before making changes. | We routinely use statistical tools to differentiate common cause variation from special cause variation in our systems and processes. | We routinely discuss and measure the degree to which our processes are stable and/or capable. We use data effectively to prevent us from tampering: overreacting and under-reacting. |
| **Becoming routine:** Systems and structures in place and documented | We regularly agree definitions of concepts and can see how this creates clarity and reduces confusion and variation in understanding. | We are beginning to analyse situations to identify the root underlying causes of variation before attempting to fix problems or make changes to our systems and processes. | We seek to differentiate between common and special causes of variation in our systems and processes. We use statistical tools to help us. | We discuss and measure the degree to which our key processes are stable and/or capable. We seek data to prevent us from tampering: overreacting and under-reacting. |
| **Early application:** Ad hoc, with some patterns | We sometimes agree definitions of concepts and can see how this reduces confusion and variation in understanding. | We sometimes look for root underlying causes of problems, rather then trying to fix the symptoms. | We recognise it is possible to differentiate between those causes of variation that are inherent to the process (common causes) and those that are not (special causes). | We are beginning to discuss whether our processes are stable and/or capable. We understand the need avoid overreacting and under-reacting. |
| **Limited application:** Event driven | We rarely define concepts to reduce confusion and variation in understanding. | We rarely distinguish between causes and symptoms of problems. | We rarely discuss the concept of variation in our systems and processes. These conversations are of little consequence or interest. | We do not know if we are under-reacting to common cause variation or overreacting to special cause variation. |

# Motivation: Removing barriers to intrinsic motivation improves performance

| | A. Remove barriers to learning and improvement | B. Build systems to enhance collaboration for improvement | C. Actively enable others | D. Reduce reliance on extrinsic motivators |
|---|---|---|---|---|
| **Embedded:** Everybody, always, everywhere | Relentless effort is applied at all levels of the school to identify and remove barriers to learning, improvement, and excellent performance. | Collaboration for improvement is the dominant mode of operation across the school and with all key stakeholders. This is reinforced and enhanced by robust school improvement processes. We regularly celebrate success. | We have robust, school wide processes to develop teacher and student capacity to manage and improve processes and relationships. Staff and students participate in and benefit from improvement. | We do not offer extrinsic rewards. |
| **Becoming routine:** Systems and structures in place and documented | Efforts are made in many parts of the school to identify and address barriers to learning, improvement, and excellent performance. | There is strong evidence of collaboration for improvement among staff, stakeholders and in classrooms. We celebrate success. | We have a school wide approach to developing teacher and student capacity to manage and improve processes and relationships. Staff and students benefit from such improvements. | Rewards are not the preferred method of acknowledging learning and good behaviour. |
| **Early application:** Ad hoc, with some patterns | Some efforts are made to identify and address barriers to learning, improvement, and excellent performance. | There is evidence of some collaboration for improvement. | Relationships across the school are supportive. There are some processes to develop capacity to manage and improve processes and relationships. | Our reward system offers prizes like gold stars, food and privileges that have nothing to do with learning. |
| **Limited application:** Event driven | We rarely identify barriers to improved performance. | Few staff and students collaborate. | Relationships in the school are predominantly based upon power and control. | Our behaviour management system punishes bad behaviour and rewards good behaviour. |

# Relationships: Strong human relationships are built through caring, communication, trust, and respect

| | | | | |
|---|---|---|---|---|
| **Embedded:** Everybody, always, everywhere | We have clear, explicit and agreed statements of values and expected behaviours, which were developed as the result of extensive dialogue among key stakeholders. The values and behaviours are current, regularly discussed and periodically reviewed. | There are robust school wide processes by which students receive continual and constructive feedback on their learning. | There are processes in place to ensure continual and constructive feedback to teachers about their teaching and how it is supporting student learning. | Processes in the school are explicitly designed to promote collaboration and constructive feedback and to minimise competition and fear. |
| **Becoming routine:** Systems and structures in place and documented | We have statements of values and expected behaviours, which were developed with input from key stakeholders. The values and behaviours are discussed some times. | Most teachers ensure there are processes by which students receive regular and constructive feedback about their learning. | There are the beginnings of systems by which teachers seek and respond to feedback from their students and their colleagues regarding their teaching and how to improve learning. | In general, people collaborate well across the school. Competition is actively discouraged and fear is reduced. School processes encourage regular and constructive feedback among stakeholders. |
| **Early application:** Ad hoc, with some patterns | We have developed a statement of school values and the desired behaviours. | Some teachers provide regular and ongoing feedback to students about their learning. | Some teachers seek student and colleague feedback to improve their teaching. | There are pockets of cooperation across the school. Competition among students and staff is not encouraged. |
| **Limited application:** Event driven | We may have school rules, but the school does not have agreed values. | Teachers provide students with results of their assessments. | Teachers don't listen to students or their colleagues. | People at this school do not collaborate well. Competition is overt. Fear is evident. Constructive feedback is rare. |
| | **A.** Agree values and behaviours | **B.** Provide feedback to students | **C.** Provide feedback to teachers | **D.** Promote cooperation over competition |

# Leadership: It is everybody's job to improve the systems and processes for which they are responsible by working with their people and role modelling the principles

| | | | | |
|---|---|---|---|---|
| **Embedded:** Everybody, always, everywhere | The development of leadership capacity of staff and students is a key strategic priority, which is fully integrated into school systems, processes, planning and resourcing. | The school's core leadership processes are identified, agreed and documented. They are subject to regular cycles of review and improvement. | Everyone role models the principles, school values and agreed behaviours. | Leaders at all levels of the school ask questions and engage in conversations that directly reference the quality improvement principles and practices. |
| **Becoming routine:** Systems and structures in place and documented | Leadership capacity development for staff and students is an explicit priority of the school. We have the beginnings of an integrated whole school approach. | Most school core leadership processes have been identified, agreed and documented. Many of these have been subject to cycles of improvement. | The behaviour of staff and students, including those in formal leadership positions, is mostly consistent with the principles, school values and philosophy. | Many staff and students ask questions and engage in conversations that directly reference quality improvement principles and practices. |
| **Early application:** Ad hoc, with some patterns | Opportunities to develop leadership potential tend to be limited to specific individuals. | A few key school leadership processes have been identified and documented. | Many people in formal leadership positions behave in a manner that is ethical and consistent with the principles, school values and philosophy. | We sometimes discuss the quality improvement principles and practices, and their implications for us and our school. |
| **Limited application:** Event driven | Leadership is largely seen as limited to those in formal positions of authority. | We have not identified the school core leadership processes. | Senior leaders tend to manage and control rather than support, inspire and enable. | We do not discuss the principles or philosophy by which we operate. |
| | **A.** Build capacity for everyone to lead improvement | **B.** Agree, document and use the core leadership processes to drive improvement | **C.** Role model the principles, school values and philosophy | **D.** Ask principle-based questions |

# Appendix 3:
# I do not work in the school education system. What can I do?

Parents, community members, policy makers and politicians don't work within the system of school education, and are unable to bring about change from within. In many cases, students are not given the opportunity to contribute to improvement either. So, what can you do if this is you?

The answer relates to asking new questions based on the principles. Given our understanding of the principles and practices described in this book, we can not only ask new questions, but we are also well equipped to listen carefully to the answers with a fresh appreciation of their significance. In many cases, we listen to what is not said. This will, no doubt, lead to more questions. By asking new questions of leaders in the system we can begin to change the conversations within and about the system of school education.

Table A3.1 presents a sample of questions that might be asked of any system of education. Guidance is also provided about what to listen for in responses to these questions.

These questions have been framed in a general sense, asking about the system, which, in this case, could be a state education system, a district, a network or cluster of schools, a school or even a classroom.

Some questions relate to the system leader, who could be anyone, including the chief executive officer, district superintendent, administrator, principal or teacher.

> By asking new questions of leaders in the system we can begin to change the conversations within and about the system of school education.

| Theme | Principle-based questions | What to listen for in the response |
|---|---|---|
| Direction | **What are the purpose and vision of the system?** How were these created and agreed? When were they last updated? How are they used? | Is there a current and mutually agreed statement of direction that is being used on a daily basis to align effort and guide decision making and action at all levels? |
| | **What are the desired values and behaviours of the system?** How were these created and agreed? When were they last updated? How are they used? | Are aspirational behaviours and values mutually agreed and explicit? To what degree are these promoted and used to ensure productive interactions and supportive relationships? |
| | **What are the principles that underpin the system's philosophy for learning and improvement?** How were these derived? How are they used? | In what theory is the improvement approach based? How does the theory align with the principles outlined in this book? |
| Leading Improvement | **What is the system leader's current approach to bringing about improvement?** What are the current priorities for improvement? How were these selected? How are key stakeholders involved? How is it going? How do you know? Can you show me? | Is there an explicit improvement process in use by the system leader? Do they have a robust evidence-based process for identifying and prioritising improvement opportunities? Is improvement actually happening? |
| | **What role does the system leader play in school and classroom improvement?** What is the role of the system leader? | To what degree are leaders engaged in managing and improving the processes for which they are responsible? Do they see this as their role? |
| | **What are you doing, personally, to improve processes and relationships?** | To what degree is the individual engaged in managing and improving the processes for which they are responsible? How are they seeking to improve the quality of relationships? |
| | **How do students contribute to school and classroom improvement?** | Are students meaningfully engaged in improvement activities? |

| Theme | Principle-based questions | What to listen for in the response |
|---|---|---|
| Student Learning | **What does the system expect students to learn while at school?**<br>How were these expectations developed?<br>Where is this documented?<br>How are they used?<br>How is the system progressing towards achieving these outcomes? | Is there a clearly defined graduate profile for each school? To what degree does it reflect the current views of the whole school community? To what degree is it being used to guide curriculum decisions? Is the school serious about achieving it and measuring progress along the way? |
| Student Learning | **How are students supported to take responsibility for their learning?**<br>How do they know what they are seeking to learn?<br>How do they track their progress? | To what degree are students responsible for their own learning — planning, setting goals, self-assessing their learning and monitoring progress over time? Do students have to wait for the teacher to tell them what to do next? Are they actively engaged in self-assessment? |
| Student Learning | **How are students supported to learn at their own pace?**<br>By what method? | Are students required to keep up, or are there student-directed processes that support them to learn whatever they need to learn next? |
| Student Learning | **How does the system deal with variation in students' prior learning and current ability levels?** | How does the system manage variation? How does it support all students to learn? How do students support one another in their learning? Is there evidence of tampering? |
| Teacher Professional Learning | **What is the process for teacher professional learning?**<br>How are their learning priorities determined? | To what degree are teachers continually learning? Are teacher learning priorities established with reference to the individual needs of the teacher (evidence based) and those of the school as a whole? Is professional learning linked to the individual performance and development process? |
| Process Management | **How are the key processes identified and documented?**<br>How are these processes improved over time?<br>How are people supported in their efforts to enact the agreed processes? | Does the system/school/classroom pay attention to identifying, documenting and following agreed processes? How is process documentation made available to those who need it? To what degree are those who use the process engaged in its ongoing review and improvement? Are there processes to document, train, and coach? |

| Theme | Principle-based questions | What to listen for in the response |
|---|---|---|
| Performance Management | **How does the system identify and respond to underperformance of schools/principals/teachers/students?** | Is there a focus upon improving the system as a whole, or simply chopping the tail of the distribution? Is there a focus on systemic improvement, or is the focus on fixing individuals? |
| | **What is the system approach to the use of rewards, punishments and consequences?** | What is the role of extrinsic motivators? |
| | **How are individuals in the system recognised for their efforts, contributions and achievements?** By what process does this occur? | To what degree does recognition of individuals play a role in building intrinsic motivation? How is recognition distinguished from praise? How is recognition distinguished from rewards and other extrinsic motivators? |

**Table A3.1 Principle-based questions for the system of education**

## Parents, community members and students

Parents, community members and students are encouraged to ask these questions of school principals and teachers. These questions can be used to shift public debate about school education. They can also prompt educators to reflect upon personal and school practices and their philosophy of learning and improvement.

Families may also find these questions useful in considering which school might be most suitable for their children. The quality of responses is likely to reflect the quality of the education on offer.

## Policy makers

Policy makers are encouraged to reflect on the degree to which the educational policy areas for which they are responsible equip and encourage schools and teachers to provide satisfactory answers to these questions. The principles and practices described in this book represent a theory of management for continual improvement. These questions explore the theory of management in use.

The responses that educators provide to these questions will, to a large degree, be reflective of the constraints imposed by policies and compliance requirements of the education systems of which they are part. Policy makers in particular have a responsibility to support (not require) schools to adopt the principles and practices of continual improvement.

In particular, they have the capacity to ensure that barriers are removed and those working in the school education system are actively enabled to deliver continual improvement.

## Politicians

Politicians are encouraged to explore these questions with their constituents and educational policy makers. The community as a whole is seeking improvement in the system of schooling and politicians play a crucial role in guiding the conversations and educational policy.

Politicians can ask key questions of the system's most senior leaders. They can encourage senior leaders to learn about and role model the principles. Politicians can also continually learn about the principles and practices, apply them, and encourage others to do the same.

Politicians can also ask of policy makers: what structures, systems and processes are in place to actively enable (not require) all schools, administrators, school leaders, teachers and students to actively engage in continual improvement?

# Appendix 4: Planning the Improvement Journey

The following Gantt chart can provide a starting point for schools wishing to plan the initial stages of their improvement journey.

It is based on the six key areas of activity described in Chapter Seven, and illustrates a sequence of activities that could be undertaken during the first two years of implementation.

Our aim is to provide you with a reference point for your planning.

Our aim in presenting this chart is not to provide a definitive program of activities, but rather to provide you with a reference point for your planning. Every school is different, and you must develop your own theory for improvement. Hopefully, this suggestion can help.

| Task/Activity | Who | T1 | T2 | T3 | T4 | T1 | T2 | T3 | T4 |
|---|---|---|---|---|---|---|---|---|---|
| **Agree and apply the principles** | | | | | | | | | |
| Agree and apply the principles in your context: | | | | | | | | | |
| • Gain stakeholder commitment to learning about and applying the quality learning approach | Principal | ▓ | | | | | | | |
| • Conduct awareness sessions to engage key stakeholders | Principal | | ▓ | | | | | | |
| • Agree the implementation plan (this Gantt chart) with key stakeholders | Principal | ▓ | | | | | | | |
| • Agree the principles for individuals and the organisation | Principal, Board, Executive | ▓ | | | | | | | |
| • Develop and implement a program of education and training for all staff | Principal, Executive | | ▓ | | | | | | |
| Ask principle-based questions | Everybody | | | ▓ | ▓ | ▓ | ▓ | ▓ | ▓ |
| **Think and act systemically** | | | | ▓ | | | | | |
| Understand, agree and document your systems: | | | | | | | | | |
| • Engage stakeholders in development of a whole school system map | Principal, Executive, Everybody | | | ▓ | | | | | |
| • Pilot development of classroom system maps | Volunteer Teachers | | | | ▓ | | | | |
| • Develop classroom system map | All Teachers | | | | | ▓ | | | |
| • Develop system maps for other sub-systems | Admin Exec. Support Staff | | | | | | ▓ | | |
| Optimise the system | Everybody | | | | | ▓ | ▓ | ▓ | ▓ |

| Task/Activity | Who | T1 | T2 | T3 | T4 | T1 | T2 | T3 | T4 |
|---|---|---|---|---|---|---|---|---|---|
| **Use data effectively** | | | | | | | | | |
| Establish measurement processes: | | | | | | | | | |
| • Refine school performance measures, reporting and use | Principal, Executive | | ▓ | | | | | | |
| • Refine school perception measures, reporting and use | Principal, Executive | | ▓ | | | | | | |
| • Refine school process measures, reporting and use | Principal, Executive | | | ▓ | ▓ | | | | |
| • Refine school input measures, reporting and use | Principal, Executive | | | ▓ | | | | | |
| • Refine classroom performance measures, reporting and use | Principal, Executive, Classroom Teachers | | | ▓ | | | | | |
| • Refine classroom perception measures, reporting and use | Principal, Executive, Classroom Teachers | | | ▓ | | | | | |
| • Refine classroom process measures, reporting and use | Principal, Executive, Classroom Teachers | | | | ▓ | ▓ | | | |
| • Refine classroom input measures, reporting and use | Principal, Executive, Classroom Teachers | | | | ▓ | | | | |
| Apply statistical thinking | | | | | | ▓ | ▓ | ▓ | |

| Task/Activity | Who | T1 | T2 | T3 | T4 | T1 | T2 | T3 | T4 |
|---|---|---|---|---|---|---|---|---|---|
| **Conduct regular self-assessment** | | | | | | | | | |
| Self-assess individual learning and behaviour: | | | | | | | | | |
| • Pilot behavioural self-assessment with the school executive | Principal, Executive | | | | ▓ | | | | |
| • Extend behavioural self-assessment to all staff | Principal, Executive, Everybody | | | | | ▓ | | | |
| • Pilot the use of capacity matrices and quality criteria in the classroom | Volunteer Classroom Teachers and Students | | | ▓ | | | | | |
| • Extend the use of capacity matrices and quality criteria to all classrooms | All Teachers | | | | | ▓ | | ▓ | |
| • Pilot the use of capacity matrices with staff | Principal, Executive Volunteers | | | | | | ▓ | | |
| • Extend the use of capacity matrices to all staff | Everybody | | | | | | | ▓ | |
| • Pilot student-led conferences | Volunteer Teachers and Students | | | | ▓ | | | | |
| • Extend the use of student-led conferences to all students | All Teachers and Students | | | | | | ▓ | | |
| Self-assess system learning and behaviour: | | | | | | | | | |
| • Pilot school self-assessment using the principles | Principal, Executive | | | | ▓ | | | | |
| • Integrate regular school self-assessment into the school planning process | Everybody | | | | | ▓ | ▓ | ▓ | |

| Task/Activity | Who | T1 | T2 | T3 | T4 | T1 | T2 | T3 | T4 |
|---|---|---|---|---|---|---|---|---|---|
| **Apply tools and the PDSA cycle to improve processes and relationships** | | | | | | | | | |
| Use the quality learning tools: | | | | | | | | | |
| • Using tools in executive and staff meetings | Principal, Executive | █ | | | | | | | |
| • Pilot the use of selected tools in classrooms | Volunteer Teachers | | █ | | | | | | |
| • Share experiences with the use of tools in the classroom | All Teaching Staff | | | █ | | | | | |
| • Extend the use of tools across all classrooms | All Teaching Staff | | | | █ | █ | █ | █ | █ |
| Establish and train improvement project teams: | | | | | | | | | |
| • Train and coach initial improvement project teams through first improvement projects | Principal, Executive | | | | | █ | █ | | |
| • Train and coach subsequent improvement project teams | Principal, Executive | | | | | | █ | █ | |
| **Capture and share the learning** | | | | | | | | | |
| Identify, document and agree key processes: | | | | | | | | | |
| • Identify and document key school and classroom processes | Principal, Executive, Admin. | | | █ | █ | █ | █ | █ | █ |
| • Review core leadership processes | Principal, Executive | | | █ | | | | | |
| Establish system documentation: | | | | | | | | | |
| • Establish a system of documentation | Principal, Admin. | | | | █ | | | | |
| • Progressively capture processes, policies and supporting documents | Everybody | | | | █ | █ | █ | █ | █ |
| • Train and coach staff in use of system documentation | Principal, Executive | | | | | █ | █ | █ | █ |

**Figure A4.1 Illustrative implementation Gantt chart**

Source: QLA

# Glossary of Operational Definitions

The following is a summary of the operation definitions of key terms discussed throughout the book.

**Capability**: the degree to which a system consistently delivers results that are within acceptable limits of variation.

**Clients**: the recipients and beneficiaries of the products produced and the services provided by an organisation.

**Common cause variation**: the variation inherent in a system, which is always present as the net result of many influences, most of which are unknown.

**Compliance**: submission to the will of others.

**Consequence**: an outcome that follows as a result of something occurring earlier.

**Daily routines**: the everyday, getting-the-job-done type of work, working in the system.

**Data**: facts, statistics or pieces of information.

**Dependent relationship**: one party exerts a dominant position over another.

**Engagement**: enthusiastic commitment of attention, effort and care.

**Extrinsic motivation**: stimuli or drive for action coming from sources external to an individual.

**Extrinsic reward**: a desired object or experience that is bestowed by sources external to the individual or group, contingent upon the individual or group having satisfied certain criteria.

**Improving systems and processes**: working on the existing system to improve it.

**Independent relationship**: each party acts with autonomy towards their individual goals.

**Innovation projects**: projects that seek to meet organisations' emerging needs through the creation of new systems and processes. Innovation projects work on the system to create new products, services, and ways of working.

**Input measures**: measures collected at the boundary of the system and quantifying key characteristics of the inputs that affect system operation. Input measures answer the question: what are the key characteristics of the inputs to the system?

**Interdependent relationship**: parties willingly collaborate to achieve individual and shared goals.

**Intrinsic motivation**: stimuli or drive for action coming from within an individual.

**Intrinsic reward**: a desired object or experience that is conferred upon an individual or group, contingent upon having satisfied certain criteria, the conference of which is independent of the influence of others.

**Leadership**: the ability to articulate a vision that causes others to move with a passion.

**Management**: the ability to organise resources and coordinate the execution of tasks necessary to reach a goal in a timely and cost effective manner.

**Measurement**: a process of assigning numbers to observations.

**Motivation**: stimuli or drive for action.

**Natural consequence**: an outcome that follows predictably from the laws of the natural world as a result of something occurring earlier.

**Objective data**: data that are derived from observation and are free of personal feelings, interpretations and prejudices.

**Operational definition**: a procedure agreed upon for translation of a concept into a measurement of some kind.

W. Edwards Deming, 1994, *The New Economics: For industry, government and education*, MIT, Massachusetts, p. 108.

**Optimisation**: "Optimisation is the process of orchestrating the efforts of all components towards achievement of the stated aim." W. Edwards Deming, 1993, *The New Economics: For industry, government and education*, MIT, Cambridge, p. 53.

**PDSA Storyboard**: a graphic organiser of tables, charts, tools and other illustrations displayed in sequence with the aim of capturing, recording, visualising and sharing the progressive activities, findings and decisions of a PDSA team.

**Perception measures**: measures collected from the stakeholders in the system and used to monitor their thoughts and opinions of the system. Perception measures answer the question: what do people think of the system?

**Performance Measures**: measures of the outcomes of a system that indicate how well the system has performed. Performance measures answer the question: how did we go?

**Plan**: the product of a planning process that articulates the intended actions to be taken in pursuit of the desired future state. A plan documents an agreed theory for action.

**Planning**: a process of making and evaluating a set of interrelated decisions, before taking action, in order to increase the likelihood of achieving some desired future state through the actions taken.

**Praise**: the act of expressing approval or commendation.

**Process**: a sequence of actions that are enacted to achieve a purpose.

**Process map**: a pictorial representation of the sequence of actions that comprise a process.

**Process measures**: measures collected within the system that are predictive of system performance and which can be used to initiate adjustments to processes. Process measures answer the question: how are we going?

**Project**: a temporary endeavour undertaken to meet specific goals and objectives with a defined beginning and end. Projects are usually subject to specific time and resource constraints.

**Punishment**: a negative or unpleasant experience imposed upon an individual or group in response to behaviour that is deemed to be unacceptable.

**Qualitative data**: data that relate to characteristics or qualities.

**Quality improvement tool**: a physical or procedural instrument used to improve quality.

**Quality learning tool**: a physical or procedural instrument used to improve the quality of learning. Quality learning tools include quality improvement tools, cooperative learning tools and the so-called thinking tools.

**Quantitative data**: data that relate to quantities.

**Rate**: to appraise or estimate something's worth or value.

**Rank**: to assign something to a particular position or classification relative to other things of the same type.

**Recognition**: respectful acknowledgement of an individual.

**Reliable**: the data are consistent when collected in different places, at different times, and by different people.

**Reward**: a desired object or experience that is conferred upon an individual or group contingent upon certain criteria being met.

**Shared vision**: a picture in the collective minds of key stakeholders for a given point of time in the future.

**Special cause variation**: variation that is unusual and unpredictable, which can be the result of a unique event or circumstance, and which can be attributed to some knowable influence. Also known as assignable cause variation.

**Stability**: a system is said to be stable when the observations fall randomly within the natural limits of variation for that system and conform to a defined distribution, frequently a normal distribution.

**Stakeholders**: individuals, groups and organisations with an interest in the activities and outcomes of a system.

**Statistic**: a number that summarises observations.

**Statistical thinking**: a philosophy of learning and action based on the following fundamental principles: all work occurs in a system of interconnected processes; variation exists in all processes; understanding and responding appropriately to variation are keys to success.

**Storyboard**: a graphic organiser of illustrations or images displayed in sequence with the aim of visualising a narrative.

**Subjective data**: data related to the thoughts, opinions and perceptions of people.

**Suppliers**: people and organisations external to the system who provide resources necessary for the system.

**System**: "A system is a network of interdependent components that work together to try to accomplish the aim of the system."

> W. Edwards Deming, 1993, *The New Economics: For industry, government and education, MIT, Cambridge*, p. 50.

**System map**: a pictorial representation of the elements that comprise a system.

**Tampering**: making changes to a system in the absence of an understanding of the nature and impact of variation affecting the system.

**Theory**: a coherent system of concepts that represents a view of how the world works. Theory can be used to make predictions about the outcomes of proposed actions.

**Tool**: a physical or procedural instrument.

**Valid**: the data are well founded and measure what they are supposed to measure.

# Annotated Bibliography

## A note about references

While it not has been our aim to write an academic text, we have endeavoured to acknowledge the sources of our ideas and provide references for further reading. To this end, we have referenced original source material where this has been available, rather than more recent writings presenting the same ideas. Many of these references are, in our view, seminal and timeless, not old.

# General references

These references continue to provide the foundation for our work and are referred to throughout this book.

W. Edwards Deming, 1982, *Out of the Crisis*, MIT, Massachusetts.

Deming's most significant summary of his approach. While it is not an easy book to read, it is a seminal work. New insights continue to emerge with each visit to its pages.

W. Edwards Deming, 1993, *The New Economics: For industry, government and education*, second edition, MIT, Massachusetts.

Deming's last book, with a strong focus on the system of profound knowledge. Much easier to read than *Out of the Crisis*. A continuing source of insight and inspiration into the theory of improvement.

David P. Langford, 2015, *Tool Time for Education*, version 15, Langford International, Montana.

A comprehensive, easy-to-use recipe book of quality improvement tools relevant to education which includes step-by-step instructions and examples of uses in the school and classroom.

Tony Miller and Gordon Hall, 2013, *Letting Go: Breathing new life into organisations*, Argyll Publishing, Glendaruel.

We had the good fortune to hear Gordon present at the Deming Research Conference in New York in 2006. In this wonderful, easy to read book, the authors capture some of the amazing work that has been taking place applying Deming's theory to the workplace in Scotland. Miller and Hall explore the origins of performance management and argue that effective leaders and managers must let go of their controlling paradigms and instead nurture the intrinsic motivation of people through management systems that actively support the human spirit, enable creativity, and allow staff to realise joy in their work.

Peter R. Scholtes, 1998, *The Leaders Handbook: A guide to inspiring your people and managing the daily workflow*, McGraw Hill, New York.

Peter Scholtes did a wonderful job of explaining Deming's work and the theory of improvement in simple terms. It is such a great book, we wish we had written it.

Myron Tribus, various papers on quality in education. Available from http://www.qla.com.au/Papers/5.

Myron Tribus authored over 30 papers on quality improvement, many with direct relevance to improving education.

# Chapter 2: Learning to Improve

Lloyd Dobyns and Claire Crawford-Mason, 1991, *Quality or Else: The revolution in world business*, Houghton Mifflin, Massachusetts.

An excellent summary of the emergence of quality as a global issue, the theory behind quality improvement, and its application across different industries.

Cecelia S. Kilian, 1992, *The World of W. Edwards Deming*, second edition, SPC Press, Tennessee.

A book that provides insight into the life of W. Edward Deming, his family, his love of music, and his work.

Thomas S. Kuhn, 1962, *The Structure of Scientific Revolutions*, University of Chicago Press, Chicago.

A seminal work on the concept of paradigms, not just in science.

Henry R. Neave, 1990, *The Deming Dimension*. SPC Press, Tennessee.

An easy to read book that clearly explains Deming's philosophy, including the system of profound knowledge.

Homer M. Sarasohn, 1997, "Progress Through a Commitment to Quality: Presentation to the 12th National Australian Quality Management Conference". Available at http://www.valuemetrics.com.au/.

A fascinating recount of the birth of quality management in Japan after the Second World War.

Homer M. Sarasohn and Charles A. Protzman, 1949, *The Fundamentals of Industrial Management: CCS management course*, electronic edition prepared by N. I. Fisher and S. J. Lavery 1998. Available at http://www.valuemetrics.com.au/.

This document provides full details of the course developed by Sarasohn and Protzman and taught to Japanese senior managers immediately after the Second World War. This course laid the foundations for the Japanese adoption of quality management as a philosophy. Parts of the course were later taught by Deming.

Walter A. Shewhart, 1931, *Economic Control of Quality of Manufactured Product*, ASQC Quality Press, Wisconsin.

This work contains, among other things, Shewhart's original exposition on statistical process control.

Walter A. Shewhart, 1986, *Statistical Method from the Viewpoint of Quality Control*, Dover, New York.

A reprint of Shewhart's seminal work, with a foreword by W. Edwards Deming. Deming devised the PDCA cycle from this work.

Myron Tribus, 1998, "The Contributions of W. Edwards Deming to the Improvement of Education". Available at http://www.qla.com.au/papers/the-contributions-of-w-edwards-deming-to-the-improvement-of-education/2112871001.

An evaluation of the impact of Deming's ideas over the 15 years to 1998. Originally published on the Deming Electronic Network.

Myron Tribus, 1993, "The Transformation of American Education to a System for Continuously Improved Learning". Available at http://www.qla.com.au/papers/transformation-of-american-education/2112870993

This paper provides a blueprint for transformation of the system of school education. It identifies eight factors that are essential for such a transformation, and explains each in detail. The paper includes some of the earliest capacity matrices developed by Tribus, outlining the learning requirements for quality management.

# Chapter 3: Working on the System

Russell L. Ackoff, 1999, *Ackoff's Best: His classic writings on management*, Wiley and Sons, New York.

An excellent all-in-one reference on systems thinking and organisations. A must read for those with an interest in the philosophy of systems thinking and management. Ackoff has been a key influence on our thinking.

Viktor E. Frankl, 1959, *Man's Search for Meaning*, Simon and Schuster, New York.

A remarkable book that highlights the importance of individuals' purpose and vision in life.

Joseph M. Juran and Frank M. Gryna, 1988, *Juran's Quality Control Handbook*, fourth edition, McGraw-Hill, New York.

A seminal reference that collates Juran's profound research and writings on quality control. A doorstop-sized tome.

# Chapter 4: Creating and Applying Theory

John Dewey, 1910, *How We Think*, D. C. Heath and Co., Boston.

John Dewey lays the foundations for what we now know as the Plan-Do-Study-Act learning and improvement cycle. The cycle is evident in his analysis of reflective thought.

Graham Hubbard, Delyth Samuel, Graeme Cocks and Simon Heap, 2007, *The First XI: Winning organisations in Australia*, John Wiley & Sons, Sydney.

An interesting study of 11 diverse Australian top-performing organisations and the elements of success that they have in common.

Masaaki Imai, 1986, *Kaizan: The key to Japan's competitive success*, McGraw Hill, New York.

A great introduction to continual quality improvement, as learned from Deming and practiced in Japanese industry.

Myron Tribus, 1993, "Quality Management in Education", *Journal for Quality and Participation*, Jan–Feb. Available at http://www.qla.com.au/papers/quality-management-in-education/2112870990.

In this paper, Tribus outlines the distinction between traditional management and quality management, and elaborates on the application of quality management to education. This is a key reference relating to the transference of quality management to an educational setting.

# Chapter 5: Using Data to Improve

Russell L. Ackoff, 2007, *Management F-Laws: How organisations really work*, Triarchy Press, Axminster.

A wonderfully irreverent and insightful reflection on contemporary management practices.

S. B. Dransfield, N. I. Fisher and N. J. Vogel, 1999, "Using Statistics and Statistical Thinking to Improve Organisational Performance", *International Statistical Review* 67:2.

An important paper that lays a firm foundation for the development of appropriate organisational performance measures based on systems thinking and value analysis.

Henry R. Neave, 1990, *The Deming Dimension*, SPC Press, Tennessee.

An easy to read book that clearly explains Deming's philosophy, including the system of profound knowledge.

Donald J Wheeler, 1993, *Understanding Variation: The key to managing chaos*, SPC Press, Tennessee.

A delightfully easy to read explanation of data in the context of system and process variation.

# Chapter 6: Improving Relationships

Stephen R. Covey, 1990, *The 7 Habits of Highly Effective People*, Simon and Schuster, New York.

A landmark reference that is as relevant today as it was when first published.

Ron Crosling, 2008, "Building Highly Effective Relationships". Available at http://www.qla.com.au/papers/5

A practical and well researched paper that describes how to build trust and effective relationships in any organisation.

Edward L. Deci and Richard Flaste, 1995, *Why We Do What We Do: Understanding self-motivation*, Penguin Books, New York.

Deci was one of the first researchers to explore intrinsic and extrinsic motivation and its impact on human behaviour. This book summarises his findings and lessons over many years. Deci's work laid the foundation for many ongoing studies and writings in the area. Daniel Pink and others draw heavily on Deci's work.

John H. Fleming and Jim Asplund, 2007, *Human Sigma: Managing the employee–customer encounter*, Gallup Press, New York.

An excellent summary of the Gallup organisation's research into employee and customer engagement.

Alfie Kohn, 1986, *No Contest: The case against competition*, Houghton Mifflin, New York.

Alfie Kohn's first book, which confronts widely-held assumptions regarding the benefits of competition.

Alfie Kohn, 1993, *Punished by Rewards: The trouble with gold stars, incentive plans, A's, praise, and other bribes*, Houghton Mifflin, New York.

A landmark book that challenges contemporary thinking about punishment and rewards as drivers of human motivation.

Hugh Mackay, 2010, *What Makes Us Tick?: The ten desires that drive us*, Hachette, Sydney.

A fascinating and contemporary exploration of human motivation by one of Australia's leading social researchers.

Abraham H. Maslow, 1998, *Maslow on Management*, John Wiley & Sons, New York.

A reprint of a journal first published in 1961, this book is an annotated collection of papers exploring different aspects of management.

Douglas McGregor, 2006, *The Human Side of Enterprise*, annotated edition, McGraw Hill, New York.

A classic reference about the assumptions people hold regarding effective ways to manage people.

Daniel H. Pink, 2009, *Drive: The surprising truths about what motivates us*, Riverhead Books, New York.

A very easy to read book that provides good coverage of the factors surrounding human motivation.

Kenneth W. Thomas, 2000, *Intrinsic Motivation at Work: What really drives employee engagement*, second edition, Berrett-Koehler, San Francisco.

A carefully researched and crafted work that builds the case for employee engagement and proposes approaches to enhance engagement in the workplace.

Uco J. Wiersma, 1992, "The Effects of Extrinsic Rewards in Intrinsic Motivation: A meta-analysis", *Journal of Occupational and Organisational Psychology* 65.

An examination of the literature and research on the impact of extrinsic motivation on intrinsic motivation.

# Chapter 7: Making Improvement Happen

Enterprise Excellence Australia, 2012, *Conversations with Rob*, DVD.

A series of explanations of the application of Deming's ideas in organisations presented in video format. Rob Palmer is a colleague of the authors and is credited with highlighting the importance of conversations as the basis for changing behaviour.

John Hattie, 2009, *Visible Learning*, Routledge, London and New York.

A groundbreaking book that synthesises over 800 meta-analyses of factors affecting student learning achievement. The findings of these analyses are consistent with the principles discussed in this book.

John Hattie, 2012, *Visible Learning for Teachers: Maximising impact on learning*, Routledge, London and New York.

A follow on to Professor Hattie's first book, this time with an emphasis on teacher practice. 'Know thy impact'.

SAI Global, 2011, *Australian Business Excellence Framework*, Sydney.

The Australian Business Excellence Framework provides a description of the elements required for organisations to achieve and sustain high levels of performance. The framework is used by many organisations for self-assessment and improvement planning. It is also the basis for the Australian Business Excellence Awards.

# List of Figures, Tables and Video Clips

## Figures

# Tables

# Video Clips

# Index

Note: Page numbers in italics indicate supplementary visual material, such as pictures, templates or videos.

CPSIA information can be obtained
at www.ICGtesting.com
Printed in the USA
LVHW071556210821
695829LV00008B/11